To Dad,

Wishing you a

Merry Xmas 1967

Bill.

CONGO KITABU

[*Photo Margrit Winzenried*

The Author with Yoma (*right centre*) and Ebu, his two constant
companions during his eighteen months' stay with the Bambuti
pygmies of North Kivu.

CONGO KITABU

BY

JEAN-PIERRE HALLET

With the editorial collaboration of
ALEX PELLE

Illustrated

HAMISH HAMILTON
LONDON

First published in Great Britain, 1965
by Hamish Hamilton Ltd
90 *Great Russell Street, London, W.C.*1
Copyright © 1965 *by Jean-Pierre Hallet*

Printed in Great Britain by
Western Printing Services Ltd, Bristol

CONTENTS

CONTENTS

ILLUSTRATIONS

ix

I

When I was a 'Bleu'

> 'How people keep correcting us when we are young!
> There's always some bad habit or another they tell
> us we ought to get over. Yet most bad habits are
> tools to help us through life.'
>
> GOETHE

'CAN you be ready to leave within a month?' the round-faced
little man asked me, with his pen poised above the paper. He
didn't bother to look up, and his bored monotone remained
unchanged.

'Of course. Can't you make it any sooner?' I said, a trifle
sharply.

Now he looked up at me—with a frown. 'We don't do things
that way here at the Ministry of Colonies. One month is the very
minimum time we need. If you knew how many papers I have to
fill out every time I send a recruit from Brussels to the Congo,
you might understand.'

'I do understand, to judge from the stack of forms I've filled
out myself. I'll be glad when I get to Africa and escape from all
these papers.'

He smiled cynically and shook his head. 'How old are you?
Twenty-two, was it?'

'Twenty-one.'

'You're just a *bleu*, Monsieur Hallet, a very raw recruit.[1]
Wherever you work in the Congo you'll find that you *never*
escape from printed forms and paperwork. Meanwhile, I advise
you to calm down and read this.'

[1] British novices (and Germans) are generally referred to as 'green'.
We Belgians and French prefer to be 'blue'. *De gustibus et coloribus non
disputandum.*

1

He handed me a little book with the title *Notions Elémentaires d'Hygiène Tropicale* printed on its light green cover. I leafed through it for a minute. Words like 'yaws', 'syphilis', 'sleeping sickness', and 'leprosy' sprang out of the text. 'Are you trying to frighten me?' I asked him. 'I've just completed a course in tropical medicine. I know all about that sort of thing.'

'That's just part of the standard procedure. So is this.' He pushed a printed form across the desk. 'Fill in the blanks and sign at the bottom, if you *really* want to go to the Congo.'

It was quite a document. 'I, Jean-Pierre Hallet, entering the service of the Ministry of Colonies on 8 March 1948 in the capacity of agronomist and sociologist, engage myself to accept any condition of climate, habitat or work that my life in the service may entail, and under no circumstances to make complaint or request for transfer without the most explicit and imperative reasons.'

I signed it without hesitation.

If I had any inkling at that moment of the strange adventures, misadventures and outright disasters I was headed for; if some menacing Belgian Nostradamus had arisen before me and declaimed, 'You are going to be riddled with tropical diseases, stabbed, speared, blasted, and perforated with poisoned arrows!' I might have thought about it for an hour or two. Then I would have signed anyway. I wanted to get back to Africa.

Although I was born in Belgium, my roots were deep in the Congolese soil. My father, André Hallet, was known as '*the painter of the Congo*' and his work was famous for its colour, atmosphere and fidelity to traditional African scenes. His landscapes and portraits hung in most European museums and many had reached America and Japan. He was a consummate artist, whose paintings had been compared to those of the Impressionist masters, but his sensitivity and his volcanic temper were equally formidable.

When I began to obtrude upon his personal African landscape, he sent my mother back to Belgium for special obstetrical attention. It was a wise precaution; on 4 August 1927, in Louvain, she suffered through a long and difficult labour to deliver a 14 lb. baby—an ordeal from which it took her six months to recover. Then, early in 1928, we went back to Africa together for a reunion with my father.

For six years I grew and lived in complete happiness and harmony with children whose skins were black. I spoke fluent Kingwana, a form of Swahili used in the eastern part of the

Congo, and after a time I refused to speak French. That was my downfall. As a struggling six-year-old, I was forcibly put on board a plane from Bukavu which carried me back to an aunt in Belgium, to a European education and to war. At fifteen, I had fought in the *Armée Blanche*—the Belgian resistance movement —and at sixteen I had enlisted in the Second Infantry Brigade of the Belgian Regular Army, in which I had served actively until the end of the war. Now, eighteen months later, I left the Brussels office of the Ministry of Colonies with the assurance that I would finally return to my African home. I was to sail in four weeks on the S.S. *Elisabethville* for Lobito in Portuguese Angola.

That meant I was headed for a post in Katanga, the southern-most province of the Congo, a destination probably chosen for me simply because my parents lived in the extreme northeast, two miles over the Congolese border in the mandated territory of Ruanda-Urundi. It was an established policy of the Adminis-tration to avoid assigning a new recruit to any post where he had close relatives; there were too many distractions, they felt, and not enough solid work. So they usually planted him at the opposite end of the Congo, where he sought even more dis-traction to escape from his loneliness.

After a month of printed forms, vaccinations, inoculations and immunizations, I finally reached Antwerp and climbed the gangway on to the *Elisabethville*. I spent most of the two weeks' voyage with a stack of books, trying to relearn Kingwana, while I read, studied and dreamed about Africa. I kept thinking of those six wonderful years of my childhood among the Banande natives of Beni, a small town west of Lake Edward on the fringe of the Ituri Forest. I remembered my startled wonder at my first sight of the pygmies, full-grown men and women only four and a half feet high—scarcely larger than my six-year-old self. Now, at 6 ft. 5 in. and 225 lb., I would tower over them by a full two feet and outweigh by a factor of more than two to one the fattest pygmy in the Ituri.

The temperature soared and the atmosphere grew increasingly dank as we passed the equator and the tenth degree of south latitude. In mid-afternoon on the fourteenth day of our journey, the ship docked at Lobito. Next day I was to take the Benguela Railway to Dilolo at the Congolese border, but for a few hours my time was my own. I roamed the streets, eager to fill my eyes with actual scenes rather than memories. I gazed down at the little native women who passed by; almost every one carried a heavy pot or bundle on her head and a big-eyed baby on her back. The babies were appealing but pathetic; the flies buzzed incessantly around their shaven heads and clustered thickly near their mouths and runny little noses.

The women had a certain dignity, dressed as they were in brightly coloured *pagnes*—a long African sarong made from a patterned cotton cloth called *kitenge*—but the Lobito men were ludicrous. Almost all wore wispy rags of European clothing; their short trousers were patched in several colours, and some of their shirts were in such incredible tatters that they appeared to be made of netting rather than cloth. Other black men, obviously much more prosperous, strolled by in trousers, long-sleeved white shirts and neckties. These were the *assimilados*—educated natives who had abandoned their tribal ways to live in imitation of the white man. Nearly all their words, expressions and gestures seemed incredibly arrogant: they had little in common with the unsophisticated Africans I remembered from my childhood.

Everywhere I looked I saw *café au lait*-coloured mulattoes, apparently the end-product of the easygoing Portuguese attitude towards racial intermarriage. I had discussed the situation with a Lisbon-born planter during the voyage to Angola, and the old man had told me with obvious pride, 'God created the white man and the black man, but the Portuguese made the mulatto.' To judge from his other remarks, and from what I had heard of Brazil, there was no real racial prejudice in any of Portugal's overseas territories; instead, the government encouraged integration and even intermarriage, in complete contrast to the South African rigid *apartheid*.

My preliminary survey of Lobito's mixed population was interrupted suddenly by a blinding torrential downpour. At this time of the year, the end of April, the rainy season was nearly over and soon there would be a complete drought until October; but now there was two or three hours' rain almost every day, each deluge followed by progressively hotter tropical sunshine.

I ran for shelter, and spent the next two hours wandering disconsolately through a European department store, searching in vain for African local colour. When the rain finally stopped, I rushed outside, just in time for a magnificent, fiery sunset. The natives swarmed through the streets again, only to vanish again within a few minutes as they left Lobito for their own villages which encircled the white man's city.

I saw little of interest in my modern hotel that evening, apart from several couples of mixed colour, but next morning, in the native market-place of Lobito, I was able to see the old Africa and the new, side by side.

It was an amazing potpourri of sights, sounds and aromas. The merchandise was displayed in several straggling lines about a hundred feet long, spread out on the ground on big coloured cloths. At least a dozen loudly competitive women headed the first line, each with a large basket of manioc flour and a tin-can measuring-cup surmounted by a conical peak of the brilliantly white flour. They looked like a series of miniature, snow-topped volcanoes. Farther on, vegetable vendors were arguing loudly about their stunted-looking cabbages, beets, sweet potatoes and corn, while another group across the aisle haggled with their customers over the price of some crude, bulging black pots and red-clay pipe-bowls. Towards the end of the line were the butchers, with their bloody, stinking gobs of meat, slippery innards and coils of viscera laid out on green plantain leaves and almost completely covered with buzzing flies.

The next crowded aisle offered an amazing agglomeration of junk. Plastic necklaces, earrings and spiral bracelets predominated, tasteless trinkets dumped on the African market to exploit the natives' love of novelty and lack of discrimination. Safety-pins also seemed very popular, both for clasping a *pagne* and as the culminating ornament on a necklace. I watched with silent amusement as a buxom girl, a dark-green scarf knotted around her kinky hair, carefully tried out several safety-pins before finally buying them.

I passed a big pile of bright-coloured padlocks and a collection of fan-shaped copper and bamboo combs, and came upon a vast number of mirrors in all sizes and shapes. A very old man was squatting on his hams and peering intently into a large hand-mirror with a yellow plastic frame. The salesman, a young *assimilado* in Western clothing, patronizingly watched his customer's obvious fascination with his own reflection. Oblivious, the old fellow started making wonderfully funny faces and burst into a loud guffaw when the reflection followed suit. Everyone in the crowded aisle turned to stare at him curiously. He stared back, tight-lipped—the very picture of aged dignity—as though nothing had happened.

I moved on and saw pile after pile of cheap plastic trinkets. Then, in surprising juxtaposition, I caught for the first time a glimpse of the real, traditional Africa. A sad-looking medicine man, a withered native of uncountable years, squatted before me with his intriguing pharmacopoiea spread out on the ground. There were teeth, claws, beaks and feathers, dried flesh, snake-skins and the mummified organs of birds and beasts—infallible remedies for the treatment and cure of wounds, mental disorders, impotence, sterility and disease. I tried a few phrases in Kingwana on him, even though I knew it was not likely to be used in this part of Africa. He muttered a few words in some other language, and held out a talisman in the palm of his knobbed, wrinkly hand—a raffia string threaded through the mummified ear of a monkey. It looked appallingly human.

The rest of my tour was an anticlimax. I inspected some big heaps of green plantain bananas in the last aisle, a long procession of spices and peppers, some roughly carved wooden utensils, sieves and a few crudely woven lidless baskets. At the end of the line were several enormous collections of dried fish, giving off an unforgettable aroma, which seemed to linger in my nostrils long afterwards.

Traversing the Angolese savannahs my train took me through Nova Lisboa, Chinguar, Silva Porto, General Machado, Vila Luso and Texeira de Sousa, lonely Portuguese outposts in an endless rolling grassland dotted with distant native villages and occasional wandering antelope. Eight hundred miles . . . and then, at last, Dilolo and the beginning of 'my' Congo. Here I received my official assignment, and as I had anticipated in Brussels, my destination was nowhere near my parents' home on the shore of Lake Kivu or the pygmy forest in the north. Instead, I was ordered to report to the District Commissioner of Haut-Lomami at Kamina, which is in Katanga, the southernmost part of the Congo.

That meant another eight hundred miles in the train before I finally found myself on the platform at Kamina. A man from the District Commissioner's office was supposed to be meeting me, but no one appeared. I waited a little uneasily and passed the time talking to a young pharmacist I had met on the train. He too was a *bleu*, but was not in government service; he had signed a contract with the big Cophaco drugstore chain. After we had discussed various diseases which we had never observed or experienced and recommended startling remedies, which we had never tested, he went off and I was left alone, feeling like a large, morose orphan.

Finally my escort, a young agronomist, arrived in a Ford pickup truck. He apologized for the delay, and made up for it at the Hôtel de la Gare where he treated me to several glasses of

Simba, an excellent and very potent Congolese beer. 'The D.C. sends his regards,' my new colleague told me in a very tough and experienced tone. (He must have been at least a year older than I was.) 'He says you are to stay here at the hotel tonight and report to his office tomorrow morning at the "Salute to the Flag"—that means 6.30 a.m.'

'Why so early?'

'That's how we run things here,' he said ominously. 'You'd better look out!'

That evening I studied my guidebook, my Swahili dictionary and several works on the history of Katanga. I was determined to give the impression of a tanned, experienced colonial and not a bright blue Belgian. The next morning I was up at 5.30, full of *café au lait* and enthusiasm. My career as a *Bwana ya l'Etat*—a government official—was about to begin, and I was anxious to wear my new uniform.

Shyly but happily, like a virgin going to her inevitable fate, I donned the khaki safari jacket, *kapitula* (tropical shorts), long khaki knee socks and sturdy walking shoes. Then, as the crowning touch, I put on The Helmet, the spectacular tropical headgear, complete with *Bula Matari* badge, of the Belgian Government. The original *Bula Matari* or 'Rock-Breaker' had been Henry Morton Stanley, the famous explorer who found Livingstone at Ujiji and played such a decisive rôle in the history of the Congo. I hope he looked more impressive in *his* helmet than I did in mine.

I took one long look in my large wardrobe mirror and decided not to take another for several years. The Helmet looked like a deformed khaki chamber-pot adorned with the shiny Dick Tracy badge known in colonial argot as the *'plaque à poules'* or 'chicken plate', because of the natives' charming custom of presenting visiting officials with a chicken, not as a bribe so much as a wily gesture of goodwill.

I took another look—against my better judgement—and shuddered. Still, I strode from my room with what I hoped was the proper air of experienced official dignity and arrived at District Headquarters just as a large group of helmeted, khaki-clad colleagues was forming a solemn line and assuming the *Garde à Vous* position. The black, red and gold banner of Belgium was about to be raised. I jumped into line beside them and tried to look as pious as they did during the ceremony.

After the military salute had been given and the bugle-call sounded I was given an enthusiastic welcome. The District

Commissioner was especially friendly, which came as a pleasant surprise. Then, as we entered his office together and he sat down before his imposing desk, a mysterious metamorphosis took place. 'Life isn't easy here,' he told me with the air of a Biblical prophet.

'I'm not looking for an easy life.'

'You young people! You come here from Brussels full of illusions and misconceptions. You never listen to people who *know*. You have to learn it all from your own experience.'

I said nothing. He was probably right, but there was no need to be so pompous about it.

'I'm going to send you on a most educational trip, Monsieur Hallet. I do this with every new recruit.'

'A trip?'

'Your first job will be to make an agricultural survey of the Baluba tribes in the Malemba Nkulu area. That's in the Mwanza Territory, about two hundred miles north-east of here. How does that sound to you?'

'It sounds wonderful!' I said eagerly. Since my talk with the clerk at the Ministry of Colonies, I had harboured a secret fear that I would find myself trapped behind a desk or running a mimeograph machine in a stuffy office.

'You'll be provided with transportation,' the D.C. continued. 'An S.T.A. pick-up truck [Service des Transports Administratifs] will come and get you tomorrow morning. The driver will take you to Mwanza, and your Territorial Administrator there will fill you in on all the details.'

As promised, a native driver named Marcel drove me to Mwanza the next day and deposited me in the local *gîte d'étape*, a sort of bungalow provided by the Government for travellers passing through bush posts. I arose next morning eager to learn the details of my first safari; but my mood changed for the worse when I met my first Territorial Administrator—or A.T. as we used to call them—a fat, unctuous individual, whom I shall call 'Grosjean'. From the moment we set eyes on each other, we got along about as well as a giraffe and a wart-hog forced into a shotgun wedding. After the A.T. had offered me a limp handshake and a forced, toothy smile, he got down to business.

'Life isn't easy here . . .' he started out, patterning his style after our mutual boss in Kamina.

'When do I leave?' I broke in, completely out of patience with the official ritual.

'Don't be so hasty, Monsieur Hallet. You'll have a rough time near the Malemba Nkulu swamps—the whole area is infested with mosquitoes and tsetse flies. Relax and take it easy while you can.'

Grosjean handed me a map on which the route of my trip was marked in an irregular circle. It was a two-week safari, and I would average about twenty miles a day. My mission was to survey the crop reserves, both those in the ground and those stored in the huts; to study the possibilities of crop extension; to report on the general sanitation conditions; and to notify the Government of all infractions against agricultural regulations.

'You'll have a good chance to get acquainted with the Baluba,' Grosjean commented. 'They're the largest tribe in the Congo with at least a dozen sub-tribes here in Katanga and farther north in Kasai. They're typical Bantu, and you'll find them fairly representative of about ten million people in the Congo. The rest of our population is made up of Sudanese in the north, Nilotics in the northeast, and Hamites in the east and Ruanda-Urundi.' The A.T. paused, eyeing me sardonically. 'Here I am,' he said, 'getting technical with you, and you don't even know what the word "Bantu" means.'

That really annoyed me, so I decided to show off. 'The Bantu are the largest and most important ethnic group of the Negroid racial stock,' I said pedantically. 'Their languages are characterized by pure Italian vowels and unchanging roots governed by prefixes. Their way of life is overwhelmingly agricultural, based on simple hoe cultivation, with some occasional hunting and fishing thrown in. The average stature is around 5 ft. 5 in. and the bodily proportions are generally harmonious—'

'Very impressive,' the A.T. interrupted, 'but none of your book-learning will do you any good in the bush.'

'I can't see where it will do any harm.'

'Time will tell. You'll be surprised at how many things you still have to learn. Good luck, Monsieur Hallet,' he added, with a last crocodile smile, 'I suspect that you'll need it.'

I began to agree with him when I went to the Territorial Depot and tried to put together the essential elements for my first safari. Tents, food, instruments, books and equipment were relatively small problems; people were very large ones. I had two *moniteurs*, foremen in charge of agricultural control, to deal with; two *polici*, native policemen; a dozen porters; an aged *pishi*, or cook; and Sylvestre, an arrogant *karani*, or native clerk, as my interpreter. He seemed competent enough, but after a few

minutes with this educated Muluba,[1] who wore long trousers
and a white shirt, it became obvious that there was going to be
trouble along the way.

I gave a simple order. Sylvestre translated it into Tshiluba, and
one of my porters looked up at me with sudden resentment.
'What did you say to that man?' I asked anxiously

'Just what *you* said, monsieur.'

I wondered, and after several similar incidents I stopped wondering and started to worry. Then I had a wonderful stroke of
luck: a skinny fourteen-year-old Luba boy, with large, intelligent eyes and what appeared to be a perpetual smile, wandered
into the Territorial Depot and stood silently watching the chaos.
Once or twice he laughed aloud and I began to feel almost
annoyed until he spoke to me in Kiswahili. Now I was overjoyed: here was an African I could talk to—with some hesitation
and fumbling, of course—but without benefit of a meddlesome
interpreter.

'Please let me come with you, *Bwana*!' he pleaded. 'I have
worked for white men before. I can be a big help!'

'Won't your parents worry if you don't come home?' I asked
in pidgin Kiswahili.

'They are dead. I live with my uncle. He doesn't care what
I do.'

'Then you can come.'

It was a wise decision: the youngster, whose name was Ngoi,
had things running on an efficient, orderly basis within minutes,
and I began to entertain the hopeful conviction that my first
safari might eventually progress beyond the walls of the Territorial Depot.

*   *   *

At 6.30 next morning, when the little caravan assembled for
departure to Malemba Nkulu, the A.T. showed up and stared
at me with obvious disapproval. 'Where's your *tipoye*?' he
demanded.

[1] Most of the prefixes of tribal names are Ba- or Wa- in the plural and
generally Mu- in the singular form. For the name of the corresponding
language, the prefix is Ki-. When the native name is used as an adjective,
no prefix is necessary. An example of correct usage: 'A *Mu*lega told me a
dirty joke in *Ki*lega about what two *Ba*lega were doing inside a Lega hut.'
Unfortunately, I cannot use the Baluba as an example, not because they
are excessively moral, but because the name of their language, Tshiluba, is
an exception to the rules.

'My *what?*'

He sighed. 'It's to ride on,' he explained. 'A kind of hammock carried on the shoulders of four porters.'

I stared at Grosjean's pot-belly until he started to redden. 'I don't ride on anyone's shoulders,' I said pointedly. 'I walk.'

'They'll have more respect for you if you use a *tipoye*.'

'I walk.'

'Look here, Monsieur Hallet! You're behaving as though you were going to reform the entire Congo in two weeks. You'll come to grief if you keep it up.'

'Don't waste your time worrying about me. I can take care of myself.'

He shrugged and walked away. Then I spoke to Ngoi, Ngoi spoke to Sylvestre, Sylvestre spoke to the porters, and we finally started to move.

I felt tremendously excited during the first couple of miles, picturing myself as an intrepid explorer setting out to face all the dangers of the mysterious 'Dark Continent'. My enthusiasm waned as we marched across twenty more hot and entirely uneventful miles of lonely savannah. By the time we pitched camp late in the afternoon, my only real feelings were fatigue and a sense of overwhelming relief.

The porters unfolded and laboriously erected the tents, dug a latrine and drainage ditch for the camp and built a temporary kitchen for Tukula, the cook. Then the policemen and monitors went to a nearby village for water and firewood. As for myself, I stood by and watched the proceedings with glum interest: I hadn't said a word since we stopped to make camp. While I had been trying to think what needed to be done, my native crew had simply gone ahead and done it.

Just before sunset I saw half a dozen strangers approaching from the direction of the village; one carried a scrawny brown chicken and another a wicker basket covered with a white cloth. A tall, middle-aged man with a large shiny medal dangling on his chest dominated the group. 'Who is that?' I asked Ngoi nervously.

'He is the *Sultani*, the chief of all the chiefs in this group of villages. He has come to greet you.'

The six Baluba walked into my camp with an easy, confident air. '*Jambo, Bwana!*' the *Sultani* said, and flashed me a blinding smile along with the classic Swahili 'Hello'. Then he made a lordly gesture and the two gift-bearers came forward. Unaware that I was committing a grave social error by taking a present

from the hand of a servant instead of gesturing to one of my own
'boys', I stepped forward to take possession of the *plaque à
poules* chicken. Before I came to my senses, and handed it to
Ngoi, the indignant bird squawked and flapped wildly in my
hands; feathers flew through the air and dung dropped on to my
left shoe. The wicker basket held a dozen eggs. Fortunately I
didn't handle it, otherwise I probably would have made an
omelet on the spot.

'Take it to the *pishi*!' I said a little too loudly. Then, as an
afterthought, I called out to him, 'And bring back a couple of
bottles of beer!'

It was the perfect gesture. The *Sultani* and I drank together
and, flanked by Ngoi and Sylvestre, I managed to keep up a
more or less sensible conversation. My first native official
seemed anxious to assure me that all went smoothly in his villages and that they weren't worthy of my expert attention. He
was very firm on both of those points. At once I saw myself as I
must have appeared in his eyes: a large, blindingly *bleu* Belgian
innocent, to be flattered, patted on the head, presented with the
traditional chicken and hustled out of the area.

I thought longingly of making a sweeping investigation, a
grand-scale exposé—perhaps of chicanery in the sweet-potato
fields or some sort of sanitary *scandale*. I toyed with the idea but
soon abandoned it. This was just an overnight stopover; my
real work was not supposed to start until twenty miles northwest at a larger and more important group of villages. The *Sultani* left, vastly pleased with the apparent success of his strata-
gems, and I consoled myself with his chicken and two of the
eggs which Tukula fried for me in canned butter. The bird was
tough and tasteless and most of the eggs were rotten.

The next thirteen days were a confusing montage of Luba
villages, cotton and sweet-potato fields, native privies and safari
camp-sites, punctuated by misunderstandings and mysteries.
Without Ngoi I would have got nowhere; my official interpreter,
Sylvestre, was almost useless. As an *évolué*—an educated or
'civilized' native—he was much too concerned with money,
clothes and social status to have any real interest in his job.

Sylvestre's dark trousers always had a knife-edged crease, his
shoes shone like twin mirrors, and his long-sleeved white shirt
was generally spotless. Such sartorial splendour was hard to
maintain on safari, and every night I heard the *évolué* shouting
in his tent as he supervised his 'boy' through the ironing and
shoe-polishing rituals. Then next morning he would emerge—an

immaculate vision, with his breast pocket full of fountain pens and mechanical pencils, with a wrist-watch on a pink plastic strap, and horn-rimmed spectacles. He was for ever taking the glasses off and polishing them with his handkerchief; once when he mislaid them, he grew almost hysterical.

'Is your sight so bad?' I asked sympathetically. 'Are they a special prescription?'

He looked surprised. 'No, monsieur,' he answered. 'I bought them in a shop.'

'Then how do you know if the lenses are ground correctly?'

'They suit me perfectly.'

I was intrigued. 'May I try them?'

'Be careful,' Sylvestre warned me. 'They cost twenty francs!'

I slipped them on and peered at him intently. It was just like looking through a window—the frames contained plain glass.

'Do things really look different to you when you put them on?' I asked him, a trifle mystified.

'No, monsieur. *I* look different. Those *bashenzi*—those ignorant natives—in this way they have more respect for me.'

Among Sylvestre's other methods for commanding respect, the most annoying was his habit of barking orders in French to uneducated Baluba who couldn't even speak Kiswahili. Then, when they stared at him blankly, he would raise his eyes to heaven, wave his beautiful hands in martyred despair, and make a great show of speaking the Luba words as slowly as if he were addressing backward children. This ridiculous procedure took so much time that I could make myself understood more quickly by sign-language.

Sylvestre did a thriving business with the natives of the different villages we visited, giving them the benefit of his intellectual opinions with paid advice on their love life, family problems and, very often, financial disputes. I was surprised to see how many apparently primitive natives were in possession of both coins and paper currency; later I learned that modern money had penetrated into nearly every Congo village and that its meaning and use were understood by natives on every educational level.

Those little interviews generally netted him five francs a time. For another ten francs Sylvestre would write an imposing letter, inscribed in a flowing hand on stationery stolen from the A.T.'s office. Underneath the Government's French-Flemish letterhead, CONGO BELGE—BELGISCH CONGO, and the typed legend *Province du Katanga, District du Haut-Lomami, Territoire de*

Mwanza, which lent an impressive official air, Sylvestre wrote passionate love-letters for his clients, threats to real or fancied enemies, and brisk business correspondence about dowries and possible lawsuits.

Sylvestre over-reached himself, however, when he started soliciting the members of my crew. The climax came when the old *pishi*, Tukula, appeared before me at breakfast, bearing a square white envelope with the inscription *Monsieur Hallet, En Route, Région Malemba Nkulu*. Since Tukula could speak a little Kiswahili, I wondered why he didn't try to talk to me, but I opened the envelope without comment. Inside I found a letter written in French on official stationery—with Tukula's scrawled signature underneath Sylvestre's careful, professional calligraphy. Literally translated, it read:

Sir, my Boss,

I have the honour very humbly to solicit of Your very high benevolence and consideration the favour of a grant of an augmentation in salary by reason of the arduous, exhausting and incessant labour which I must perform without the elementary benefit of a servant destined to vulgar enterprises such as the peeling of potatoes and carrots and the onions which make me weep, and finally, what is totally incompatible with my dignity as the grandson of Chief Kalungula, washing the dishes and preparing the cookfire.

In the hope of being favoured by a very generous response to my legitimate supplication, I ask You to believe, Sir my Boss, in the assurance of my most lofty, profound, faithful and devoted consideration.

As I read, the cook watched me with an air of confident expectation, evidently convinced that such an eloquent appeal would stir my generous emotions.

'Do you want a *majibu*?' I asked. 'A written answer?'

'*Ndio!*' Tukula answered excitedly. 'Yes!'

I picked up a stub of red pencil from the table and wrote in crude block letters across the bottom of that beautiful epistle, 'HAPANA'—a large Swahili 'No'. I handed it back to him saying, 'Next time you want to ask me something, just talk to me about it.'

'*Bwana*,' the cook said mournfully, 'I paid Sylvestre fifteen francs for that letter. He said it was sure to work.'

'Well,' I pointed out, 'if you can afford such expensive letters, you certainly don't need a raise.'

That incident led to war between Tukula and Sylvestre. Since the letter had failed to move me, the cook demanded his money back. Sylvestre defended himself on the basis of white colonial exploitation, casting me in the traditional rôle of the brutal Belgian slave trader, too callous to be swayed by even the most flowery prose. Coming from him this was a strange argument; he had received a free education from the Belgians and was making a very decent salary, about five times more than Tukula, whom he mulcted so zealously, and at least seven times more than Ngoi, whom he treated with utter contempt.

Ngoi was ignorant and 'uncivilized' compared to Sylvestre. He owned neither white shirt nor fountain pen nor shiny shoes; but he was always good-natured, reliable and full of enthusiastic curiosity. In all of those characteristics, I preferred him vastly to the *karani* and his fellow-*évolués*, though there were, of course, a few who were much less vain and superficial.

*   *   *

On the last day of our safari, we entered the village of Kitereke about twenty miles from Mwanza. My eye was attracted immediately by the sight of a native tailor, pedalling away at an archaic Singer sewing machine. Beside him, an old woman stood watching in silence, her eyes wide with wonder at the miracle by by which two pieces of calico cloth became one. 'He is almost as powerful as the medicine man,' Ngoi explained gravely. A few steps away I saw the *magazini*, a sort of Central African general store, selling nails, soap, hoes, axes, petrol, cotton cloth and clothing in the loudest colours and patterns, alarm clocks, junk jewellery, bow-ties, and all the necessities for the new way of life which seemed to be sweeping over Africa.

Yet much of the past remained, like a vivid echo of my childhood memories. The dark thatched roofs of the houses were splashed with brilliant white where manioc roots were drying. The women still stood in poses of almost classic dignity, rigidly upright, pounding the dried roots with giant mortars and pestles, the young girls strained the resulting flour into flat trays through a kind of primitive sieve with a framework of rough wood and a screen made out of *moustiquaire*—mosquito netting.

That word *moustiquaire* gave Ngoi and the rest of the natives tremendous trouble. No matter how they tried, it always came out with an extra syllable in the middle: *moustiquetaire*. The native tongue plays wonderful tricks with the French language: *allumette* is converted into *limeti*; *avion* becomes *ambio*; *serpent*

comes out *seripan*; and, ironically, *civilisé* is transmuted to
sifilisé.

Not far away from the straining operations, a fat old Luba
lady was making *bukari*—manioc dough—the Congolese
natives' most important staple food. The procedure was simple:
she mixed flour and water in a big metal pot, added a little salt
and a pinch of 'starter', covered it with a banana leaf and set it
aside to ferment. When she got up for a moment to reach for
another pot, I saw for the first time the beautiful little four-
legged stool she had been sitting on—an amazing piece of work:
the legs were carved in the form of four human figures, and as I
knelt to examine it, I realized that the whole intricate carving
was made from a single piece of wood, according to the fine
traditions of the past.

'I must buy this!' I told Ngoi excitedly.

'It is very old, *Bwana*. They make better chairs now, just like
the white man's. Come, I will show you.'

He started to walk away. 'I don't want a white man's
chair,' I insisted. 'I want a Luba stool—that one!' Ngoi
rolled his eyes in bewilderment but surrendered, and we turned
back.

But the stool had vanished, somewhere beneath the broad
bottom and flowing *pagne* of that vast Luba lady. She was very
fond of the stool, it developed. Either that or she was extremely
shrewd. After half an hour of cunning negotiations I was five
hundred francs lighter, the lady was sitting on the ground count-
ing my money, and I had acquired the very first of five thousand
traditional African artifacts which would ultimately become the
largest private collection of its kind in the world.

That night in Kitereke, I lay on my canvas cot and did a great
deal of thinking. It was terribly hot and I was a little depressed
that my first safari was coming to an end. I thought of the several
hundred Baluba I had met during the past two weeks and, realizing how very little I knew about them, tried to make plans for
the future. Language must come first, that was obvious. Later, it
would be possible to learn the customs and traditions, and the
complex magico-religious beliefs of the people. But beyond that,
I wanted to reach the hidden mind and soul of the Baluba, to
understand their strength and weakness, and to help them. I was
a raw recuit, a mere *bleu*, but I felt certain of one thing: Africa's
real future would never materialize if we tried to make imitation
white men of the natives, to clothe them in our own irrelevant
political, economic and religious philosophies as well as our

cast-off garments. They needed material and social aid, but *within the framework of their own traditions.*

My goal would be achieved neither by standing aloof, as the member of a 'superior, civilized' race, nor by enforcing any rigid system of regulations and punishments, and certainly not by riding in a *tipoye* and playing *Bwana Mukubwa*—Africa's version of India's *pukka sahib*—the Great Master. Yet I could see, even now, that the opposite attitude would be even less effective; being soft-hearted and unrealistic would spoil the natives beyond recognition. They would certainly take advantage of my weakness and I would lose whatever influence and power I had to help them. The great problem in being a novice 'paternalist' obviously lay in finding some reasonable compromise between stifling discipline and foolish indulgence. I knew that it wouldn't be easy.

I kept thinking about this as I turned and tossed on my narrow cot. Then I turned over once too often and the canvas fabric ripped along its entire length. I was dumped unceremoniously into the metal framework which promptly caved in, trapping me like a latter-day Laocoön in its cold, serpentine embrace. I lay there for a moment in an attitude of startled imbecility. Then, trying to sit up and free myself from the trap, I managed to fall between the two halves of the framework. As I went down, I instinctively snatched at the mosquito netting; it tore loose from the top of the tent and descended with me, yard after yard of filmy white cloth entangling me in its folds.

I thought of calling for help and decided against it. Not only was I involved in a grotesque tangle of bedframe and *moustiquaire*, but I was entirely naked. My career to date had been undistinguished enough; I didn't want to lose the last shreds of my official dignity. Grimly determined, I struggled, freed myself and searched through the endless folds of gauze for my pyjama trousers. I saw them and snatched, not realizing they were tangled in the framework. Once more came the familiar sound of ripping cloth and one pyjama-leg was two feet shorter.

I put them on anyway and ran to the flap of the tent. 'Ngoi!' I shouted. 'Ngoi!' My call was answered by hundreds of hungry mosquitoes that screamed with shrill delight as they zeroed in. 'Ngoi!' I shouted again. Then, half-crazed by that massive insect attack, I rushed back into my tent for the crumpled *moustiquaire*. I picked it up and pulled, trying to untangle the mess, and there was another sound of ripping cloth. I groaned, cursed, draped the two pieces of netting over my head and shoulders, and dashed out through the tent-flap again—only to collide with Ngoi and Tukula, both coming to my aid.

They went over backwards. The old cook looked up and saw, looming over him, an enormous spectral form, its lower parts clothed in an oddly tattered garment, its head draped in a mysterious white veil. It was obviously the evil spirit of a dead Muluba.

Tukula shrieked and fainted on the spot. Ngoi was round-eyed as he stared at the ghost and its victim; then, recognizing me, he collapsed into fits of hysterical laughter, rolling on the ground beside the motionless cook. People came running from every direction and I ran too—back into my tent. I sat down very warily on a folding chair and tried to invent some kind of reasonable explanation while I listened to the excited *brouhaha* of voices outside. Then the tumult died down, I heard soft footsteps padding away and Ngoi came in.

He stared at the wreckage of my cot and sat down at my feet. 'Don't look so sad, *Bwana*,' he said consolingly. 'I'm sorry I laughed at you.'

'I don't blame you for that. Is Tukula all right?'

He laughed. 'I let him lie on the ground while I talked to the others. Then I kicked him and he woke up. He is still as foolish as ever.'

'What did you tell the people?'

'I told them that Tukula walked in his sleep and had a bad dream. He screamed, you ran out to see what was happening and bumped into him. Everyone listened to the story and went back to bed. Nobody knows what really happened except you and me.'

I gazed down at him, admiring his quick resourcefulness. Then I had a disturbing thought. 'What about Tukula? He'll talk.'

'I told you, *Bwana*, don't worry! I made *him* think that he had a bad dream. Now he feels sorry for making so much noise, so he has built a nice fire to chase the mosquitoes and asks if you will come out and sit with us.'

I felt terribly guilty, but I knew that Tukula would forget the whole thing in a day or two. On the other hand, if the entire camp learned the truth of the matter, the story would certainly get back to Grosjean in Mwanza. The A.T. would tell the story to everyone he met, probably with an introduction like 'Guess what happened to the last *bleu* that Kamina unloaded on me.'

'*Akisanti sana*,' I said gravely, a heartfelt Swahili Thank you. Then Ngoi and I went outside to console the confused and extremely penitent cook. The three of us squatted as near the fire as possible, anxious to avoid not only the mosquitoes but the flies, fleas, moths, beetles and crickets of the buzzing African night. Tukula nodded timidly, Ngoi grinned with a wonderfully knowing look and I smiled back at my two new friends with an emotion entirely new to me, and one from which I would quickly recover: humility.

2

Red Blood and Black Water

Uwakiz'ubusore aba agize Imana—'Give thanks to
God if you live long enough to grow old.'

TUTSI PROVERB

'YOU look as if you had a bad night, Monsieur Hallet. Any
trouble?'

'No trouble at all. Everything went very smoothly.'

'Glad to hear it,' the A.T. remarked. 'You'd be surprised if
I told you some of the things that have happened on a new
man's first safari. I'm always having damned trouble with *bleus*.'

I was anxious to change the subject. 'I'm making excellent
progress with the languages. My Kiswahili is coming back
stronger every day, and I've already managed to pick up some
of the basic principles of Tshiluba. I think I'll be able to deal
with the natives directly in three or four months.'

'That sounds far too optimistic. It took *me* nearly two years
to learn Tshiluba.'

I refrained from the obvious comment. 'What happens now?
Do I go right out again?'

'You have a maximum of three days to write up your activity
report. Then I'm going to send you back to the bush.' Grosjean
got up and took a step towards the big map on the wall. 'I'll
show you where you'll be going.'

I joined him at the map and he traced a crooked route with
his forefinger through the area north of Mwanza. 'It's a much
longer safari than the first one,' he remarked. 'You'll be out for
forty-five days. You'll inspect fifty-eight native villages. And
you'll walk about three hundred miles—unless you want a
tipoye.'

'I'll walk.'

20

'At the upper limits of the Mwanza Territory, you'll cross the Lualaba River by pirogue.[1] Then you'll head towards the road that runs between Manono and Mitwaba. Fifty miles south of Manono, a territorial truck will be waiting for you, *if* you arrive on schedule. Otherwise, you'll have the opportunity to do some more walking. You seem to enjoy it well enough.'

'I do. I prefer any kind of activity to sitting behind a desk.'

Grosjean smiled at me like a gloating piranha fish. 'You can use Van Geel's desk in the next room for your activity report. He's out on safari. I suggest that you get started on it right away.'

Three days later, after Homeric struggles with an old Remington typewriter, I produced a document entitled *Rapport sur la Situation Agricole de la Région Malemba Nkulu*. All five of the territory's native clerks had watched with lofty condescension as I typed on the roller instead of the paper, put the carbons in backwards and forgot to release the shift-lock. '. . . to think that *he's* coming here to civilize us!' I overhead one of the *évolués* remark from the next room. Then he clattered away furiously on his own machine, apparently bent on proving that a direct ratio existed between typing speed and degree of civilization.

When at last I escaped from the territorial office, I started to gather my personnel, supplies and equipment for the forty-five-day safari. Then I ran into what at first appeared to be a minor difficulty at the local dispensary: the supply of drugs was very low, and the *Infirmier*, the native male nurse on duty, said that no new supplies were expected for a fortnight, when the Sector Doctor's requisition would come through. I couldn't equip my safari without leaving the native population of Mwanza dangerously short of drugs, especially the all-important quinine.

I explained the situation to the A.T., and he sent me to a Catholic Mission about six miles away, to see if I could get the necessary supplies there. The mission doctor, a pleasant young nun, could provide everything I needed with one important exception: quinine. Her stock was very low and she could give me only half the quantity I needed. She promised, however, to send the rest on to me within two weeks via the A.T.

'Don't worry about it,' Grosjean assured me, when I returned to the post. 'I'll send it on by a special courier—I'll take care of it personally. Now, will you please get out of Mwanza before I lose my patience? You're half a day late.'

[1] A dug-out canoe.

*　　*　　*

The first week of safari was relatively uneventful. Then, on our eighth day out, we reached the village of Goy Mani. After seven nights in a tent, I was looking forward to sleeping in the local *gîte d'étape*, but it was occupied. The tenant was a tall man with light blue eyes, remarkably skinny legs and a cigarette perpetually dangling from his lip. He introduced himself as Franz Van Geel, a territorial agent from Mwanza.

'Van Geel?' I said curiously. 'Why, I was using your desk last week, and your typewriter. That "A" key really needs fixing!'

He smiled stiffly at the unexpected remark. 'Let's discuss it at dinner,' he suggested, 'after you pitch your tent. I think you'll be surprised at the kind of table I keep.'

I was. Victor, Van Geel's *pishi*, prepared a wonderful chicken in white sauce with tinned mushrooms which bore no resemblance to Tukula's unappetizing *plaque à poules* messes. We washed it down with two bottles of *Simba* beer and had tinned peaches for dessert. Then, as Victor was clearing the table, Van Geel let out a loud, deliberate belch. 'We Flemings, we really know how to live,' he said expansively. 'You Walloons are much more easily satisfied.'

I sighed. Even here in the Congo, it was impossible to escape the everlasting conflict of Fleming versus Walloon. In Belgium, where racial discrimination is obviously impossible, prejudice exists on a linguistic and regional basis. About 55 per cent of the population are Flemings, who occupy the northwestern half of Belgium, and are a stolid, stubborn, hard-working, often fanatically Catholic people who speak a Low German dialect similar to Dutch. The French-speaking Walloons in the southeast are less determined and industrious, but much more artistic and good-natured. Each section of the population has its stronghold: Antwerp for the Flemings and Liége for the Walloons. They meet—and often mate—in Brussels, where they have produced a half-and-half breed and a peculiar argot, both called 'Brusseleer'. The favourite local oath is *Podferdomme!* —a hearty Brussels 'Dammit!' I myself am one of these half-breeds, with a Walloon father from Liége and a Flemish mother from Louvain, so I can look at both sides with some objectivity.

'*Ik ben in Leuven geboren,*' I explained to Van Geel in Flemish, '*mais j'aime parler, manger et faire l'amour en français.*'

'At least you're not a full-blooded Walloon,' he said dryly, 'so maybe you won't be offended if I tell you a little joke.'

'A joke? Let's hear it.'

THE DIVINE KING OF THE BAKUBA (SOUTH CENTRAL CONGO)
Bope Mopinji II, wearing his cowrie-encrusted ceremonial dress,
with some of his court.

BAMBUTI PYGMIES

(*Top left*) Women roofing a hut with *mangungu* leaves.
(*Top right*) A typical pygmy of the Efe tribe, North Kivu, Congo.
(*Below*) Men and women dancing in their traditionally separate circles.

'It seems that the Antwerp Zoo made an unusual addition to
its monkey-house. The new cage wasn't large, but it drew a
tremendous crowd. All the Flemings gathered to watch the new
tenant sitting making monkey-faces and trying to look smart.
But they had to hold their noses because he smelled so bad.'
Van Geel paused, hoping to stimulate my curiosity.

Obediently I asked, 'What was in the cage?'

'A Walloon!' he barked triumphantly and burst into howls of
laughter.

I laughed briefly, to please him, and launched into a joke of
my own, a story I had heard just before I left Brussels: 'There
was once a Congolese *évolué* who arrived by plane on his first
visit to Belgium. He took a taxi at Melsbroek airport and, as the
cab sped into Brussels, asked the driver, "How is it that I see
houses, streets and factories wherever I look? Where is the
bush?" "We have none," the driver explained. The Congolese
stared at him. "If there's no bush," he said in bewilderment,
"then where do you put the Flemings?" '[1]

My joke hit Van Geel a little too hard. He was, after all, a
typical *petit flamand* in a bush post. The lines of his face
hardened and the rest of the evening's conversation had a
decidedly frigid edge.

Next morning I was awakened by a loud noise, a sharp crack
repeated eight times. It stopped. Then there was another
sequence of eight staccato sounds. I dressed quickly and rushed
out to see what was going on. I shall never forget the sight. A
Luba native lay face down on the ground, his *pagne* drawn up
to expose his naked buttocks. A powerful soldier stood over
him, brandishing the *fimbo*, a murderous whip made from the
dried and stretched penis of a hippo or buffalo—the same lethal
instrument which the South Africans call the *sjambok*.

Every time it cracked and slashed, as the soldier wielded it
with all his force, the *fimbo* cut deeply into the muscles of the
man's buttocks, leaving thin red lines of blood that trickled
down his thighs. The soldier was obviously trying to strike the

[1] Most Congolese, like the travelling native in the story, have a relatively
poor opinion of the Flemings. The *évolué* class (and the semi-*évolués*) have
been educated in French and distrust the harsh, alien sounds of Flemish.
Whenever two Flemings converse in their native language, every sensitive
évolué within earshot assumes that they are making derogatory remarks
against him. (Often, they are.) The worker class is even more antagonistic,
since the zealous Flemings fill many minor supervisory positions, and
badger the natives to work as hard as themselves.

same spot repeatedly to make the punishment even more painful. Horrified, I watched as the whip descended twice more.
Then the victim pulled himself to his feet and started to stagger
away. 'Wait a minute!' the soldier called out. 'You forgot to
say "Thank you." That's part of your punishment.' The
Muluba obediently mumbled 'Thank you' as he limped away,
dark streaks of blood staining his *pagne.*

That last little refinement was worse than the blows. I moved
forward quickly as a fresh soldier took over and gestured to the
next native who waited at the head of a long, apprehensive line.
Then I saw Van Geel, lounging on the steps of the *gîte,* calmly
watching the proceedings. He smiled at me. '*Bonjour,*' he said,
'*avez-vous bien dormi?*'

'Never mind how I slept! Can you tell me what the hell is the
matter with you, allowing something like this to go on?'

He looked at me with astonishment. 'What are you talking
about?'

'That.'

'That is *fimbo nane.* Don't tell me you have never seen it
before? *Mijn God,* you really have more to learn than I
thought!'

The whip cracked again and I shuddered as though it were
striking my own flesh. 'Van Geel!' I cried furiously. 'How can
you tolerate it?'

'I don't tolerate it: I'm ordering it. It's the only thing they
understand. *Fimbo nane* means "eight blows", that's the legal
maximum. A few years ago it was twelve; in the past it was
twenty, and when the great native chiefs used it, without any
control, they sometimes gave the whip to five strong men in
succession until, after fifty or sixty blows, the criminal usually
died. To avoid that *we* control the punishment now. It's really
the only way to get anything done around here.'

The *fimbo* cracked again. Van Geel watched my face contort.
'Oh, I know how you feel,' he said. 'I didn't approve of it
myself when I started working with these people six years ago.
I tried everything else, but the natives just laughed at me! *They*
said I should use the whip on their own people—the ones who
were lazy or stole or refused to pay their taxes.'

The *fimbo* cracked again, for the eighth time, and another
Muluba struggled to his feet. Blood ran down his legs in jagged
red lines. I saw blood on his chin and realized that he had
bitten clean through his lower lip. The next culprit stepped forward towards the man with the whip.

'Order them to stop,' I said abruptly. 'If you don't, I'll step between them and put an end to it myself. If you try to interfere, you'll have to fight me.'

'Are you crazy? Do you want to destroy all local respect for authority? We can't fight in front of the natives!'

I started towards the man with the *fimbo*. 'All right,' Van Geel called hastily, 'you win. I can't permit a scandal of this kind.' Then he shouted an order to the soldiers. The long line of waiting Baluba wavered and broke, the territorial agent watched with rising fury as they wandered off, chattering to each other incredulously. When the last native was out of sight, he turned to me. 'Don't ever try that again,' he said venomously. 'Stupid *bleu!*'

At that, my own anger boiled over. '*Petit crétin!*' I shouted, seizing him by the lapels and twisting the cloth around his throat until his face started to purple. 'If I ever catch you doing that again, I'll break you in half!' He struggled to speak, but I tightened the pressure on his throat. 'You make me sick, Van Geel! You talk about leading the natives away from savagery, and then introduce them to your own hypocritical brand of it. Regulated, sanitary savagery, that's all your little system is!' Then I turned him loose with a gesture of disgust.

He coughed and finally caught his breath. 'They're just big children!' he cried hoarsely. 'They don't understand talk. You have to beat them. You'll find that out some day!'

'Of course they're children—but is *that* your idea of how to teach a child? Is the *fimbo* an instrument of paternal love and understanding?'

'You'll find out,' he repeated, 'sooner or later.' He turned and walked back to the *gîte*.

I started to walk away, but Sylvestre blocked my path. '*Excusez-moi*, monsieur,' he said politely. 'May I tell you a little something?'

'What is it?'

'You don't seem to be aware of our customs. Those natives really need the *fimbo* to keep them in line!'

'Those "natives"? What do you think *you* are, Sylvestre? A Belgian? An English lord? A white hunter?'

The *évolué* stared at me angrily through his windowpane spectacles, raised his head proudly and answered, 'I am a civilized man, monsieur.'

'Is your behind civilized too? Is it any different from theirs? Can't you imagine how you'd feel if you got eight good cracks?'

'You can't talk to me like that!' he exploded. 'It's against the law to inflict corporal punishment on an *évolué.*'

'The law protects you. But what about them? They're your own brothers!'

'They're no brothers of mine! They're just *bashenzi*—bush natives!'

'Monsieur Sylvestre,' I said wearily, *'allez vous promener!'*

He walked off indignantly and spent the rest of the day telling everyone in Goy Mani about my brutality, while Van Geel was brooding about my weak sentimentality. Apparently, I was doomed to controversy with A.T.'s *évolués*, Flemings and nearly everyone else. The only people who liked me, it seemed, were the *bashenzi.*

Early next morning I had a final confrontation with Van Geel. 'I'm giving in to you because I don't want any more trouble,' he said coldly. 'You've done enough damage here. But I intend to make an official complaint against you to the District Commissioner in Kamina. You'll see how much this will cost you—I have friends, Monsieur Hallet.'

I stared into his angry pale-blue eyes. 'Listen, Van Geel! If you start any trouble, I'll catch up with you sooner or later. You'll find yourself stretched out on your belly, my friend, and you'll learn what a *fimbo* can really do, in the old native style. I swear it!'

Van Geel's official complaint never materialized. A year later the Government reduced *fimbo nane* to *fimbo* six, and progressively to *fimbo* four and two. In 1955 flogging was completely suppressed in the Congo (over the indignant protests of many traditional native chiefs) while it remained a legal punishment in many countries of the civilized world. I was deeply relieved to see the end of the *fimbo*, but as the native crime-rate rose sharply in every part of the Congo, I began to appreciate the practical necessity which had driven some government officials to use it. Van Geel and the others like him were not villains; they were desperate men trying to cope with the age-old indolence, indifference and delinquency of the people for whom they were directly responsible. They were profoundly wrong in their methods, which lacked imagination or subtlety, but the deep-seated problems which had forced white men to adopt the natives' own *fimbo* were undeniably real, and they remained.

*　　*　　*

We left the Goy Mani area four days later, headed east towards another cluster of villages. After several days at the new camp-site, and a seemingly endless round of inspections, we were ready to move on; but a minor trouble developed at the last moment: my toes started to itch with maddening insistency.

I tried to ignore it for a while, but finally took off my socks and inspected my feet. I was horrified to find several small pale bulges near my toenails, which I recognized, from textbook illustrations, as one of tropical Africa's most loathsome pests: *Sarcopsylla penetrans*, the infamous 'jigger-flea'. The female parasites, less than a millimetre long, had burrowed beneath my skin and now their abdomens were swelling to vast proportions with crops of eggs. Each might grow to the size of a small pea and, if untreated, would develop into an abscess. I was still peering disgustedly at my feet when Ngoi came into my tent. '*Funza*,' he said promptly. 'They hide under your skin. Do you want me to take them out?'

I was curious to see his technique, but a little wary. 'Are you sure you know what to do?' I asked him.

'Don't worry, *Bwana*. It's easy. Just give me a needle.'

Working very slowly and carefully with a steel darning-needle, he opened the skin and exposed the sacs where the insects were embedded. Taking exquisite pains, he removed every one of them intact and crushed them between his fingers, wiping his hands on his tattered trousers. Then, asking me to wait a minute, he darted out and came back with Tukula. The *pishi* smiled at me foolishly while he rolled a big quid of tobacco between his jaws. I smiled back, a little perplexed.

'Hold up your foot, *Bwana*,' Ngoi directed me. I obeyed and he pointed to it. 'Spit on it!' he told Tukula.

By the time the cook had finished bathing my toes with dark brown saliva, I understood what the two Baluba were doing. The tobacco juice was an antiseptic and, as it turned out, an effective one. The little holes in my feet healed quickly. But soon I had a new problem to worry about. Three weeks had gone by, no special courier had arrived from Mwanza and my supply of quinine was nearly exhausted. I waited impatiently for another two days and then decided to send a porter back to the post with an urgent message for Grosjean. The young Muluba took the envelope from my hand and inserted it carefully into a short length of split bamboo.

'Why is he doing that?' I asked Ngoi.

'To keep it clean, *Bwana*. If he held it in his hand, your paper might get full of sweat and dirt.'

Touched, I gave the porter a friendly slap on the back and wished him good luck. He must have had it, since I later learned that he made it back to Mwanza in four days, only to find when he reached the Territorial Office that Grosjean wasn't there. The A.T. was on safari, and my message passed through the hands of several subordinates before ending up in a filing-cabinet. The package of quinine, which the nun had forwarded to him nearly two weeks before, stayed where it was: in the A.T.'s desk; he had completely forgotten it.

Meanwhile, my caravan continued to move towards the Lualaba River. By now we had been out a full month, and it was five days since I had taken my last dose of quinine. We crossed the Lualaba in several pirogues; the river was nearly a mile wide at this point, but very placid, so that the long crossing was accomplished without any real difficulties. All the same, I felt terribly tired that evening and had no appetite for dinner. Next morning, after an unnaturally long sleep, I felt horribly sick: my neck was stiff, my head ached and a terrible vertigo seized me as I tried to get up. I fell back and lay there, sweating and shaking uncontrollably, a typical victim of malaria.

I stayed in bed all day. Tukula several times brought me soup and begged me to eat it, but the thought of food revolted me. I slept very badly that night and next day was amazed to find that I felt even worse. I hadn't thought it possible. The stiffness had spread through all of my muscles, I vomited repeatedly and the malarial paroxysms grew more prolonged and violent.

Remembering something I had heard from the young pharmacist at Kamina, I tried a supposedly infallible remedy and I drank a whole bottle of Johnny Walker whisky. Sweating horribly, I lay in an alcoholic stupor for hours, my mind wandering through a crazy landscape where African antelope and lions promenaded through the prim streets of Brussels and Louvain. Eventually I fell asleep and spent another restless night punctuated by nightmares.

In the morning, feeling the need to urinate, I groped unsteadily for the aluminium pot which Tukula had left for me. I found myself sitting there a moment later, shivering violently as I stared at a dark red pool in the bottom and terrible words came to my mind—*hématurie* . . . *la fièvre bilieuse hémoglobinurique* . . . blackwater fever.'

It was a sentence of death.

Blackwater fever was an enigma, difficult to treat even under optimum conditions in a European hospital. Even the causative organism was unknown.[1] Some authorities took the classical view that the disease was a severe and aberrant form of subtertian malaria, aggravated by overwork, under-eating and too much quinine—a factor which certainly didn't apply in my case. Among several questions left unanswered by this theory is the perplexing fact that blackwater fever frequently occurs in regions where malaria is either very rare or completely unknown. Whatever the cause, there was no argument about the prognosis: it was grim and usually fatal.

I knew that my one chance of survival was to remain absolutely quiet. Every movement only hastened the destructive processes going on inside my heart, liver and kidneys. I wasted a few minutes thinking about Grosjean in Mwanza, wondering why he hadn't sent the quinine. Then I forced myself to examine the situation as dispassionately as possible.

I was two hundred miles from medical aid, trapped in a little tent on the east bank of the Lualaba River. If I tried to move, the disease would kill me very quickly; if I remained here, it would take longer but would probably kill me in the end. Logic told me that I was going to die; my youth, will and ambition all rebelled against that conclusion. 'I am *not* going to die!' I whispered to myself. 'I refuse.' Then I lay there for a long while, trying to form a plan while still capable of rational thought.

'Ngoi!' I called out finally. 'Ngoi!' He didn't come. I waited, and soon became aware of a pressing need. Slowly, painfully, I rose to one elbow and reached for the battered pot. This time the result was even darker and more ominous. I stared at it with grim disgust, and then looked up to see Ngoi watching me from the tent-flap. His silence was significant: 'I'll fix everything!' and 'Don't worry, *Bwana*!' had been his favourite phrases. Now he said nothing.

'Listen very carefully,' I told him. 'Soon I may not be able to talk, so you must remember everything I say. I have to go

[1] The question remains unsettled. The modern school of tropical medicine claims that blackwater fever is a specific disease, probably caused by a protozoan parasite, *Piroplasma* (=*Babesia*). Species of this same organism are responsible for the 'Texas fever' of cattle in the United States and 'redwater cattle fever' in South Africa. The presence of the malarial parasites, especially *Plasmodium falciparum*, in about 80 per cent of cases of blackwater fever may be coincidental rather than causative, just as the bacon accompanies but scarcely gives birth to the eggs.

back to my own people, they can help me. Tell the men to build a litter. Make sure they start work on it at once and tomorrow morning we must start out for the road to Manono. If we leave very early, we can reach the road before it grows dark.'

'There is a white man, *Bwana*. A forester. He lives near the road. One of the *polici* spoke of him. Maybe the white man can help you.'

'That is wonderful news. Bring me the paper and pencil from the table and I will write him a letter. Then you can send a porter with it to the white man.'

I raised myself to one elbow again and scrawled a desperate message. I was appalled to see how my fingers trembled as I tried to write and noticed for the first time, as my hand rested on the white paper, how very yellow my skin had become. '*Ictère*,' I said to myself, 'jaundice . . . renal insufficiency.' Then I lay back, shivering horribly; Ngoi tucked the blankets round me.

'Tomorrow morning,' I repeated. 'Even if I cannot speak, even if I seem to be dying, you must see that we leave early in the morning!'

'Try to sleep, *Bwana*. I will send the porter. The men will make a strong litter to hold you. We will reach the road.'

Ngoi left. I huddled under my blankets, shivering so violently that the little cot trembled and swayed. The pot, again . . . and again . . . and again. 'Polyuria', the medical books called it, excessive secretion of urine. I felt terrible revulsion. I was nauseated and I rocked with spasms of bilious green vomiting. Exhausted, I tried to sleep. It was impossible. A dull stupor alternated with my paroxysms and I was moving farther and farther away from reality. As the sun set, I entered into a grotesque eternity of darkness and delirium.

I fought many phantoms that night. I returned to Mwanza and confronted Grosjean with his broken promise. I found Van Geel beating an old Muluba and wrenched the *fimbo* from his hand. Soon he lay sobbing on the ground while I struck him repeatedly with the murderous whip. Sylvestre sat in the background and laughed while he wrote interminable letters with a pen dipped in blood.

Suddenly the scene shifted to the market-place at Lobito. The old medicine man had a mysterious talisman in the palm of his withered hand—it was the cure for my sickness, I knew it! He drifted away and I saw myself back in the little Brussels office, signing a printed form. The words flowed slowly across the paper . . . 'I shall make no complaint or request for transfer . . .'

The office shattered into a million kaleidoscopic fragments of coloured glass which reassembled slowly into an incredibly beautiful scene: I was on the shore of Lake Kivu, walking towards the open door of my father's villa, and everything was perfect. Then suddenly, violently, the landscape changed. The blue lake turned into a sea of blood swarming with huge proto-zoan forms, the sky rained acid green and the earth shook with vast, sickening spasms . . .

I was still delirious when they put me on the wickerwork litter in the morning. 'Is this a *tipoye*?' I thought dizzily, as the four Baluba picked up the supporting poles. 'I shouldn't ride in a *tipoye*. . . . I'm not a fat pig like Grosjean or a brute like Van Geel!' I started to struggle and Sylvestre came to peer at me curiously. I struck out at him wildly. He ran away, terrified, and Ngoi rushed to my side.

'Please, *Bwana*,' he begged me. 'Please lie quietly or you will hurt yourself.'

I stared at him and nearly struck out again. Then recognition came and some awareness of my situation. 'That was Ngoi,' I told myself firmly. 'This is a stretcher, not a *tipoye*. And you must lie quietly, or you will die.'

The trip was a waking nightmare. The porters struggled with the clumsy litter along the narrow trails through the tree-clad savannah. They laboured up hills and stumbled down steep slopes; several times I nearly fell out when one of them tripped. It was strange how my mind alternated between lucidity and delirium: for a while I classified the trees and shrubs along the trail; then, as the fever rose again, I would find myself battling with the spectres of Grosjean and Van Geel.

'Sleep, *Bwana*! Please sleep!' Ngoi pleaded.

I couldn't. I was trapped somewhere between the fever's grotesque fantasies and the jerky, swaying, nauseating reality. Hours passed before I finally slept. I awoke when the porters set the litter down on the shoulder of the Manono-Mitwaba road. I opened my eyes and stared into a red sun hanging a few degrees above the horizon. 'Where is the white man?' I asked weakly.

'He's not here yet,' Ngoi answered uncertainly.

We waited; gradually hope waned. About half an hour after it grew dark there was a mechanical roar and we saw two beams of brilliant white light. Ngoi shouted and, waving his arms frantically, ran into the road, almost directly into the path of a

huge truck. It swerved, rocked and screeched to a halt. Furious,
the native driver jumped out of the cab and ran after the boy.
Then he saw me lying on the dust of the shoulder.

'Ask him where he's going,' I called out.

The driver answered my question directly. 'To the Géomines
plant at Manono,' he said in Kiswahili.

'Can you take me to the hospital there?'

He nodded, my porters lifted the stretcher into the truck, and
I joined a load of office supplies intended for the big tin mine.
'I'm coming with you,' Ngoi said firmly. I hesitated; I didn't
want to leave him behind but I had to face facts. It would be
cruel to take him into a strange territory. Whatever happened
to me in Manono, I would be in no position to take care of him.

I tried to explain, but he refused to listen. 'I'm not afraid,' he
insisted. 'I'm coming with you.' I searched for a reason he would
accept. 'My books and equipment,' I said suddenly, 'I know you
will get them to Mwanza for me. Who else could I trust?' Ngoi's
eyes shone with pride. 'Don't worry, *Bwana!*' he cried. 'I'll take
good care of everything!' Then he jumped off the truck, shouted
to the driver, and it lurched into motion.

A couple of hours later it deposited a delirious young
agronomist at the hospital in Manono. The doctors examined
him, shook their heads and decided it was a case for specialists.
Next morning a Géomines plane flew the unconscious body to
Elisabethville, where specialists at the Hôpital des Européens
inspected the wreckage and shook their own heads. Then they
sent a telegram to Kisenyi, in Ruanda-Urundi, inviting the
family to attend the last rites.

Several days later, when I opened my eyes for the first time
since leaving Manono, my father was sitting beside the bed. His
face was tired and terribly drawn. I knew what he was thinking:
it was our first meeting in many years and he felt sure that it
would be our last. Still, he made an heroic effort to smile, and I
managed to whisper a few words, trying to reassure him. Then,
very tired, I closed my eyes again and drifted back into the coma.

I hovered between life and death for two more days, while the
doctors dosed me with atrabrine, cinchonine and arsenic and
pumped in several gallons of whole blood. Then, gradually, my
pale-green complexion improved and I recovered sufficiently to
criticize their technique. In revenge, they inundated me with
milk, broth and a small ocean of orange juice.

One month later, forty pounds lighter, I escaped from bed at
Elisabethville, intending to go to Mwanza, where I anticipated

a reunion with Ngoi and further trouble with the A.T., Sylvestre and Van Geel. But fate intervened in the guise of a doctor, a District Commissioner, and several million fish . . . So I never returned to my first territory, where I had been successively blue, yellow and green.

3

The Kingdom of God on Earth

Ichobey boy, yachiki ilolonkudi—'Only the eyes tell
the truth, not the stories one hears.'

KUBA PROVERB

WHEN I left the Hôpital des Européens, the Medical Chief
ordered fifteen days of complete rest, and at least three months
of semi-sedentary work, to effect a full recovery. When I presented myself, pale but reasonably alive, to the District Commissioner of Elisabethville, my convalescent assignment came
as a shock—a course of studies at the Station de Recherches
Scientifiques Piscicoles of the Mission Piscicole du Congo Belge.
Upon completion of this course I would acquire an astonishing
title—Fish Counsellor.

The Central Government had created the Mission Piscicole to
conserve, develop and fully exploit the Congo's piscine re-
sources. Now, as a part of the *Plan Décennal*—the enormous ten-
year development plan that was just getting under way—the
Scientific Fish Farming Research Station at Elisabethville was
expected to play an important rôle in handling one of Central
Africa's most serious problems: the conspicuous lack of animal
protein in the natives' diet. Artificial ponds were to be built
throughout the Congo, and existing natural waters restocked with
the most hardy, prolific and protein-rich freshwater fish, especially
species of the cichlid *Tilapia*, a distant relative of the perch.

I completed my watery studies, earned my picturesque title
and was assigned to Sakania in the Katanga highlands, about
140 miles southeast of Elisabethville on the frontier of Northern
Rhodesia—where there wasn't a fish in sight. There were, however, more than ten thousand Balamba natives who needed

34

technical supervision and aid for their plantations of staple and industrial crops. I spent several months working among them and developed some real innovations in the field of agricultural propaganda, encouraging the natives to improve and expand their cultivation. Then, just as I was beginning to settle down, the Sector Doctor decided that Sakania's relatively high altitude might strain my weakened system and I was transferred to Mweka, in the neighbouring province of Kasai.

Mweka was over a thousand miles from Sakania, and the heavy February rains had transformed some stretches of the road into thick, muddy *poto-poto*. Nevertheless, I made the trip in three days, speeding north along the Route Prince Léopold in my spattered Chevy pickup. As I entered Kasai, my new province, I found a vast, low-lying, tree-clad savannah, rich in cotton, coffee, corn, rubber, diamonds and *Elaeis* palms. Mweka, my new territorial headquarters, proved to be an ordinary bush post with a thoughtful, soft-spoken A.T.

'I'm afraid your new job will be fairly routine,' he told me. 'You're to supervise the agricultural work in the Kuba villages of the Mweka area. If the natives deviate too far from the established programme, you'll have to fine them or send them to jail. You must have a fairly good idea of what's involved.'

I did. The Bakuba would probably differ little from other Congolese tribes in their agricultural philosophy, or lack of it. Central African natives have little idea of planning: nature is taken for granted, often with tragic results; one bad season can create a devastating famine. To prevent such catastrophes the Government required every H.A.V. (Homme Adulte Valide, or able-bodied man) to cultivate at least an acre and a half of non-seasonal crops, such as manioc and sweet potatoes, to constitute a permanent reserve of food in the soil. The natives resented this regulation and usually tried to ignore or get round it.

'About those fines and jail sentences,' I said. 'I'd rather not use them.'

'Why not?'

'I never found them necessary, either in Mwanza or Sakania, and when I saw other people use them I didn't like the results. If a native is sentenced to jail, he thinks it's a wonderful, well-fed holiday—it has the very opposite of a corrective effect. If he's fined, he complains to his relatives about the "white man's injustice" until they make a little contribution. Sometimes he even makes a profit on the deal.'

'That's true,' he admitted, 'but what else can we do?'

'I've used psychological persuasion to very good effect. A silent, mysterious attitude works wonders with unsophisticated people, and a little subtle intimidation can be more effective than outright threats. Magic is even better.'

'Magic?' he smiled at me, perplexed. 'What do you mean?'

'Card tricks, disappearing coins, any kind of conjuring trick. That sort of thing really impressed the natives down in Sakania.'

My new A.T. burst out laughing. 'It's a hell of a way to grow sweet potatoes, but I'm all for it, provided it works. Still, I should warn you: the Bakuba probably have more magicians per square mile than any tribe in the Congo. You'll have some stiff competition.'

*   *   *

A few days later, I set out from Mweka on my first journey into the great Kingdom of the Bakuba, a colourful, complicated sociopolitical organism, with a history dating back probably to the beginning of the thirteenth century. At that time, according to Kuba legend, the world was created by their first king, Chembe, who was God Himself. During the next 750 years, 124 *Nyimi*, or Divine Kings, had succeeded to the throne. Now some eighty-five thousand of Chembe's descendants—a nation of wonderful sculptors and weavers—were living in the big triangle of land between the Sankuru and Kasai rivers, under the joint juris-diction of the Belgian Colonial Government and their current Divine King, Bope Mopinje II, the Nyimi Bushongo, also called Chembe Kunji—God on Earth.

The first Bakuba I met were my new *karani* and *pishi*. The interpreter, François Ndugulu, an earnest young *évolué* who planned to become a lawyer and perhaps even a judge of the local native tribunal, read and studied incessantly; his manners were relatively unaffected and he turned a fairly tolerant eye on his own people—something extremely rare for an educated native. Mbodo, the *pishi*, was a small wiry man with tribal tattoos on his temples. He spoke excellent Swahili, wore skin-tight khaki shorts and showed far more interest in women than in cooking.

Bulape, my first Kuba village, was very nearly my last. In quick succession, I had a contest with a wily magician, an affair with a pneumatic lady, and an encounter with a very sharp knife.

Like most Congolese villages, it consisted of two rows of windowless, rectangular huts with a big clearing in the middle. But some features were strictly a part of Kuba tradition. The village was laid out on an east–west axis. Each sector, north and south, had its own leader, respectively the *Mbambi* and the *Mbengi*, each with far more power than the 'mayor' or nominal chief, a puppet-ruler called the *Kum a Boro*. The huts were unusually large and ornate, with walls of palm-stems and leaves woven together in time-honoured geometric designs and gabled roofs thatched with palm fronds. Each hut had two doorways with very high thresholds, one in front and one at the side, and at the back a cylinder-shaped silo on stilts for storing grain.

Bulape's most unusual feature was that, like all Kuba villages and unlike any others in the Congo, it was *movable*. The huts had no foundations; central pillars of wood, planted deeply in the ground, supported the ridgepoles. When a Mukuba decided to move, he simply cut down the central pillar, slid six long poles under the hut, and found twelve strong men to carry it.

The people of Bulape were as beautifully built as their houses, and some bore the same geometric designs carved in their flesh. The women, especially, were adorned with profusions of ornamental scars on their foreheads, temples, necks, breasts and legs. The intriguing patterns moved, swayed and bounced freely, since their only clothing was a length of raffia cloth wound round the body from the waist to the knees. The children wore little raffia ropes round their waists, sometimes with an amulet, but never with a loincloth or other garment suspended from them. It was quite an original fashion—a belt and no trousers. The men dressed more elaborately, although their scar-patterns were simple—the tribal tattoo on the temples, and sometimes chevrons and half-moons on the shoulders and chest. They wore kilt-like raffia *pagnes* which fell to their knees in deep, gracious folds, with a ceremonial knife at the right side. On their heads were funny little cone-shaped raffia bonnets, some with small clapperless bells attached by long iron needles. According to François, the silent bells were supposed to jingle in the world of ghosts and spirits at every step the wearer took. He explained that it was almost a kind of prayer—a Kasai equivalent of Tibetan prayer-wheels, Jewish *mezuzoth*, or Catholic candles.

The black complexions of both men and women had a peculiar ruddy tinge because their bodies were covered with dark orange-red *ngula* powder, the Congo's favourite cosmetic.[1] Most of them were busy with *palabres*—endless arguments and gossip —but here and there, several pairs of men squatted on either side of carved wooden boards nimbly dropping bean-sized pebbles into a series of saucer-shaped hollows. They were playing *lela*, the most popular game in Black Africa, which, according to Kuba tradition, was invented by their greatest king, Shamba Bolongongo, over three hundred years ago.

I wandered around Bulape a little longer, before I headed for the *gîte*, while François and the rest of my crew drifted through the village to find lodging. In five minutes' time I was singing *Auprès de ma blonde* in a little round shack behind the bungalow, underneath a galvanized-iron bucket which released a cascade of cold water; an hour later I sat down to a steaming dinner.

'Very good,' I remarked to Mbodo, 'but take it easy on the *pili-pili*. I like red pepper on my chicken, but not as much as that!'

'I'm sorry, *Bwana*. I was worried and my hand slipped.'

'What do you have to worry about?'

'My father is very ill and I think he will die. If that happens, I can take over his hut and his land! Tonight I shall find out; I am going to see the *nganga*.'

It was my first opportunity to watch the notorious Kuba magicians in action. So, later that evening, accompanied by François, I stood with my back against an old *Elaeis* palm tree in the centre of the village, watching thirty Bakuba who squatted in a circle round a blazing fire. Twenty feet away from me, Mbodo was cowering anxiously before an impressive, mysterious figure, whom François called the *mikando*, or 'assistant

---

[1] *Ngula* powder, obtained from the *tukula* tree (*Pterocarpus tinctorius*), is stored in beautifully carved wooden boxes or pressed into *bongotol*, small ingots which the women make by mixing the powder with clay and a little palm oil, forming it into geometrical shapes and incising them with designs. *Bongotol* were extremely important in the people's daily lives—as money, dowries and offerings placed in the graves of the newly dead. The colour of the *ngula* is highly significant: red is the nearly universal symbol of love and happiness among primitive peoples everywhere. Black, obtained from charcoal powder, enjoys a similar status with some Bantu tribes and the pygmies. Unlike ourselves, almost all Africans agree that white, derived from a clay called *pembe*, is associated with death and sorrow, hence they use it for funeral ceremonies and generally explain that, since a negro is very light in colour at birth, he must be made white again to be reborn. Only thus can he join his dead friends and relatives who, as disembodied spirits, have once again become white.

magician'. Spotted genet skins were draped around the *mikando*'s waist, their tails dangling over his checkered *pagne*. His ankles were loaded with brass bangles and a carved wooden whistle, sometimes used to summon the rain, was tucked into his belt. He stared at Mbodo compellingly.

'Is my father going to die?' the *pishi* asked in a quavering voice.

No answer. Instead, the magician reached under his dangling genet skins and pulled out the *itombwa*, a divining instrument which looked like a small, flat-backed wooden crocodile. Some *itombwa* resemble other animals—lizards, chameleons, pangolins or dogs—but almost all have in common a strange feature: on its upper side the wooden animal has the hint of a face, and when it is held upright, it looks strikingly human.

The *mikando* squatted down, holding the *itombwa* in his left hand and a greasy wooden disc in his right. He stroked the flat back of the crocodile with the disc while he repeated the ancient magical phrases, a rapid-fire chant which continued for several minutes. Suddenly he stopped, turned the carving on end and held it high in the air. Mbodo sucked in his breath, the villagers muttered in awe; and I saw that the disc was stuck fast to the little figure's back.

'The *itombwa* has summoned the Spirits of Water,' François told me gravely. 'They are the ghosts of the dead, who must be present at any real divination. Now the *ngomo ibalo* will make the big ceremony. He is the chief magician.'

A weird figure moved from the shadows into the flickering firelight, a big man with a leopard-skin girdle, bands of cowrie shells round his shins, and a pagoda-like hat with strings of copper bells jingling as he walked. In his right hand he carried a large, lightly carved buffalo horn, the *ishike nganga*.

He squatted. Then slowly, suspensefully, he tilted the magic horn. Several white bones rolled on to the ground; they looked like parts of a human hand. He paused, savouring the effect on his audience, before he jiggled the horn again; now a couple of leopard claws tumbled out, followed by a red parrot feather that drifted into the fire. The villagers murmured and the *nganga* waited for almost a full minute, allowing the tension to mount. Then, when he shook the horn for the third time, a round black object—a headless goliath beetle—fell to the ground. He picked it up, held it in the palm of his hand, and stared at it melodramatically. 'Your father will die!' he told the trembling Mbodo.

'If the first beetle to drop out of the horn had a head,' François explained knowingly, 'the old man would get better. The beetles are always supposed to speak the truth. That is why we call them *Mutu wa Chembe*—the men of God.'

'Isn't it obvious that the magician must cut off some of the heads himself, before he puts them into the horn?'

'That makes no difference. You *wazungu* don't understand how magic works.'

'Most of us don't,' I answered. 'but I am a white *nganga*!'

He eyed me sceptically.

'Tell the people that I will show them a new kind of magic, a trick that none of their *nganga* can ever perform!'

François spoke in Lokuba to the crowd of squatting men. They stared at me, and the *ngomo ibolo* tossed his head with a jealous jangle of bells. I moved closer to the fire and asked for my props: a knife, a banana leaf and a blanket. I had some trouble getting the blanket: the only man in the crowd who was wearing one refused to surrender it when I announced that I would pass a knife through the centre without making a hole in it.

'He says the blanket cost sixty francs,' François explained, 'and it's almost new. He doesn't think you're a real magician and he's afraid you'll spoil it.'

'Tell him I will buy him ten new ones if I hurt it in any way.'

That had the desired effect. He gave me the blanket and I selected two volunteers to hold either end while I stood behind it, the knife in my right hand, the banana leaf directly over the cloth in my left. The crowd started to murmur when the tip of the knife suddenly burst through the leaf. Then they gasped with astonishment as the blade and hilt emerged, the knife fell to the ground, and I raised the mangled leaf with a big gesture, revealing—an intact blanket.

During the next few days the people of Bulape worked their fields with unheard-of enthusiasm, anxious to please such a powerful *nganga*. François treated me with increased respect and Mbodo spent most of his spare time trying to solve the great knife-and-blanket mystery and imitate some of my card-tricks. He never succeeded, but that only increased his ambition.

'*Bwana*, I have a surprise for you!' he told me one evening in the big clearing.

'What is it? Can you make the ace of spades jump out of the pack?'

He grinned. 'This is something different. I had a long talk with the *Kum a Boro* and we made some arrangements for you. No one should sleep alone, *Bwana*.'

'I can make my own arrangements. If I see a woman I like, I know what to do about it.'

'But, *Bwana*—'

I turned and walked off, annoyed at his officious attitude. I went to the *gîte*, walked in and lit the Coleman lamp . . . only to discover three timidly smiling young girls sitting in a row along the edge of my bed. They were almost entirely naked. 'Mbodo!' I shouted. '*Kuya!*—Come here!'

The cook materialized a moment later. 'You found the surprise!' he cried happily.

'I certainly have. Now, will you please tell the girls to leave?'

'All of them?'

'Yes, *all* of them.'

Mbodo looked shocked. 'You can't do that, *Bwana*! I tried to explain before but you wouldn't let me. They are the *Kum a Boro*'s daughters. If you refuse, he'll take it as an insult.'

'Am I supposed to sleep with all three of them?'

'Not unless you want to. You can pick whichever you like best. She will be very proud to sleep with a white *nganga*.'

'Won't the other two be insulted?'

'Oh, no. They will understand. Besides, if they look too sad, François and I will take good care of them.'

I went back into the *gîte* and made my choice, a shapely girl of sixteen—the oldest of the three—with exceptionally ornate scar-patterns. Her name was Ishisha. It was a wonderful opportunity to make some ethnographic observations on the motifs of Kuba tattooing, but after a few minutes I turned off the Coleman lamp.

*   *   *

Next morning my prestige stood even higher in the village of Bulape. Everyone smiled at me congenially as I emerged from the *gîte*. François smiled. Mbodo smiled. The *Kum a Boro*, who was now our informal father-in-law, smiled at the three of us with fond paternal pride. We were one big happy family. Then I marched off to the fields with my usual crew to begin another exhausting day of inspections.

It was quite a job, checking the quality and quantity of the

production, ferreting out any bacterial, fungus or insect invasions, and seeing that the proper crops were rotated according
to schedule. During the first year after a new parcel of land had
been cleared, bananas and manioc were supposed to be planted.
Harvesting began during the second and finished during the
third. Then, in the first season of the fourth year, corn, gourds
and beans were seeded, and during the second season, cotton.
In the fifth year both cotton and peanuts were grown; afterwards the land was supposed to lie fallow for at least ten years.

Cotton was the big cash crop around Mweka, as in much of
the Congo, and was strictly a native enterprise, sponsored by
private Belgian companies and controlled by the Colonial
Government. Since 1921 Europeans had been prohibited from
planting cotton, thus ensuring a substantial source of revenue
for the native families, who found it relatively easy to cultivate,
and encouraging them to remain in their villages rather than
migrate to the already crowded cities.

By now seven hundred thousand of those families were
producing nearly forty-seven thousand tons of raw fibre
annually, and the Congo's *per capita* cotton production was the
third highest in the world. Every family was the sole owner of its
crops until the sponsoring company sold them in the international market. Thus, under the Belgian paternalists—often
denounced as 'slave traders'—the natives were independent
planters, pocketing their own profits, quite unlike the negroes
in the cotton fields of the American South.

To control the health, quality and quantity of the native
planters' crops, I worked like a slave myself, walking from fifteen
to twenty miles a day under the scorching Congolese sun between endless rows of the white and violet flowering cotton. I
had to watch for plant bugs, 'tea mosquitoes', 'red bugs', red
spider mites, *Fusarium* fungus and such bacterial invasions as
angular leaf spot. Yet I must have spent at least a quarter of
my time arguing with the natives, trying to badger them into
working actively for their own profit. By five in the afternoon,
when I headed back to the village, I was a corpse-like heap of
sweat, dust, leaves, pollen, insects and aggravation.

I revived in the evenings, when I divided my time between
learning Lokuba from François, mystifying Mbodo, and enjoying Ishisha. Every night, when I retired into the *gîte*, I found
her in my bed, with her dark head on my pillow. She took our
continuing soirées as a matter of course and I never declined:
after all, it put me in a unique position to study bilateral rela-

tions *à la* Bakuba as opposed to the conventional ups and downs of European sex.

One evening while we were rather preoccupied, I became aware of a tremendous racket. I rose, jumped into my *kapitula* and rushed outside to find a shrieking mob of Bakuba surrounding two men who were rolling on the ground. One had a knife, the other had a long slash in his shoulder; both were covered with blood.

I recognized the knife-wielder as Bikuri, a husky, quick-tempered blacksmith who had sold me some iron bells the day before. He was obviously drunk on *malafu*, the native palm wine which often drives men into hysterical rages. 'Bikuri!' I shouted. 'Stop it!'

'Kill him!' roared the crowd. 'Kill him!'

The smith swiped at the other man with his seven-inch *goribi* and just missed planting the straight single-edged blade in his chest. I sprang forward and grabbed Bikuri's shoulders, trying to pull him away. In the excitement, a flailing leg hooked me behind the knee and down I crashed into the tangle of perspiring bodies, just in time to intercept another thrust of the knife. The sharp blade plunged into my right thigh. Bikuri stared at me, shocked, until his clenched hand opened slowly and let go the hilt. The he pushed himself away, suddenly realizing that he had wounded a white man.

I wrenched at the knife, which had bitten deeply into my femur, and pulled it free. Blood was streaming from a three-inch wound and my leg nearly buckled under me as I stood up. I searched the silent, frightened crowd of Bakuba with my eyes until I spotted François, who was standing, appalled, on the far fringe. 'Tell the chief to have Bikuri tied up in his hut,' I ordered, 'and bring the wounded man to the *gîte*.' Then I limped off, pressing a handkerchief to the wound.

I entered the *gîte*, bleeding dramatically. Ishisha gasped and bolted out of my bed with a torrent of unintelligible questions. 'Oh, shut up!' I exploded, as I rummaged through my medical chest for a piece of rubber tubing to use as a tourniquet; then Bikuri's victim came in, clutching his bloody shoulder, and I began to dress his wound.

I washed the long shallow slash with a solution of Dettol antiseptic that should have stung him terribly, but he never even twitched. I dried it with a clean compress, dusted it with sulfa powder and made a spectacular bandage round his shoulder and chest. Finally, I presented him with a stimulant—half a pint of

Black and White whisky. He gave me no thanks; but his eyes brightened and he left with an expression of complete devotion . . . to the bottle.

My patient had been more than stoic, but when I poured the strong antiseptic into my own wound, the pain was terrific. I dried it, used sulfa powder liberally, and sewed it up with some khaki thread. Then I bandaged the aching thigh and hobbled to bed, where Ishisha obligingly made room for me. I spent a restless night, for several reasons.

In the morning I held a big conference—via François—with the *Kum a Boro*, the *Mbambi*, the *Mbengi*, Bikuri and his victim, a rival smith from the next village, all of whom were astonished to learn that I had no intention of sending Bikuri to jail. Instead, I severely reprimanded him, publicly shaming him for his drunkenness and cowardice in attacking an unarmed man. Whether or not my words had a lasting effect is debatable, but imprisonment would certainly have been a serious mistake, breaking his ties with the village of his birth and exposing him to permanent corruption.

I stayed in Bulape until my wounded leg was fit for real travelling, and then, a week later, limped out with my crew for an eighteen-mile trek to the next stop. The leg ached horribly, but I consoled myself with a Kuba proverb I had learned from François: *Dema ikuna kamagachin kushumudi*—Ignore a pain and it flies away. It worked, up to a point.

I reached the next big group of villages . . . and the next . . . and the next . . . and almost before I knew it, six months had passed, I had visited more than two hundred Kuba villages, dealt with about ten thousand people, and finally mastered the difficult, little-known language. It was September 1949, and I was entitled to two weeks' leave. I decided to spend it at Mushenge, the capital of the ancient Kuba Kingdom, where I was eager to get acquainted with one of the strangest socio-political organisms in the world: the Royal Court of the Divine Nyimi Bushongo, Bope Mopinje II, still known to his eighty-five thousand adoring subjects as Chembe Kunji—God on Earth.

*   *   *

Mushenge proved to be a rather large village, with extremely ornate huts and an enormous *lupangu*—a complicated labyrinth of bamboo palisades containing the inner sanctum of the Royal Court. I entered the maze and meandered uncertainly through a series of blind alleys. No one was in sight but I heard distant voices and worked my way towards them, with many stops and starts, until I turned a corner and suddenly found a hut.

A young boy stood just outside the doorway, leaning his back against the wall and whittling a stick of wood. A few feet away two men squatted on the ground playing *lela*. The boy stared curiously, but the men crouched over their board pretending not to see me, obviously playing the game of social prestige as well as *lela*. I joined in by pretending to ignore them and introducing myself to the boy.

'My father is a very busy man,' he explained. 'He is the Royal Eagle Keeper and his friend is the Head Snake Charmer. They are both *kolomo*—officials of the court.'

'Surely such an important man as your father,' I said loudly, 'can arrange an interview with the Nyimi.'

The boy shook his head emphatically. 'Only the Kimi Kambu can do that.'

'The Kimi Kambu?'

'He is the Prime Minister and First Judge, a very great and powerful person. I have to talk to my father about it.'

I waited while he squatted down and whispered into the older man's ear. The Royal Eagle Keeper had been following our conversation very closely, but the whispered repetition was a tribute to his high social status as well as a mark of filial respect. 'My father says I can take you to the Kimi Kambu,' the boy finally announced, 'but it won't do you much good. The Nyimi has been ill for the past few days and isn't seeing anyone. We can go now, but first I have to get my *ilondo*.'

He rushed into the hut, returning in a moment with a large ceremonial sabre in a soft raffia scabbard hanging from his left shoulder. He explained that it would be a serious breach of court etiquette for any subject to approach the King's palace without it.

We passed through interlacing palisades with a few scattered huts, winding our way towards the centre of the *lupangu*. The bamboo panels became more intricate, woven with different shades of palm leaves and grasses to achieve the traditional geometric patterns. Wall followed wall until we arrived in a little courtyard occupied by a large hut, where I waited nearly a quarter of an hour while the Kuba Prime Minister donned his elaborate ceremonial dress.

He finally emerged, a magnificent figure wearing a rich chequered *pagne* edged at the hem with velvet-like raffia cloth and a fringe of little raffia balls; his waist was girdled with a leopard skin, a belt of the fibre balls and a knotted sash of cowrie shells.[1] A huge necklace of cowries criss-crossed his chest and heavy bands of the shells sheathed his wrists and ankles. The crowning touch was a white plume in his *lukete*— the little raffia bonnet—and a ceremonial bell.

The Kimi Kambu spoke to me rather arrogantly. 'The King is sick, but in two or three days he will be better. You may see him on the afternoon of the third day, two hours before sunset.'

'Good. In the meantime, can *you* spend a few hours with me? I'd like to find out about some old Kuba legends and traditions.'

He seemed astonished. 'I have no time for such trifles,' he said loudly. 'I am very busy with matters of state. But this boy can take you to see the Moaridi. It's his job to talk.'

The Moaridi, who lived at the other end of the *lupangu*, was the Kuba Custodian and Narrator of Royal Legend. He was a wonderful, knowing old man, who looked like a black version of Field-Marshal Montgomery. He knew more about Kuba history, mythology and gossip than any man in Mushenge. We talked first about the ailing King, since I was anxious to learn the extent of the royal powers.

The Hungarian explorer Emile Torday, who made a pioneer visit to the old Kuba Kingdom at the beginning of the present century, described the great Nyimi Bushongo as a bizarre figure hedged in by complex ritual prohibitions. As King of the Bakuba, he was the one political link between the four administrative provinces and the many sub-tribes of his realm. As Chembe Kunji—God on Earth—he was the sacred figure uniting his people with their dead ancestors' spirits. As the

[1] Cowrie shells (*Cypraea moneta*) were originally obtained from the shores of the Indian Ocean and introduced into tropical Africa by Egyptian and Arab traders. Once widely used for money and as ornaments, in some of the more remote areas they still serve as currency. The cowrie shell is reputed to have been originally a fertility symbol, because of its obvious resemblance to the female sex organ. (For the same reason, the Greeks had associated the innocent mollusc with Aphrodite, their own fertility goddess, and later with the cult of Cybele, the Great Mother.) Then, because of their scarcity, they came to be used as money, and, inevitably, as symbols of power. In Kasai they were used to decorate ceremonial clothing and masks, especially the spectacular *mashamboy* masks worn first by chieftains in honour of departed heroes and later by professional dancers. Until fifty years ago, they were the only currency used in Kasai except for the ingots of *bongotol*. It sometimes took two hundred thousand cowrie shells to buy a wife. Each shell had to be counted over to the bride's father or uncle before the marriage contract was final.

symbolic embodiment of the entire nation, his health, prosperity and power were magically reflected in all his people.

To safeguard his divine virtues, the Nyimi was forbidden to touch the ground, to come into contact with blood, or to be seen by a woman in the act of eating. He sat on a living human throne—a wretched slave called the Ipona—and was not allowed to die a natural death. Instead, whenever a King was believed to be mortally ill, he was ritually smothered by his eldest son, the Buimbi or Heir Presumptive. Then his body was ceremonially buried with sometimes as many as two thousand living slaves beside it.

Many of these customs, the Moaridi complained, had either been suppressed or abandoned. Of the King's most striking royal privileges, one remained: he had a vast army of wives, never fewer than one for every day in the year, and sometimes as many as eight hundred. They were scattered all over his kingdom, with about a hundred generally in residence at Mushenge. The King married for politics, profit or pleasure, and usually managed to combine the three.

The results could be seen all round me. Virtually every man in the kingdom must have had his share of royal blood, since several Nyimi of the past were each reputed to have fathered as many as ten thousand children. The most potent of all, the Moaridi confided, begat three sons during one heroic night.

'How can you be sure,' I asked, 'that the King made all three babies in one night?'

'Three sons were born to him on the same day,' he said proudly, 'by three different women. That means he did it six times in one night, since once is not enough to make a baby. Only when a man takes a woman twice, without waiting too long, can he fill her with a child.'

Certainly the Moaridi deserved his title as Custodian and Narrator of Royal Legend.

We spent another hour or two discussing a more academic matter, the complicated administrative structure of the Kuba realm, and most of the next day arguing about religion and magic. Since my first visit to Bulape, I had seen the *itombwa* ceremony performed several times, both with and without the magic horn and decapitated beetles, and had met a whole series of specialized sorcerers: the *Iluka*, or Hunting Magicians, without whose aid no pious Mukuba could bring down an antelope or a bird; the *Bilumbi*, or War Magicians, who claimed the power to turn bullets into water and blunt the sharp edge of a spear; the *Imbamba*, who ferreted out buried charms which were spreading an evil influence through the village; the *Phomba*, who recovered stolen property; and the *Geshi*, who were supposed to cure sterility and expedite cases of difficult childbirth.

The word used most often by all these picturesque charlatans was *moena*, the evil spirits. The *moena*, I was told repeatedly, can possess a man with or without his knowledge and force him to spread a fatal influence among his friends and neighbours, a Kasai version of the 'evil eye'. Thus, if a Mukuba died without apparent cause, he was believed to have succumbed to the hellish powers incarnated in one of his fellow villagers. A 'witch hunt' began, *itombwa* divination was used to reveal the culprit, and some unfortunate man would on occasion be subjected to ordeal by poison. This was a simple matter: the victim was forced to drink the *ipomi* poison from a consecrated horn. If he vomited up the poison and lived, he was innocent; if it stayed down and he died, he was, of course, guilty.

This same ordeal by poison, practised by many Congolese tribes, had probably been claiming at least fifty thousand lives a year until the Belgians managed to suppress its widespread use. Add to that figure the vast number of victims of cannibalism and human sacrifice, and one reaches the appalling conclusion that the number of deaths from ritual murder exceeded those from natural causes. That was the tragedy of the past; but yet, even in the present century, the entire sub-continent of Black Africa, with an estimated 175,000,000 people, was preoccupied by fear of the *moena*, or *bazimu*, as many Congolese tribes called them.

'Where do they come from?' I asked the Moaridi. 'Where do they live? And why do they want to torment people?'

He thought for a long time. 'Man is made of four different parts: *Lo*, the body; *Ilo*, the double; *N'Shanga*, the soul; and *Lume-Lume*, the shade. When the body dies, the soul hides in the womb of a woman until it is sprinkled with the Water of God [human semen]. Then the soul is born again in the child that grows in the belly. *Ilo*, the double, visits the living in dreams, but *Lume-Lume* dies with the body. Sometimes there is a fifth part, the *moena*, the phantom, or evil spirit. It is present only in wicked men. When the body dies, the *moena* escapes and hunts for a new home. It keeps searching until it settles down in a living man. He must be discovered and destroyed!'

'Is there no other way to control the evil spirits?'

'They can be trapped in the bones of the dead, but only if they are burned by a powerful *nganga*. Otherwise, the possessed man must be revealed by the *itombwa* and the Beetles of God.'

'But why doesn't God do something about it? Why does He tolerate such evil?'

The old man sighed. 'God doesn't care about us any more. He made the world and everything in it, but afterwards He got tired of the whole thing. So He flew up into the sky.'

'Tell me the story,' I urged.

'In the beginning, the world was made out of shadows. There was no life on the earth or in the water, only *Chembe*, who ruled in the middle of nothing. God was shaped like a man, but He was very tall and He was white. One day He felt a terrible pain in His stomach and started to vomit. He threw up the sun, the moon and the stars. That is how light was born. The sun shone, the waters started to dry and banks of sand showed above the surface, but there were no animals or plants. God didn't like that, so He started to vomit again. First He threw up the leopard, *Koy Chembe*—the cleverest beast of them all—then *Pongo Chembe*, the crested eagle; *Ganda Chembe*, the crocodile; *Yo Chembe*, the minnow; and *Kono Chembe*, the tortoise. *Tsetse Chembe*, the lightning, came next—an animal shaped like a black leopard with a flaming tail. After that, *Nyanyi Chembe*, the white heron, flew out of God's mouth, along with the scarab beetle and *Budi Chembe*, the goat. Finally, God vomited man.

'Then the animals God had created went to work to fill up the world. The white heron vomited all of the birds except the hawk, the crocodile threw up the snakes and the lizards, the goat made all the horned beasts, and the lizards vomited all the beasts without horns. Every fish in the world came from the mouth of the little fish *Yo*, and the scarab beetle threw up the rest of the insects, except the grasshoppers. The serpents made *them*.

'Afterwards, one of God's sons, Nyonye Ngana, vomited all the termites. It was a wonderful deed, but it killed him. So, to show their gratitude, the white ants searched the inside of the earth for rich black soil. Then they brought it to the surface to cover the barren sand and bury their father with honour. Another of God's sons, Chonganda, vomited a tiny plant, and all the world's green things grew from its seed. His brother, Chedi Chembe, tried as hard as he could, but he only threw up the hawk.

'After the world was finished, God visited our villages, saying to each of them: "Look at the wonderful things I have made. They all belong to you, on one condition—there is a single

animal you may not eat. I leave you free to enjoy the rest."
Thus, He gave us our *ikina bari* [food taboos], so that men
would learn to control themselves. But He forgot to visit some
of the villages and they received no *ikina*. Those men are like
savage beasts: they eat all things and their blood is not pure.

'God looked on the world He had made and He liked it,
except for one thing. The lightning—the black leopard with the
tail of fire—was an evil beast who loved to do mischief. God
chased her and she hid in the sky, but then men couldn't make
fire. So He must let her return once in a while, even though she
makes trouble.

'Now Chembe's work was really finished, so He flew up into
the sky. He has never come back, though we sometimes see Him
in dreams. So we know that God has forgotten us. But we have
our King, who is Chembe Kunji—our God on Earth.'

*   *   *

I met 'God on Earth' two days later, when thirteen Kuba
courtiers ceremonially escorted me through the last mazes of the
lupangu to the large hut called the 'palace'. Bowing low, they
ushered me into the presence of His Majesty, Bope Mopinje II,
the Nyimi Bushongo, who, since 25 November 1939, had been
the 124th Monarch of the Divine Kuba Dynasty.

Bope was obviously ill. Dressed in a simple *pagne*, he lay on a
massive wooden bed padded with woven palm fronds, surrounded by a retinue of pages who included his son, the Buimbi,
or Crown Prince. The King was short, with a round head and
flabby, almost feminine breasts; he must have weighed over 20
stone. He stared at me with a mixture of weak curiosity and
regal disdain. I stared back and uttered a few polite phrases in
Lokuba. He gave a grunt of surprise and mumbled the ritual
answers.

Then I ceremonially presented my gift, two bottles of Johnny
Walker whisky, which the A.T. had advised was the only
acceptable tribute. Bope flicked a fat finger to one of his
attendants, who handed me in return an ornately carved tobacco
pipe—one of the King's own—and a big square of raffia cloth
embroidered by one of his wives.

The interview was officially over. The thirteen courtiers
escorted me from the royal presence and I made my way out of
the *lupangu*, disillusioned about the King, but delighted with
my new treasures.

The 18-inch pipe was carved from *bungawa* wood; its bone

mouthpiece was made from a monkey's tibia, and a strong, expressively carved hand held the decorated bowl. Like almost every Kuba artifact, it was incised with geometric patterns; red *ngula* powder filled the grooves, producing an exquisite patina.

The raffia cloth was a glowing two-foot square of black, brown and *ngula* red, with an intricate design and a soft, luxurious texture. As a fabric, it was unrivalled by anything made on the African continent and was treasured in museums all over the world as 'Kasai velvet'. The Bakuba call it *musese*, and have a wonderful legend that it was first created by Kashashi, chief wife of King Shamba Bolongongo (1600–20), who is credited with having invented not only the art of weaving and the game of *lela*, but most of the old Kuba proverbs.

I spent two more days in the old Moaridi's company, while he introduced me to many of the King's *kolomo*—a wildly diversified collection of picturesque officials and dignitaries. I met a representative sampling of the Judicial Functionaries, twenty-one solemn judges whose last resort was the *itombwa*; the five Military Functionaries, comic-opera generals who could never agree; the six Treasury Functionaries, who kept a sharp eye on cowrie shells, *bongotol* and Congolese francs; and the thirty-three Representative Functionaries, who included delegates and deputies from the four provinces, from the Kuba sub-tribes, and from all the individual arts and crafts; wood-carvers, weavers, blacksmiths, musicians, singers, dancers, salt-makers, hunters, fishers, boat-builders, oil-pressers, mat-makers, net-weavers, tailors and rope-makers. I even met the Nybilimbi, who officially represents the fathers of twins.[1]

Besides these, there were still the Court Dignitaries to be considered, numbering fifty-seven. I urged the Moaridi to be selective, and he responded by introducing me to a fascinating medley of drummers, heralds, cup-bearers, carpet-spreaders and marimba-players. Finally I met the lowest dignitary of the Kuba Court: the Ipona—the King's living throne.

In the past the Ipona had been forced to crouch on his hands and knees so that the King could sit on his back. Now he had

---

[1] Unlike most African tribes, the Bakuba look upon the birth of twins as an omen of good fortune, and reserve certain political offices for twins or their fathers. Albino children are also considered lucky, and are very well cared for. Monsters and congenital cripples receive very different treatment: the eastern Bangongo bury them alive; the western sub-tribes deny doing so, but one never sees deformed children among them.

the title but no job, so spent most of his time playing *lela*. He was probably the luckiest man in Kasai: when the 20-stone Nyimi put on his elaborate court dress, his total weight must have approached a quarter of a ton. The little Ipona would have been squashed flat.

I was lucky enough to see the King in all of his ceremonial finery before I left the Kuba capital. Bope had hauled himself out of bed, in spite of his illness, to preside over an important *kolomo* wedding. Now, looking very weary, though his face was thickly coated with red *ngula* powder, he sat on a stool in front of his 'palace', dressed in a costume so fantastic that I doubt whether he could have stood up in it.

The Divine King was covered from head to foot with tiny white cowrie shells. They were encrusted on his headdress, sewn in patterns on his red raffia robe and embroidered all over his spats. Round his waist was a huge sash of the little shells; his neck and chest were hung with great bands of them, his arms were loaded with shell bracelets, and even his gloves, his spear and the scabbard of his ceremonial sword were studded with them. From his headdress sprouted a wild crown of feathers, a clapper-less bell and something which looked like a stick of cotton candy. Another ceremonial bell dangled between his knees over the heavy copper bangles sheathing his shins, while on his cowrie-covered chest a leopard-tooth necklace competed for attention with a shiny medal engraved with the head of Albert I, King of the Belgians.

I left the Kuba Royal Court, dazzled by the sight of its treasures, and spent the rest of my holiday on a collecting trip through the Mweka-Mushenge villages. By the time it was over I had spent every franc I had saved during my first two years in government service, and my truck was loaded with a wonderful variety of drums, stools, knives, adzes, spears, swords, masks, flutes, *itombwa*, drinking-horns, cups, *bongotol*, seventy-five powder boxes, and beautifully carved clysters. I had thirty magnificent *musese*, old and new, and by a wonderful stroke of luck I had managed to find one of the *lukengo*—impressive wooden statues commemorating all the important Kuba kings since the end of the sixteenth century. Only eighteen of these royal effigies had previously been discovered: eight were in national museums and ten in private collections. Now I had the nineteenth.

Three months and two safaris after I had unpacked my treasures in Mweka, it was time to pack them again. I had repeatedly applied to work with the Bambuti pygmies in North Kivu, and the Government had finally given me a transfer, not to North, but to South Kivu, with its notorious cannibal tribes.

So, in January 1950, I climbed into my heavily loaded Chevy pickup, turned my nose northeast and drove away from the Kingdom of God on Earth. As I approached the limits of the territory I passed a young Mukuba riding a decrepit bicycle. He wore a black dinner jacket fastened with safety pins, with two shiny fountain pens in his breast-pocket and a wine-red trilby hat. I waved to him and he spat on the ground.

The people of Mweka and Mushenge were becoming 'civilized'.

4

Land of the Man-Eaters

'The God of the cannibals will be a cannibal, of the crusaders a crusader, and of the merchants a merchant.'

RALPH WALDO EMERSON

SHABUNDA, my new territory, lay in the heart of a region called Maniema, a tract of equatorial forest and timbered savannah, with a singularly turbulent history. Racked by sleeping sickness, smallpox and periodic famines, its people had suffered two terrible scourges: Arab slave traders invading from the east, and their own insatiable, age-old cannibalism. The very word Maniema means 'Man-Eaters'.

Sir Richard Burton saw only the fringes of the region in 1858 when he and John Speke discovered Lake Tanganyika. He described its tribesmen as human wolves devouring each other, people who called themselves *nyama*—'the meat'—and spoke of their Arab and native despots as *kisu*—'the knife'. Livingstone penetrated farther in 1869, witnessed incredible scenes, and cried out at Kasongo, 'The blood runs in horrible waves! I am overcome, nauseated by all this human blood!' Henry Morton Stanley, who arrived in Maniema in 1876, five years after finding Livingstone at Ujiji, was more cynical. 'These savages', he remarked, 'would consider a whole congress of bishops and missionaries from only one viewpoint: roast beef!'

Lieutenant Verney Lovett Cameron, leading the Royal Geographical Society's expedition of 1873, rejoiced that he was too thin to be worth eating and described how the natives devoured diseased corpses as well as newly murdered men, macerating the bodies in water until the flesh was nearly putrefied and then

54

[*Photos Shell*

LANDSCAPES OF RUANDA-URUNDI (NOW RWANDA AND BURUNDI)

(*Top left*) Anti-erosion terraces between Ruhengeri and Astrida.
(*Top right*) The Rugesi Falls.
(*Below left*) Lake Luhondo (alt. 5,786 ft.).
(*Below right*) Muhutu herdsman watching over his Tutsi master's cattle.

MASAI WARRIORS

The man on the left wears a lion's mane *olowuaru*; the other's head-dress is the ostrich-feather *isidan*. Their buffalo-hide shields are painted with symbols of their clans and honours.

eating it raw. This peculiar practice is supposed to have accounted for the cannibals' characteristic aroma, the notorious 'Bouquet of Maniema'. He concluded by quoting a popular native chant:

> The flesh of man is good,
> The flesh of woman is bad;
> She's only fit to eat
> When there's nothing else to be had!

Thus, Balega, Basongola and Babinja tribes of Maniema had been devouring each other for a great many years when, towards the middle of the nineteenth century, the Arab traders of Zanzibar invaded Central Africa, looking for ivory and slaves.

Slavery had long been established among the negroes themselves, and ancient Egyptian, Carthaginian and Sudanese kings had made limited domestic use of slaves, but the Arabs were the first to put the slave trade on an organized commercial basis. They shipped millions of Sudanese and East African negroes from Zanzibar and the other great markets of the coast to Arabia, Persia, India and even China, aided by their protégés, the Swahilis (or, in the Congo, Bangwana), 'arabized' natives who embraced Islam and betrayed their brothers for the love of Allah, trade goods and money.

Some Swahili were pure negroes; others were of mixed Arab-negro blood; all followed the Koran, wore the red fez and the white robe called the *djellabah,* and spoke the *lingua franca* Swahili, a mixture of elements from Bantu and Semitic. Their treachery and rapacity were notorious: even the deeply humanitarian Dr. Livingstone was so repelled by the Swahili merchants that he described them, in a November 1871 letter to James Gordon Bennett, in the very strongest of terms:

> ... these nigger Moslems must have slaves, and they assaulted market people and villages, and made captives, chiefly of women and children. . . . I had no idea before how bloodthirsty men can be when they can pour out the blood of their fellow men in safety. . . .

Between them, the Arabs and negroes had enjoyed an almost complete monopoly for more than a thousand years. Then competition arrived for the pagan and Moslem slave traders, in the guise of Christian slave traders from civilized Europe. They were less bloodthirsty, but they compensated for it by amazing hypocrisy. A recent publication, *Tropical Africa*,[1] has described them wonderfully well:

> Catholic, Anglican, Calvinist, Lutheran . . . much as they might quarrel among themselves, they could at least agree about the advantages to be gained from slaving; in that respect they quarrelled only about who should gain the most. They maintained their piety throughout. For it was easy to demonstrate that to remove the African from his heathen environment and expose him to Christian influences would be greatly to the advantage of his immortal soul; and meantime there was money to be made.

The Portuguese arrived first, in the fifteenth century, working their way round the west coast of Africa until they encountered and squabbled with the Arabs on the east. They retreated, leaving a large colony in Mozambique, and concentrated most of their subsequent efforts in the west. There they gathered up hordes of negroes—future servants for the great lords and ladies of Lisbon, field hands for their enormous new colony of Brazil, and merchandise for the insatiable slave markets of the West Indies. From Angola and the Congo alone, during the next four hundred years, Portugal sent an estimated five million slaves to the Americas.

The Spaniards were the next interested party. To provide manpower for the mines and plantations of their growing colonies, they had tried to enslave the American Indians, but soon gave up the idea, for the Indians, proud, implacable warriors who preferred to die fighting rather than live in fetters, had none of the essential qualities for slave-status. So Spain contented itself with exterminating the natives of the New World and their remarkable cultures, and commissioned the Portuguese—who were decimating the Old World—to furnish the requisite slaves.

In the seventeenth century the other great European powers broke the Portuguese monopoly and elbowed their way into the trade. Soon virtually every civilized nation was fighting for its share of raw material and markets. The west coast of Africa was solid with English, Dutch, Swedish, German, Danish, French, Portuguese and, eventually, Yankee slave traders. It was one of the world's most profitable businesses: the purchase price of a full-grown man in a Congolese village was about two shillings, a figure multiplied fifteen hundred times if and when he reached

[1] *Life*, World Library (New York, 1962).

the United States, where the average market value of a negro was £150 (and up to £450 just before the close of the Civil War).

Among them, the west coast slave traders managed to deplete the population of the African continent by an estimated twenty-five to fifty million people. About fifteen million survived to reach the New World. The rest had been massacred in the *razzia* —the great raids of the slavers, or perished during the long marches from the interior; or died in the *barracoons*—the slave depots of the coast; or expired in the stinking holds of the ships. Then, in 1850, Brazil prohibited further importation of slaves, and when slavery ended in the United States with the defeat of the South in 1865, the West African trade came to a halt.

The Arabs still flourished in the east, sending their slaves to the continuing Oriental market. In fact, during the first half of the nineteenth century, they had been expanding their operations towards the centre of the continent. By 1830 they reached Tabora in Tanganyika, and twenty years later they were solidly established at Ujiji and other strategic bases on the shore of Lake Tanganyika. From these strongholds they raided Maniema, Ruanda-Urundi and even Katanga, where they sometimes came face to face with Portuguese slavers from the west. Then, in 1860, the Arabs settled in Maniema, at Nyangwe on the banks of the Lualaba River. They brought their three most persuasive arguments with them: the whip, the gun and the iron collar.

Every year an estimated three hundred thousand men, women and children of the Maniema tribes either perished in the raids or started on the long march to Zanzibar a thousand miles away. Only seventy thousand arrived. As for the rest, the German explorer Georg Schweinfurth wrote, 'All over Africa, dried human skeletons show where the slave trader has passed.'

A Belgian 'White Father', Père Wynck, saw one of those infamous caravans arriving at Ujiji and described the scene unforgettably. He spoke of the 'living skeletons' which came out of Maniema, riddled by starvation and disease, tied together by a cord run through their pierced ears, and recounted how the dead or dying were thrown into the bush between Lake Tanganyika and the Ujiji slave market in such incredible numbers that the hyaenas, sickened of human flesh, turned away from the feast.

His report, and the testimony of many other missionaries and explorers, especially Dr. Livingstone and Sir Samuel Baker, horrified the civilized world. In 1888 Cardinal Lavigerie, Archbishop of Algiers, preached against slavery in the cathedrals of Paris, London and Brussels. Nothing came of it in Paris or

London, but a year later the Brussels conferences for the aboli-
tion of slavery began, and in 1892 the Moslems met their first
real opposition in Maniema: King Leopold II of Belgium,
Sovereign of the Congo Free State, declared war on the Arab
slavers.

It was a tall order. The realm of Tippo Tip, infamous 'King
of Maniema', had no intention of surrendering lightly, and the
'King' himself prudently departed for Zanzibar before the
fighting began. But he left an intricate network of friends and
relations in charge: his son Séfu at Kasongo, his cousin Bwana
Nzige (the 'Grasshopper') at Kabambare, his nephew Rachid
at Stanley Falls, and his former slave Gongo Lutete far to the
west at Gandu. At Nyangwe the wily old chief Munie Mohara
commanded ten thousand men; Nserera held the *boma*, or
fortress, at Riba-Riba (now Lokandu); 'Rumaliza the Ravager'
ruled Lake Tanganyika, the Arabs' 'Sea of Ujiji'.

Among them they had more than thirty thousand riflemen at
their disposal, while the forces of the newly formed Congo Free
State numbered only twelve hundred, commanded by a handful
of Belgian officers. The odds were impossible, nearly thirty
to one.

Yet odds meant nothing to those daring pioneers, especially
Captain Francis Dhanis, a Belgian-Irish half-breed, who
manœuvred his pitifully small army with rare tactical genius.
He defeated Gongo Lutete, and when Séfu's forces attacked
him, Dhanis killed a thousand of the enemy and took more than
a thousand prisoners. He lost only two of his own men. A
month later, at the head of six Belgian officers and 450 native
troops, Dhanis had the audacity to attack Munie Mohara's ten
thousand riflemen and to win. He went on to take Nyangwe and
Kasongo, and to inflict a terrible defeat on 'Rumaliza the Ravager', who fled to the east.

The war lasted two years; on 22 September 1894 the last
Arab *boma* surrendered and Maniema was finally free. Dhanis
returned in triumph to Belgium and the King made him a baron.

Others were less fortunate: at Kasongo, on my way to Shabunda, I had seen their impressive monument, a column of
rough brown masonry flanked by four large bronze shields and
four blocks of stone indicating the points of the compass. Beneath it lay the bodies of Major Ponthier, Lieutenant Baron de
Heusch and Captain de Wouters d'Oplinter, all of whom died
fighting Rumaliza, Sultan of Ujiji. The remains of Lieutenant
Lippens and Second Lieutenant de Bruyne were enshrined in the

same crypt. The two Belgian officers had been tortured and murdered by Séfu, their bodies had been terribly mutilated and the Moslems had cut off their hands and feet.

For the Arabs, who sometimes built triumphal arches framed with putrefying hands, this was almost a pious gesture, since they were merely carrying out the Koran injunction: 'The reward of those who make war against God and His Apostle, and strive after violence on the earth, is that they shall be slaughtered or crucified, or their hands cut off and their feet on alternate sides. . . .'

Other heroes of the Arab campaign lie in the Pioneers' Cemetery at Nyangwe, but Arthur Hodister and the members of his mission were never buried. They were massacred by Maniema natives who delivered their heads to their master, the Arab chieftain Nserera. Their bodies were eaten, a common fate for white and negro dead. Dr. Sidney Langford Hinde, an Englishman attached to Dhanis' forces, summed up this aspect vividly:

> What struck me the most strongly during all these expeditions was the number of partially cut-up bodies which I encountered for miles in every direction. Some of them lacked the hands and the feet; others had slices taken out of the thighs or elsewhere; still others lacked the intestines or the head, according to the taste of each savage.

Such was the old Maniema, the blood-drenched 'Land of the Man-Eaters', which Leopold's pioneers gave their lives to liberate. The war they fought so courageously against such impossible odds has been ignored almost completely in most books in the English language, but as that great English administrator, Sir Harry Johnston, remarked, the Belgian campaign against the Arabs was 'one of the most extraordinary chapters in African history'.

Perhaps the most moving tribute came from a Congolese native, who wrote:

> When we pass the graves of those heroes who gave their lives for our safety, and thanks to whom we can now utter the words 'independence and autonomy', let us be silent for a few moments and bow our heads respectfully in their memory. . . . Other countries more powerful than Belgium remained indifferent to our fate and left us to perish. Belgium, moved by a very sincere and humanitarian idealism, came to our help, and with the assistance of doughty native fighters, was able to rout the enemy, to eradicate disease, to teach us

and to eliminate certain barbarous practices from our customs, thus restoring our human dignity and turning us into free, happy, vigorous civilized men.

Incredibly, the author of those words was Patrice Lumumba. He wrote them in 1958,[1] before he became a tragic victim of the Communist brain-washing which taught him, by a supreme irony, to call the Belgians 'slave-traders'.

*   *   *

When I came to Maniema, more than half a century after these events, it seemed at first that the grim past was forgotten. Yet, as in many other parts of the Congo, the people still secretly followed their old ways. My new A.T. warned me to keep my eyes open for evidence of cannibalism among the local Balega tribesmen and to arrest any natives who might still be practising the forbidden rituals of the Bwamé Secret Society, which the Government had been trying to suppress since 1916.

For four months, I saw no trace of either. Then, in a strange succession of events, I met a band of contemporary Maniema cannibals, unwittingly became one of them, found the Bwamé cult flourishing underground and instead of reporting it, became one of its members.

It all began when I made a quick safari into the bush, trying to find some Lega masks and figures for my collection. I was about ten miles east of Penekusu, a village about fifty miles south of Shabunda, accompanied by three porters, when I stumbled across a small forest encampment where a dozen young boys, looked after by two old women, were living in ritual isolation, preparing for their circumcision ceremonies.

The entire camp was suffused with a wonderful aroma of simmering meat from a big black pot. The smell nearly drove me wild: I had eaten nothing all day except a handful of peanuts and a banana. 'What's in the pot?' I asked one of my porters, a husky fellow named Mogudu.

He spoke for some time with an old woman who was stirring the stew. Then he turned and said briskly, '*Nungu.*'

'That's quite a big pot for a porcupine,' I remarked.

'Two porcupines, *Bwana*. Big ones!'

Nungu was regarded throughout Black Africa as a dish for gourmets so I pitched in without hesitation when the old woman skewered several chunks, let them drip against the side of the pot

[1] *Le Congo—Terre d'Avenir—Est-Il Menacé?*, translated by Graham Heath as *Congo, My Country* (New York: Frederick A. Praeger, 1962).

and plopped them down in front of me on a banana-leaf plate. They were big, irregularly shaped gobbets of meat—fine-grained, pinkish-grey, and boneless; they tasted a little like veal and a little like suckling pig, but much better than either. I remember thinking they must have come from an extremely large porcupine.

A moment later, she brought us a wooden bowl full of *bukari* and a smaller bowl of sauce that she ladled out of the black pot. Following the Bantu style of dining, I pinched off a piece of the manioc dough with my thumb and forefinger, kneaded it into a ball, punched a deep trough in the ball with my thumb, forming a dough spoon, and used it to dip up the savoury sauce. Then I ate the spoon and went on to make and devour a dozen more, between bites of the succulent meat.

'How do you like it?' Mogudu asked me.

'*Iko mutamu!*—It's delicious! And very tender. Are you sure it's porcupine?'

The porter nodded, with his mouth full. His eyes gleamed with pleasure and the three tattooed lines on each of his cheeks made him look like a chocolate-coloured cat with big black whiskers. He seemed rather nervous and kept glancing at me sideways; still, I suspected nothing: we had both been terribly hungry and his excitement seemed quite natural.

I felt wonderfully satisfied and relaxed afterwards, until later in the evening, when I was questioning one of the young candidates for circumcision about the impending rituals. He was a small, skinny twelve-year-old with reddish-coloured hair—a symptom of *kwashiorkor*, the protein-deficiency disease which affects so many children in tropical Africa. He spoke very slowly, in mixed Kilega and Kingwana, and appeared to be slightly retarded.

'Just before we are cut,' the child told me, 'we have to drink the *mududawa*. That is *malafu*—palm-wine—mixed with *majivu ya mtu*, ashes from human bones. The bones of a young boy are the best, but this time it will come from a girl.'

'How do you know?'

'It's all been arranged. Two days ago a man in the next village threw his wife out of the hut because she couldn't have babies. She went mad and ran into the bush. When my uncle found the girl, he grabbed her and cut her throat. She didn't even try to fight.'

'Your uncle did *that*?'

'She would have died anyway, *Bwana*. Afterwards, he

brought the body here on his shoulder. We cut the meat off her bones and burned them, along with the guts and the brain, until they turned into white ashes. Then we put the ashes in a special little basket and my uncle took it to the *muchawi* in the village. The magician will mix the ashes with wine when the time comes to cut us.'

'What did you do with the flesh?'

'What everyone does with it,' he said, gesturing towards the black pot. 'We ate it.' Then, suddenly realizing that he had said too much, he stared at me in terror.

I suppose I should have felt violent physical or emotional revulsion to learn that the 'porcupine' meat in my stomach had once been human flesh. I must admit I experienced no such reaction. What did horrify and enrage me was to think how the unfortunate dazed girl had been murdered, as casually as the natives kill an antelope or a bird. That seemed far more important than the fate of her dead body.

Murder for meat had once been a regular feature of life in the Congo, at every cultural level. In the northeast the long-headed Mangbetu and the Azande, whose neighbours called them the Niam-Niam, or 'meat-people', had smoked their victims' flesh and doted on human fat, which they considered to be as intoxicating as alcohol. In the west the Basoko tribe used to make a kind of *shish kebab* from alternating pieces of human kidney and breast, while the Bapoto sold living men piece by piece: they marked each area of the captive's body with coloured clay as a buyer selected his favourite cut of meat; then, when all the parts had been sold, the living jigsaw puzzle was carved up and its pieces were distributed to the impatient purchasers. The Bangala preferred riper meat and for many years guard had to be kept on the cemeteries of Léopoldville to prevent them from exhuming and devouring the corpses.

The reason why cannibalism had been endemic throughout the Congo as in much of tropical Africa, was not that the natives were depraved or sadistic but simply because their bodies craved the human meat which custom and tradition had taught them to accept. 'Morality is the custom of one's country and the current feeling of one's peers,' Samuel Butler once remarked. 'Cannibalism is moral in a cannibal country.'

Moreover, the Africans were not alone in their strange morality. Cannibalism, in one form or another, had been reported among the North and South American Indians, Eskimos, Australian aborigines, Polynesians and Melanesians. All had some strange theories concerning the magical virtues of human meat—that the liver was rich in courage, the ears contained intelligence or the testicles strength—but the basic motive for cannibalism, wherever it happened, was always hunger, the oldest and most natural animal impulse. To satisfy that hunger, even by killing and devouring other human beings, was certainly less reprehensible than the crimes of 'civilized' men, who kill more subtly and cynically for money or power . . . and always by the most efficient, up-to-date and well-organized means.

My little band of Maniema cannibals were terrified when they discovered that one of their members had talked. They were sure that I would report them and that they faced the prospect of long terms in jail. But knowing how pointless that kind of punishment was, I took no official action. Instead, I talked to them patiently, tried to explain the meaning of their crimes, and threatened them with terrible retribution, personal, magic and supernatural, if they ever repeated the offence.

They listened to me with apparent compliance, as their countrymen had done for the past half-century, and every single one of them swore that he would never eat human flesh again. They may well have kept their promise—for a while.

*　　*　　*

On our next safari to the bush country south of Shabunda, we stopped at the little village of Kitamba where my porter Mogudu introduced me to his aged uncle, a shrivelled man in a monkey-skin loincloth, wearing a necklace of five dangling leopard teeth and a fez-shaped monkey-skin hat decorated with cowrie shells, mussels and hyrax teeth. Mogudu, who had become friendly and confiding since I hadn't reported him for his part in the *nungu* incident, boasted to me that the old man was what he called an A-Tumba-Yananio—the highest-ranking dignitary of the Bwamé Secret Society in the village of Kitamba.

The A-Tumba-Yananio was wary of me at first, but at Mogudu's urging, finally consented to answer some questions.

'What does a man have to do before he can join Bwamé?' was the first thing I asked.

'He must have enough money to pay his initiation fee,' the old man said bluntly.

This was no great surprise. In virtually all secret societies, African or otherwise, admission and promotion are on a strictly monetary basis. 'How much does it cost?' I prodded him.

'A man has to pay five hundred francs to be initiated as a

Mwamé,' he explained grumpily. 'That is the lowest rank. He can pay it in money, meat, iron, kola nuts, bracelets or beer—but money is best. Then, when he moves up to the next rank, the Mpala, he has to pay twice as much. When he becomes a Yananio, like me, he has to pay four times as much, and if he wants to become a Kindi—one of our big chiefs—it costs him five thousand francs!'

'Are there any other requirements?'

'Well, his wife has to join with him. Every time he buys himself a new rank, she moves up too. That means he has to pay for her promotions, but it doesn't cost as much for women as for men.'

That was an interesting sidelight. Most African secret societies, I knew, refused to admit women and parallel female societies arose mainly concerned with human and agricultural fertility rituals. Others admitted women to extremely limited participation, and only a few, like the Ndembo Society of the Lower Congo, were completely mixed.

'Do they ever get the money back after they become members?' I asked.

'Of course not! But they get lots of free meat and beer from the people who don't belong. Sometimes the villagers don't want to give it to us, but they usually change their minds. Otherwise they get big trouble!'

'What happens to them?' The old man was silent. I quickly changed the subject. 'What kind of rituals do you perform?' He looked scandalized. 'Do you have any special Bwamé carvings or masks here in Kitamba?' I persisted. His reaction grew even more frigid and he stalked off with extreme dignity into his small, leaf-thatched hut.

'You shouldn't have asked him questions like that,' Mogudu rebuked me. 'He can't talk about those things to anyone who isn't a member—especially a white man. You know how the *wazungu* feel about Bwamé!'

The old man's fears were certainly justified. More than thirty years before, when the Government had outlawed Bwamé, the Catholic Missions of Maniema had joined in, denouncing the society's masks and figurines as 'heathen idols'. Since merely possessing them was enough to implicate a man in the eyes of the law, many members threw their carved emblems of rank into the nearest stream, buried them in the soil or abandoned them in the forest. The boldest Bwamé adepts hid them in the recesses of their huts and hoped to avoid discovery.

It was a serious mistake on the Central Government's part, caused, as such errors usually were, by incomplete information about local problems. The Bwamé Society had gradually come into being among the Balega tribesmen of the Shabunda, Pangi and Mwenga territories as a means of counteracting the despotism of the *nene-kisi*, or tribal chiefs. Thus, like the Tenda Society of French Guinea, it had served a useful political purpose; it was also the great repository of Lega tribal traditions. During a period of increasing contact with Europeans, Bwamé alone could have preserved those traditions and ensured the survival of Lega art, the purest, most abstract and expressive native sculpture in the Congo.

I had already acquired about fifty of their small statues and masks: strange, contemplative, concave faces in yellowed ivory and shiny brown wood which seemed like a fusion of negro and modern art. All were somehow connected with unknown Bwamé rituals, but their exact significance was virtually unknown. Apparently, the only way to find this out was to become a member of Bwamé.

'It's impossible,' Mogudu said flatly, his tattooed cat whiskers quivering indignantly. 'They would never accept a white member, not even you.'

'Why should my colour keep me out? I'll pay the initiation fee.'

'But *Bwana*,' he protested, 'they'd be afraid you might report them to the government. None of them would trust you for a minute!'

'Tell them about the "porcupine". I didn't report that, and it was much more serious. And say something about my magic. They might let me join if they know I'm a white *muchawi*.'

'Well, I'll try, but I don't expect it will be any use.'

Mogudu sighed and walked towards his uncle's hut; I waited at least fifteen minutes while they argued. Then, when the pair emerged, shaking their heads together, I took the offensive. 'I have decided to join Bwamé,' I informed the old man imperiously.

He stared at me, shocked. 'Nothing can be decided yet. First the *mpala* must discuss the question among them and then the A-Tumba-Kindi—our Supreme Chief—will make the final decision. It will take time. This has never happened to us before; the *wazungu* have always tried to destroy Bwamé and now they want to join it!'

'I am not like the other *wazungu*. Your people have seen some of my magic; they will tell you about it.'

The A-Tumba-Yananio nodded stiffly. 'I have heard about the mysterious knife and the cloth which is never cut. It is very strange.'

'I have other magic.' I stared down intently into his eyes.

'Very well,' he said quickly, 'I will talk to the Kindi.'

I heard no more for five days. Then a very excited Mogudu came and announced that the top-ranking dignitaries of the Society had agreed to admit their first white candidate. The ceremony was to take place next day, but there was one small problem: they demanded a fee of 2,500 francs—five times the usual tariff for initiation to the lowest grade.

'That's robbery!' I exploded. 'Whom do they think they're dealing with? A child? An innocent? A tourist?'

Mogudu smiled apologetically. 'That is what they decided. They say you are a rich man. You have a truck and three pairs of shoes, and you change your shirt every day. They say it would be dishonourable for you to pay less, and they don't want to insult you.'

'Well, 2,500 francs is a lot of money, but I daresay it's worth it.

'You have to bring beer, too. For the initiation ceremony.'

'Don't they have any *pombe* of their own?'

'Yes, but this is something special. If you bring them *wazungu* beer in real bottles, no one will ever forget it.'

'All right, we'll pick up a case of *Simba* before we go to Kitamba.'

'There's one other thing, *Bwana*. The ceremony can only take place in the village of a Kindi. That means we will have to go to Kiakupa, about twenty miles away. Then the Kindi of Kiakupa can make you a member.'

'What will he do?'

'You'll see. I'm not supposed to tell you anything about it.'

Next morning Mogudu and I drove to Kitamba, where I installed the A-Tumba-Yananio in the front seat and seven boisterous Bwamé in the back. They sang lustily all the way, but stopped abruptly when we arrived. Obviously important preliminary steps had already been taken: no women or children were in sight and at least four-fifths of the men had prudently disappeared into the bush. Only bona fide male members of Bwamé could attend the initiation of a new member. Most of my brothers-elect were lounging in the *baraza*—the big open hut that served as a central meeting-place for the entire village, but they stopped chattering, rose to their feet and stared at me gravely as our little party approached.

In the foreground Kiakupa's supreme Bwamé chief stood like a monument of the old Africa that was passing away. The A-Tumba-Kindi wore a leopard-skin loincloth and a magnificent necklace of leopard and lion teeth, interposed with glass beads and copper spirals, with a curious man-shaped ivory amulet that was framed between two pairs of extremely large lion teeth at the bottom; his braided rattan hat was covered with cowrie shells and its peak adorned with the tuft of hair from an elephant's tail.

In the centre of the *baraza* were four symbolic objects and now, as the ceremony began, the A-Tumba-Kindi explained each one. First he waggled a stick of bamboo at me: 'As soon as you have been initiated, you may leave your people and found your own village.' Then he gestured at a slender *ficus* bough: 'This is a branch of the *mugumu* tree. When you build your village, you will plant the *mugumu*. Make loincloths from its beaten bark and do not dress in any other cloth, for the *mugumu* is the true guardian of Bwamé.'

That could be a problem.

'When a brother passes by,' the Kindi told me, waving at a basketful of meat and bananas, 'you will always give him to eat.' I nodded, a little dubious at the prospect of having to feed up to two or three thousand of my Bwamé brethren, especially on my anaemic salary. Then the Kindi came to the 'beer clause', the one element present in virtually every African initiation oath, dowry arrangement or blood brotherhood. He pointed at the fourth object, a pot of *pombe*, and said, very emphatically, 'You will always have enough beer on hand to satisfy the thirst of your brothers!'

Then he formally proclaimed me a Mwamé and gave me the insignia of my rank, the *mpita*, a conical rattan cap with two rows of cowrie shells. Since the *mpita* was more than six inches tall but much too narrow for my head, it wobbled grotesquely on top. The Kindi stared up at the seven-foot apparition with obvious dismay.

'You must never remove the *mpita*,' he told me gravely. 'If you do, you will die.'

'I cannot wear it among the *wazungu*—'

'None of us can,' he said quickly. 'We understand that.'

'But what it the wind blows it off? Will I die if that happens?'

He glared at me angrily, although my question had been quite logical. Then he made what he obviously considered to be a major decision: I could wear a raffia chin-strap to secure my *mpita*, even though that was usually a prerogative of the higher ranks. It proved to be a questionable privilege, for the chinstrap was beautifully decorated with cowrie shells, but so short I could hardly open my mouth.

Once the hat problem had been settled, the Kindi leaned forward with an impressively mystical air, reciting in a tense monotone the 'secrets' of the Bwamé Society. Many were cast in the form of bizarre proverbs, so obscure and symbolic that I searched in vain for a meaning. Others were intelligible but extremely complex; for example, there was an elaborate set of food taboos varying according to the phases of the moon and the locale. Had I tried to follow them seriously, I would have needed a pocket chart to determine whether it was safe to consume porcupine meat in Kitamba during a new moon or completely forbidden to eat eggs in Shabunda during the same phase. Nevertheless, the Kindi rattled off the endless variants with no trouble—a striking example of the African natives' remarkable powers of memory.

Many of the 'secrets' were connected with sex, including a special magic formula to be recited before having intercourse with a woman. It was guaranteed to reinforce any Bwamé member's potency and augment his wife's fertility. Unfortunately, most of the secrets in this category are unprintable.

Towards the end, the Kindi recited a long list of the Bwamé Society's most illustrious members, and I recognized with some amusement the name of a very formal and pompous *évolué* whom I knew—he was one of the clerks in the District Commissioner's office. Then the Kindi named, and inveighed against, the Society's outstanding enemies, black and white alike, and forbade me, under pain of atrocious death, to betray the secrets to any of them. That list included the District Commissioner himself and my own A.T. in Shabunda.

After the Kindi had divulged the last peculiar 'secret', we went on to more important matters: beer, beef, bananas and *bukari*. There was plenty of beer, both my own case of *Simba* and several pots of *pombe*; the 'beef' was excellent antelope meat and not spurious porcupine; the bananas were roasted; and the *bukari* was warm and sticky. The big basket of meat and bananas was empty within half an hour, the beer took a little longer. Then, half-tipsy, I drove the Kitamba delegation back to their own village, and a few miles later deposited an almost unconscious Mogudu at our camp.

I took part in several more Bwamé ceremonies, all of which

ended on an alcoholic note, before I returned to Shabunda to file my monthly report. I felt almost tempted to interpolate among the eternal statistics on coffee, manioc and cotton a much more stimulating account of my progress as an *évolué* member of a black secret society. It would have been delightful to see what consternation this would have produced. But I didn't need to go looking for trouble: it came to me.

'Information has reached me,' my A.T. said pompously, 'to the effect that you have acquired a number of Lega statues and masks. Is this true?'

'Yes. I also have some beautiful ivory spoons and ceremonial knives. What's wrong with that?'

'Those objects are almost always associated with the illegal Bwamé Society. You should know that. They practically never sell them to a white man.'

'What are you suggesting?'

'Just this, Monsieur Hallet. I don't intend to tolerate any thugs or fanatics in this territory. I suspect that you've been fraternizing with members of Bwamé, yet you've never reported any illegal activities to this office. Am I correct?'

'If I see any "illegal activities" endangering the security of this territory, you can be sure I'll report it.'

With that honest but evasive answer, I left. Had the A.T. known at that moment that he was dealing not only with a suspected fellow-traveller of the Society but a full-fledged Mwamé, complete with chin-strap, he probably would have had apoplexy.

Native secret societies had acquired a bad name in the Congo, although most of them were relatively peaceful organizations; this was simply because a few, like the notorious Anyoto, or 'Leopard Men' of the northeast Congo, had been dedicated assassins spreading terror and death. The Anyoto Society apparently originated among the Mabudu tribe in the Wamba area of the Ituri Forest, and after infiltrating the Mambela Society of the Babali tribe, the sect had gradually spread south to Avakubi, Irumu, Bafwasende, and even Beni on the southeast edge of the forest, leaving a trail of mutilated bodies in its wake.

The Anyoto masqueraded grotesquely in bark-cloth tunics and hoods marked with black spots and rings to resemble a leopard's skin. The tail of a real leopard dangled from the human leopard's rear, attached to a belt which held other important accessories: a small earthenware pot, a stick carved in the shape of a leopard's paw, and a very sharp knife. He blew into the pot to mimic the leopard's muffled snarl, pressed the stick into the soft earth surrounding his victim's body to copy the animal's spoor, and used the knife to sever his prey's carotid arteries. The final tool was an iron bracelet equipped with four dangling knives: when his hand was extended, the blades were concealed under the wearer's palm, but when he made a fist they jutted out between his clenched fingers, like a leopard's claws.

The Anyoto hunted at dusk, prowling forest paths or picking off victims at the edges of plantations and villages. Like their animal prototypes, they rarely attempted to kill strong young men who could put up a real fight. Instead, they hunted old men, children and especially women, and often, as an initiation requirement, murdered their own close relatives. Like the leopard, the Anyoto attacked from the rear, slashing their prey with incredible fury. But then they usually gave themselves away, for the human leopards did something no real leopard could ever do: they cut off their female victims' breasts.

Sometimes the severed breasts were taken to the local Anyoto leader as proof of successful murder, sometimes they were eaten. As a final touch, the Leopard Men often tore the eyes out of their kill for use in making *dawa* or ritual medicine: they were simmered in a pot containing the claw-knives and the Anyoto drank the resulting mess, convinced that this grisly procedure gave them the power to see in the dark. Then daylight came, and like the legendary werewolves of Europe, the Leopard Men went calmly about their business—smiling, polite and even friendly.

In later years, when I talked to Babali tribesmen who had been jailed for complicity in Anyoto killings, I found that their strange behaviour was partially explained by their almost complete lack of what civilized men call a conscience. 'If the crime is successful,' one explained to me, 'and everyone thinks it's a leopard, why should the real killer worry? He should be proud of himself for taking everybody in!'

The behaviour of the Leopard Men's intended prey may seem equally strange: they are terror-stricken and yet, when they suspect or even have definite knowledge that one of their fellows is an Anyoto killer, they will not report him. They are afraid of reprisal, of the supernatural aura surrounding the Society and, most tragic of all, of the white authorities who are desperately anxious to help them.

At the end of the nineteenth century the Anyoto were at their most powerful, killing thousands of victims every year. In 1909, only a year after the Belgian Congo was formally created, more than fifty Leopard Men killers were jailed and hanged at Avakubi, where the local authorities had sworn to put an end to the reign of Anyoto terror. During the next two decades, sporadic Anyoto killings probably accounted for at least a hundred deaths a year, and even as late as 1934 Leopard Men in the Beni region killed forty-two natives in three months. By 1960 the Belgian Colonial Government had succeeded in extirpating them almost completely. Then 'independence' came to the Congo and, as did so many other barbaric traditions, the cult of the Leopard Men sprang back to life.

Similar leopard societies had flourished in Kenya, Angola and West Africa, especially the Mendi cult of Sierra Leone, whose members, motivated by ritual cannibalism, had spread death and supernatural terror among their neighbours. 'Crocodile Men' had infested parts of the Congo and 'Hyaena Men', the notorious Mfisi Society, had arisen in East Africa.

Kenya's Mau Mau rule by fear, but are not a real secret society so much as a terrorist sect, whose crimes are inspired by calculated political and even racist goals. The Mau Mau of course have their 'secrets' and their incredibly ugly initiation oaths; but the Kikuyu natives are often *forced* to take the oaths, unlike the members of a real secret society, who enter voluntarily and even pay for the privilege to gain social prestige and power in their villages.

There are basic motives in secret societies of the civilized world. We, too, have had our pathological sects like the Russian Flagellants and Skoptsi who castrated themselves to achieve salvation; bands of religious or political fanatics like the Islamic Shiahs and Ismailians, the American Ku Klux Klan and the Spanish Garduna; professional murderers like the Assassins of the Near East; the Hindu Thugs, who killed for Bhowani, the Black Goddess; the Italian-American Mafia, who kill for money and revenge.

In China, the secret societies known as *tongs* have grown in power until they have actually taken over the reins of government. The Kuomintang, or Nationalist Party of China, headed today by Chiang Kai-shek, was founded by Dr. Sun Yat-sen, a member of the Hung or Triad Society, the largest secret society in the world, founded at Rozan in A.D. 386 by the Buddhist patriarch Hwui-yin and powerful even today. The Triad admits men and women to membership, initiates them with ritual

blood-drinking and indoctrinates them with a catechism stress-
ing mystical numbers and secret poems. It has figured notor-
iously in the gambling, opium and prostitution industries of
the Orient, and its members have been extremely influential
in 'Free China'. Ironically, the Kuomintang's opponent, the
Chinese Communist Party of Mao Tse-tung, was also organized originally as a secret society. China has, in fact, been
honeycombed with secret societies for two thousand years. The
Carnation Eyebrows, the Copper Horses, the Iron Shins, the
Eight Dragons, the Three Incense Sticks, and the Fists for
Righteous Harmony (the famous Boxers) have been only a few.

*   *   *

I dug deeper into Bwamé during the next few months, trying
to achieve a real understanding of its peculiar traditions and
acquire some of its emblems of rank for my ethnological collection, especially the A-Tumba-Kindi's magnificent necklace. Obtaining this took nearly a fortnight of concentrated persuasion
and a collection of presents that cost me nearly £70. I felt a little
guilty when I took it from the Kindi's hands in exchange for the
things he demanded—a bicycle, a sewing machine and an assortment of Western clothing—but I knew it would eventually have
been lost or destroyed, as with so many other Lega treasures.

Learning more of Bwamé traditions was a slower, more complicated process. I had made enough notes for several technical
papers, but I realized that it would take a lifetime of patient
work to absorb and understand their elaborate symbolic rituals.
But I took a big step forward when I was actually able to witness
one of the most important Bwamé ceremonies: the initiation of
a Kindi.

Theoretically, as a member of the very lowest echelon, I was
forbidden to be present, but Mogudu's uncle intervened on my
behalf: it was his own initiation, to the rank of Kindi-Kiaziba-
Yende, and he wanted me to help him finance it. He had saved
three thousand francs of his own, so needed only two thousand
more to pay for the new rank. As Mogudu made very clear, his
uncle had expressed complete confidence in 'his white brother's
goodwill'.

Though I was running short of money since buying the Kindi's
necklace and needed cash for my forthcoming holiday, I knew
I would never see such a ceremony in the ordinary course of
events, so handed the two thousand francs over to Mogudu's
uncle. A week later, at Kiakupa, where the initiation took place,

I was rewarded by an extraordinary spectacle, complete with a small orchestra of drums and tom-toms, a choir of noisy singers and some of the strangest dances in the Congo.

A group of small ivory and wooden statuettes lay on the ground in the centre of a circle of Bwamé dancers, who stamped and shuffled round the mysterious figures; then, one by one, picked up the statues and danced with them. Some of the higher-ranking men had tiny masks tucked into their belts; they held the statues in one hand, and as the rapture of the dance overcame them, snatched the masks from their belts and pressed them to their sweating foreheads, almost as though they were trying to impregnate themselves with some mystical powers.

The younger men danced with their eyes open, but some of their elders seemed in a trance, with eyes closed and an expression of deep devotion on their faces. The faces of the statues and masks had a similarly ecstatic look about them, with closed 'coffee-grain' eyes, carved in high relief, which hinted also of the mysterious cowrie shell.

Some of the statues had wonderful names and meanings. The one called *musansala* had two heads and his wooden body was pierced in three places. '*Katanda ali musaga musansala gwa muitile,*' the dancers proclaimed in Kilega—'This is a man who has a fine appearance but a wicked heart!' The *kakinga* statuette depicted a voluptuous woman. 'Her breasts are firm,' the men chanted, 'and she has a big dowry—but who knows if her nature is good or bad?' '*Samatwe mabile kumukongo kwa monene nzagu*'—'He knows everything and sees all at once'—this, of a two-faced, four-eyed statue associated with hunting rituals.

One by one, the enraptured Bwamé danced with the sacred statues and left them on the ground in front of the newly initiated Kindi. Afterwards, there was a ritual fire-dance, in which every performer tried to light pieces of wood from a firebrand held by a man in the centre. They never succeeded, but that was part of the plan, for the whole thing was supposed to symbolize the power of authority—Bwamé authority—and the relative ignorance of youth. Just as the dance ended, the performers stopped in their tracks as an excited hunter ran out of the bush and burst into the *baraza*.

'*Nkoka!*' he cried. '*Nkoka!* There is a pangolin caught in one of the traps! The sacred *nkoka* is dead!'

First there was general confusion. Then the A-Tumba-Kindi ordered two of his men to go into the bush and bring back the corpse. Half an hour later they returned, carrying the body of the dead pangolin on a litter of branches. It had strangled itself trying to escape from a slip-noose wire: the tiny pointed head was half-severed and dabbled with dried blood where the taut wire had torn the neck. The Bwamé dignitaries stared respectfully at the archaic scaled mammal, the most sacred creature in Lega tradition. It looked like an elongated pine cone and had four short legs armed with massive claws.[1]

'The animal-which-nobody-hunts has been killed,' the Kindi said loudly. 'Now we will all die too, unless we remove the curse of *nkoka*'s death. Prepare for the ceremony!'

The firebrand and the sticks of wood were put aside. A ritual knife with a copper blade was thrust under the scales of the dead pangolin's back, and about twenty-five Bwamé paraded round the corpse in their traditional circle, stamping on the ground, swinging their shoulders and from time to time making strange gestures.

'They are pretending to eat the pangolin's meat,' Mogudu's uncle explained, 'just as we will all eat it soon.'

'Isn't the meat forbidden?'

'If men hunt and kill the *nkoka* to eat his flesh, they are cursed. But if they cause his death without wanting to, they are cursed if they *don't* eat his flesh. That is the law.'

As I wrestled with the logic of this answer, little groups of three or four men ran from the circle to touch the roofs of their houses. '*Nkoka* taught us the lesson of his wonderful roof!' the

---

[1] The pangolin is almost as great a mystery to science as it is to the Balega. It was formerly erroneously lumped with armadillos, tree sloths, anteaters and the aardvark, in a hodgepodge zoological order called *Edentata*—'toothless ones'. That was quite wrong, since tree sloths and aardvarks and armadillos all have teeth, armadillos up to a hundred— more than any other land-mammal. Both anteaters and pangolins (who eat only termites) are without teeth, but there the resemblance ends. Pangolins are now grouped in a lonely little order of their own, *Pholidota*, with three species in South East Asia and four in Africa south of the Sahara. Their imbricated 'scales' are formed (like the rhino's horn) from compacted hair, and hair grows very sparsely between them. Their feet are armed with powerful claws, used for burrowing and to smash open termite nests; the tongue is extremely long, and the animal has anal glands like those of a skunk. When really frightened he rolls into a compact ball, presenting the enemy with the hard edges of his erected scales. The pangolin's status as a sacred animal is undoubtedly due to his weird, prehistoric appearance, as with the chameleon, the hornbill and the monitor lizards, which are all deeply feared throughout Black Africa.

dancers cried. 'We saw him and learned how to make our own roofs. Without *nkoka*, the rain would kill us!' Their hands lingered on the big *mangungu* leaves that thatched the roofs of their houses—leaves which overlapped like the pangolin's scales. '*Nkoka* taught us the lesson of his back!' the dancers repeated ecstatically, before rejoining the circle.

Unfortunately, the pangolin hadn't taught the lesson as well as he might. Roofs of Lega huts had a deplorable tendency to disintegrate; whenever I found untended coffee fields, the owner's eternal justification was 'I was busy mending my roof.'

At last the strange ritual was finished, and the pangolin was ceremonially lowered into his last resting-place: a big black cooking-pot. He was boiled for about an hour, his scales were removed and his flesh was cut into pieces for distribution to the expectant Bwamé. Each man received a cut of pangolin meat corresponding with his hierarchic position: the A-Tumba-Kindi, the highest official, had the privilege of eating the heart; as the most junior on the scene I was given a one-inch cube of pink flesh from the pangolin's rear.

It was extremely tough and tasted peculiarly bitter. I chewed it interminably and made a little vow to respect the pangolin's sacred person for ever after.

Then there was a final dance, a mock combat with wooden stools, and the Bwamé ceremonies were over. The members hid their precious statues and masks in the huts. The A-Tumba-Kindi changed from his leopard-skin loincloth into a pair of khaki shorts, and the uninitiated people of Kiakupa crept back into their village. All that remained of the strange rituals were a charred stick of wood and a few scattered pangolin scales.

As I climbed into my waiting Chevy pickup, which seemed suddenly like some armoured animal from another world, I knocked my conical *mpita* against the roof. The chin-strap broke, with a shower of little cowries, and the rattan hat fell to the floor. I picked it up, and placed it very carefully on the seat beside me. Then I drove off towards Kitamba.

The long day was over and I was a white man again . . . at least for a while.

5

A Glimpse of the Grand Forest

> '... These areas are inhabited by pygmies. This is no
> myth, there actually exists a small tribe, and even
> their houses are small. Their habits are said to be
> those of Troglodytes.'
>
> ARISTOTLE, 'NATURAL HISTORY', 330 B.C.

LAKE KIVU, Kisenyi, Beni and the Ituri Forest—I marked the
route on my map, jumped into my truck and drove eastward.
It was June 1950, I had two weeks' leave and after two years in
the Congo was finally headed towards my family in Kisenyi
and a reunion with the shadowy little figures remembered from
my childhood: the Bambuti pygmies.

The Chevy and I crossed at least forty bridges and then, two
hundred miles east of Shabunda, we started to spiral downwards along a series of hairpin bends which led to Lake Kivu
and the first of my dreams. In the foreground Bukavu, a town
of villas and wonderful gardens, rambled over five small penin-
sulas lying like a green hand stretching its fingers into the water.
Beyond, the Ruzizi River started on its wild journey south, and
the distant hills of Ruanda climbed in tormented folds from the
deep blue lake.

I was entering the Graben or Central Rift Valley, a gigantic
crack in the crust of the earth stretching 869 miles from the
Zambezi River in Mozambique to the Nile in northern Uganda.
Twenty-five miles wide, rimmed by towering mountains and
active volcanoes, the immense crevasse separates the equatorial
rain forest of the Congo from East Africa's burning savannahs,
and holds between its serrated walls the long chain of Central
African lakes: Nyasa, Tanganyika, Kivu, Edward and Albert.

Farther east, Victoria, the largest lake on the continent, broods alone in a separate basin, before giving birth to the Nile; to the southwest, equally isolated, lie Bangweulu and Moëro, the shallow, swampy lakes which are the ultimate source of the Congo River.

Victoria is an inland sea bigger than Ireland. Tanganyika is the longest, deepest and most impressive: an undulating 404-mile-long ribbon, whose depth is nearly a mile. Kivu, with 879 square miles, is one of the smallest, but at an altitude of 4,789 feet is the highest lake in Central Africa, and one of the most delightful. To one who came, as I did, from the interior of the Congo, the shores of Lake Kivu seemed like a temperate paradise a few miles south of the equator.

I turned left at Bukavu and headed towards the eight giant Virunga volcanoes at the northern end of the lake. Two of them, Nyamulagira (10,022 feet) and Nyiragongo (11,381 feet), had erupted only two years before. The other six, Karisimbi (14,786 feet), Mikeno (14,557 feet), Muhavura (13,540 feet), Visoke (12,175 feet), Sabinio (11,486 feet) and Gahinga (11,400 feet), were apparently extinct, and along with several hundred smaller craters lay passively across the entire width of the Rift Valley, quietly separating the basins of the Nile and Congo rivers.

I passed Sake at the northern tip of the lake, and the road cut its way through the crumpled black waves of an enormous lava field. Ten miles later, I reached the twin towns of Goma-Kisenyi on the Congolese border. I crossed into Ruanda and a few minutes later stopped the Chevy in front of a Provençal villa on a little hill overlooking the shore of the lake in Kisenyi.

'*Mon Dieu!*' my mother screamed wildly, abandoning her sewing machine in the *baraza*. '*Voilà Jean-Pierre!*' She ran forward and seized me, sobbing with emotion and inundating me with tears and kisses.

'*Bonjour*,' I said with a smile. 'You're looking very well.'

She smiled with satisfaction and patted her hair. Then we tiptoed through the house to the large studio where my father, André Hallet, was hard at work on his latest painting. I intended to give him a little surprise.

His back was turned and he was jabbing furiously at a canvas as he put the finishing touches to a study in oils of a 'Watusi' dancer. I stood for a moment, admiring his energy. Then, suddenly realizing that someone was watching him paint, which he detested, he whirled round angrily, scowling at me from under his shaggy eyebrows. He recognized me, and in a moment the taut lines of his face melted into an expression of incredulous pleasure.

'*Sacré nom d'un chien!*' he cried, laying down his brush. 'What a surprise!'

'I see your style hasn't changed,' I said dryly and took a few steps forward to embrace him.

We spent four wonderful days together in Kisenyi and then I headed north again, driving along the famous 'Road of Beauty' which leads to Albert National Park, Lake Edward, the Ruwenzori Mountains and the Grand Forest. At Rutshuru, forty-five miles from Goma, I put the last banana and coffee plantations behind me. Then, after crossing the Ruindi River, the road zigzagged up into the Mitumba Mountains, following the contours of the Congo-Nile Divide as it climbed the Kabasha and Matembe Escarpments, swinging around fantastic curves to the summit at 8,202 feet.

At Alimbongo I drove through a high-altitude forest of bamboo and lichens; at Lubero, the highest administrative centre in the Congo, I tasted the local fresh strawberries and whipped cream; and near Butembo I saw neat European plantations of coffee *arabica*, quinine and pyrethrum, all high-altitude crops. Then the road dipped again, and forty-five minutes later I came to Beni, the little town where I had spent six exciting years as a child. I drove on and seven miles north of Beni, finally reached my goal: I saw and touched the first trees of the Grand Forest.

Here were 25,000 square miles of the earth's surface which rarely see the sun, an incredible outburst of vegetation spreading from the mouth of the Aruwimi River in the west almost to Lake Albert and the slopes of Ruwenzori in the east. The ancient Egyptians called it the 'Land of Trees'. Others have known it as the 'Pygmy Forest,' the 'Stanley Forest', the 'Great Congo Forest', the 'Aruwimi' or 'Ituri Forest', or, most fitting of all, the 'Grand Forest' of the Congo.

African mahoganies and cedars, *limba* and parasol trees, ebony, teak and a host of others with no familiar names, grow to enormous dimensions, some towering up to 160 feet. Below, in the underbrush, immense flowering lianas compete with Phoenix and Raphia palms, dangling aerial roots, ferns, shrubs and occasional masses of lichen to wrest life from the damp mossy floor.

This green universe belongs to the lemur, the elephant shrew, the hyrax, the miniature antelope, the pangolin, the leopard, the forest elephant, and red buffalo—and a fantastic variety of snakes. This is the dark, little-known retreat of the Congo's rarest and most elusive mammal, the okapi, and the home of the oldest, smallest and most primitive human race: the Bambuti pygmies.[1]

In modern times the Bambuti were discovered by Dr. Georg Schweinfurth, the German explorer, in 1870 when he led an expedition into the Uele district of the northeast Congo and visited the cannibal Mangbetu tribe. He found several strange little men at King Munza's court and immediately realized that they were not negroes but members of an entirely different race: true, pure-blooded Bambuti pygmies, the same mysterious people the Egyptians had discovered more than four thousand years before.

'The-little-men-from-the-land-of-trees-and-spirits-at-the-foot-of-the-mountains-of-the-moon-who-dance-the-dance-of-the-gods' was what the Egyptians called the Bambuti whose Grand Forest lies west of the Ruwenzori range, the classical 'Mountains of the Moon'. Egyptian artists carved recognizable pygmies in the bas-reliefs of Fifth Dynasty tombs at Sakkara, dating from 2700 B.C., and during the Sixth Dynasty Pharaoh Pepi II rejoiced wildly—and worried—when Herkhuf, Prince of Elephantine, captured a live pygmy in the 'Land of Akhtin' far to the south.

'. . . When he goes down with you to the vessel,' the Pharaoh warned Herkhuf in an excited letter, 'appoint trusty people who shall be about him on each side of the vessel; take care lest he

---

[1] Among racial pygmies, there are two distinct groups without any apparent connection, the Asiatic Negritos and the African Bambuti. The Negritos, including the Andaman Islanders, the Semang from Malaya and Sumatra, the Aëta from the Philippine Islands, and the Tapiro of New Guinea, are slightly taller and often show traces of Mongoloid blood. Some of them use the blowgun, an Asiatic or South American weapon, often mistakenly attributed to the Africans. 'Bambuti', in the broad sense, includes ten thousand pygmies who inhabit the equatorial forests of Gabon and Cameroun where they are known under many local names. More properly speaking, the word should be restricted to some twenty-five thousand true, pure-blooded pygmies of the Congo's Ituri Forest. African 'pygmoids', hybrid negro-pygmy groups, include the Batwa of Kivu and Ruanda-Urundi, the Babinga of the Ubangi District, and the Batswa of Equator. The 'pygmiform' peoples are far less clear cut, Bantu or Sudanese tribes heavily infused with Bambuti characteristics because of their penchant for taking pygmy wives.

fall in the water. When he sleeps at night, appoint again trusty
people who shall sleep about him in his tent: inspect ten times a
night! My Majesty desires to see this pygmy more than the
produce of Sinai and of Punt.'

Pharaoh's letter is engraved on the façade of Herkhuf's
tomb, so the enterprising Egyptian traveller must have succeeded in foiling any attempt the pygmy may have made to
escape and brought him as a precious curiosity to the Pharaoh's
court.

Nearly two thousand years later Homer referred to the
African pygmies and described in the *Iliad* their fantastic war
with the cranes. Aristotle accepted them as an established fact,
but was wrong in describing them as troglodytes, or cave-
dwellers. Herodotus, in the second book of his History, regaled
his readers with a strange ragoût of pygmies, deserts and crocodiles.

Misunderstandings and legends multiplied until the thirteenth
century when Albertus Magnus, *Doctor Universalis* of Cologne,
sought to clear away the confusion. The pygmies, he stated, have
no art, philosophy, morals or sense of shame. They have babies
at the age of three and die in their eighth year. They stand only
one ell (27 inches) tall. '*Utrum pygmaei sint homines?*' asked the
most noted Christian scholar of his age—'Are pygmies people?'
His answer was a stern negative.

The world seems to have held to that opinion for the next
seven centuries. Only a few years ago, pygmies were still being
reviled by tourists who had spent a week or two in the Grand
Forest during a 'Cook's Tour' of Africa—and then wrote books
about it. According to those self-styled authorities, the Bambuti
were 'vicious, immoral dwarfs' less than four feet tall, who had
been driven into hiding in the Ituri Forest where they continued
to practise cannibalism and 'black magic'.

All these reports were completely wrong, but it took me some
time to determine the extent to which the Bambuti have been
misunderstood and abused.

My first little contact was a nearly classic example of what
happens when a pygmy meets a white man in the equatorial
forest, but with a slightly different ending from usual. I was
about ten miles north of Beni when five tiny brown men, ranging
in height from 4 ft. 5 in. to 4 ft. 10 in., suddenly materialized
beside the road. They carried small bows and arrows, but were
obviously hunting only one thing: tourists.

'Pygmy! Pygmy!' the little men shouted their advertising

slogan as they stood in a line at the side of the road. When I stopped they rushed towards the truck, again and again repeating the word 'Pygmy!' interposed with cries of 'Picture, one dollar!' When I tried to talk with them in Kingwana they changed their tune and begged for *matabish*, the universal word in Black Africa for a 'tip'.

'Where is your camp?' I asked. 'Can I come and meet your people?'

'*Matabish! Matabish!*' they implored, insistently thrusting out their palms.

I drew back, remembering the proud, independent Bambuti of my childhood. None of them, I felt sure, would have begged on the road. *They* were the pygmies I wanted to meet again, these tourist-hunters were not. I drove on.

I met a few similar little groups as I travelled through great stretches of pygmy territory, driving from Beni to Mambasa and Nia-Nia and eventually to Paulis where I spent three days getting to know the handsome Mangbetu tribe, descendants of King Munza's gourmet cannibals. Then I turned back to the pygmy country again, determined to find at least a few Bambuti not completely corrupted by money and shiny trinkets.

After a few more encounters with *matabish*-seekers on the road, I decided to stop at the next Bantu village, Ofay, and confer with the local chief of the Balese, a small people who were obviously on intimate terms with the pygmies. I drove into the centre of the village and a crowd of smiling children rushed to greet me. Soon the adults' curiosity got the better of them and they, too, gathered round in an excited circle.

'*Jambo! Kapita iko wapi?*' I asked politely. 'Hello! Where is your chief?'

A very cocky-looking young man stepped forward. '*Mi, iko kapita,*' he announced loudly. 'I am the chief.'

I knew he was lying. He sniffed money in my pocket and was after it. 'Are you the chief's son?' I asked tactfully.

Several Balese sniggered. A much older man stepped forward and pushed the pretender aside. 'The chief is away on safari,' he said. 'I am his brother Mulume, and I am in charge while he is gone.'

'Well, Mulume, perhaps you can help me. I want to visit a real pygmy camp, far away from the road.'

'That would be very hard for a white man to do. It's much easier to meet the ones on the road.'

'I'm looking for pygmies who don't know the word pygmy,' I explained, 'real forest Bambuti who don't go begging for money.'

'Have you no money?' Mulume's big almond-shaped eyes stared up at me suspiciously. Just over five feet tall, he looked almost like a wary pygmy himself.

'I have money, and I'll pay you well, but you'll have to earn it.'

'Real forest pygmies are very hard to find,' Mulume sighed. 'There are fewer and fewer each year. But I know of a hidden camp a few miles away. How much will you give me to take you there?'

We haggled politely for ten minutes before Mulume agreed to accept two hundred francs for his services. Strutting a little before the admiring villagers, he marched after me with a military air, climbed into my beat-up Chevy as though it were a Rolls-Royce, and grinned with pleasure as I stepped on the gas and we shot out of Ofay.

'I rode in a truck once before,' he confided, 'but they made me sit in the back. That was when they took me to the *muzungu* jail in Bunia.'

'Oh? What for?'

'I had a little fight with my cousin. He stole one of my chickens and then he bragged about it, so I cut down his bananas. He complained to the Territorial Agent in Irumu, and they put *both* of us in jail, him for the chicken and me for the bananas. But they didn't whip us with the *fimbo* and the food was pretty good.'

'Did it teach you a lesson?'

'Yes, I learned how to play cards.'

I smiled, in spite of myself. Then I realized that we must have driven at least three or four miles down the road. 'How far is it the Bambuti camp?' I asked.

'A little farther. Then we have to walk for an hour.'

This estimate proved wildly inaccurate. It was only after ten more miles in the Chevy and a three-hour walk over dark, narrow trails that we finally reached our goal: a small clearing which held five little huts thatched with *mangungu* leaves, ragged hemispheres no more than four and a half feet high with entrances less than two feet above the ground. They looked like beehives or untidy green igloos. A campfire burned under a crude pot full of skinny white roots, and a half-woven basket lay on the ground nearby. There was no one in sight.

'The pygmies saw you coming and ran away,' Mulume said glumly.

'Do you think they went far?'

'No. They're hiding in the bush, watching us.'

'Call out and explain that I just want to make friends.'

Mulume shouted at the tangled mass of vegetation in a mixture of Kilese, his own tongue, and Kimbuti, the strange staccato language of the pygmies. His tone was abrupt and commanding, but nobody bothered to answer. 'We may have to wait for a while,' he said, 'but they'll come back soon. I buy meat from them sometimes and they know me pretty well.'

We sat on the trunk of a fallen tree and waited for half an hour. Then, finally, two little men emerged from the bush and walked slowly and very cautiously towards us. One, with an antelope-skin quiver slung on his back, held a bow and arrow; the other carried a four-foot elephant spear with a sharp, shiny eighteen-inch blade. Twenty feet away, they stopped.

'Don't stand up, *Bwana*,' Mulume warned me, 'or you may scare them. They're not used to seeing a white man, especially such a big one.'

'Tell them I want to see the rest of the people.'

'Wait here and I'll try. But don't stand up!'

Mulume walked slowly towards the two pygmies with a broad, reassuring smile. There was a long exchange of alien syllables and what seemed like a minor argument. Then he returned.

'They want a stalk of bananas,' he explained. 'They say that if we bring them bananas, they will come back into camp.'

'Tell them that I will bring *two* stalks of bananas tomorrow, if they come back now.'

Mulume said a few words, and a moment later he and the older man struck their right hands together as a sign of agreement. At once pygmies started to materialize out of the forest, and I was soon surrounded by eighteen men and women, watching me warily from a distance of about ten feet.

Their eyes were big, wide and beautifully expressive. Their heads were relatively large, much rounder than those of the narrow-skulled Bantu, and set on a short, robust neck. Their noses were very broad and flat, with a deeply depressed bridge, and the mouth beneath was just as wide as the flaring nostrils, with rather narrow lips. Their hair was very peculiar: tightly coiled little tufts with almost bare skin in between, the famous 'peppercorn' formation found in another small and primitive but totally unrelated people, the Bushmen of South Africa's

Kalahari Desert, apparently a mixed Negroid-Mongoloid race believed to have come from Central or North Central Africa, and originally from Asia.

One of the older ones had a little black beard and nearly all the men, unlike the negroes, had relatively dense body hair, pepper-corn tufts covering most of the torso. The men's breasts were slightly more developed than in other races, whereas the women's breasts, although negroid in form, were relatively smaller, higher and farther apart.

The bosom, the slightly shorter stature and the absence of body hair were the women's only feminine features: their faces showed virtually no difference from the men's. Evidently this did not unduly bother their husbands, since six of the ten women had a tiny baby clinging to the left hip, and there were five older children clutching their parents' arms, hands or knees, according to their size.

Both men and women had the bulging, tight-skinned bellies which result from a diet too rich in starch; the children's abdomens were even more prominent and most of their navels protruded. The adults wore the *milumba*, a little *ficus* bark loin-cloth, and absolutely nothing else: no ornaments, no paint, and no tattooing. The children, all below the age of puberty, wore no clothing at all, except that some of the oldest ones sported funny little ropes round their waists, like the young Bakuba of Kasai. The three naked young boys showed, for their age, an unusually well-developed penis with a very long prepuce.

'Tell them to forget that I'm here,' I said to Mulume after the Bambuti and I had been inspecting each other for about five minutes. 'They can go back to their work round the camp.'

'They don't want to work any more. They'd rather watch you.'

'Try to explain that I'm here to watch *them*. I'd like to see how they cook, and weave baskets, and build those *mangungu* huts. Can't you make them understand that?'

For an hour I argued with Mulume and he argued with the pygmies, but in the end I decided to leave and come back next morning with the bananas, in the hope they would then behave more naturally.

We got back to the car just before darkness suddenly fell. In the Ituri Forest, only a few miles north of the equator, twilight is extremely short and night comes on almost instantaneously. I flicked on the headlights, Mulume cackled with delight and we drove back to Ofay. He proved a wonderful host: I spent the night in Mulume's hut, on Mulume's bed (with Mulume's daughter), and rose at six next morning, mosquito-bitten but happy. The only thing Mulume didn't provide was breakfast: like most Central African tribes, the Balese eat one meal a day, generally in the evening.

I haggled with a villager for three spindly stalks of plantain bananas and finally settled for fifty francs. Then I hired two porters to carry the sixty-pound load of fruit, and four hours later, we finally arrived back at the pygmy camp.

This time the pygmies didn't run. Instead, they gathered round us very closely, to get a good look at the bananas. This confirmed something I had suspected the day before: the Bambuti possess a peculiar body odour, quite different from that of their Bantu neighbours, and much more pronounced. The two porters left on their long walk back to Ofay, and the bananas were hauled off in silence by three determined pygmy women. The old man with the scraggly black beard directed the operation, very officiously.

'Is he the chief?' I asked Mulume.

'Bambuti don't have chiefs,' my guide explained. 'He is the elder of the camp. He is called Moyoga.'

The old man heard his name spoken, turned, and asked Mulume a question.

'Do you want to see a pygmy dance?' Mulume translated.

'They dance in the morning?'

'No. At sunset. But Moyoga will make them dance now if you want them to.'

'That's just what I don't want. Try to explain, Mulume. Ask them to behave naturally.'

'What shall I tell them to do?'

'Why don't you ask them to build us a hut? Then we can spend the night here.'

'You want to sleep in a pygmy hut?' Mulume was completely astonished. He sighed with exaggerated resignation and translated my words to the pygmies. He was obviously humiliated by the prospect of spending a night in a *mangungu* hut. The pygmies, too, were astounded by the idea. Several of them burst out laughing as they pointed first at the minuscule huts and then at me. I was two feet taller than the houses as well as the people. Moyoga, his beard waggling furiously, made a little discourse on the subject and Mulume sourly translated. 'He says you'll never get in, *Bwana*. And even if you do, you'll never get out.'

'Tell them I can fold myself up, but ask them to make the doorway a foot higher than usual.'

Moyoga nodded, and his people disappeared into the forest to fetch wood, lianas and *mangungu* leaves for my new residence. 'The women usually do all the hut-building work,' Mulume told me. 'As this hut has to be bigger, the men are helping them gather the wood. But the women will build the house by themselves, you can be sure of that.' He was right. When the Bambuti straggled back a little while later, loaded with pygmy construction supplies, the men relapsed into idleness while their wives went to work. Occasionally a man would wander over to give his advice, but he never offered to help.

Two old women started the hut-building job, moving with really surprising co-ordination and dexterity. Each took a flexible sapling eight feet long, sharpened at the heavier end. They pounded the saplings firmly into the damp, yielding earth, about nine feet apart, trampled the loose soil back into place, walked towards one another bending the saplings down, overlapped them and lashed them together with ropy lianas, forming a crude arch about five feet tall. They repeated this simple technique, making a second arch parallel to the first about two feet away, and then set up a third, at right angles, lashing it tightly where it passed over and bisected the first two elements of the frame. Smaller saplings were then driven into the earth about a foot apart all round the circumference and lashed to the main structure, except for a gap for the doorway.

Once the skeleton of the hut had been completed, two old women wove horizontal strips of liana, about twelve inches apart, through the vertical framework. Meanwhile the other women were sitting on the ground sorting out a big pile of *mangungu* leaves and notching the thick, fleshy stem of each leaf to form a hook by which it would be fastened to the liana web. The two little girls worked on a smaller pile, weaving them together with string made from *kekele*, rattan, into narrow green mats.

I could see no difference between the sixteen-inch leaves and those used by the Balega of my own territory. In fact the *mangungu*, technically called *phrynium*, is found almost everywhere in the equatorial forest. I asked Mulume what the pygmies called this extremely important plant and he answered, 'Some of the old men say "*kerenu*". That is the real Kimbuti word. But most of the pygmies say "*mangungu*" just like everyone else. It used to be much harder to talk to them, but now the Bambuti have learned a few of our words.'

'Sometimes you can guess what they're saying without knowing *any* of the words.' I pointed to the two hard-working old women, one of whom was obviously reaching boiling-point as old Moyoga, with a wealth of gesture, criticized her very competent work. 'That is Moyoga's wife,' Mulume explained. 'Her name is Dereke. She has a very bad temper, even worse than most pygmy women. I think she has evil spirits inside.'

A moment later, when Moyoga pretended to adjust a few strands of liana, the 'evil spirits' escaped, and Dereke lost her temper completely. She launched into a wild salvo of Kimbuti abuse, and when Moyoga tried to answer back she snatched a bunch of *mangungu* leaves up by their long stems and slapped him across the back with them.

I was astonished. With any other people in the Congo, a wife who dared talk back to her husband would have been soundly beaten. If a woman had actually struck her husband, with a leaf or anything else, she would probably not have lived to tell the story.

Things were certainly very different here. Moyoga retreated, took up a new observation post about thirty feet away and pulled out a little tobacco pipe from the belt of his loincloth. He lit it with an air of indifference and pitying condescension, reminding me irresistibly of the old saying, 'When a man takes a wife, he no longer dreads Hell.'

Soon my new house was ready to receive its *mangungu* thatch. Starting at the bottom, as if they were shingling a roof, Dereke and the other old woman fastened a row of inverted leaves to the liana ropes, hooking them into position with the notched stem and carefully overlapping the edges. Each successive tier was shingled into place over the row before, and when they finally reached the summit, Dereke added a final crown of leaves with the stems tied together on top.

Evidently the pygmies, like my Bwamé friends from Maniema, had studied the lesson of the pangolin's imbricated back.

Now my house was complete, a shaggy green dome about five feet high and nine feet in diameter, built in less than three hours by two tiny old women whose only equipment consisted of a small, single-edged knife. At least I thought it was complete—until Dereke asked my guide a solemn question. 'She wants to know whether to build a partition,' Mulume translated. 'What for?'

'So we can each have a room of our own.'

'Do you want a partition?'

'No, *Bwana*. You don't smell bad, and without one we'll have more room.'

'Then I don't want one either.'

I crept through the doorway on my hands and knees to inspect my new dwelling. It was dark, damp and extremely confining. I couldn't stand up at all, and was able to sit only in a few square feet in the centre. I felt like a dinosaur embryo trapped in a chicken's egg. I crept out again while the pygmies tittered with laughter, wondering how Mulume and I would manage to spend a whole night in that cramped, uncomfortable hut. I was still speculating about the problem two hours later when I tasted my first pygmy meal: turtle meat and roast bananas.

I'd brought the bananas myself, but the turtle appeared as a surprise. He was a water terrapin about ten inches long, dull green, with a few little orange stripes on his cheeks. His webbed feet paddled aimlessly in the air. He was tightly clutched in the hands of an eight-year-old boy who came running excitedly back to the camp after his solitary hunt in the forest.

The youngster received a hero's reception. The pygmies apparently loved turtle flesh, and they all heaped praises on the grinning, naked child while he told the story of his hunt. One of the women built a fire under a black clay pot and two others fetched some bananas to stick in the hot coals. They all seemed terribly hungry.

I was hungry myself, but the scene that followed took the edge off my appetite.

Moyoga produced a little ivory hammer with a dark brown patina, a tool generally used for beating out bark cloth, and pounded away on the turtle's carapace. A big crack appeared along the middle of the shell, with smaller ones on the sides. Moyoga gave it a few more taps, and then, just as he would peel a fruit, carefully picked the shell away until the turtle was naked: a flattened hemisphere of white flesh that gradually turned first pink and then a dark bloody red. Moyoga handed it to the expectant boy. While the rest of the pygmies looked on enviously, the child opened the turtle's belly with his knife and probed around with his little brown fingers until he found his reward: three soft leathery white eggs. He kept the biggest for himself, gave one to his younger brother and respectfully handed the third to Moyoga. The two boys devoured theirs almost immediately, but the old man stared at his prize for a long ecstatic moment before he bit into it. Then he stood there, rolling his eyes with delight, while a little trail of viscous yolk dripped down his beard.

Meanwhile the mutilated turtle lay on the ground, stripped of its shell, its belly laid open, its eggs ripped out and devoured. It was still alive.

A man picked it up by a forefoot and tossed it into the black pot. The naked turtle paddled desperately when it hit the boiling water. Its eyeballs congealed and its flesh started to turn grey, but five minutes later the webbed feet were still moving feebly. At last the tortured animal died.

I stared at the pygmy band as they crouched around the black pot, waiting to share the meat. They had watched the turtle's silent convulsions without any sign of emotion, other than appetite. It never occurred to them that they might have killed the animal first; yet there was no real cruelty involved, only ignorance and a profound lack of imagination. To the pygmies, or virtually any Central African tribe, an animal is merely a running, walking, flying or crawling piece of meat, mindless, emotionless, something to be hunted and eaten, unless of course it was feared as either totem or taboo. What happened to it between the hunting and the eating was of absolutely no consequence.

Mulume watched the turtle's prolonged agonies with exactly the same attitude as the pygmies, even though he had seen a little more of the civilized world. It was a feeling, or lack of feeling, totally alien to our own concept of humane behaviour—complete indifference to the suffering of animals other than ourselves.

After the turtle had boiled for an hour in the pot, a shrunken, miserable little piece of meat that looked as though it could never have been alive, Moyoga skewered the cooked flesh on a pointed stick and placed it on a *mangungu* mat. Then, with a pompous air, he started to carve.

The first piece was a little grey gobbet of meat, pink on the inside, which came from the turtle's rear. Moyoga gazed at it lovingly, put it in his mouth and chewed it with slow, deliberate pleasure. Then he asked Mulume a question. 'He wants to know which part you like best,' Mulume translated. I stared at the shrunken turtle. I hadn't eaten for thirty hours, but that made the prospect no more appetizing. 'Tell Moyoga I don't care. It's up to him.' Mulume interpreted, and the pygmy elder cut off another chunk of the turtle's behind. It was a pitifully small morsel, but I resisted the temptation to swallow it whole. I chewed it politely, in spite of its strong, unpleasant flavour, and Moyoga smiled with the satisfaction of an indulgent host. The rest of the turtle was cut up, distributed and devoured and then each of us had a couple of roast plantain bananas.

I felt hungrier than ever, but the pygmies patted their bellies, evidently quite satisfied by this strange, inadequate meal. Then they danced, grouping themselves in two circles—an inner ring of men, an outer band of women and children—which revolved slowly round the big camp-fire. As they revolved, the men blew a simple tune on their *malinga*—little flute-whistles made from *matete* or 'false bamboo' (*Pennisetum*), a savannah-loving plant which grows on the fringes of the forest. Hour after hour, the two circles continued to spin slowly and the weird *malinga* music went on and on. I watched, almost hypnotized, while the tireless Bambuti danced in the same circles that Herkhuf, the Egyptian, had seen more than four thousand years before.

Eventually, when my eyelids drooped, I crept wearily into my *mangungu* hut. Mulume followed. It was pitch-dark inside but in such a small space we had no trouble finding our mats. Mulume stretched out and was asleep in five minutes. As for me, I must have turned and twisted on the short *mangungu* mat for more than an hour, listening to the strange cries of the living forest. The crickets and frogs droned in the background while the owls and lemurs delivered their solos. Occasionally a hyrax screamed with a noise like grinding prehistoric gears, or a band of monkeys woke and squabbled high in the trees. I thought about leopards prowling through the night, but when I finally drifted off to sleep, the most menacing sounds I had heard were Mulume's snores.

By the time I crept out through my three-foot doorway next morning—like a shaggy St. Bernard leaving its kennel—the camp was full of excited preparations. It was just a little past dawn, the day promised to be clear and sunny, and the pygmies had decided to go hunting. The men sat in front of their huts, checking their equipment, sharpening iron arrow points on a large whetstone and refeathering some of the shafts. One fitted a new string to his bow. Then they whistled and three dogs came bounding up to their masters. They were skinny long-legged creatures, about the size of terriers, with long pointed ears, curly tails and short-haired, yellowish-brown coats spotted with white. They seemed good-natured and amiable, spending most of their time prowling for food at the edge of the camp. They were definitely not pets and none even had a name; they were simply *ebo*—dog—the pygmies' only domesticated animal, a tool for hunting originally obtained from the negro tribes and now one of their most valued possessions. I watched curiously as flattened wooden bells mounted on strips of hide, and looking rather like castanets, were hung round the animals' necks. The reason they were essential for tracking down game is that the pygmies' dogs were completely mute, unable to bark or even to howl, apparently members of the same stock which produced the famous 'barkless basenji'.

The men formed themselves into two separate hunting parties: three men and one dog marched off into the forest together, while four men took the other two dogs in the opposite direction. All the men and the two older boys who trailed after them sang, shouted and chattered incessantly. Long after they had disappeared into the bush, I could still hear the incredible racket.

'Why do they make so much noise?' I asked Mulume. 'Aren't they afraid they'll frighten the animals away?'

'That is the only way they can keep together while they look for the game. When they find something, they stop all the chatter. Then they make sounds like a monkey or bird to signal each other while they close in for the kill.'

When the men's cries faded away in the distance, the women got ready to leave on a hunt of their own; some were sharpening knives at the whetstone; others took up big, crudely woven carrying-baskets, with a strap that encircled their foreheads, and slung them over their backs. As usual, most of them carried a big-eyed baby on the left hip. They trudged off into the forest together, followed by the two little girls and the smallest boy, making an even noisier exit than the men. The pygmy camp was completely deserted. After several hours of poking about the little *mangungu* huts and talking to Mulume, I began to grow terribly hungry. 'Why don't we try and follow the hunters?' I suggested. 'I can still hear them shouting, so they can't be too far away.'

His answer was quick and emphatic. 'You're wearing *kapitula*, *Bwana*. If you try to go through that tangled bush in your shorts you'll tear your legs and get festering sores. Besides, no one can hunt with the pygmies. They travel through places where real men can't follow.'

'What do you mean by real men?'

'Pygmies aren't people,' Mulume said firmly, drawing himself up to his full height, about 5 ft. 1 in. 'Not like the Balese or anyone else.'

'Why not?'

'They don't know how to make beer or pots or real houses. They don't know how to plant seeds or grow bananas. They don't even believe in magic. They're just like smart little monkeys who have learned how to talk and hunt.'

'But your own people take pygmy wives,' I pointed out. 'I saw two or three in your village.'

'That's different. It's good business.'

'What do you mean, "good business"?'

'If a man wants to buy a Lese wife, he may have to give six or seven goats to her father. That costs over three thousand francs! But he can get a pygmy woman for a dog, a chicken and a spear-blade. That costs less than a hundred francs, so he has plenty of money left over to buy nice things.'

'What kind of things?'

'You know, *Bwana* . . . all the things they sell at the *magazini*. White men's clothes and bottles of beer, even a bicycle if a man really gets rich. How can we ever buy things like that if we have to spend all of our money on wives?'

'But apart from the question of money, do you like pygmy girls as well as your own women?'

'No. But they give us more babies and work much harder. Besides, a man's real wives are always happy when he buys a pygmy girl. They know that she'll do most of the work.'

'What would happen if a Lese woman married a pygmy man?'

Mulume stared at me in shocked surprise. 'That could never happen, *Bwana*. The husband must be the woman's master—how could a pygmy be a master when he isn't even a man? Besides, how could he pay her dowry?'

'Look, Mulume, I'm running out of patience. You keep saying that pygmies aren't men, just because they have no money and don't know how to plant bananas and build houses. Don't you think they could learn—if someone bothered to teach them?'

'Bambuti? Plant crops? Live in real houses?' Mulume shook his head with a condescending smile. 'That will never happen, *Bwana*. They don't want to do things like that, and no one could ever teach them. They will always be the same, just as you see them now, because . . . well, just because they are pygmies.'

I argued with Mulume for at least three hours, but nothing I said made a dent in his deep-seated racial prejudice. His own people, the Balese, were a small, insignificant tribe without any real cultural distinction, one of the least artistic and progressive peoples in Orientale province. Only a few days before, farther to the north, I had seen the Mangbetu, who, despite their canni-bal record, were a robust, handsome and very intelligent people. Their pottery and sculpture were both of a high level, and some of their monumental old houses without parallel in tropical Africa: immense, beautifully decorated structures 150 feet long by 60 feet wide, with peaked roofs 60 feet high. Now Mulume bragged of *his* people's houses, which no pygmy could ever build, and I remembered Ofay, his village, with its banal little dwell-ings. Compared to the great Mangbetu structures, Mulume's cherished houses were no better than the pygmies' *mangungu* huts.

To make the situation even more ludicrous, Mulume's people were themselves part pygmy, small in stature, and steadily growing smaller, due to their calculated policy of taking 'economical' pygmy wives. At 5 ft. 1 in., Mulume was only three inches taller than Abue, the biggest pygmy in camp, and far blacker; his physique was less sturdy and his cultural superior-ity was quite limited. Yet, as far as he was concerned, the Bambuti were 'smart little monkeys' and Mulume was a man.

It was a classic example of active racial prejudice—small people preening themselves at the expense of even smaller ones —but negroes were usually the victims and not the culprits. Of course, in the Congo it was only the least confident and success-ful of the whites among the Greeks, Portuguese and Flemings, and even a few Walloons, who made a point of demonstrating their 'superiority' over the negroes. In the United States, and in every country with a negro population, the situation was probably just about the same.

But, ironically, here in the Grand Forest where the negroes found themselves living in close contact with a more primitive race, they seized the opportunity to exercise a little prejudice of their own. As one might have expected, it was the physically small and culturally backward tribes like the Balese who tried to assert their so-called superiority over the pygmies, while the highly advanced Mangbetu showed far less racial prejudice.

We were still arguing about it when the first band of Bambuti returned from the forest, rejoicing noisily in the success of their hunt. Abue, the tall pygmy, walked in front with the game slung on his back. It was an animal the Bambuti call *mede*—the fifteen-pound forest antelope (*Cephalophus sylvicultur*)—an elegant creature with two little pointed horns, a dark brown coat and a few white spots, the same animal known to most forest peoples of the eastern Congo as *mboloko*.

I took a few steps forward to congratulate the band of returning pygmies who followed Abue and the blood-stained *mboloko*, but I stopped short when I saw what old Moyoga was carrying in his hand, a living animal impaled on the shaft of a wooden-tipped arrow. It was a potto, a strange little lemur that looked like a deformed furry baby with enormous saucer-like eyes. It was whimpering softly with pain. One look at that potto was far more disturbing than the entire scene with the turtle. 'Tell them to kill it,' I ordered Mulume.

'They won't like that, *Bwana*. Besides, the *a'bede* will die after a while.'

I took one more look at the potto and reached a decision. I made a point of never carrying a weapon of any kind—except my two hands. So I walked up to Moyoga, pulled the knife from his belt and cut the potto's throat. The old pygmy stared at me, shocked, and the others murmured in astonishment.

'I told you they wouldn't like it,' Mulume said. 'Now the *a'bede* will lose all his blood. If the blood stays in the flesh, then the food is much stronger.'

There was no point in answering.

Later the *mboloko* was butchered. The tiny antelope was laid on his back in the centre of a large banana leaf, skinned and cut into pieces. Abue, the hunter who made the kill, received one foreleg, about a pound and a half of meat. Moyoga presented the other foreleg to me, and the rest of the meat was reserved for the hunters, women and children. The intestines, a tangle of dark blood and foul-smelling excrement, were tossed into a dirty basket and carefully set aside. I did not find out the reason for this until the second hunting party returned.

They came creeping back into camp very quietly, empty-handed. None of them spoke more than a few words. Even their dogs were silent: the humiliated hunters had stuffed the animals' wooden bells with grass to silence the mocking 'clip-clop' sound of the hunt. The three little men drooped visibly as they walked past their exuberant friends and sat down at the edge of the clearing. Moyoga gestured and the youngest boy in the camp picked up the dirty basket, trotted over to the morose trio and presented them with the antelope's stinking guts. It was their share of the meat.

Now the *mboloko* was completely divided, but the cooking didn't begin until the pygmy women returned from their long trip into the forest. Singing, screaming and shouting, in spite of their obvious fatigue, the little women trudged into camp, bent almost double under their heavily loaded baskets, which they had probably carried for three or four miles, each weighing half as much as its bearer. The women set down the baskets with obvious relief, and I could see that the carrying straps had left deep marks across their foreheads. I watched them empty and carefully sort the edible cargo—roots, tubers, mushrooms, nuts, frogs, mice, snails, caterpillars, tree-slugs and honey-ants—from such non-comestibles as lianas, *ficus* bark and *mangungu* leaves.

The women built fires and all the camp's cooking utensils were pressed into service, three black pots with chipped, lop-sided rims. The antelope meat went into the two largest, along with the tiny potto, and the vegetable contents of the women's baskets pell-mell into the third. A few condiments were added to the boiling water, including salt, some large, mysterious-looking brown seeds, and an ominous quantity of *pili-pili*—little red chili peppers.

Mulume pointed at the three simmering pots. 'Look, *Bwana*,' he said. 'This proves that these little pygmies wouldn't be eating so well if it weren't for my people.'

I answered as patiently as I could. 'What do you mean?'

'Long ago, before my grandfather was born, the pygmies had no fire. They ate everything raw, just as animals do. We showed them how to build fires by rubbing two sticks and how to cook meat in water. But they never learned how to do anything else.' Mulume gestured again. 'This band of pygmies traded those pots from my brother. They got the *pili-pili* and the salt from me, and bother us all the time for bananas.'

'What did you get in exchange?'

Mulume shrugged. 'Just meat.'

'How much meat did they have to give you for one of those pots?'

'One big *mboloko*.'

'But you can sell the *mboloko* for at least a hundred francs, and the pot is only worth twenty.'

'Well, *Bwana*, we have to make money on the deal.'

That really enraged me. Here I was, in the heart of the Congo's Grand Forest, trying to catch a glimpse of an unspoiled,

primeval people, and all I heard was the word 'money'. Was
this what the white man had done to Black Africa, the Arab,
Greek and Portuguese traders with their cheap trinkets and
trade goods? I ate my *mboloko* meat without enthusiasm, in
spite of my hunger, and even swallowed a piece of the martyred potto before I realized what I was eating. I was lost in
thought, staring at the pygmies, watching their every word and
gesture, trying to see with their eyes and feel with their emotions.
They were much more than 'smart little monkeys', as Mulume
called them, or 'filthy little beggars'—a phrase I'd heard from a
British tourist in Mambasa. They were small, primitive, and
unwashed, there was no denying that, but they were *men*. Some
day, I swore to myself, I would help them to prove it.

*   *   *

I spent another night in my little *mangungu* hut, sleeping
sporadically between Mulume's snores. The next morning I had
to leave: I had only two days' leave left and a 650-mile drive
back to Shabunda. I said my good-byes to Moyoga, Dereke,
Abue and the rest of the pygmy band, and then, as I left the
clearing, turned for a long backward look. The last thing I saw
was the shaggy green hut where I'd spent the past two nights.
If I could, I would have taken it with me.

Four hours later I left Mulume at the 'civilized' village of
Ofay, and began the long drive. Everything went wrong. I had a
puncture near Beni, a blown gasket which kept me waiting
nearly a whole day in Goma, and distributor trouble thirty
miles west of Bukavu. After a year and a half in the bush, the
Chevy was just about ready for the scrap heap.

When I arrived, nearly thirty-six hours late, in Shabunda, my
A.T. was waiting for me, eager to pick a quarrel.

'Monsieur Hallet,' he demanded ominously, 'where the hell
have you been?'

'Car trouble. I just got back from around Mambasa in Orientale. I spent a few days there with the pygmies.'

'Pygmies?' He shook his head with a deprecating smile. 'What
a waste of time!'

That little remark added fuel to my personal fires. Next day I
sent in another urgent request to be transferred to any post in
the Ituri Forest where I could work with the pygmies. Five
weeks later, after a series of pitched battles with my Flemish
A.T., I received a telegram from Bukavu which I read with
surprise, disappointment and growing curiosity. My request for

a transfer had been approved, and the Government, as usual, had operated in accordance with its traditional spirit of contradiction: I'd asked for the smallest and my new work was to be with the tallest people in Africa—the Giant Watusi of Ruanda-Urundi.

6

A Hole in the Floor of Heaven

> *Umututsi umusembereza hakweru akagutera mu mbere*—'Let a Mututsi come in through the door and he'll soon take over your house.'
>
> RUANDA-URUNDI PROVERB

ACCORDING to native legend, the first civilized inhabitants of Ruanda-Urundi were three celestial beings who fell through a hole in the floor of the sky. They brought with them the secrets of working metal and cultivating the soil, and were accompanied in their unexpected descent by a cow, a bull, a ram, a ewe, a rooster and a chicken. The savage natives of the country knelt down before them and swore to become the loyal and tireless servants of the *Ybimanuka*, the wonderful 'Envoys of Heaven'.

In less poetic terms, what probably happened some time before the end of the fifteenth century was that a tribe of eccentric Hamites known as the Batutsi emigrated from the north, bringing with them their herds of long-horned cattle, and managed, successively, to mystify, hoodwink and completely dominate a tribe of Bantu agriculturists called the Bahutu.

Then the Batutsi cattle barons settled in Ruanda-Urundi and spent the next five centuries drinking beer, casting spells on each other, composing poems in honour of their cows and playing their two favourite games: politics and *igisoro*—the *lela* game which allegedly got its start in Kasai. They neither worked metal nor cultivated the soil, but lived instead in feudal splendour, supported by the work of their awe-struck Bantu servants. In fact, they performed no manual labour at all for five hundred indolent years.

98

The Batutsi were intelligent, ambitious and wonderfully proud. They were aloof but always polite, complete masters of their emotions, never permitting themselves to show either anger or familiarity. They were shrewd diplomats, who loved to give an impression of profound magnanimity but were in their hearts without scruples or mercy. Their arrogance was unsurpassed, their elegance and eloquence unparalleled. They were Central Africa's most successful 'confidence men', and probably the most skilful, experienced liars in the world. Tucked away in their remote little mountain fortress, they considered their territory to be not only the most powerful and civilized realm on earth but the absolute centre of the physical universe. They believed their own propaganda: they were the Lord's Chosen People, the descendants of the *Ybimanuka* who fell through the hole in the sky, elected to reign for ever.

These were the Batutsi, the feudal lords who dominated Central Africa's smallest, strangest land. But according to recent reports emanating from tourist agencies and film producers, Ruanda-Urundi is ruled by an entirely different tribe: the world-famous 'Watusi'.

The 'Watusi', according to Hollywood legend, are a race of 'Noble Giants' at least seven or even eight feet tall. Their impressive physical stature is accompanied by a correspondingly lofty moral code, resulting in a purity of mind, body and spirit never before seen on the 'Dark Continent'. All are of royal blood, princes descended from the ancient Egyptian Pharaohs; intrepid warriors who are unconquerable but always merciful to their fallen enemies; Central African knights who exhibit their chivalrous skills by engaging in ritual duels at a capital city which looks like King Arthur's Court, although it is situated very near 'King Solomon's Mines'.

Incredibly, the indolent, beer-drinking politicians and poets called the Batutsi, averaging 5 ft. 10 in. tall, and the energetic, incorruptible seven-foot 'Watusi' warriors are one and the same.

As usual, the 'Dark Continent' is dark only because there are so many misconceptions about its people and their remarkable history. In this case, as in so many others, the truth is more intriguing than either the native or the cinematic legend.

*   *   *

The Batutsi may have reached their new home by falling from heaven, but for mere mortals the trip was immensely more difficult. The Central Rift Valley, with its glacier-clad mountains, active volcanoes and chain of magnificent lakes, remained one of Africa's last mysteries. The subject of wild speculation and unsuccessful expeditions for thousands of years, somewhere in its embrace it held the answer to one of the most intriguing problems ever to obsess men's minds: the ultimate source of the Nile.

The ancient Egyptians, Persians and Greeks played with the question endlessly. Then, in about the year A.D. 60, Nero sent two centurions on a special expedition to find the answer; they could get no farther than the great Sudanese marshes and had to return. But a few years earlier, a Greek merchant named Diogenes seems to have come considerably closer. He travelled inland from the east coast of Africa, and after a twenty-five-day journey reached two great lakes and a range of snow-covered mountains. Diogenes told his tale to Marinus of Tyre, a Syrian geographer, whose written account intrigued the civilized world. A hundred years later Ptolemy of Alexandria expanded on the story and produced a theory that the two southern lakes were fed by melting snows from what he called *Lunae Montes*, the 'Mountains of the Moon'.

This phrase captured the imagination of all who heard it, and for more than a thousand years men talked of the wonderful 'Mountains of the Moon', the legendary 'Lake of Cataracts', the mysterious 'Lake of Crocodiles', and, of course, the ultimate source of the Nile. Then, during the fifteenth and sixteenth centuries, Portuguese explorers began to invade the east coast of Africa, and in the seventeenth century two Portuguese priests actually visited the source of the Blue Nile at Lake Tsana in Abyssinia. In 1770 James Bruce, the Scottish explorer, traced the Blue Nile to its confluence with the White, and claimed that the question was definitely settled.

But the Blue Nile, or Bahr-el-Azrak, as the Arabs call it, is shorter and far less important than Bahr-el-Abiad, the White River, whose source lies far to the south. During the next century a Belgian, Adolphe Linant, explored the White Nile to a point 132 miles south of Khartoum. In nearly two thousand years, he was the first white man to reach that spot. Egyptians, Frenchmen, Turks, Germans and Englishmen continued the march from the north; but the Central Rift Valley was finally penetrated, as one might have expected, from the east.

The Arabs, who had gradually been infiltrating westward from

their great base at Zanzibar, reached Lake Tanganyika around
1845. They called it Bahari, 'The Sea'. Munie Mohara and
'Rumaliza the Ravager' installed themselves at Ujiji on the
eastern shore of the lake, and established bases at Nyanza-Lac,
Rumonge and Usumbura to the north. The Arabs were, of
course, exploring for profit rather than knowledge; they were
interested in a new source of slaves, which they found in
Maniema, and not in the source of the Nile.

It was 1858 before the first Europeans, still searching for the
answer to the ancient question, finally arrived in the Central Rift
Valley. Sir Richard Burton and his companion John Speke
struggled westward along the trails of the Arab slavers, quarrel-
ling all the way, until they discovered, officially, both Lake
Tanganyika and Ruanda-Urundi.

Sailing north from Ujiji, Burton and Speke landed at the little
Urundi port of Nyanza-Lac on 14 April 1858, where Burton
commented sourly on the inhospitality, insolence and inebriety
of the natives. Speke, who went farther north along the fringes
of Ruanda until he discovered the Kagera River, the most
remote headstream of the Nile, and the calm expanse of Lake
Victoria, commented significantly on the 'huge pots of *pombe*'—
beer!—that he saw along the way, and on the 'thousands and
thousands of cows'.

Thirteen years after Burton and Speke reached Nyanza-Lac,
an even more historic event occurred forty miles farther south;
Stanley 'found' Livingstone where the heroic doctor had finally
come to a halt in Ujiji after his own unsuccessful search for the
source of the Nile. After their classic dialogue had been spoken,
'*Boula Matari*', the 'rock-breaker', and '*Baba Daoud*', 'Papa
David', journeyed together to the northern tip of the lake, where
they discovered the outlet of the Ruzizi River and made a brief
foray into Urundi. Unfortunately, they had no opportunity to
comment on either the people, the cows or the beer, for they
left hurriedly under a rain of arrows and stones. Stanley cocked
his gun and threatened to fire, but the doctor persuaded him not
to return the Urundi salutation.

David Livingstone died in 1873, and the first caravan of
French 'White Fathers' arrived at his old Ujiji headquarters six
years later, eager to continue the dedicated missionary's work.
Fathers Deniaud and Augier, accompanied by the Belgian
Sergeant d'Hoop, went north to Urundi and founded a mission
at Rumonge. All three were massacred in May 1881 when Munie
Mohara's Arab slavers incited the natives to murder; four other

missionary attempts were made in the next few years. All failed, with the connivance of the Arabs.

Then the Germans arrived and became the first white men to strike out beyond Lake Tanganyika and penetrate the mountainous interior. Dr. Oskar Baumann traversed Urundi in 1892; two years later Count Adolph von Goetzen succeeded in crossing Ruanda and in discovering another great body of water: Lake Kivu. More of their countrymen followed, and Ruanda-Urundi was absorbed into the former German East Africa, which was divided at the end of the first World War into two very unequal parts: Tanganyika, with an area of over 300,000 square miles, was awarded to Great Britain; Ruanda-Urundi, more than fifteen times smaller, but with a population more than half as great, became a Belgian mandate.

What did the Belgians find in Ruanda-Urundi? Problem piled on problem, a patchwork of enigmas. Here were 22,000 square miles of *terra incognita*, a labyrinth of jagged peaks and gullied hills, an African Tibet rimmed with lakes of ethereal beauty, threatened by active volcanoes, a country with barren, eroded soil, an erratic climate and unnavigable rivers, ravaged by disease and periodic famines, and yet, paradoxically, with the densest population south of the Sahara.

But the people they found were the greatest paradox, enigma and problem. There were three different tribes in Ruanda-Urundi, each with marked physical and cultural distinctions: Batutsi, Bahutu and pygmoid Batwa. The three were united in a strange feudal system in which the Batutsi functioned as lords, the Bahutu did all the work, and the Batwa were pariahs. From a political point of view, however, the situation was different. There were two warring kingdoms: Ruanda, to the north, with a three-ply population of Batutsi, Bahutu and Batwa welded into one people, the Banyarwanda, who spoke one language, Kinyarwanda; and Urundi, to the south, with its composite population, the Barundi, and its Bantu language, Kirundi. Each country was ruled by a Mwami, a Divine King, who controlled life and death from a royal court infested with opportunistic lackeys and clever magicians.

The court was the centre of superstition and sorcery, but all the people in Ruanda-Urundi were obsessed with magic. They spoke of evil spirits, jealous and malign, when great plagues of smallpox and sleeping sickness swept over them or epidemics of anthrax and rinderpest killed the precious cattle. They opened the entrails of rams, bulls or roosters, and sought favourable omens, when drought and famine reduced them to living skeletons covered with phagodenic ulcers. With amulets, talismans and potions they tried to wrench a living from a soil denuded of trees, gullied by erosion, and exhausted by overgrazing, deliberate brush fires and irrational cultivation. Then, when their magic failed, they tortured and murdered each other by the most agonizing means: impalement on wooden stakes, drowning, dismemberment, blinding, scalping, bastinado, crucifixion, and amputation of hands, feet and genital organs.

These were the land and the people that Belgium found at the close of the first World War. She had undertaken, without any possibility of profit, to heal, feed, educate and guide them towards social and political autonomy. Now, only thirty years later, I was about to find out how well she had succeeded.

*   *   *

Ruyigi, my new post in eastern Urundi, consisted of hundreds of green and brown hills scored with parallel horizontal lines where rows of ditches had been dug and hay planted beside them. That was the Colonial Government's simple but very effective weapon in the grand-scale battle against soil erosion. Eucalyptus, silk oak, black wattle and cypress grew in irregular clumps on the rocky slopes and summits of the hills. Almost every tree had been deliberately planted as a part of the reafforestation programme. Between the stands of timber, the hills were chequered with cultivated fields and garnished with banana groves. Scattered among the vegetation, depending on the size of the hill, were anywhere from five to fifty huts, looking like enormous beehives with conical grass roofs.

Each hill resembled the next, from one end of the territory to the other; it was hard to tell where the adjoining territories began and Ruyigi left off. In fact, virtually all of Ruanda-Urundi consisted of similar hills, no matter how far you travelled. It was an up-and-down world, composed of thickly settled, intensively cultivated hills and almost uninhabited valleys where cattle pastures alternated with sweet-potato and manioc fields. There were no villages. Each native family lived in a conical hillside hut, surrounded by hedged cattle kraals and courtyards which they called *rugo*; these in turn were surrounded by banana groves, small coffee plantations and a few patches of tobacco, taro and gourds. The whole establishment, hut, *rugo* and fields, was known as an *itongo*.

Roughly eleven out of every twelve *itongo* were inhabited by the Bahutu, sturdy, hard-working men in soiled, wildly patched khaki shorts or ragged *pagnes* who spent their days planting, hoeing or herding cattle. The twelfth *itongo* harboured the Batutsi, a very different breed; tall, elegant men in immaculate white or brightly coloured togas who spent most of their time either puffing on long clay pipes or sipping beer through a straw. A third people, the pygmoid Batwa, lived on the hills in other regions of Ruanda-Urundi, but there were virtually no Batwa here in Ruyigi; only the Tutsi lords and their Hutu vassals.

Their social status and way of life were, of course, utterly different. Nevertheless, Batutsi and Bahutu were healthy, well fed and apparently relatively civilized. Coming, as I did, from the vast, sparsely populated forests and savannahs of the Congo, where more than 600 different tribes lived in widely scattered villages, I was startled by the terraced hills of Ruanda-Urundi, tenanted by only three kinds of people. It seemed more like Switzerland than Central Africa.

That was a charming theory, but after a few months in Ruyigi I reached a very different conclusion: Ruanda-Urundi might have looked like a black version of Switzerland, but its people weren't yet ready to make cuckoo-clocks.

In spite of the general well-being, superstition and sorcery still infested the hills of Urundi. Every *itongo* had, in addition to its Tutsi or Hutu owners, a full crew of *bazimu*, invisible spirits and ghosts, who had to be feared, honoured and at all costs propitiated so that human life might survive. To deal with those supernatural beings, the people resorted to the services of the *bafumu*, the glib, ingenious, money-grubbing magicians.

During those first months in Ruyigi, as I walked from one hill to the next, I often rubbed shoulders with the agricultural magicians. I was busy checking the quality, extent and growth cycle of the crops, inspecting the natives' food reserves, and instructing each family in the difficult art of cultivating coffee *arabica*: planting, mulching, pruning, treatment of all its endless diseases, harvesting, drying, depulping and grading the beans. In addition, I supervised the anti-erosion campaign and showed the natives where and how to plant timber trees for the best results. While I was about it, I kept my eye on the local sanitation, dropping helpful hints on how to make septic holes and suggesting that cow-dung was more useful in the coffee fields than in the *rugo*.

The people of Ruyigi weren't impressed: the magicians' job

seemed to them far more important than mine. Not only did the *bafumu* prevent the banana trees from being struck by stray bolts of lightning, but they dealt confidently with all the evil omens lurking in fields, bushes and groves.

Thus, when the first bunch of bananas ripened in a new grove, the anxious native who owned the *itongo* called an *umufumu* to the scene. The magician gave him a shot of evil-tasting stuff known as *isubyo*—the exorcizing liquid which he dispensed like patent medicine; then they cut down the unfortunate tree and heaved it over a precipice. Afterwards, they usually had a little beer-party in the newly purified grove.

The first time I saw that performance, I was outraged. It was a perfectly healthy tree which had taken eighteen months to reach bearing age. When I tried to intervene, I was confronted with an angry magician and an even angrier client. If the ceremony were not allowed to proceed, they explained, the man would certainly die. After nearly an hour's argument I realized I was wasting my time. The ceremony proceeded. I stood by quietly and watched as the *umufumu* went about the peculiar job of disenchanting bananas by a wide variety of picturesque methods.

Immediate action was necessary when a tree presented its cluster of fruit from the side rather than the top. Usually, the magician told his client to cut the accursed fruit, anoint it with magic herbs and bury it in the ground at a spot where two paths crossed. This would allow the bananas to vent their evil on an innocent passer-by, and the owner of the grove would avoid the curse. If a bunch of bananas grew too heavy for its stalk and fell to the ground, a rare event, it was even more serious. Obviously, the owner's other fruit—his children—were being threatened with sudden death. To prevent this, the man was forbidden to have sexual relations with his wife until he had called in a magician and had a stiff jolt of exorcizing liquid.

Sometimes an *umufumu* burned magic herbs to stimulate the growth of the trees, or buried the skulls of *inguge*—baboons— in the soil of the grove. Once I watched an old Hutu magician burn about three pounds of *agahuza*, little herring-like fish that came all the way from Lake Tanganyika where the Congolese called them *ndagala*. The theory behind this smelly operation was that the potent fumes of the burning fish would penetrate into the banana trees, which would then have as many babies as the herring.

From the natives' point of view, bananas definitely seemed to be the most delicate and dangerous product of the soil. But important rituals also were connected with the cultivation of beans, corn, manioc, peanuts, gourds, peas, and especially sorghum. I took notes on all of those ceremonies during the day and studied the difficult Kirundi language at night (with the aid of several charming teachers). In between, I watched and gradually began to understand the strange and fascinating social life of Ruyigi, the endless struggle for wealth, power and status.

In Ruanda-Urundi, those three words could be translated by only one: *inka*—the cow, an animal not here considered sacred but the prime element of the country's social and economic life. To become rich, a Muhutu had to acquire at least two or three cows. Power and prestige followed. Would-be servants flocked to his *rugo*, eager to work without pay, providing only that they might some day be given a calf. Then the farmer laid down his hoe, decked himself out in a spotless toga, and became Central Africa's version of the English country gentleman. He now considered himself a 'Mututsi', and eventually was accepted as such by the ruling caste. If he was rich enough, he even acquired a pure-blooded Tutsi wife. Conversely, a Mututsi who fumbled and somehow managed to lose all his own cows descended the social ladder. If he had wealthy relatives, they usually helped him, simply because they wanted to maintain their own prestige. If not, he lived on his wife's labour or sponged off the Bahutu. He still refrained from manual work, but eventually he forfeited all of his authority and privileges and became no better than a Muhutu himself.

This really astonished me, for I had believed the Batutsi to be a tribe in the ordinary sense of the word, characterized by a culture of their own, and, moreover, with a very distinctive physique. Undoubtedly that had been the case in the past, but social changes and interbreeding were slowly altering the picture. Now, in addition to the tall, skinny Hamites, the 'True Batutsi', I began to discover short, stocky Batutsi with thoroughly Bantu features, and, of course, at least two or three cows.

There was an old Kirundi proverb which summed up the situation very concisely: *Ntihakundana abangana, hakundana abanganya*—Equals don't fraternize with each other, but only with those who are equally rich. Obviously, in Urundi, as in so many other parts of the world, there were only two really significant tribes: the rich and the poor.

In that sense, the system wasn't entirely feudal. The four million Bahutu of Ruanda-Urundi had an incentive to work: the prospect, however hazy or remote, of some day becoming Tutsi lords and working no longer. The four hundred thousand 'Batutsi' had an even stronger incentive to scheme. Roughly thirty thousand were pure-blooded, true Batutsi; the rest were either of mixed blood or were merely rich Bahutu who 'passed' for Batutsi. They were a social body whose numbers and status were subject to drastic change depending on the extent of their fortunes. So each man engaged in constant manœuvres to increase his own share of the country's million cattle; he could not afford to rest on his laurels in a society where cut-throat competition was the rule.

Thus, a shrewd Mututsi chose his wife for her good connections, and pressed his relatives, friends and even his Hutu vassals for gifts. He made complicated, clever deals concerning his cattle and, above all, advanced his fortunes by currying favour with sub-chiefs, chiefs, nobles and even the King, fawning on the missionaries and cultivating opportune friendships with government officials.

In the past, to further his plots, the ambitious Mututsi employed magicians to cast spells on his enemies, or hired assassins to stab them, snipe at them with arrows, or poison their beer. *Nta umenya akabindi kazamwica* was another favourite Tutsi proverb—Nobody knows which pot of beer will kill him. Nowadays such methods were rarely employed, for fear of the Belgian Government, but unexplained accidents continued.

On a higher level than these individual manœuvres were the political intrigues of the rich and powerful families. The most notorious of these was the Bezi-Batare feud which had threatened to pull the country apart for a century: the struggle for possession of Urundi's symbol of state, the Karyenda—the wonderful Royal Drum. Never beaten, but indispensable for the conduct of the monarchy's highest affairs, the Karyenda had six smaller drums supporting its authority, and, remarkably, a devoted human wife, the Mukakaryenda, a vestal virgin wedded to the Royal Drum, who spent her spare time looking after Semasaka, one of the two Royal Bulls.[1]

[1] The Karinga or Royal Drum of Ruanda was considered even more sacred. A perpetual flame burned in its honour, and the people saluted it just as they greeted the King, with three hand-claps. The drum ranked equally with Rusanga, the Royal Bull, and both were the King's equal in status. As in Urundi, the Royal Drum of Ruanda had a group of smaller colleagues, *ingabe*, or 'little royal drums'. None had a wife, but their guardians, the Biru, were the most powerful officials of the former royal

The Bezi family, led by Mwambutsa IV, the present Mwami or King of Urundi, was currently in possession of the Royal Drum. The Batare, descended from a collateral line, schemed continually to oust Mwambutsa, install their own Mwami and seize control of the Drum. The Belgian Government supported Mwambutsa and tried to keep the 'pretenders' quiet. It was the only way to maintain law and order, but the Batare were not easily discouraged. They had openly rebelled twice during the past thirty years, and their leaders were still busily hatching intrigues and plots.

'Stay out of native politics!' my new A.T. had warned me on my first day in Ruyigi. 'If you get involved in the Bezi-Batare feud you're in for trouble.'

His advice was sound, and was not difficult to follow. To my disappointment, the two local chiefs I dealt with made no attempt to involve me in their intrigues, although Joseph Ndikumwami, the newly appointed Chief of Buhumuza, belonged to the Bezi family, and Johanni Kashirahamwe, the Chief of Buyogoma, was a prominent member of the Batare. They were rivals, of course, but they always met with typically suave Tutsi smiles and elegant phrases.

As time passed, I found myself being drawn closer and closer to Johanni, but not for political reasons. He was much older than his Bezi colleague, and knew far more about the customs and traditions of Urundi. Moreover, since he spoke fluent Kiswahili —rare for a native in this part of the country—I could really enjoy our meetings.

From Johanni I learned of the old royal court, the Ibwami, where the colourful kings of the past had lived in despotic splendour. It was a huge, complex establishment containing hundreds of huts, but had no permanent location. Each new Mwami who took possession of the Royal Drum had to consult the magicians to determine the most propitious site for his court. The old Ibwami had to be abandoned when the reigning monarch died; otherwise, his indignant ghost would come back to haunt his successor.

Here in the Ibwami the Divine King of Urundi lived an

court. The drums, never permitted to touch the soil, sat on stools or were carried on wickerwork hammocks. Several times a year, they were sprinkled with the fresh bull's blood, as a result of which the drums and their baskets thickly encrusted with blackened magic blood. These baskets contained the *ibikondo*—the severed, smoked testicles of enemy kings killed in pre-colonial wars.

elaborate ritual existence surrounded by a fantastic rabble of more than two thousand scheming souls: chiefs and sub-chiefs, magicians, medicine men, dancers, minstrels, musicians, wives, concubines and depraved young boys.[1] Even the pygmoid Batwa, generally barred from respectable society, had their place at the court, as hangmen, assassins and jesters.

Like the Divine King of the Bakuba, whom I had met in Kasai, the person of the Mwami was surrounded by an intricate network of religious taboos. He was forbidden to eat, drink, smoke or spit in public, or to cross the threshold of the royal hut without submitting to the magicians' ritual purifications. His very name was sacred and every one of his actions was supposed to have a direct effect on his kingdom. If the Mwami was caught in a sudden shower of rain, the country would suffer from drought. If he stumbled, the country would undoubtedly blunder and lose some of its land. The only remedy for the disaster was for the Mwami to turn back and retrace his steps; the curse would then be lifted.

The Mwami had previously enjoyed many imposing titles: Lord of the Cows and the Drums, Master of Earth and Heaven, Prince of the Streams and Pastures, Dispenser of Justice, Eminent Proprietor, Supreme Autocrat and Hierarchic Monarch. He was the Lord, Ever Just, Good and Magnificent, the image of God his Father.

That was past history, Johanni repeated, with a sigh. The present Mwami had no divine virtues, he was only a man. Worse still, he was one of the infamous Bezi, a false king who had stolen the Royal Drum.

A few weeks later, I was able to see just how divine or infamous the King of Urundi was. The chain of events began when my aged Chevy yet again broke down. I tinkered with it until it would run again, but it was obviously a lost cause, and I set out on a quick trip to Usumbura to look for a replacement. The engine knocked, the radiator bubbled and the suspension squeaked for 108 worried miles until I reached 'Usa', the capital city of Ruanda-Urundi at the northeast tip of Lake Tanganyika, where I made an extensive tour of the local garages, loudly advertising the virtues of my decrepit truck. Of course, no one believed me, but I managed to make a fairly decent deal for a

---

[1] Sodomy was an established institution at the old royal courts of Ruanda and Urundi. The chief victims seem to have been the Ntore dancers, a *corps de ballet* composed of young men and boys, all sons of nobles or chiefs.

brand-new Chevrolet pickup. The dark blue body was sleek, the upholstery pristine, and the engine purred like a big contented cat. I might have purred myself if it hadn't cost so much.

I spent two days in Usa, taking a good look at native life in Ruanda-Urundi's largest town. It was very different from my pastoral Ruyigi. Here the people lived in mud or brick houses, clustered together in the native quarter at the northern end of the town. This they called the 'Belge', a term which struck me as ironic, though I had often heard it used in the Congo. Apparently, the people chose the name for their part of the town because it represented their concept of European living. To judge from what I saw, their idea of the new life consisted mainly of drinking in bars instead of drinking at home.

There were scores of little native cafés, shabby huts with shakily lettered signs painted on the dry mud walls: *Chez François*, *Au Clair de la Lune* and *Café du Crépuscule* were only a few. All were equipped with hand-wound gramophones that squealed out rhumbas and sambas. The men danced with each other, not for homosexual reasons, but because their women were busy working at home. All the bars were terribly crowded, but the Government's social and recreational centres, created for the natives' benefit, were virtually deserted. Here there were only a few Swahili, sombre-looking men wearing the red fez and long white robes. (I suppose they were sombre because the Koran forbade them to drink.)

A final ironic note was an admirable immense swimming-pool donated by one of the European firms of Usumbura for the natives' exclusive use. It was more than twice as large as the Europeans' swimming-pool, which was always packed, and, like the social centres, it was almost deserted. The well-meaning altruists had ignored the obvious fact that the natives had little interest in swimming and even less in sunbathing.

Returning from Usumbura, I stopped first in Kitega to pay my respects to the Resident, then, since Johanni had whetted my curiosity, I made a short detour to visit the King of Urundi.

The Mwami's 'palace', just a couple of miles from Kitega, turned out to be a comfortable European dwelling, a square brick house tucked away among the trees and shrubs of a large park and almost hidden in purple bougainvillaea. There were no guards at the door, I simply walked in and wandered through the *baraza*, where I admired a fan-shaped display of traditional Urundi spears. Within a few minutes a white-robed 'boy' appeared and ushered me into the drawing-room, a large chamber filled to the brim with gifts and souvenirs the Mwami had received from visiting European dignitaries or acquired on his several trips to Belgium.

The whole atmosphere was surprising: there was wonderful crystal from Val-St-Lambert, oil paintings of calm European landscapes, and thick, ornately patterned carpets. Every surface was covered with intricate Bruges or Brussels lace and crowded with ormolu *objets d'art*. I remembered a portrait which my father had painted many years before of the youthful King dressed in leopard skins, monkey fur and intricate Tutsi bead-work. Now that same man, Mwambutsa IV-Bangiricenge, fif-teenth Mwami of Urundi, was entering the room; a stocky, dignified figure about 5 ft. 10 in. tall, dressed in a well-cut business suit with a red and black striped tie.

'*Bienvenue! Asseyez-vous, s'il vous plaît,*' he said smoothly, with a vile accent and a warm, wonderful smile.

'*Bonjour*, Mwambutsa. *Je me présente:* Jean-Pierre Hallet,' I said, as we shook hands. Then I lowered myself cautiously into a delicate Regency chair while I took a good look at the current Lord of the Cows and the Drums.

The Mwami was, of course, regarded as a Mututsi, but to judge from his physical characteristics there was obviously a strong Hutu element in his ancestry. His lips were rather thick and his nose lacked the high Tutsi arch. He was virtually bald and his face was round, with a smooth, almost feminine fore-head. He looked much less like a king than my Batare friend Johanni Kashirahamwe, but his manner was cordial and extremely self-assured.

'Are you related to André Hallet?' the Mwami asked me.

'I am his son.'

'He is a great artist, a strange character but a very good man. If you are his son, I must welcome you once again, *Bwana* Hallet.'

That word really surprised me. It seemed very strange to be called *Bwana* by a Divine King whose ancestors had fallen from Heaven. This was, however, the Mwami's usual style when speaking to a Belgian official; it was probably his way of expressing respect to a government which on several occasions had saved not only his Royal Drum but his life. We talked for an hour or so, mostly about Ruyigi. Then, by way of an experi-ment, I remarked casually, 'I've had a great deal of help from Johanni Kashirahamwe. Do you know him?'

Mwambutsa favoured me with an easy smile. 'Kashirahamwe?

Let me see. Oh, you must mean that Mutare chief from Buyo-goma. I understand he's a pretty good fellow.'

This was a typical Tutsi reaction: as the reigning head of the Bezi, Mwambutsa probably would have been delighted to cut out Johanni's liver—but would never have admitted it. We talked a little longer and, as I was leaving, the Mwami announced his intention to visit me in Ruyigi. Had I then known what a lively companion the King of Urundi could be, when surrounded by beer, women and song, I would have been even more appreciative. Mwambutsa and I were later to have many wonderful rambles together throughout pastoral Urundi, but all we said now was a formal '*Kwa heri!*'—'Go with happiness!' the Kiswahili farewell.

Back in Ruyigi that evening, I picked up a few bottles of beer and drove to the lonely little brick house where Johanni Kashi-rahamwe maintained his social prestige as a chief. I gave him my bottles of white man's beer, and he presented me with the specialty of his household, a big pot of *ubuki*, delicious native beer brewed from honey. When we had settled down, each with his favourite drink, I dropped my second conversational bomb-shell of the day.

'I met the Mwami today,' I said innocently. 'He was extremely pleasant.'

Johanni stared at me intently. '*Uruciye munsi ntamenya ikiru-limo,*' he remarked. 'The walls of the house don't tell you what's going on inside.'

'That's a very interesting proverb. Don't you think the King was sincere?'

'It is only a proverb, *Bwana* Hallet. It means whatever you wish.'

After that, Johanni seemed a little remote. Obviously, he hadn't appreciated my friendly appraisal of the Mwami. But as he drank my beer, he grew more and more amiable. We talked for a while about non-controversial matters, local super-stitions which Johanni, a baptized Christian, officially censured but privately practised. Then we veered to the subject of inter-tribal relations. Rather to my annoyance, Johanni made the usual arrogant Tutsi remarks about the Bahutu.

'How can you possibly justify feelings like that?' I said hotly. 'What makes you think you're any better than they?'

'It is well known that my people are divine,' Johanni answered calmly. 'Anyone who knows the history of our race can tell you the story.'

'I've heard talk about that before. But you're a Christian. Do you really believe it?'

He glared at me. He was half-tipsy by now and beginning to show it. 'The first Mututsi came from the sky!' he said emphatically. 'His father was Imana—God himself—and his mother was named Gasani. His birth was a miracle! Do you want to know how it happened?'

I nodded quietly.

'Life in the sky was very beautiful,' Johanni said, a far-away look in his eyes. 'There was no hunger, disease or death. But even so, Gasani wasn't happy, for she was barren. She begged Imana to help her. God listened to that weeping woman and was moved by her tears.

'So he took a piece of clay, wetted it with spittle from his own tongue, and shaped it into the form of a child. "You must hide it in a pot of milk," Imana told the woman. "If you keep the pot filled with fresh milk for nine months, the child will come to life. But you mustn't tell anyone how I made this child for you! Do you promise?"

'Gasani promised, nine months passed, and then, just as Imana had told her, the clay child awakened and started to cry. She gave him the name Sabizeze. Then Imana made a brother and sister for Sabizeze so that the little boy wouldn't be lonely.

'Now Gasani, the mother of God's children, had a sister who was just as barren as she was. When that woman saw Gasani's beautiful children, she gave her sister no peace, trying to find her secret. Then one day she tricked her sister into drinking too much beer, and Gasani told her the story. She whispered very quietly, but you cannot fool Imana! He knew at once, the moment the words were spoken. Outraged, he searched throughout Heaven for the children of Gasani. He found them at last, returning from the hunt. Then Imana made a great hole in the floor of Heaven, and the poor children fell through that hole on to the barren earth.

'It was a terrible world! After ten days they were so sick with hunger and cold that they begged Imana to forgive them. They thought they were dying. So God sent a streak of lightning from the clouds to make a fire in the grass. Then, next day, seeds and plants fell through the hole in the sky: beans, peas, corn, sorghum and bananas. And on the third day the hole opened again and tools rained down upon the earth. "Imana has helped us!" the children cried. Then they picked up the tools and started to work.'

'Work with tools?' I interrupted. 'How could they do that? Weren't they really Batutsi?'

'That is how the story goes. I don't understand it myself.'

'Oh. Well, what happened next?'

'Batwa and Bahutu were already on the earth,' Johanni continued. 'They lived like savages in poverty and ignorance. But the Ibimanuka, those who fell from Heaven, were kindly and generous. They shared their heritage and, in gratitude, the savages became their servants.

'Imana looked down upon his children and he was pleased with them. So he sent a Mutabazi, a beautiful angel, to pay them a visit. When the children saw the angel fly down on wings of thunder, they were terrified. "Do not fear me!' the Angel of God told them. "Imana has sent me to help you. Ask what you wish."

'The children asked for a cow, a bull, a ram, a ewe, a rooster and a chicken. Imana smiled, and the animals fell from the clouds! While they were admiring those beautiful animals, the Angel told the children that God would permit them to mate with each other, even though they came from the same womb. Then the children cried out with joy and began to people the earth.

'Mutabazi, the Angel of God, stayed on the earth for many years to help people with their troubles. But then, one day, evil men seized the Angel and nailed him to a tree with iron spikes! Imana pulled out the spikes and healed the Angel's wounds. Then he sent a terrible storm from the sky which blew the poor Angel back to Heaven.

'That was a long time ago . . . but the Angel comes back again and again. He sends his spirit into the body of each new Mwame so that the Mwame himself is the Angel of God.'

'Where did the Batwa and Bahutu come from?' I asked softly. 'You said they were already in the forest when the children fell from the sky.'

'Imana made them too, but he was tired that day. His hand slipped as he fashioned their bodies. They were ugly and stupid, and God was tempted to destroy them. But he decided to save them: to help us and to be our servants.'

I certainly didn't like that explanation. But I didn't try to argue with the confident Mututsi. There was too much I wanted to learn. 'If Imana is good,' I asked him, 'and if Imana made all men, then why is there evil in the world?'

'The *bazimu*,' Johanni whispered, with half-closed eyes, 'the dead, the ghosts of the departed! They move from their world to ours whenever it pleases them. Sometimes they take vengeance on those who forget them. And there are others in the world of spirits who spread evil wherever they pass, but these are not the ghosts of our fathers! They are demons, strange shapes made from pieces of many different animals. Even the magicians cannot appease them.'

Johanni shuddered, and suddenly sat up very straight in his chair. 'That is what most of my people have always believed,' he said gravely, 'but today some of the *évolués* say it is only a legend.'

'It sounds almost as if it came from the Christian Bible. . . . Johanni, are you sure that the missionaries' teachings haven't been mixed into your people's stories?'

'Oh, no,' he answered very quickly. 'That is a very old Tutsi legend. It hasn't changed in a hundred years. The missionaries don't like it. They say we should give up our own legends and believe in theirs, but nobody really wants to, their stories don't even mention the Batutsi!'

'You're a Christian though, aren't you?'

'Yes, but I'm still a Mututsi.'

I often thought about that comment afterwards. As I learned more and more of their language and customs, I found myself speculating endlessly about the strange creation myth Johanni had told me and the real origin of the Batutsi.

According to most authorities, the Batutsi were an ethnological mystery. Were they negroes as some scholars claimed, with a heavy dash of Hamitic blood? Or were they really Hamites with a long history of Bantu intermarriage? This question has never been resolved, but the fact remains that the Bantu-speaking Batutsi are obviously linked with the Hamites, a very complex division of the white racial stock.

Scattered over all of North Africa these pastoral Hamites include the Somali, the Galla, the Nubians, the gypsy-like Peuls, and the Falasha, the famous 'Black Jews' of Abyssinia. The typical Hamite is lean, sinewy, light brown, with a Grecian or even Roman nose, thin lips and a straight jaw. He speaks a terribly complicated language related to Coptic and, more distantly, to the Semitic tongues, usually scorns agricultural labour and shows an exaggerated preoccupation with everything that pertains to the cow.

About ten centuries ago the tall, handsome Hamites started to wander down from the north in vast migrations that left traces of their blood and pastoral culture even in South Africa among the Xosa and the Zulu. During the progress of those successive waves, the warrior Masai were washed up on the shore of British East Africa, the Biblical-looking Bahima drifted through the countries surrounding the great lakes, and as a final eddy, the much-disputed ancestors of the Batutsi wound up in Ruanda-Urundi.

That was a reasonably sound theory, but to say that the Batutsi were Hamites was to evade the real issue. Almost no ethnological term was quite so confused or ambiguous. Moreover, that convenient word obscured a fascinating question: the Batutsi's remarkable cultural resemblances to the Jews.

This idea may seem startling, but the evidence weighs heavily in its favour and many eminent scholars have supported it, including Baumann and Westermann, A. Moeller, Monseigneur Gorju and R. Bourgeois, the former Resident of Ruanda, who wrote a definitive three-volume study of its people. The Batutsi, who have often been described as displaced Egyptians, show very little in their physique, customs or traditions to suggest any more than a superficial resemblance to the ancient people of Egypt; they seem, instead, to be the descendants of pre-Mosaic Hebrews who have intermingled with negroes and even adopted their language, but who still retain many of the physical characteristics of the white racial stock and the cultural traits of the Jews. According to some theorists, their remote ancestors were the Hyksos shepherds, the 'pastoral kings' who invaded the Nile Delta in 1800 B.C.; according to others, they came from Arabia, Persia or the regions near the Caspian Sea.

That is theory, but what I saw in Ruyigi and the rest of Ruanda-Urundi is fact. Here was a people whose religion forbade them to eat either pork or the flesh of goats; they were not permitted to mix meat and milk, and their slaughtered cattle had to be bled, kosher-fashion, before the meat could be eaten. They made no graven images, no representations of any person, animal or thing; instead, they restricted themselves to pure geometric designs. They rendered homage to serpents, like the children of Moses (Numbers xxi, 8; 2 Kings xviii, 4), venerated the moon like the Israelites of old (Numbers xxviii, 11), and had incredible horror of manual work, especially anything that had to do with the soil—a sentiment often expressed in the Old Testament (Genesis iii, 23, iv, 3–5; Exodus i, 14).

When I read of those strange customs and saw them in action, I began to feel sure of the Batutsi's Hebrew connections. The fact that they spoke a Bantu language was easily explained: like so many other conquering peoples, they had adopted the speech of the conquered, intermarried to a certain extent and acquired some of the physical and cultural characteristics they professed to despise. The absence of circumcision, a practice shared by Egyptians and Semites alike, was not of major importance. The ancestors of the Batutsi had apparently parted company with their fellows some time before God and Abraham sealed their bloody covenant (Genesis xvii, 9–12), and much later, when the circumcised Arabs and Swahili spread the ritual among most of the Central African tribes, the isolated, self-assured Batutsi rejected it.

After hundreds of years in Ruanda-Urundi, the old customs still remained, permeating all of Tutsi life with a strange, utterly non-Bantu flavour. One which baffled me for a long time was the practice of placing an earthenware pot on the summit of a newly completed hut. No one could tell me why it was done; it was merely an 'old Tutsi custom'. I worried about those pots for a long time until I read Bourgeois' monumental work and discovered that Ethiopia's 'Black Jews' usually place an earthenware pot on the summit of their synagogues.

That did it. Having become completely intrigued with the question of Hamites and Semites, I decided to see them for myself. I was eligible for six months' leave, for it was September 1951, and I had spent three years in government service. So, with only a vague notion of where I was going when I drove away from Ruyigi, I set out on a haphazard safari through Kenya, Ethiopia, the Sudan and Egypt.

Eventually I wandered on to Kenya's vast Masai reservation, and it was there that I found and faced the first significant challenge of my twenty-four-year-old life.

7

I Spear the Lion!

Nanu o-le-papa; ten aä ten apok, enne-weji—'I am the son of my father; whether I die or conquer, it will be in this place.'

MASAI WARRIOR'S OATH

THE first Masai warrior I saw was a vision of classic dignity and grace, daubed from head to foot with a mixture of red ochre and sheep fat. Everything about him was red: his face, with its aquiline nose and narrow lips; his hair, braided into long skinny pigtails that hung down on his shoulders; his torso, his limbs, even his sole garment, a simple six-foot length of calico cloth knotted on the right shoulder.

A light wind flapped at the ochred robe, and I saw the magnificent sinewy body beneath, naked except for a hide belt at his waist, a single strand of multicoloured glass beads at the neck, and two or three copper bracelets on his wrists. A wide ring of the brilliant beads passed through the top of each ear, and smaller brass-weighted rings hung from the long loops of stretched skin which once had been his ear lobes. A sword, sheathed in a red leather scabbard, dangled at his right side, and he held a long-bladed spear in his right hand. On his feet were crude leather sandals, something I had never seen among the tribesmen of the Congo and Ruanda-Urundi, who went barefoot.

He stood motionless, watching several young Masai boys driving a herd of cattle across the thorn-bush savannah; skinny unhealthy-looking animals, with short horns, hanging dewlaps and prominent humps to testify to their zebu ancestry. He paid almost no attention as I drove past about twenty feet away.

118

A LEOPARD KILLED BY HAND

The Author with the skin of the 7 ft., 120 lb. male leopard which he killed after a half-hour struggle in the North Kivu district in January 1957.

TALKING TO BAMBUTI AT THE PIONEER AGRICULTURAL
SETTLEMENT, OR PAYSANNAT, AT NAITI

THE AUTHOR AT EBIKEBA WITH BEROKA, AN 18-YEAR-OLD
PYGMY WOMAN WHO IS COOKING BANANAS IN FRONT OF
HER HUT

When he saw me wave to him from the cab, his only reaction was to assume an even more dignified, self-assured and aloof pose.

After that, I passed several groups of warriors, women and children along the road to Narok at the northern end of Kenya's vast Masai reservation. With their aura of freedom and unspoiled natural grace, they all impressed me deeply. But half an hour later, when I arrived at Narok itself, the classic place 'to see the Masai', I found a collection of *dukah*, cheap little Hindu stores with barred windows, and a gang of sensitive, arrogant, 'educated' natives who once had been Masai.

I watched a tall man posturing on the veranda of one store and haranguing a group of his own people while his Hindu boss nodded approvingly. This 'Masai' wore long trousers and a R.A.F. corporal's ragged military tunic. He had removed the rings of beads from his ears, and the empty loops of skin hung down on either side of his face, looking incredibly ugly. A cigarette dangled from his lips, and he had on a broken Mickey Mouse wrist-watch, probably a gift from a passing American tourist.

I took a long look at this modern Masai leader and the other 'civilized' tribesmen loitering about the *dukah*. Some wore plastic sunglasses, several were chewing gum. One man, on a bright green bicycle, wobbled back and forth down the dusty road until he eventually ran into a tree. Remembering the seemingly unspoiled people I had seen along the road, I decided to get the hell out of Narok.

I spent the next three days in Nairobi, visiting the Coryndon Museum and the McMillan Memorial Library, where I spoke to experts on Masai life, customs and history. My big question was very simple: Where, in the thirty-eight thousand square miles of the Masai reservation, would I be most likely to find among a hundred thousand semi-nomadic people, those tribesmen who still followed traditional ways, relatively untouched by civilization?

They answered that question and many others. I left, armed with a small black notebook containing several dozen Masai phrases and a crude map of my suggested route. I drove first to Lake Magadi, about sixty miles southwest of Nairobi. Leaving the road behind, I pulled out my compass and headed due south towards the Tanganyika border, bouncing my way across the untracked barren savannah.

I saw herds of wildebeest and zebra grazing in the distance but no sign of people or cattle. A few miles later there were some deserted huts; it was only after I had driven for about two hours that I caught sight of a large *emparnat*—a traditional Masai village—about three hundred yards to the east. I saw first the *esita*, a tangled thorn-bush fence, about eight feet high, round the huts and kraals. As I came closer, I could see people: a crowd of women, children and elderly men who came forward in silence, staring with astonishment as the Chevy and I materialized next to their village.

Some were smeared with rancid red-ochred sheep fat; others revealed the natural chocolate colour of their skin. Several old men were wrapped in grey or black woollen blankets which must have come from the little trading post at Magadi. The adults wore *enkamuke*, crude leather sandals, and the children went barefoot. Most of them lacked their lower central incisor teeth, which, according to custom, the Masai remove with a knife. All of them, men, women and children, had shaven heads. Their naked scalps were alive with flies, as were the babies' faces. Some of the women looked as if they had short black beards, but the beards flew away, buzzing, when they brushed at their chins.

In spite of the flies and the smell, the women were slim, dignified figures, clad in reddish-grey robes that covered them almost completely from the shoulders to well below the knees. Almost all wore two or three necklaces, large flat collars of brilliant glass beads, as well as big-beaded rings through the tops of their ears and beaded leather plaques with dangling copper ornaments suspended from their stretched ear lobes. Spiral bracelets of heavy brass, copper, iron or even aluminium wire were wound round their shins, wrists and upper arms.

No one spoke; for a long moment we stared at each other uneasily. Then I consulted my little black notebook to find an appropriate phrase. '*Loo papaai! Entasupa!*' I declaimed to a group of three wary-looking old men—'O fathers! My greetings!'

They peered at me with increased astonishment. '*Ipa!*' one answered faintly.

I felt wonderfully encouraged. '*Kokoo! Takuenya!*' I said suavely to a withered old woman. 'Greetings, Grandmother!'

'*Iko!*' she answered immediately, the feminine form of *Ipa!*

'*Eero! Supa!*' I said to a small boy hiding behind his mother's legs. He refused to answer. Undismayed, I was about to continue with specialized greetings to Masai of every age, sex and

status. Then a sturdy middle-aged man with a slight military
air walked up to me. '*Apaayia! Supa!*' I said, and waited
eagerly for the traditional '*Ipa!*'

'*Jambo, Bwana,*' he said in the easy, familiar Swahili. 'My
name is Masaka. Can I help you?'

I was a little disappointed to hear those banal-sounding
words in a Masai village, but it was just as well, since I had
nearly exhausted my Nilo-Hamitic conversational gamut.

'Where did you learn Swahili?' I asked.

'At Magadi. I worked in a shop for a while, but I didn't like
it. So I came back to live here. Sometimes I work for hunters or
travellers who need a guide in Masailand.'

'Then you will work for me, Masaka, and help me to meet
your people. I shall pay you well.'

'*Eé! Eé!*' he replied—an eager Masai 'yes'—forgetting his
Swahili in the excitement of the moment.

'I want to spend a little time in your village. Shall we talk to
the chief?'

'He went to the *manyata* to see the *muran*.'

That really intrigued me. I knew that the *muran* (or *moran*, as
they are sometimes called) were warriors, and I had some hazy
notions about the *manyata*. According to all I had heard, it was
a special warrior village resembling to some extent the ancient
Roman gladiator schools. 'Where is the *manyata*?' I asked my
new guide.

He pointed to the south. 'One day's walk from here, *Bwana*.'

'Good, we shall go there tomorrow. Now I would like to see
your village and settle down for the night.'

Masaka and I walked through one of the four openings in the
thorn-bush *esita*; the aloof but curious crowd followed. The
village reeked of cattle dung and fermenting urine. The huts, set
back along the perimeter of the enclosure, were rounded oblongs
made of branches plastered with dung and clay. In the centre a
much smaller circle of thorn bush enclosed the sheep pens. The
area between the huts and the central pens was the *emboo*, a
large filthy cattle kraal occupying most of the village. In the
late afternoon it was almost empty, but from distant lowing
sounds I knew that the wandering herds of cattle would soon
be home to join the permanent herd of several million flies.

Inside, the huts were even worse, with very low doors and
no windows. Smouldering fires emitted suffocating clouds of
smoke which, combined with the reek of dung-plastered walls
and dung-covered floors, made the atmosphere completely

intolerable. The air seemed almost solid with flies. A sickly-looking calf mooed at me from the shadows and I backed out, bumping my head on the low entrance.

My original enthusiasm at the idea of sleeping in a Masai hut was gone. 'Where can I pitch my tent?' I asked Masaka. 'Things seem a little too crowded here.'

He pointed to a tall cassia tree with a top like an open parasol, about a hundred feet from the village. 'Over there, *Bwana*. I will help you.'

Masaka had obviously had some experience in erecting a large tent, but two men helping us had no idea how to go about it. They struggled with the heavy canvas, becoming increasingly baffled, and one started to mutter irritably. '*Ingik!*' he said several times, with increasing annoyance.

'What does that word mean, Masaka?'

'I don't want to tell you, *Bwana*. He is a dirty old man, or else he wouldn't use such a word in front of a stranger.'

'Come on, Masaka! What does it mean?'

'It is our word for human excrement. We say it sometimes when we get angry.'

Apparently, the Nilo-Hamitic language of the Masai wasn't quite as alien as it seemed.

'Do you want me to find you a cook?' Masaka asked, once the tent problem had been solved.

'No. From now on, I shall eat only what the Masai eat.'

He looked troubled. 'We live on only three things,' he explained gravely. '*Kule, osarge* and *enkiringo*—milk, blood and meat.'

'Then those are what I want to eat and drink.'

'White men don't do that. No *Musunkui* would ever drink fresh warm blood from the veins of our cattle as we do.'

'If you bleed a cow now, I shall prove that I tell you the truth.'

'We only bleed cows in the morning. But I can give you some fresh milk.'

'*Ashe*,' I answered, Masai for 'Thank you'.

Masaka looked surprised, then he smiled with obvious pleasure. It was the first Masai smile I had seen, and it was a beautiful sight, despite his missing lower incisors. Ten minutes later, we were drinking milk together from a small calabash—a very rich, ivory-coloured milk with a slightly acid taste, presumably because the Masai wash almost everything, including their bodies, with *inkulak*—strong-smelling cow urine. The flavour was unusual, but I drained the milk with real enjoyment.

It was the first significant step in my attempt to share the life of the Masai.

Afterwards, we moved to the *enkima*, a large fire built behind a thorn-bush windbreak about a hundred feet from the village. There, surrounded by a circle of squatting, impassive elders, I riddled my new friend with questions. 'What makes the Masai so different from everyone else?' was the first thing I asked him.

'We are the only people who really know how to live,' Masaka told me. 'We are not like the Kikuyu or the Wakamba who plant things in the ground: they are not warriors even when they fight. They have no *manyata* and they know nothing about cattle or God. We have one word for all of those ignorant people: *Ol-Meeki*. That means the savages or the natives.'

'What do you think of the white people you've seen?'

'We used to call them *Il-Ojuju*, the hairy ones, because they are not civilized enough to shave their heads and bodies. Now we say *Il-Ashumpa* like the Kikuyu, or *Il-Musunku* like the Swahili. The white people know a little more than the natives, but still they are not Masai.'

'That may be true, but now they are ruling your country. How did that happen?'

'Well, *Bwana*, it's a long story. We Masai came to this country about a hundred lifetimes ago from Endigir.' Masaka pointed to the north. 'Three other peoples lived with us there: the Dorobo, the Kunono and the Kikuyu. God told the Dorobo to live by hunting wild beasts. He gave iron to the Kunono and taught them how to be blacksmiths. He sent the Kikuyu to live in the mountains where they learned to eat grass. Then he gave all the cattle in the world to the Masai. He let down a long strip of hide, and the beautiful cows walked down on it, one by one, from the top of Heaven.'

'Other people have herds of cows,' I pointed out. 'How do you account for it?'

'I told you the way it was when the world began, *Bwana*. Later, when things got mixed up, we began to find natives who *said* they owned cows. We knew at once that the cattle were either stolen or found, so we made war and raided to get back our God-given property. We killed the Wakamba and the Kikuyu who dared to resist us, then we killed the Arabs when they tried to take us for slaves. We even killed most of the Masai who ate grass like the natives. Those were the good old days. But then we had lots of trouble.'

'What happened?'

'The medicine men! *Il-oibonok!* They made civil war among the people, trying to get control of the cattle. We killed each other, just as we'd killed the natives. The smallpox came and more of our people died. The rinderpest came and killed a lot of the cattle. As we grew weaker, the Kikuyu and the Wakamba took their revenge. More of our people died in the fighting. Then there were terrible famines. After all these things had happened, the white men came to our country and put an end to the wars between the Masai and the natives. They made us stop raiding. They even made us stop fighting each other! That was a very strange thing to do, because real men can only be happy if they are warriors.'

'How does a Masai man become a warrior, Masaka?'

His answer was confused and evasive, as it so often is at first when dealing with almost any of Africa's tribes. His fanciful explanations showed that Masaka was more interested in trying to please me than in telling the truth. Then, when I tripped him up with some relevant counter-questions, he began to give me the real story. But the subject proved so complex and bizarre that I didn't really understand the situation until I had talked repeatedly to Masaka and a few other Masai during the weeks that followed. A picture then emerged of the Masai's little-known, rigidly compartmented lives, which is unique, not merely in Africa, but throughout the world.

According to classic but now fading Masai tradition, there were six different stages in the lives of men. First they were *inkera*, children, who spent their days helping to herd cattle and sheep. Then at puberty they became *ilamala*, candidates for circumcision. Boys of this age banded together and wandered from village to village, dancing, singing, and asking for presents like honey and hyrax-skin robes. Nobody refused. They took their presents to the medicine men and asked them to make arrangements for the ceremonies of circumcision. Circumcision ceremonies, among the Masai, were very difficult to organize and sometimes it took almost a year. First, all the councils of elders had to agree, which always took time. Even though the boys were permitted to make love with young, unmarried women, the delays made them very impatient. Then, still before the circumcision, the ceremony of seizing the ox by the horns had to be conducted. The ox had to be perfectly black, without a single defect. A special village had to be built for the festivities. *Ilamala* gathered from every corner of Masailand, but only those boys were allowed to compete whose fathers had taken part in a

similar ritual during their own youth. The boys stood in a row
behind the starting-line, and the elders brought the ox into the
village. Then, at a signal, all the boys raced to the black ox and
tried to grab him by the horns or the hump. As soon as two
succeeded, the boys of their own clans tried to protect them
while the other youths did their best to force them away and
take their places. It was very rough sport: many were wounded,
sometimes a few were killed. Afterwards, the ox was slaughtered
and everyone shared the meat. Then the boys returned to their
native villages and waited—sometimes as long as another two
years—to be circumcised.

The reason for this further delay was involved and peculiar.
Circumcision, and the slaughtering of Masai cattle, could be
performed only by a Dorobo, a member of a strange hunting
tribe. The Dorobo circumcisers travelled slowly from village to
village, and the youths had to wait for them.

When they finally arrived, each candidate's mother shaved his
head and gave him new sandals and a robe made of the skins
of four young rams. Next day, wearing this ceremonial clothing,
he sat on an oxhide outside his mother's hut, determined to
appear completely unmoved while the Dorobo performed the
operation, for he knew that any outcry would mark him for
ever as a coward and that his mother would be beaten with a
stick. He spent the next five or six days in the hut, eating ram's
meat and fat, until the wound started to heal over, at which
time he left home to enter the third stage of his life: he became
one of *ilaibartak*, the novices, a phase sometimes lasting up to
two years.

Novices roamed the country in bands, shooting all kinds of
birds with bows and arrows. Their favourite trophies were preserved in a most bizarre fashion: the birds' entrails were scooped
out, their bodies stuffed with grass and tied on to the novice's
hair. The birds were never removed, and the boys went on adding more, until their heads bristled with brilliantly coloured
feathers. Custom forbade them to put *ereko*, the red ochre, on
their bodies, only plain fat, and they were allowed no sexual
relations. When this period drew to a close, the novices
assembled in groups and each boy's mother publicly shaved off
his hair, also removing the stuffed birds. Then his father gave
him the three most important material things in his life: *arem*,
olalem and *elongo*—spear, sword and shield—to show that he
was ready to become one of the strongest and bravest men in the
world—*il-muran*, the warriors of the Masai.

The next nine years—*ilbarnot*, which means being junior *muran*—was the most exciting time in a man's whole life. It started immediately after the shaving ceremony, when the new warriors went off together in groups, each with his mother and his own herd of cows, to build their *manyata*. The mothers usually took their young children as well, especially girls. The women built huts for the warriors and performed such work as milking, gathering wood and hauling water. The girls helped them a little, but were mainly occupied as companions and lovers for the junior *muran*. Free love in the *manyata* was general, but in all other respects strict military discipline reigned. Junior warriors were not allowed to smoke or drink beer, and had to practise their skills every day. During the entire nine years, they were forbidden to cut their hair: instead, they braided it into *iltaikan*, the classic warrior pigtails.

Yet another head-shaving brought this period to a close, and they entered the fifth stage of their lives to become *ilmorijo*, or senior *muran*. Once again special ceremonies marked the occasion, a sort of grand 'graduation', or *unoto*, held every seven years and sometimes involving up to five hundred mature junior warriors. A special village, containing either thirty-nine or forty-nine hide-covered huts, according to the number of elected leaders, was built, and an enormous circular dung-and-mud-plastered hut—*osingira*—served as a 'clubhouse'. The *osingira*, where no women or boys were ever admitted, was sometimes fifty feet across and could hold four hundred men.

Within its dung-covered walls was a magic cesspool into which every *muran* was obliged to urinate as soon as he entered the hut. If he had ever secretly dishonoured the warrior's moral code, the *muran* knew he would die the moment his urine splashed into the hole. After passing this singular test, the men were entitled to participate in all the singing, dancing, feasting and beer drinking. The ceremonies lasted nine days; on the tenth, they were shaved, becoming senior *muran*.

In this new capacity they built a separate *manyata* and were permitted to marry, acquiring as many wives as they could afford, though the wives were not allowed to live at the senior warriors' village. Two or three years later, when the next group of junior warriors was ready to move up, the seniors left their *manyata* and went to live in their wives' villages.

This brought them to the sixth and final stage of their lives: they were now *ilmoruak*—the elders—exercising advisory and judicial authority over women, children and cattle.

This was the gist of the long, complicated story which I put together gradually. Even on that first night, as I sat by the fire with Masaka, one question struck me as extremely important. 'How can there really be warriors now when the white men will not let your people make war?'

'It is very difficult, *Bwana*. *Nkirisa*—the English—don't even want us to have our *manyata*. For a while they made it against the law. Now they let us live where we please, but they talk all the time against the *manyata*. Because of that, the time of being a warrior is growing shorter and shorter. Today, most men become elders only four or five years after the ceremony of circumcision. That is not the way life should be! A man always wants to remain a warrior just as long as he possibly can.'

'But how, Masaka? *How?*'

'When they made us stop raiding and killing the natives, we Masai found a new way to fight. The warriors practised *ola-mayio*—the lion hunt—to prove their courage. Together, the *muran* went out to battle against *olngatuny*—our enemy the lion—who kills the cattle and sheep. Sometimes they hunted another terrible enemy, *olkeri*, the leopard. They were all brave, but the two most honoured warriors were those who threw the first spear and grabbed the lion's tail. Then, about twenty years ago, the junior *muran* grew even more daring. They started to duel with the lion single-handed, armed only with the spear, the sword and the shield. Most of the time, the lion won the duel and the man died. But sometimes, maybe once in every three duels, the warrior won and killed the lion. That made him a hero for the rest of his life. It was the most exciting and wonderful thing in the world . . . and then the white men told us we had to stop. They were worried that too many young warriors would be killed.'

'*Did* you stop?'

'Mostly. They put us in prison when they caught us, and no Masai can live long like that! But a few of the young warriors still try to do it, in spite of the penalties. That is because we Masai have two things that the white men and the natives lack: *empijan* and *olwuasa*, courage and pride.'

There was a long silence after Masaka uttered those words. For me it was a moment of sadness for I was deeply moved by the tragedy of the Masai, a warrior people who were gradually losing their main reason for living, because of the inexorable arrival of civilization. Moreover, I felt a certain shame: there was truth in what Masaka said about the white man's lack of courage and pride, at least in our time. Most of our lives lacked meaning or choice, as we clung to such banal realities as our jobs, our families and what we regard as 'fun'. Many of us pass through life without facing a single real challenge, a gamble with pain or death for what the Masai call *engisisata*, 'the glory'. Instead, we waste precious time making money or spending it, live with our own fear and mediocrity until we grow old and feeble, and then die, still clutching at the mockeries of our existence.

With some such thoughts in mind, I made my decision: whatever the cost I was going to prove to the Masai and, even more important, to myself that I had what these wonderful people called *empijan* and *olwuasa*. 'Masaka,' I said gravely, 'I am going to kill a lion, single-handed, with a spear.'

'What? Oh, *Bwana*, you must be joking!'

'No, I mean it. If the warriors at the *manyata* will teach me how to handle their weapons, I will duel with the lion.'

'But the lion will probably win.'

'I'll take my chances.'

'And then my village will get into trouble. We will all go to prison if we let a white man be killed.'

'Masaka, I am not an Englishman. I come from a different country; my government doesn't even know that I'm here. No one will come to look for me if I never return. If the lion wins, you can let him eat me. If he doesn't like white man's meat, then the hyenas can have a good time.'

Masaka looked appalled. 'It's getting very late, *Bwana*,' he said nervously. 'Why don't you sleep on the idea? When you get up in the morning, perhaps we'll both have forgotten. It will be just as though you had said nothing at all.'

'I will sleep, but I will not forget. I am going to spear a lion.'

*   *   *

Masaka was waiting as I stepped out of my tent next morn-morning. '*Jambo, Bwana*,' he said brightly. 'Do you want me to help with your breakfast?'

'Yes, I'd like to drink some fresh blood. Afterwards, we'll talk some more about the lion.'

He rolled his eyes upwards with an expression of baffled consternation, and softly exclaimed '*Na-Ai! Na-Ai!*'

'What does that mean?'

'It is a little Masai prayer—"O Sky!" I am asking our God to watch over you.'

'*Ashe*, Masaka. I am happy to be your friend.'

We walked together to the village where the cattle were still in their kraal. 'Which cow do you want to drink from?' he asked. 'You can choose any one which has two little slits on the left ear. That is my special mark. The brand on the animal's flanks shows the clan.'

I took a good look at the scraggy-looking cows, a far cry from the well-groomed cattle of the Batutsi. None seemed particularly appealing. 'You choose for me.'

'Then you will have Kerete. She is my favourite cow.'

The fact that the Masai gave names to their cattle came as a surprise. In Urundi the Batutsi lavished far more care on their beautiful long-horned cows, but never bothered to give any of them a name.

Kerete, an elderly black and white cow, with one blind eye, struggled briefly while two young boys grappled her into position and Masaka tied a leather thong round her neck. He tightened it until the jugular vein swelled prominently. Then one of the boys handed him a crude bow about two feet long and a small arrow; the wooden tip of the arrow he placed against the swollen blood vessel; he pulled the bowstring back about an inch, released it, and the arrow point penetrated just far enough to open the vein.

He caught the surge of blood in a long oval gourd, and passed it to me with the traditional two-handed gesture. The blood was thick and dark red, with a froth of bubbles on top. The flavour was very strong, and of course there was the inevitable aftertaste of urine; otherwise it wasn't too bad. I drank half of it, about a pint, and looked round to see the people's reaction. They were all staring at me intently. I smiled, sipped a little more blood, and handed the gourd back to Masaka with my customary '*Ashe!*' He drained the rest.

'What do you think of it?' he asked curiously.

'It's excellent. It makes me feel strong enough to kill a lion.'

'Are you really sure, *Bwana*, you want to try it?'

'Yes.'

'Then I will take you to the *manyata*. Maybe you will succeed.'

We struck the tent, Masaka said good-bye to his three wives, and we bounced off towards the south, while he explained very carefully that he had told no one in the village about my intentions—not even his wives.

'Aren't you worried about leaving your wives behind?' I asked. 'We may be gone for some time.'

'No, their lovers will take good care of them,' he said, very matter-of-factly.

'Don't you mind?'

'Not as long as the lovers are married men. Of course, if any of my wives fooled around with an uninitiated boy, I'd give her a beating and pour sheep's urine over the bruises. That would really teach her a lesson! But I have no right to be jealous if she makes love with a married man.'

'But what happens if your wives decide they prefer their lovers to you?'

'Nothing. They enjoy themselves, but they are still my wives. We Masai have no divorce.'

The Masai obviously had a strict but peculiar moral code, in which marriage was not the end of individual liberty. On the contrary, it seemed to be only the beginning.

After driving very slowly across the rocky savannah for more than two hours we reached the *manyata*. It was situated somewhere east of Lake Natron, in Kenya or, more probably, just over the border in Tanganyika. Physically it was much like the *emparnat* I'd left behind me, though rather larger: a circle of thorn bush surrounding some fifteen huts and a big kraal. There were women and children here—and many young girls—as well as a few visiting elders. But overshadowing all the rest were the young Masai warriors, whose lithe, elegant presence filled the *manyata*.

The junior *muran* ranged in age from 16 to 30; their average height must have been about 5 ft. 8 in. All were smeared with red-ochre sheep fat from the top of their pigtail hair-dos to the tips of their sandalled toes, and each carried a shiny, sharp, long-bladed spear. They stared up at me with self-assured curiosity and magnificent hauteur.

'*Lo murran! Entasupa!*' I delivered another of the classic salutations.

'*Ipa!*' they chorused, looking surprised and rather pleased.

'*Masaka*,' I said, 'tell them why I am here. Tell them about the lion.'

'Oh, no, *Bwana*, I can't do it just like that. First they must be prepared: I have to explain. Otherwise, they will think we are both mad.'

'All right, Masaka. Tell them I am tired of the white man's life, that I want to be a real friend of the Masai. Explain that I want to stay here for a fortnight at least.'

He launched into a complicated Masai oration. I sat on a big

stone and watched the warriors' faces while they listened. Their
first reactions did not seem favourable: several of them spat on
the ground. Then they argued for a long time among themselves,
while Masaka tried to slip in a few words edgewise. Finally, their
expressions grew more friendly and I felt sure that they would
tolerate my presence in the *manyata*. I was right, but their
reason was disillusioning.

'You can stay here,' he explained. 'They didn't like the idea
at first, but I made them understand how strange you are and
what fun it would be to watch you.'

I had no intention of playing court jester to the Masai, but
still, it would give me a chance to prove what I was fit for. 'All
right, Masaka. But why did they spit on the ground?'

'That was only to show their surprise. They didn't mean
anything bad.'

'Did you talk to them about the lion?'

'Not yet. All in good time. For the present they told me to
wish you welcome and asked where you want to sleep. I explained about the tent and they are anxious to see it. Most of
them cannot understand about a cloth house that can be built
in half an hour.'

'Where can we pitch the tent?'

'They are going to push back the *esita* next to the chief's hut.
That will make room.'

I watched as the *muran* took some long sticks and prodded
away at the bristling thorn bush until they had made a kind of
alcove. Then, with many amazed comments, they helped us with
the cumbersome canvas. The way they worked with their hands
pleased me enormously, for in Ruanda-Urundi no Mututsi
would dream of doing the manual labour which the Masai
seemed almost to enjoy. Now I began to realize more than ever
the great gulf between the Masai and the Batutsi, in spite of their
shared Hamitic blood and some cultural similarities. Where the
Batutsi were arrogant, the Masai were merely self-assured and
aloof; where the Batutsi were devious and full of duplicity, the
Masai were open and honest.

Dr. Sidney Hinde, first British Resident of the Masai Reservation (in about the year 1900), had summed up their character
very concisely: 'As a race they are intelligent and truthful, and
a grown Masai will neither thieve nor lie. He may refuse to
answer a question, but once given, his word can be depended on.'
That innate sense of integrity distinguishes the Masai from the
vast majority of African tribes and, to be completely objective,

from most Europeans and Americans. In this and several other respects they strikingly resemble the American Indians, especially the Blackfoot and Sioux of the Great Plains, who live on the New World's equivalent of the East African savannahs.

Significantly, there are almost no 'rice Christians' among the Masai. The efforts of both Catholic and Protestant missionaries to convert them have ended in failure, in contrast to some regions of the Congo where the missions are the most powerful local authority, not only in spiritual matters but in social life, systematically suppressing traditional customs and offering, unlike the medical missionaries, no real material aid. The Masai had obstinately resisted that kind of harassment, because of their ironclad personal ethics and morality: I felt sure that if I really succeeded in gaining their friendship I would always know where I stood with them.

I spent the rest of that first day at the *manyata* watching the warriors practise swordplay and spear-thrusts while the old women patched the huts with *imodiok*, fresh cattle-dung. Dinner consisted of about a quart of rich milk, and next morning breakfast was another pint of fresh blood, both tinged with the familiar flavour of cow's urine. The warriors watched my blood-drinking ceremony with astonishment, and one shot a quick question at Masaka, who translated for me. 'He wants to know why you don't eat white men's food. I told him that you want to live like a Masai, that you even want to learn how to use a spear.'

'Did you explain about the lion?'

'Not yet! All in good time!'

'No, Masaka. *Now.*'

'*Eé! Eé!* As you say, *Bwana.* I will try.'

Assuming a very dignified pose, Masaka delivered an earnest speech that must have lasted half an hour. Towards the end I caught two significant words: *arem*, the spear, and *olngatuny*, the lion. The warriors' reaction was extremely disconcerting: they burst out laughing. A tall man with a terribly scarred belly made a short, incisive-sounding comment, and the laughter increased.

I began to grow angry. 'Who is that man, Masaka? What did he say?'

'His name is Konoko. He said that you'd better load your gun. That is the only way a white man can kill a lion. The other *muran* believe him, for he's the only warrior in this *manyata* who has ever faced a lion single-handed and won.'

I walked over to the scarred warrior and stared intently into his eyes. 'Tell him, Masaka,' I said slowly, 'that I don't even own a gun.' Then I added, with conscious but sincere bravura, words I knew a Masai would certainly understand. 'I will duel with the lion alone, just as you did, with a Masai spear and a buffalo-hide shield. When it is over, I will either be a man alive or a man dead, but a *man*. Whatever happens, I will not leave this place until it is finished.'

Masaka translated, and all of the junior *muran* stared at me without speaking. Finally Konoko gravely intoned a few words. 'He says you are young and strong, *Bwana*, but that you are not a Masai. He doesn't really think you can do it, but would like to find out for sure. He will even train you himself.'

'*Ashe!*' I said, unconsciously offering Konoko my hand. To my great surprise, he shook it vigorously, a custom rarely practised by the natives of the Congo and little more common in Ruanda-Urundi.

During the next three weeks Konoko and I became almost like brothers, although neither spoke the other's language. Masaka usually squatted beside us to translate, always with a few wry comments of his own. In some ways he seemed almost like a shaven, red-ochred version of my own father. Virtually everything the three of us did was involved with the *arem*, *olalem* and *elongo*, the traditional weapons Konoko gave me, none of which was made by the Masai.

The *arem*, or spear, was forged by the Kunono, a blacksmith caste regarded almost as pariahs, who bought iron ore from the Swahili or smelted the nuggets they found in streams. The result was a soft, badly tempered metal, which they made into knives, cattle bells, ornaments and spears. The *olalem*, or sword, was obtained from the Kikuyu or, more recently, from the trading posts which imported blades made in Birmingham. The *elongo*, or shield, was made by the Dorobo hunters from buffalo skin stretched on a wooden frame. On it the Masai *muran* painted brilliant designs in red, black and white, showing clan, territory and individual honours.

Most of my interest centred, of course, on the spear, a thin, flexible three-foot iron blade connected by a six-inch wooden shaft to an iron butt about three feet long. The result was a heavy but well-balanced weapon which felt very good in my hand. Konoko presented it to me with a ceremonial flourish and a rousing little speech. 'He wants me to tell you,' Masaka explained, 'that he has never before seen a man as tall as his spear.

So he has decided to give you a Masai name. He will call you Arem, the spear.'

I was delighted, and during the next three weeks of intensive training did my best to deserve the name. I must have thrown the heavy spear more than two thousand times, while holding the twenty-pound shield in my left hand. My target was a six-foot stick about four inches thick, to one end of which Konoko had fastened with bark ropes a cylindrical bundle of dry grass, which was supposed to resemble a lion.

The target's wooden centre represented either the lion's sternum or ribs. If I struck that hard core with my spear, the soft, narrow blade was badly bent; if I missed it completely and struck the hard-packed soil the result was the same. The only good cast was one which passed through a six-inch grass radius on either side of the wooden core; that was difficult, since the target was always moving towards me, just like a charging lion. Our method was simple. Konoko stood eight or nine feet away, holding the stick with its round shaggy target on top. Simultaneously, he let it fall forward and jumped to one side as I hurled the spear. The first four times I tried, I missed the target completely. On the next few attempts I managed to nick the edge. Then my aim seemed to improve, but the result was no better: I hit the wooden core of the target and bent the blade. It was only on the twentieth try that I made a really perfect cast through the bundle of grass that represented *ol-tau*, the lion's heart, a feat I duplicated only ten times in the next hundred casts I made that day.

After a fortnight's practice nine out of every ten casts of the spear which I made at a distance of eight feet were accurate. At that distance my degree of precision just about equalled Konoko's, but at fifteen and twenty feet he was still more skilful. At twenty-five feet neither of us could achieve any real precision.

The meaning of these statistics seemed very simple: the closer I was to the lion, the more chance I had to strike the right spot with the maximum degree of force. Of course that theory had its limitations; if I waited a fraction of a second too long, I wouldn't have time for a quick leap to the side or the rear. Thus, I might make a perfect cast only to find myself pinned underneath a speared lion who was quite capable of tearing me to pieces while he died.

That was what had happened to my brother-in-arms Konoko, who still had terrible scars to prove it. He hadn't jumped quickly enough, and the wounded lion had crashed down on top of him. His upraised shield had protected his face and chest, but the lion's claws had laid open his belly. Another *muran* had rushed up at once and grabbed the lion by the base of his tail. This distracted the lion and gave Konoko a chance to leap to his feet, pull the spear from the lion's chest and strike again, more accurately. Only then, as the lion died, did Konoko look down and see coils of his own intestines dangling from his lacerated belly.

That sight, which might have frightened a civilized man into his grave, did not really bother Konoko. He watched calmly while his companions washed the bloody intestines, stuffed them back into place, and poured a quart of sheep fat into the wound. Then they sewed him together with sinew from the back of an ox. Throughout the proceedings, I was told, Konoko made no outcry, but endured everything with stoic indifference.[1]

Knowing that I might soon be submitting to Masai surgery myself Konoko's wound seemed almost like a personal warning. Yet somehow I felt completely confident, even when Konoko and Masaka said they were prepared to give me the standard funeral rites for a Masai warrior who died in battle.

'If the lion kills you,' Masaka said, very gravely, 'we will not let him eat you without first making the proper ceremonial arrangements.'

'*Ashe!*' I said, with somewhat forced gratitude.

'We will chase the lion away or kill him if he refuses to leave. Then we will place you on your left side with your legs drawn up, your head to the north and your face turned towards the east. We will bend your left arm under your head as a cushion

---

[1] The African's extraordinary capacity to endure pain and survive physical ordeal is established fact. Primitive surgery involving setting broken bones, amputations, circumcision, and elaborate, repeated scarification is always performed without any form of anaesthetic. Some physiologists, such as Dr. J. M. Habig (*Initiation à l'Afrique*, Brussels, 1948), believe that this high pain threshold results from a nervous system which has a great number of autonomic centres and few dermal ramifications. It would appear also that the lack of a regular summer and winter rhythm vitiates the nervous system. Thus, pain originating in one part of the body apparently is not transmitted to other neural centres and has surprisingly little impact on the brain. This type of nervous organization places the African in perfect balance with his tropical milieu, unlike white settlers who have to go through a long and never entirely successful period of acclimatization. They remain energetic, nervous and unstable; the natives are calm, patient and enduring. But these same qualities which in the long run help the natives to survive, encourage passive indolence; the white man's sometimes self-destroying nervous energy leads to dynamic action.

and fold your right arm over your chest with the hand on the heart. Then we will take a last long look at your body and return to the *manyata* in single file, singing sad songs in honour of your courage. Soon, all Masailand will know the wonderful story of Arem, the first white man to duel with a lion. You will have even more glory dead than if you survive!'

'What other ceremonies will there be?' I asked. 'Will you bury my body?'

'No, we bury only medicine men or very rich elders. We build cairns of stones over their bodies. Then, as soon as they rot, their souls turn into snakes and return to the homes of their Masai children. That is why we do not kill serpents if they enter our huts: we know they are really our fathers who have returned to protect us.'

'Is there a chance that I might turn into a snake?'

'How could you, *Bwana*? Your body will not be buried. If we don't kill the lion, maybe he will come back and eat you. Otherwise the hyenas will do the job, just as they do for most of our own people. But that doesn't really matter: the important thing is that we leave your body in the correct position.'

'I see.'

'As a final tribute to your memory, we will taste neither milk nor meat for three days. We will drink only blood, in honour of Arem, our dead fellow warrior.'

As he spoke those words, my friend trembled with emotion. 'Masaka,' I pointed out gently, 'I'm not dead yet.'

'You will be.'

'*Ingik!*' I said angrily. 'I don't like that kind of talk!' Both Masai stared at me with amazement when I used their own smelly curse. 'Look, Masaka,' I continued, 'I have confidence in myself, I handle my spear like a Masai, and I feel certain that I'm going to win. Tell Konoko I want to duel with the lion as soon as possible. I'm ready for it now, and I'm tired of waiting.'

When Masaka had translated my words, Konoko answered, 'Arem, there are two groups of lions near the *manyata*. One of the warriors saw them this morning, and we are eager to make a hunt. If you feel sure that you're ready, there is no reason to wait. Maybe it would even be lucky to go tomorrow; we are now in the period of the green days.'

'The green days? What does that mean?'

Masaka pointed to the sky and said, '*Iloonyori*, the green days of the moon, when it is fat and perfectly round! That is the best time to conduct any important affairs.'

'Very well. Tell Konoko that I wish to go on a green day. I will duel with the lion tomorrow, and I will win.'

The answer to this rather bombastic declaration was a little deflating. 'Konoko says you are his friend and he wishes you luck, but he still wants to be honest; he doesn't believe you can do it. He asks you, before you give your final decision, to think about one of our Masai proverbs: "*Melang olambu ennongoto.*"'

'What does it mean?'

'Loud talk won't get you across the dangerous valley.'

* * *

On the morning of the *olamayio*, making no pretence of going about their normal activities, the Masai gathered in large groups, whispering, talking or laughing, seething with restrained excitement. Konoko, who was going to lead my warrior escort, made an unusual gesture as a mark of his friendship: he solemnly put on his *olowuaru*, a magnificent headdress made from the mane of the lion he had conquered alone. Three other *muran* followed suit, donning their own *olowuaru*; these were men who had won the mane at a collective hunt when they threw the first spear. The rest of the warriors sported the ostrich-feather headdresses which the Masai call *isidan*. All these precious ornaments were normally reserved for the *unoto* ceremony. As a final surprising touch, Masaka volunteered to join the warrior escort despite his status as an elder, and after a brief discussion he was accepted. This made him so happy he actually started to shake.

Seventeen other men accompanied Konoko and Masaka, making a total of nineteen *muran*. That figure has a special significance for the Masai because it contains the mystical number nine; the fact that there were nineteen Masai *plus* me instead of nineteen Masai *including* me, emphasized that I hadn't proved anything yet, either to Konoko or the rest of the *muran*.

They seemed to be taking me seriously, and were even willing to accept the fact that a white man might face a lion without a gun. As to how I would face it, they were obviously reserving their judgement. They knew the vast difference between throwing a spear at a grass target and throwing that same spear at the hurtling four-hundredweight package of claws, teeth and powerful muscles they called *olngatuny*. Hitting the target required a keen eye and a strong right shoulder; killing the lion demanded a great deal more: judgement, guts, and absolute presence of mind. They weren't quite sure that a white man could possibly have those elementary Masai virtues. Neither, I must admit, was I.

As we prepared to leave the *manyata*, the *muran* unknotted their calico robes, dropped them down, and belted them at the waist. Most of them had added fresh red ochre and sheep fat to their faces and bodies; all wore beautiful headdresses and carried brilliantly painted shields. Seeing that vivid colour and splendour, I felt like a drab white pigeon among peacocks, a bareheaded alien in rumpled khaki *kapitula* and shirt.

When the last warrior had put the finishing touches to his personal décor, we left the *manyata* in single file. Konoko led the long line, I followed, Masaka came next. We walked for four or five hours, passing several herds of zebra, wildebeest and Thomson's gazelle before we spotted a couple of lions in the distance, lying near a clump of thorn bushes.

As soon as we saw them, we advanced and spread out, trying to make a ring round them. This was the usual Masai strategy, but each time we got any closer than two or three hundred feet, they retreated. Their attitude was entirely different from that of the fearless, confident lions in the national parks of the Congo, Uganda and Kenya, who were aware of their complete security; these animals obviously knew and feared the Masai. While this explained their actions, it still seemed strange to see lions running from men.

We spent a few more hours trying to trap them in a circle formed by our bodies and shields. At the end of the afternoon we abandoned the chase and settled down to make the *olpul*, our temporary encampment, for which the Masai chose a big clump of thorn bushes, in the centre of which they carved a clear space, swinging their *olalem* like machetes. To cut wood for the fire they used their keen-edged shortswords. The fire itself was obtained by *aipiru*, the classical African method of rotating a hard round vertical stick (the 'male') at high speed against a softer flat piece of wood (the 'female').

I was terribly tired after trying to keep up with the Masai all day, and ravenously hungry. The high-protein meal was the perfect diet for warriors and one of the main reasons why the Masai were not only endowed with splendid physiques but were virtually immune from dental decay. Theodore Roosevelt, who travelled to Masailand, remarked in 1911: 'I hate to shock the vegetarians, but I am bound to say that these people, who never eat anything but meat, blood and milk, are as hearty and strong a set of people as I have ever seen in my life.' Forty years later I was beginning to find out just how hearty they were. I had lost twenty pounds during the past three weeks, trying to live the life of a Masai warrior, but I'd gained something more: I was in prime physical, mental and emotional condition, ready for my first real initiation to life.

None of us slept more than a couple of hours that night. It was very cold in spite of the big campfire, and we were all eager to continue the hunt. About 5.30 a.m. Konoko sent two parties of *muran* out to scout the terrain; two hours later one returned, extremely excited. They had spotted a second group of lions, three males holed up in a big clump of bushes. Two of the cats were small, but one was full-grown, with a beautiful mane.

When the second scouting party joined us, we set out moving almost at the double. We were at the lions' hide-out in an hour, and Konoko sent ten *muran* to beat the back of the bush. The rest of us waited with shields upraised, attempting to block the lions' escape route. Almost as soon as the beaters began, the three cats burst out of the thorn bush. Two got away; the third was trapped within the network of bodies and shields. He stood, one of the small ones, a 250-pounder, without a mane, turning his head from side to side in nervous confusion.

Konoko pointed with his spear at the young lion. '*Tara!*' he said. 'Kill him!'

Instead, I pointed my spear at the larger lion, who had come to a halt about a hundred yards away. He must have weighed easily 400 pounds. '*Kitok!*' I answered, 'the big one!'

Konoko stared at me, almost angrily. Then he called out an order and our circle broke into two files. The smaller lion bolted across the savannah and we set out after the big one. We chased him for almost an hour; then, exasperated, he sat down to take a breather in the shadow of a cassia tree, giving us a chance to surround him. Realizing he was trapped, the huge lion sprang to his feet, snarling, furious, and ready to charge the circle. Nineteen Masai warriors answered him, yelling like Apaches.

The lion drew back, obviously frightened. His head swayed slowly as he looked for a gap in the ring of howling Masai, and he padded nervously around the cassia tree. Quickly, the circle grew tighter and tighter until the nineteen men stood only two or three feet apart, forming a human chain roughly thirty-five feet in diameter.

From any point in the circle, I knew, the lion could reach me in two giant springs as I entered. I watched him for a moment while I wiped the sweat away from my eyes and rubbed my sweaty palms in the dirt. Then, with my buffalo-hide shield gripped in my left hand and the spear in my right, I leaped into the arena. '*Simba!*' I shouted, reverting to Swahili. '*Simba!* Come here!'

The lion ran back and forth nervously, about ten feet away from me. The Masai slowly raised their own spears to protect the circle, and I waited for the lion to charge. He refused. I stepped forward and shouted again. Immediately he sprang in the opposite direction—a great twelve-foot leap that toppled my friend Masaka like an ochre-coloured tenpin. Then he streaked off across the savannah.

I rushed to Masaka's side, feeling sick with apprehension. He lay, motionless, under his shield. Then I felt overwhelming relief as he rose to his feet, breathing a little hard: the marks of the lion's claws were deeply engraved on the painted buffalo hide, but not on his skin. '*Adoshi!*' he cried ecstatically as he passed his fingers over the torn shield. '*Adoshi! Eng-Ai!*'

More determined than ever, we set out again in two parallel rows to pursue the big lion. It took nearly two hours to trap him this time. He was growing more and more wary. Again the circle tightened round him and the Masai screamed with excitement. Then, just as before, I leaped into the human arena, intent on making the lion charge me. He retreated and threatened to spring at the other side of the circle. The Masai brandished their shields and shouted a chorus of violent abuse. He backed up and looked around very uneasily. He was about twenty-five feet away from me and still refused to charge me.

I waited for him, nearly exhausted by hours of violent exertion. My shirt and shorts were soaked with sweat, my breath came in gasps, my heart was pounding against my ribs with terrible force. I was at the very limit of my endurance and I knew it. Yet, strangely, I felt happier and more completely alive than I had at any other moment of my life. I balanced the spear in my right hand, vibrating it slightly in the style of the *muran*. Growing impatient, I shifted the spear to my left hand, picked up a pebble and tossed it at the lion's magnificent head. It struck him just under the left eye. That did it. He grunted deeply, turned, and started towards me. I knew he was going to charge.

Quickly, I shifted the spear back to my right hand, drew back my arm, and raised the shield to cover my chest. The lion stopped about ten feet away and stared at me with half-open mouth and baffled but furious eyes. I felt a moment of infinite pity for the great golden beauty I was about to destroy. Then I took a step forward with my left foot, crouched, and drew back my spear-arm even further. The lion's hindquarters trembled and his tail started to twitch. The *muran* stopped screaming and there was utter silence. Then he leaped towards me, as a cat springs on a mouse.

I felt no fear, only vast excitement. I looked for the spot, found it, and at the highest point of the lion's spring, threw the spear with all my strength. Then, as lion and spear met in mid-air, I leaped wildly to one side. The lion completed his arc, the heavy butt of the spear struck the ground, and the impact forced the blade even more deeply into his chest. He landed precisely where I had been standing less than a second before.

He rolled over, howling with pain and rage, as he struggled to reach me. I backed off carefully, unsheathing my *olalem*. He swiped at the sword, and once his claws clicked on the metal as he crawled after me with at least two feet of the iron blade in his chest. The protruding spear-butt swung slowly from side to side under his great head. He followed me for nearly thirty feet while the circle moved with us. Then he fell on his side, his head stiffened, his mouth lolled open, his eyes dulled, and he died.

The Masai burst into a wild orgy of joy. They shrieked, sang and jumped high into the air like men released from a catapult. Two of the warriors started to shake violently and foam at the mouth, one barking like a dog as saliva dripped from his chin; then both fell to the ground in a stupor. The Masai call this strange hysterical fit *apush*; it sometimes results from drinking decoctions of tree bark and powdered berries; on other occasions, such as this, intense emotion is enough to produce a fit.

I stood beside the dead lion, watching their strange performance. Then Konoko stepped towards me with a broad, wonderful smile and gathered me into his arms. After the embrace, he stepped back, spat in his palm and offered to shake. I grinned, spat in my own palm, and pumped his hand vigorously. I started to laugh when I saw that my shirt was smeared with red-ochred sheep fat from Konoko's body. It was the mark of a Masai.

'*Ara ol-Maasani!*' I shouted, almost crazy with joy. 'I am a Masai!'

Konoko stared at me with his beautiful honest eyes and then gave me the highest tribute of my life. '*Ira ol-Maasani!*' he echoed gravely. 'You *are* a Masai!'

After that, he unsheathed his sword and severed the lion's tail. He pulled my spear out of the lion's breast and examined the blade: it was very slightly bent. He straightened the soft iron with his fingers and passed the blade under the surface of the severed tail until the upper half was sheathed with the tawny skin. Then he handed the spear to me, with its token of triumph. It dripped blood, and the tassel of hair at the top waved like a Masai flag.

Ecstatic, the dancing, singing *muran* leaped forward, one by one, to touch alternately the bloody tail and my right shoulder. Soon I was spattered with lion's blood and I received another generous dose of red-ochred sheep fat when Masaka embraced me. The celebration went on for fully fifteen jubilant minutes; the Masai calmed down, temporarily, and turned their attention to the lion's corpse.

Since no one had interfered in the duel, as I'd requested beforehand, I was entitled to the whole thing: mane, skin and tail. To the hyaenas would go the rest of the body, excepting the heart, which the *muran* usually ate with ceremonial relish. Each member of the warrior escort would receive one of the lion's eighteen massive claws. The nineteenth man, Konoko, was beyond minor trophies: he had already achieved the supreme honour.

Konoko left two men behind to skin the lion. The rest of us lined up, single file, for the triumphal return to the *manyata*. But now, instead of walking, the Masai ran all the way, laughing, singing and shouting victorious cries. Again I had a hard time keeping up, but I was happy to see them run. A slow homeward march would have had only one meaning: my body, neatly arranged of course, was lying on the savannah, waiting for the hyaenas.

The people at the *manyata* heard us coming and several *muran* raced out to greet us. They stared at me with almost religious respect, touched the bloody tail on my spear, and slapped at my right shoulder. Then they let down their robes and belted them at the waist, a gesture which made them feel as though they were almost a part of the hunting party.

At the *manyata* I received a rather unsettling welcome. Nine young girls were waiting for me just inside the thorn-bush circle, each with a gourd in her hand and a warm, beckoning smile. I smiled back, flattered by what I considered the Masai women's tribute to my powers (even though nine was going a trifle too far, in spite of the number's magical implications). The girls giggled, shrieked, rushed forward, reached up, and ceremonially emptied the gourds over my head. Milk, tinged with urine, cascaded down my face and inundated my clothing. I stood there in astonishment with milk dripping out of my ears, while the girls fondled my spear-arm and shoulder. Then, singing and clapping their hands, my nine young bacchantes disappeared into the crowd.

The other Masai danced around me, slapping away at the magic shoulder. Some had been busy patching their huts and their hands were covered with brownish-grey cow dung. It contrasted very effectively with the smears of orange-red ochre, the ivory-coloured milk, and the scarlet spatters of lion's blood. I looked almost like a reflection of the flamboyant East African sunset that flooded the western sky.

Within a few minutes the entire *manyata* was at fever pitch. The big kraal rang with ecstatic songs and the ground seemed to rock as forty Masai jumped up and down like human pistons. I watched, almost hypnotized. Then, feeling hot and tacky, I took off my stinking Technicolor shirt and tossed it on to the ground. Half a dozen *muran* pounced on it, pulling in every direction until they tore it to pieces. Then, smiling with satisfaction, each rolled his fragment into a small soggy ball and tucked it into his belt as a magic talisman.

An hour later, during a brief lull in the party, I went to my tent, took a quick bath with my canvas bucket of water, and put on fresh *kapitula*. As I finished two young girls arrived, each clutching a small gourd. Fortunately they had no intention of emptying the contents over my head: they were merely bringing me dinner. I drank the porridge-like mixture of milk and blood with enjoyment, handed over the gourds and waited for them to leave. They didn't. Instead, they made it obvious that they wanted to prove their admiration for a man who had duelled with a lion. I hesitated. Then, as a gesture of respect to my brother (and sister) Masai, I decided to accept their personal form of appreciation.

Afterwards, when I stepped out of my tent into the brilliant moonlight, a new dance was just beginning: the classic Masai *numba*. In a ring round the big kraal twelve warriors were jumping up and down with perfectly synchronized movements once every fifteen seconds. I watched them until Masaka came and invited me to join in. Surprised and delighted, I slipped into the circle between two of my hunting colleagues and tried to copy their style. I was quickly disillusioned concerning my future as a Masai dancer: my companions bounced majestically at least three feet into the air, like men rebounding from an invisible trampoline, while I could hardly reach half that height.

The only things at all comparable to musical instruments in the *manyata* were two beautiful black spirals about three feet long, the horns of the greater kudu. The sound they produced was far from melodic, a deep sour blast that punctuated, like a foghorn, the *muran*'s unending chorus of '*Hooo! Hooo! Hooo!*'

After an hour of dancing, I staggered off to my tent, completely exhausted, and collapsed on to my Masai bed. Then a familiar voice spoke some Swahili words. It was Masaka, standing just outside the tent flap with the moonlight gleaming on his shaven, red-ochred head.

'Which girls do you want, Arem?' he repeated. 'Tonight you are entitled to make a free choice. That is one of the rewards we give a brave warrior.'

'I don't want any girls. I just want to sleep.'

'But that is one of our customs.'

'Look, Masaka, I'm tired. I must have walked and run at least fifteen miles today. I speared a lion, got nine gourds of milk over my head, and learned how to dance the *numba*. And I've already proved with two girls how much I respect Masai customs. Isn't that enough for one day?'

*   *   *

A week later, when the green days of the moon were past, I left the Masai *manyata* and drove north towards Nairobi. I brought with me my spear, my sword, my shield, the mane and skin of my lion, and a thousand memories of the wonderful people among whom I had lived for a while as Arem. Never again have I met human beings with so much dignity, integrity and rock-solid courage.

There was one final thing I brought with me, immaterial but far more precious: the hard-earned right to say, for the rest of my life, the rich and deeply significant words: *Ara ol-Maasani*— 'I am a Masai.'

8

I Marry Ndagizye

Ndaguha iruta ndagukunze—'One "I give you" is worth more than one "I love you".'

TUTSI PROVERB

'Do you consent to give your child as a blood-bride to my son?'

My adopted Tutsi father asked the question. My intended father-in-law hesitated before answering. I waited expectantly and my bride-to-be smiled at me, showing teeth beautifully white against an ebony skin.

'*Ego*,' the old man finally answered. 'Yes. I give my permission for the marriage.' Then the four of us passed a big calabash from hand to hand and sipped banana beer through a long sorghum straw.

From that moment my fate was sealed, first in beer and later in blood. Three years had passed since my initiation to the Masai tribe, and I was now about to become a Mututsi. This time no heroic exploits were required, only a contract of marriage. Yet the new relationship promised to be almost as dangerous as my East African adventure, for a very different reason. Konoko, my Masai brother, had been simple, honest and completely outspoken. My tall Tutsi bride Ndagizye was much more complex: six feet three inches of devious wiles, fully equipped with large expressive eyes, a hooked nose, a glib tongue and a large, perpetually itching palm.

We made a striking couple as we sat down together on the ceremonial mat and the wedding ritual began, especially since my bride was a man.

*　　*　　*

When I returned to Ruanda-Urundi in February 1952, the only thing further from my mind than getting married had been the incredible possibility that I might some day find myself marrying a *man*. After leaving Masailand, I had travelled through Ethiopia, the Sudan and Egypt, driving north along the Nile Valley with many, many stops. I had seen Addis Ababa, Khartoum, where the two Niles meet, and the impressive antiquities of Aswân, Ombo, Kôm, Luxor, Girga and Cairo. More important to me than temples and pyramids was to be meeting the living people of the northeastern deserts and savannahs, the strange complex of cattle-loving Hamites, who had sprung from the same ethnic roots as my own Masai and Batutsi.

In Cairo I sold my truck and flew to Europe to spend the rest of my six-months' leave in a cold climate. This was standard procedure for government workers, who, after several years in a tropical environment, generally start to show signs of nervous and physical deterioration.

As usual, I went to extremes. Having started my journey near the equator, I ended it north of the Arctic Circle in Lapland. Though the landscape, the people and the fauna there naturally differed wildly from anything I had seen in Central Africa, I was surprised to find several striking parallels, above all, the people's almost complete economic dependence on their cattle. Back in Africa cattle meant cows, whether you said *inka* like the Batutsi, *inkishu* like the Masai, or *inkomo* like the Zulu. In Lapland, however, cattle meant reindeer, and you had your choice of more than three hundred native names for the large, morose, lichen-eating animals.

I spent nearly three months in the grey Arctic expanses, watching the Lapps rope, ride, milk, butcher, skin and eat their peculiar cattle. Then everything turned into Technicolor again when I flew back to Africa, landed at the airport in Bukavu, equipped myself with another Chevrolet and drove back to southern Burundi, where I spent the next three years working and watching Batutsi and Bahutu demonstrate their own complete obsession with a more conventional kind of cattle.

'*Ntakirut'inka*' was the one piece of proverbial wisdom on the tip of everyone's tongue: 'Nothing surpasses the cow.'

Though such an attitude may evoke visions of India's sacred cows, the comparison would be entirely invalid. To the pious Hindu the cow symbolizes all living creatures, especially sanctified motherhood. Thus, an act of violence against a cow is a direct affront to God. The milk can be used, principally in the form of the watery butter called *ghee*, but the meat must never be eaten, even when the animal has died of natural causes. To the pious Mututsi, on the other hand, cow is virtually the only meat which his religion *permits* him to eat. However, milk and butter, *amata* and *amavuta*, are used far more widely, since the Mututsi rarely slaughters his cattle. He too regards them as symbols, but scarcely as symbols of nature or God. To him the cows represent, above all, social status, sanctified money.

It would be more to the point to compare the Tutsi cow with the American car. Cattle provide the people of Ruanda-Urundi with just the same precisely graded system of mooing status symbols.

First are the *inyambo*, the royal cattle of the Mwami, some of which are entrusted to the keeping of the great Tutsi nobles. The *inyambo* are remarkable for the length and contour of their horns, their shapely forms, their docility and their dandified walk. These elite cows provide neither meat nor milk : their sole function is to be beautiful. Their coats are cleaned, brushed and rubbed with butter several times a day ; their tails are amputated and replaced by more decorative fibre panaches ; and their horns are shaped into perfect lyre-like forms by repeated massage with heated banana bark. They are the custom-made Rolls-Royces of Ruanda-Urundi.

The *bigarama*, or long-horned cows of the lesser Tutsi nobles, the *imirizo*, owned by Tutsi chiefs, the *inkuku*, the skinny, short-horned cattle of the bourgeois Batutsi, and finally the *inkungu*, or hornless cows, form a descending scale. All must be observed, approached and handled with extreme care. Everyone knows that if a cow sees her owner naked in his hut, he will certainly die unless he sells her at once to a stranger ; if a cow touches the ground with her horns when she lies down, her owner will lose all he possesses ; if a cow should uncover a human skull during her ramblings round the pasture, that cow and all her descendants will certainly die.

If cattle are to be protected from disease, sorcery and theft, it is forbidden to shave while cows are passing, burn wood on which a drop of milk has fallen, mine iron ore in a pasture, use a broom in the cattle enclosure or cut your hair in the kraal. On the other hand, it is wise to plant aloes and euphorbias at the entrance to the kraal, play on the flute at twilight (it will put a spell on cattle thieves), and let the nail grow very long on the little finger of your left hand (if you do this, you will have many cattle and they will never be stolen).

*   *   *

I spent a year at Ruyigi before I was transferred to a new post, Rutana, seventy miles to the southwest. At both posts I spent most of my spare time studying the people and their customs, trying to understand and even to enter their complicated social world. Then, unexpectedly, in January 1955, I jumped right into that world—feet first—when I married Ndagizye.

Like my initiation to the Masai, the Great Tutsi Affair took place as I started six months' leave. This time I was headed for northern Ruanda, where I planned to spend a month visiting the Virunga volcanoes, the Albert National Park, the Ituri Forest and the Ruwenzori massif—the famous Mountains of the Moon. Then I would drive east to Mombasa, travel by boat to Zanzibar and Madagascar, and fly from there to Ceylon, Bombay, Athens, Rome, Nice, Paris, Casablanca, Marrakesh, Brazzaville and Léopoldville. Back in Burundi, I would then start work at another new post, Bururi, twenty miles east of Lake Tanganyika.

At the beginning of this seventeen-thousand-mile trip, I drove to my parents' home in Kisenyi, which I intended to use as a base of operations. We had one of our typical sweet-and-sour reunions, including a picturesque three-cornered argument and a ceremonial dinner of *ragoût de mouton*, the family's favourite Belgian dish. Next day my father returned to his easel (behind a locked door), my mother consoled herself with her sewing machine and I set out on a short excursion to Ntereko Hill, near the old Catholic Mission of Nyundo, where I planned to hunt up some authentic Ruanda weapons for my collection.

Once at Ntereko Hill, I strolled lazily through the fields and banana groves, passing from one hut to the next as I chatted with the natives. Then, to my surprise, I ran into an old acquaintance from Ruhengeri, about thirty miles to the east. It was Ndagizye.

'*Mwaramutseho, Bwana Ale, mumeze mute?*' he said, with his customary suave smile. 'Good morning, Mr. Hallet. How are you?'

'I'm fine, my friend. What are you doing so far away from home?'

'Oh, I just came to see my father and my wife's uncle about some cattle. Those old men aren't easy to deal with, they want too much money! But at least they have some very good beer.'

'Beer? That sounds splendid. You know, Ndagizye, it's a very hot day . . .'

He took the hint. 'Why don't you come to my father's hut? Then you can try some of our beer and meet my family too.'

A moment later I entered one of the big hive-shaped huts where I met, in turn, Ndagizye's old father Mutukware, his wife's uncle, Munteregwa, and his young wife Maliya, a good-looking girl with a light brown complexion, dressed in a dark red pagne that emphasized her provocative bosom but failed to hide her typically broad Tutsi rear. 'She came with me to carry the bananas I brought to my father,' Ndagizye explained. 'When he gives me a present, she will carry it back home.'

While we men sat down on little round stools, Maliya served each of us a calabash of *inzoga*—native beer that was about 10 per cent alcohol—with a long sorghum straw. The conversation was slow at first, but as they put down more and more beer, the two old men became loquacious. It was a real treat to hear them; they knew every detail of the past complicated intrigues woven by the dominant Tutsi families of Astrida and Nyanza, and gloated over every act of murder, incest or political chicanery that had taken place at the Royal Court of the Mwami.

'It isn't the king who kills you, it's his court,' Munteregwa declared gravely at the end of a long and very bloody story.

'That is a powerful proverb,' Mutukware answered, 'but it isn't always true. Remember, "*Imbwa ntitinyirwa amenyo iti-nyirwa shebuja!*"—"Don't fear the teeth of the dogs but watch out for their master!"'

'I once saw something in Astrida which makes nonsense of that proverb!' Munteregwa said angrily. 'There were two men who had joined themselves in the *ubunyiwanyi* ritual. Later they quarrelled, and one of them complained to the Mwami—'

'What is the *ubunyiwanyi* ritual?' I interrupted.

'The pact of blood,' he explained, 'the marriage between two men. It unites them more closely than brothers or father and son or even husband and wife. It can only be performed by a secret ceremony between strangers, men of different clans.'

That was altogether too much for my insatiable curiosity about the complex character and customs of the Batutsi. Yet I knew that I had almost no chance to witness this strange ritual unless I became a participant. The idea was irresistible. 'Munteregwa,' I said suddenly, 'you've told me that the two men must be strangers. Well, can you find two bloods more different than Ndagizye's and mine? Can we make the pact between us?'

He stared at me completely dumbfounded. 'No Mututsi has ever joined himself to a white man in the blood marriage—'

'I will do it!' Ndagizye interrupted, with surprising eagerness. '*Bwana* and I have been good friends, but now I can be his *umugeni w'amaraso*. That means the "bride of blood",' he explained, turning to me.

'Are you really sure you want to marry my son?' asked old Mutukware. 'It is a very serious matter: a man can always get rid of his wife, but he can never divorce his *umugeni w'amaraso*.'

'Can you tell me all about it?'

He explained the general procedures; I listened, very attentively, and agreed. Then Munteregwa raised an objection. 'I don't see how we can do it. The ceremony must be conducted by the fathers of the two men. Mutukware is here for his son Ndagizye. Where is *your* father?'

'In Kisenyi.'

'Will he come here?'

I pictured my father, as I had last seen him. 'I don't think so,' I said quickly.

'Then you cannot get married.'

I was temporarily baffled but quickly put forward a new idea. 'Why don't you adopt me?' I asked the old Mututsi. 'If you do that, you can act as my father and give my hand in marriage.'

There was another moment's silence. Munteregwa obviously wasn't too enthusiastic about the prospect of acquiring an inquisitive ethnologist as an adopted son. Then Ndagizye gave him a long hard look, and the old man gave his consent. Immediately, Mutukware rushed to fetch another pot of *inzoga*. As with all Tutsi ceremonies, my adoption was to be formalized in beer. He dipped up a half-gourdful, inserted a fresh sorghum straw and presented it to me with both hands, holding it until I had sipped up a long draught, which I promptly spat out on to the ground. The two old men smiled their approval; I had remembered to make the appropriate Tutsi gesture: when you accept a libation of beer, you must first offer a taste to the thirsty household spirits by spitting on the ground.

After appeasing the spirits, I appeased myself. Then, making the same two-handed gesture, I offered the gourd of *inzoga* to my intended bride. He sipped happily and handed the beer over to his prospective father-in-law, Munteregwa. Munteregwa sipped and transferred the gourd to *my* prospective father-in-law, Mutukware. By this time only a drop of beer was left in

[*Photos Margrit Winzenried*

THE FIRST PYGMY SCHOOL, AT EBIKEBA

DRUMMING UP BUSINESS AT KISENYI

(*Top*) The Author's Central African Curio Shop.
(*Centre*) View from the shop door.
(*Below*) Three glimpses of the Tutsi drummer.

the bottom of the gourd. Mutukware peered at it sadly. Then he called his daughter-in-law Maliya, who had been sitting quietly in the shadows at the other side of the hut in accordance with the admirable Tutsi custom, which forbids women to interfere in the decisions of men. Maliya sipped daintily, and I watched with growing interest. I was entitled to: after all, I was her future husband-in-law.

After that round of ceremonial beers, Ndagizye and I were officially engaged. We celebrated our new status with a few non-ceremonial beers and decided to hold the ceremony next day. Then, a little tipsy and completely enthused about my impending wedding, I drove home to Kisenyi and told my father the whole story.

'Are you completely mad?' he exploded. 'Do you have any idea of what you're getting into?'

'It's perfectly all right. Mutukware explained all the details.'

'But why? Why in the world do you *want* to?'

'It's the only way I can investigate the *ubunyiwanyi* ritual. I'm determined to find out what's really involved.'

He threw his hands up in despair.

I returned to Ntereko Hill at noon the next day. I walked under the plaintain banana trees towards Mutukware's big hut. I paused in front of the *rugo* and loudly announced my presence, as Tutsi custom demands. The men of the family came out to greet me, ushered me inside and, inevitably, we began the long, complicated wedding ritual with a drink of beer.

For the next phase Ndagizye and I sat together on a ceremonial mat in a screened-off portion of the hut. Our fathers sat in front of us, and Munteregwa produced a little stiletto-like tool called a *kimwa*, with which he made a shallow incision in the skins of our abdomens, just a little to the right of the navel. Then, using the point of the *kimwa*, he placed several drops of Ndagizye's blood on my tongue and of my blood on the tongue of my bride. We both swallowed the blood immediately, washing it down with a big swig of sorghum beer.

This time we didn't spit, for that would have been a rejection of the *igihango*, the 'pact of blood'.

Munteregwa passed the *kimwa* slowly back and forth across the palm of his left hand while he recited the terms of the lengthy pact to Ndagizye. Then he handed the little stiletto over to Mutukware, and my future father-in-law made the same gesture while solemnly announcing the *igihango* to me:

'Ubp, amgraso ya Ndagizye ali mu mitsi yawe, ygbaye amgraso yawe rwose, ibygfite n'byawe, umugore wa Ndagizye abaye umugore wawe, incuti ze, abanzi be babaye abawe ugomba kumufasha muli byose, mu makuba no mu bukire, bitabaye bityo igihango kizakwica.'

'Now the blood of Ndagizye runs through your veins, it has become your own blood, all that he has belongs to you, the wife of Ndagizye has become your wife, his friends and his enemies have become your own, you must help him in all circumstances, in misfortune as well as in prosperity, otherwise the pact will kill you.'

Then he recited the various clauses, an involved oral contract, which committed Ndagizye and me to share our women, food and cattle; to join forces in time of famine, disease and danger, and to hide each other from the police. The eighth clause forbade us to steal each other's cattle, poison each other's children or burn down each other's huts. Each of the first eighteen clauses was followed by a warning to my bride and myself of what would happen if either of us broke the marriage contract: *'Igihango kizakwica!'*, 'May this pact kill you!'

When Mutukware recited the nineteenth and final clause, which he obviously considered the most important, his voice trembled with emotion as he intoned the Kinyarwanda words, *'Umushigisha inzoga uyifite, igihango kizakwica'*, 'If you have beer and do not share it, may this pact kill you!'

The old man then gave me the *kimwa* so that I might make my solemn vow. Passing the little stiletto over the palm of my left hand, I recited the ritual sentence Munteregwa had taught me, 'If I break my word, let me be killed by this pact of blood!'

Then I gave the stiletto to Ndagizye, who made the same gesture and pronounced the same ominous speech. We lay down together for a moment on the mat, embracing each other in a purely symbolic act of mystical marriage. Each of us repeated the words 'Here is what I give you before you leave the mat', and we exchanged gifts. Ndagizye presented me with a beautifully decorated basket that must have taken Maliya at least two months to weave. I gave him a note for five hundred Congolese francs, folded in two and tastefully wrapped in a banana-bark envelope.

Afterwards each of us took the *kimwa* and shaved a tuft of hair from his head as a sign that we would shave each other in future. Then we placed the blade on our foreheads to show that if either of us were wounded in the head we both would bleed. A final touch of the little stiletto to our toes was a promise that we would never fail to help each other remove jigger-fleas from under our toenails. Finally we both went outside into the *rugo* for the ritual fight, the final phase of the wedding ceremony.[1] We struggled together in a sweaty bear-hug, repeating the traditional sentence, 'If we argue with each other, we shall make friends again very soon.' Then I lifted Ndagizye on to my back and walked in a little circle reciting, 'On the day you are ill, I will carry you to the hospital.' That day was nearly with us. When Ndagizye lifted me on to his back, he staggered and nearly fell. At 6 ft. 3 in. he was only two inches shorter than I, but he had the typical skinny Mututsi physique and weighed only ten stone, compared with my seventeen. He tottered round the *rugo* for a moment, gasping his vow, and set me down with obvious relief. Then we finished the beer, and rather tipsily pressed our abdomens together in the ritual salute of blood spouses, once again promising our eternal devotion.

Thus, I married Ndagizye, a young Mututsi of northwest Ruanda, in an irrevocable ceremony of blood, uniting my fortunes with his for the span of both our lifetimes, sworn never to betray or forget him lest I be punished with poverty, sterility, death or the loathsome *amahumana* skin disease.

*   *   *

The honeymoon was soon over. Within a month I discovered that I was a misguided idealist and Ndagizye a calculating gold-digger. Every time I returned to Kisenyi from an expedition, I found him waiting on my doorstep with an eloquent demand for money. My Tutsi bride relieved me of two thousand francs in three weeks. Then came the climax.

I had just brought back from Ruwenzori an interesting collection of specimen plants, and was intending to spend a lazy day

[1] Rwanda wedding ceremonies for the more conventional type of marriage, between a man and a woman, are also climaxed by a ritual fight. This presents the bridegroom with a unique and slippery challenge, since the bride is thickly smeared from head to foot with rancid butter. The groom applies all his strength and agility to trying to consummate the marriage, while the bride attempts to throw him out of bed. She rarely succeeds, especially since the man often cheats by putting sand on the palms of his hands. When he finally manages to seize, subdue and possess her, he shouts at the top of his voice '*Mulampe impundu, Ndarongoye!*' 'Rejoice, I have got her!' Should he omit this ritual cry, his marriage would not be valid.

around the *baraza* before leaving on the long drive to Mombasa on the east coast. I wasn't expecting marital difficulties, since Ndagizye had gone back to Ruhengeri during my absence. But the native grapevine is wonderfully efficient and once again my blood-bride turned up on my doorstep with a suavely expectant smile, having hitch-hiked the thirty miles from Ruhengeri.

'My *impfizi* has just died!' he announced dramatically.

'Your bull? That is a terrible thing. You have my sympathy.'

'It is important for your good luck that the bull be replaced at once.'

'*My* good luck? Why?'

'Otherwise my cows will calve no longer. My herd will dwindle and your own fortune will wane. Our destinies are united, like our blood.'

Ndagizye stared at me with arrogant confidence. I had given him my word, and he knew he had me in a corner.

'A bull's quite expensive—' I began.

'I know. That is why I have brought you a beautiful present in return. You will love it!'

'Where is it?'

'I grew tired carrying it. So I left it on Muranzi Hill, at the bull dealer's.'

Since Muranzi Hill is situated far to the south of Kisenyi, and Ndagizye's home lay to the east, there was a certain lack of logic in his explanation. I told him that I would be short of cash until I sold my truck in Mombasa.

'Remember the *igihango*! If you don't help me in my time of trouble, the pact will kill you! That would make me very sad.'

It was forty miles to Muranzi Hill along a bad road, and though the drive must have taken an hour and a half, Ndagizye never stopped talking all the way—about bulls. 'To the Batutsi,' he explained, 'the bull is the same thing as the king. When a new Mwami takes over the Royal Drum, a special bull must be chosen as his sign. This animal, Rusanga, cannot be black, red or chestnut. He must have a big chest, a noble bearing and horns shaped like the crescent moon. The end of his tail must be intact. When the Mwami dies, his body is wrapped in the hide of Rusanga. Then, as the flesh of the king is made eternal by the slow fires, the meat of the Royal Bull is burned beside him. Only thus can the king be born again in his proper flesh, as a leopard. If the Royal Bull should sicken or weaken with age, he must be killed. Then his body is burned on a great fire. When the ashes are buried, *umutabataba* trees [*ficus elastica*] must be planted so that none will forget the spot where he lies. The next day a new Royal Bull is chosen.'

I nodded, remembering that in Urundi, too, the body of the Mwami was mummified, to be reincarnated, however, as a lion. Moreover, Urundi was blessed with not one but two Royal Bulls: Mukabura, 'The Leader', and Semasaka, 'The Father of Sorghum'. Mukabura had a harem of thirty cows for his pleasure; Semasaka had only seven, but he was compensated by the attentions of a human vestal virgin, the Mukakaryenda.

Ndagizye went on to examine the question of the *impfizi*, or ordinary' bulls, which usually gave their owners much trouble. If two bulls fight at a watering place, one may fall in. That is a very good sign; the owner of the watering hole will never lose his land. But if one of the bulls is killed during the fight, he must be buried on the spot where he falls. Then the landowner must hire a *musizi*, a troubadour, to compose a special poem for the burial of the bull. Unless he does this, he will lose everything he owns!'

Incredibly, there was an entire school of poetry in Rwanda devoted to the praise of cattle. Some of these compositions, known as *umuzinge*, had over four hundred verses; a special poem was always composed for the *indatwa*, 'the prettiest cow in the herd'.

'If a bull attacks his owner, the animal must be slain with a spear, or else the man will die. But if a bull attacks the *wife* of his owner, the bull must not be killed. Instead, the woman must leave her husband's house at once. The marriage is over! If a bull lies down in his own dung, you must never force him to move. If you do, your land will dwindle away. If a bull stares at his owner while the man is making water, one of that man's children will die!'

Ndagizye went on, and on. All that tradition and poetry eventually cost me 3,800 Congolese francs when Ndagizye chose his bull, a placid brown animal about five years old. Afterwards, with a grandiose gesture, he produced my gift. It was an *ingabo*, a brand-new, brightly painted shield, worth about a hundred Congolese francs. 'Isn't it beautiful?' he said, with a charming smile. 'I was sure that you'd like it.'

Words were useless. I forced myself to smile back, and left my blood-bride standing proudly beside his new bull, ready for the long trek home. That evening, in Kisenyi, I told my father the whole story. He enjoyed it immensely. 'If you'll stop looking for

Masai brothers and Tutsi brides,' he said sarcastically, 'you might find out that your own family have a few good qualities.'

'But it's the only way to *know* the Africans,' I insisted.

'You'll get to know them too well, Jean-Pierre. Ndagizye is a Mututsi of the old breed. He'll take the shirt off your back if he can.'

I laughed at this absurd prophecy, but as things turned out it was little more than three years until Ndagizye exactly fulfilled it

9

A Chimp in the Garden of Eden

Urazinduka ntutanga rwuba—'You may get up before dawn, but destiny gets up before you.'

KIRUNDI PROVERB

DURING the scorching Burundi summer of 1955, I had many new people and events to divert me. Two were of lasting significance. I built my own green 'Garden of Eden', and for the first time explored the understanding and emotions of a 'wild animal'—an activity which was to become a major part of my life.

The idea of making my own Eden—a carefully balanced sanctuary of tropical African plants and animals—had gradually developed in my mind during the previous seven years. On my recent ascent of the Ruwenzori Mountains, my imagination had caught fire when I saw the unearthly, moss-draped forests of dragon-trees, bamboo and fern-pines, and the giant tree heathers, Senecios and Lobelias. Their prolific beauty came back to me each time I looked at a certain hill behind the Bururi post: its steep and dusty slopes were burned clean and deeply gullied by erosion.

There were many difficulties, especially since the nearest sizeable spring located high enough to water the upper part of my proposed garden was three miles away. I would have to survey the terrain, build a small dam, and excavate an irrigation ditch two feet deep and three miles long. In the garden itself, enormous holes would have to be dug, to let the water spread into a series of pools, streams and small waterfalls. Only then would it be possible to start planting on a grand scale and, gradually, to introduce animals.

157

It took me two days to survey the land and another three for a crew of forty-five convicts from Bururi prison to dig the three-mile trench and excavate thirteen large pools. The following week we made at least thirty expeditions to a fine gallery forest five miles away to collect ferns, shrubs, and trees (some of them thirty feet tall), as well as enough leaf mould and topsoil to cover the entire surface of the garden. Fertilizer was still lacking, so I told the pastoral population of Bururi I would pay ten francs a basket for all the cattle, sheep or goat dung they could bring me the following Saturday morning. When the time came I found more than two hundred natives waiting for me, from withered grandmothers down to naked little children; all clutched baskets of assorted sizes but similar smells. The noisy, spirited session occupied the rest of the day and soon passed into local history as '*Soko y'amase ya Bwana Ale*'—'Monsieur Hallet's S— Market'.

By evening I had three tons of excellent fertilizer at my disposal. The convicts spread it evenly throughout the garden, with almost immediate results. The dung drew flies and the flies, plus some scattered grains of corn and rice, attracted birds: orioles, wagtails, ibis, red Bengali finches, quail, and even a solitary strutting *umusambi*, an elegant crested crane. Lizards and snakes followed, including handsome green banana snakes and a militant horned viper. Then the first mammals put in a fleeting appearance: rabbits and *impongo*, the bushbuck antelope.

I stocked the ponds with frogs, toads and turtles, and offered to purchase any small animals the natives of Bururi might succeed in catching. The net result was only three turtles, two porcupines, and one small monkey. Then, in mid-October, I had a great surprise. A tall Hutu *évolué* pulled up in a three-ton coffee truck and announced he had a *sokomutu* for sale. In Swahili that means, literally, 'man of the market-place', the name which the chimpanzee has earned because of his shrewd, garrulous nature. I expected to see a small, immature animal. Instead, in the back of the truck, there was an enormous, full-grown male chimp, trussed up in a squatting position inside the folds of a heavy hunting net. It was difficult in the circumstances to tell his exact size, but he must have been about 4 ft. 6 in. tall and probably weighed about 11 stone.

Obviously I could not turn such a powerful animal loose in my garden. Regretfully, I decided to refuse the offer, though the price of three hundred fancs was extremely low. Then I noticed, through the endless folds of netting, that the chimp had a suppurating wound on his right wrist. 'How did that happen?' I asked the driver.

'Some natives caught him in the bush near Rumonge three days ago. They were hunting for antelope, and saw a band of *sokomutu* fooling around in the trees. A branch cracked and this one fell, you can see how heavy he is; the fall knocked him out and they wrapped him up in the net. Then, while they were carrying him home, he woke up, stuck his hand through the mesh, and caught one of the men by the arm. The native hit him on the wrist with a machete to make him let go.'

'That wound is badly infected. It may kill him.'

'Why else do you think I'm asking only three hundred francs? If he dies, you won't lose much, but if he gets better, you'll have made a really smart deal.'

That shrewd remark annoyed me, but I didn't bother to argue. The situation was clear: unless I intervened, the chimp would probably die a slow, agonizing death while his owner drove from place to place, trying to sell him.

The money changed hands, the *évolué* smiled knowingly, and, with the help of my new 'boy', André, I unloaded the heavy bundle of netting from the back of the truck. We carried it to the garage and set it down in a corner. Then I sent André back to his work in the kitchen, locked the door from the inside, and picked up a sharp knife.

The chimp was considerably smaller than I, but much stronger. Even with one disabled hand, he was quite capable of breaking most of my bones. Yet he was certainly intelligent, following my every move with his big, weary-looking brown eyes. Now I decided to bank on that obvious intelligence— equivalent to that of a three-year-old human child—and cut him free from the confining net.

I squatted down next to him, trying to explain by my gestures and calm way of speaking that my intentions were completely friendly. I talked to him for about ten minutes, showing him the net and the knife; as I spoke I realized that I had to give the big chimp a name. I decided to call him Joseph, per- haps because it suggested the proverbially good-natured Belgian peasant.

Joseph listened attentively. He looked at me with pleading eyes and strained at the tight folds of the net. Then he hooted with astonishment when I gave him a little pat on the head and a big kiss on the nose. Apparently he was unaccustomed to the Gallic temperament.

The first part of his body I freed was the right hand. I examined it closely and found that the injury was even more serious than I had thought. The wound smelled very bad, almost gangrenous; the fingers were stiff and swollen. Joseph winced with pain as I touched the hand, but he showed neither anger nor alarm. That encouraged me to go on, so I freed his legs, watching him carefully. He didn't make a move. Then, starting at his hips and working towards the top, I cut through the many layers which were wound round his body. He remained very quiet, even when I cut the ropes which imprisoned his arms in the last folds of netting. That was where the real danger lay: like most animals, chimpanzees practically never bite before they catch hold of their prey.

Now the net lay in a circle at Joseph's feet. Although he was completely free, he remained motionless for several minutes. Finally, pushing his big lips forward as far as they would go, he saluted me with a rising crescendo of hoots, climaxed by a suave, diplomatic smile. I hooted back at him, with a matching smile of my own. He stared at me intently. Then, still in a squatting position, he moved towards me slowly, with a drawn, melancholy expression on his face. He raised his right hand, peered at it, and gestured at the wound. I extended my own right hand and, very carefully, he rested his swollen fingers in my palm, letting out a little grunt that sounded like a long-drawn-out *oooooh*.

I must have held the hand for five minutes, examining it from every angle while I tried to determine the exact extent of the wound and the infection. Joseph watched very closely, shifting his gaze with mine while he hooted a soft running commentary. His understanding and confidence were complete, until I tried to leave the garage to fetch my medical kit from the house. Then the big chimp shrieked like an abandoned baby and leaped for the closing door. I tried to force it shut behind me, until I saw his injured hand jutting out through the crack. I opened the door a little wider to free it, Joseph gave a terrific shove, I was catapulted backwards, and he shot out of the garage. He stopped about two hundred feet away and sat down, screaming hysterically. I went after him, but the moment I came within reach, he jumped up and retreated. This happened several times, and then, almost before I knew it, the chimp and I were at large in the 'Garden of Eden'.

Joseph sat down on a big rock peering anxiously from side to side, as though he was trying to find something. I walked towards him slowly, expecting another retreat, but to my surprise, he let me close the gap and take him by the left hand. I squeezed it tightly in my own, trying to give him the illusion of my superior strength and authority. Then I pulled him up by the hand and we walked out of Eden together.

Back in the garage, I led Joseph to one of the corners and sat down opposite him. After a moment, he sat down himself and watched me quietly. 'Stay here!' I said loudly, holding one finger up in front of his nose. He seemed to be impressed by the gesture, but as soon as I got up to leave he tried to follow. I pushed him back and we both sat down again . . . and again . . . and again . . . for more than hour. Then, finally, he capitulated and decided to stay in the corner. I left in a hurry, padlocking the door from the outside. I heard Joseph start to cry piteously, but tried not to listen.

I went to the Territorial Office to hunt up the Sector Veterinarian. I found that he wasn't expected in Bururi until next day, so left an urgent message and returned to my house for some elementary medical supplies: gauze bandage, hydrogen peroxide, alcohol ether, a bowl of water, and some antibiotic powder. I knew how serious Joseph's condition was, and the danger of waiting even a day without taking action.

When I returned to the garage, the chimp was waiting near the door. This time he made no attempt to escape, but scrambled into the corner and sat down, anxious to please me. He remained quiet and entirely submissive, even when I put the bowl underneath his hand and started to wash the wound. Towards the end, when I probed at the deepest parts of the infection, he pulled the hand away. I didn't try to stop him, knowing how terribly painful the entire procedure had been. Joseph inspected the wrist, holding it very close to his eyes while he turned it slowly from side to side, and then put his hand back in mine with a gesture of complete confidence.

When the wound was clean, I covered the entire area with sulfa powder and wrapped the wrist in about twenty feet of bandage, hoping that at least four or five feet would remain in place. Then I left, and there were no pitiful cries. That seemed suspicious. I went back: Joseph, of course, was fingering and biting his bandage, trying to tear it off. I pulled his good hand away. He ignored me and went straight back to it. I pulled the hand away again, and he persisted. I spoke to him harshly and gave him a little tap on the cheek. That made him cry, but he left the bandage alone.

Later that evening, when I brought him some food, the gauze was still on his wrist, but it was red with blood. After he had nibbled lackadaisically on several biscuits and a banana, I changed the dressing. Again he was quiet and showed no sign of fear or resentment. Then, when I tried to leave, the chimp surprised me with some entirely new tactics; he followed, seized my hand, and pulled me into his customary corner. I sat down obediently, curious to discover his intentions. He sat down next to me, leaning heavily against my side, and grunted with satisfaction.

Nothing happened for a long while, and I started to doze. I woke up with a jerk as something tickled my chin. It was Joseph. Quietly, very carefully, he was examining the topography of my face with his fingers. I peered at him through half-closed eyelids while he checked all of the various bumps and holes. He pulled my lips out one at a time to inspect my teeth, and tried to force one of his thick fingers into my nose. I snorted loudly, and he transferred his attention to my hair. He played with it for a while until he became sleepy and his head nodded towards my shoulder. Then he put his big left hand in my lap and held it there, open and expectant, until I clasped it in my own. We slept together in that position until morning.

The next day I took care of some routine business while I waited anxiously for Dr. Stack, the Sector Veterinarian, to arrive in Bururi. When he finally showed up, around three in the afternoon, I explained the urgency of the situation and asked him to treat Joseph.

'A full-grown male chimp? A wild ape?' he said incredulously. 'Don't you know how vicious those beasts are? He'd try to kill me the moment I touched him!'

'I've already washed and bandaged his hand. He was perfectly quiet.'

'It's too dangerous. I won't have anything to do with it.' The vet turned and hurried back into the Territorial Office.

I followed. 'The animal needs help,' I insisted, 'and you're a vet; it's your job to help animals.'

'Cattle, sheep, swine and goats,' he snapped. 'That's what I get paid for. Not apes.'

'Won't you at least take a look at him? I'll administer the treatment myself, whatever you suggest.'

'No. It's out of the question.'

It was not until noon the following day that he finally agreed to examine Joseph. The argument nearly began all over again when the vet looked in at the garage window. 'That animal is almost as big as a gorilla!' he said. 'If you think I'm mad enough to step into the same room with a monster like that—'

'Watch. Keep looking through the window. You'll see how gentle he is.'

I went inside and handled the huge chimp, making him sit and stand, and even putting my hand between his teeth. That demonstration soothed the vet's worst fears but he was still extremely wary: he insisted that I keep my own body between himself and his patient at all times. Joseph sensed the man's apprehension and it made him nervous; still, he trusted me and submitted to the awkward examination.

'Wet gangrene,' the vet said immediately. 'There's only one way to save the animal. That hand will have to be amputated, two or three inches above the wrist.'

'No, that's not possible—'

'You asked for my professional advice. You practically forced me to give it. Now you have it, and it's *your* decision. If you can give him enough anaesthetic to put him under, I'll perform the operation myself, even though it isn't my job. But for God's sake, Monsieur Hallet, let's get out of here before this animal runs amok! If you have to think about it, you can do your thinking outside.'

I did, and I found the idea appalling. I pictured that large, gentle animal with an abbreviated stump instead of a right hand. His physical beauty and balance would be destroyed; he would spend the rest of his life in pathetic confusion. No other creature on earth would feel the loss of a hand so keenly, except, perhaps, a man. 'It's intolerable,' I said finally, 'even if it has to be done.'

'You're too sentimental, Monsieur Hallet, like an old lady with a sick Pekingese.'

'I'm concerned about the animal's future. What kind of life can he have, here or anywhere else?'

'Why don't you give him to the IRSAC Research Institute at Katana? They'll be happy to get him. They'll perform the operation, and take good care of him afterwards. I'm sure that if you can transport him to IRSAC's branch in Astrida, they'll rush him to Katana right away.'

'That sounds like the only solution, but still, I don't like it.'

*   *   *

An hour later, after I had injected Joseph with a massive dose of penicillin, the chimp and I were *en route* to Astrida, more than two hundred miles away. Frightened at first by the sight of my new Studebaker truck, once I persuaded him to enter the cab he gave very little trouble. He didn't like the rope I'd put around his waist to eliminate the possibility of escape, and fussed with it apathetically. Otherwise, he was very quiet as he sat beside me. His fever was mounting, in spite of the antibiotics.

When we reached the IRSAC station several hours later, the loitering natives panicked. '*Sokomutu! Sokomutu!*' they screamed as they fled into the building. Then three or four white men came out very hesitantly, and watched as I eased the big chimp out of the cab and walked towards them with his left hand in my right and the rope in my other hand. They were reluctant, but after a long conversation, one of the men finally took over the rope. A moment later, I said good-bye to Joseph, my calm, intelligent friend of two days' duration whom the rest of the world hated or feared as a 'wild' animal.

Instinctively I extended my left hand, he stretched out his own, and the two of us—ape and man—shook hands together like brothers. In less than a week, I myself was to meet the same destiny from which I had tried to rescue Joseph.

10

'Route Fière': The Road of Challenge

> *Quod facere ausa mea est, non audet scribere, dextra*
> —'What my right hand has dared to do, it does not
> dare to write.'
>
> OVID, 'HEROIDES', ELEG. XII

AT Burundi's administrative headquarters in Kitega, on my
way back from Astrida next morning, I learned that severe,
unrelieved famine had broken out in the Mosso and had already
taken an unknown number of lives.

What was 'the Mosso'? Imagine a scorched parallelogram a
hundred miles long and twenty miles wide formed by the rolling
hills and ramified valleys of the Malagarasi River, in the extreme
southeastern end of Burundi. Populate its lightly timbered
savannahs and thickets of false bamboo with antelope, wart-
hog and bands of insolent baboons; add lions, leopards, wild
dogs, civets, genets, servals—and a few men.

In the past, the population had been far more dense. Then, as
in much of tropical Africa, the tsetse flies had come, carrying
trypanosomiasis—sleeping sickness. The people withered and
died in vast numbers; their cattle, succumbing to nagana, the
bovine form of the disease, died with them. When the Belgians
took over they launched a systematic programme to stamp out
trypanosomiasis, and their efforts were remarkably successful
in spite of periodic reinfection from neighbouring Tanganyika,
where sleeping sickness was endemic. Now virtually no cows but
a few thousand people remained in the Mosso, sturdy pygmoids,
averaging five feet tall who tried to eke out a living on the worst
farming land in Ruanda-Urundi.

Most of the time they succeeded. But now there appeared to

165

be serious trouble in the *Chefferie* of South Mosso. Officials here at Kitega had taken immediate action, wiring the Government's Nioka depot, four hundred miles away, for emergency rations. But Nioka's big warehouses were almost empty, depleted by other famine-stricken areas, so Kitega's urgent request for fifteen tons of beans had gone to the bottom of a long waiting-list, with an estimated delay of two to three weeks.

I had got to know the Bamosso people during my service at Ruyigi and Rutana and could not stand by and shrug philosophically while they starved to death. So, instead of stopping at Bururi, I went to see for myself how bad the situation actually was. Within a couple of hours, still only on the fringe of the South Mosso, I had seen enough to convince me. The hills had seemed as I came along to be completely deserted, but as I walked from one *itongo* to the next, I found emaciated old men and women sitting in their huts quietly waiting to die. I gave them what food I had with me, tinned beef and biscuits, which they devoured like predatory skeletons.

'Where are the rest of your people?' I asked.

'Three died. Two women and a little boy. Then the others left for the bush to make a camp there and look for game. But the animals have been starving just as we have. Their water-holes have turned into dust, and they too have gone away. Even if the people find any game, they are too weak for real hunting. They will die, just as I will.'

'How did this happen?'

'Our dry season usually lasts through the two moons of *Mwandagaro* and *Nyakanga* [July and August]. This year we didn't even get rain in *Rwirabura* [June]. That is when we most need it to ripen our beans, corn, eleusine and sorghum. So most of our crops burned up.'

'What about your manioc and sweet potatoes? The drought couldn't have killed them.'

'We hoped to eat them, *Bwana*, to live on them until the rains came. But the wild animals raided our crops! Warthogs rooted up the potatoes and antelope ate the manioc leaves. When nothing was left, the animals went away. Then we really began to starve! Most of us ate our seed, but a few men managed to hold out. They planted their seed when *Gituguto* [September] came, hoping that rain would fall. Three days later, we had a little sprinkle, and the seeds sprouted. Then there was no more rain for two weeks. The little green things burned up and died. After that, we knew that we would die too.'

I was appalled by the old man's passive fatalism. 'Why didn't you send a message?' I asked. 'If you had, help would have come long before now.'

'I can't write. And I'm too old to walk.'

'Surely some of your people can write. Why didn't *they* send word?'

'I had three sons,' he said bitterly, 'who all went to school. *They* learned how to read and write and never again went hunting or picked up a hoe. It made them ashamed. When I tried to make them work, they called me a stupid old *mushenzi*, a bush native! Then they ran away to get jobs with the white men. I never saw them again. That is what happens whenever people become educated: they go away and never come back to the Mosso.'

The old man wasn't entirely right. Later that day, in the trading-centre of Butana, I found several educated natives, *évolués* in white shirts and long trousers, who had made a long, difficult trip to the Mosso, with sacks of beans strapped to their bicycles which they were now hawking at fifty francs a kilo, ten times the normal price. The few Bamosso who had any money were buying; the others, with saliva shining at the corners of their mouths, simply watched the *évolués* dole out the red beans with tin measuring-cups. One, a tall half-breed Mututsi with patent-leather shoes and a red necktie, was not even bothering to fill the cup to the brim.

I walked up to him. 'I'm a government official—' I began.

'Where's your uniform? And your helmet?'

'I don't wear a uniform, but that's none of your business. I want to talk to you about those beans. You know very well you're asking ten times the maximum price permitted in native markets.'

'I brought those beans all the way from Rutana! I'm entitled to get as much as I can for them!'

'He's right! declared a short, stocky *évolue* with horn-rimmed glasses and a maroon hat, who looked very much like a Mumosso.

'Listen to me!' I shouted. 'All of you! You're going to sell those beans for five francs a kilo, or not at all!'

They stared at me. Then the tall Tutsi half-breed spat on the ground. 'You can't make me do that,' he said. 'I'm taking my beans back where they came from.' He closed his sack, shouldered it, and started to walk towards the waiting bicycles; his four colleagues followed suit.

I walked after them, angrily. 'Can't you see these people are starving?'

'That isn't our business,' he said, tying the heavy sack back on to the bicycle. 'Why do you think we paid good money for those beans, to give them away? We came here to make a profit!'

'Profit?' I kicked the sack contemptuously.

It burst; some thirty pounds of red beans showered to the ground. The watching Bamosso gasped and leaped forward, clawing at the precious food. The big Tutsi swore and pushed the frantic little people aside, trying to protect his merchandise. I grabbed him by his red necktie.

'They may as well pick up the beans,' I told him. 'You're not going to take a single one away with you.'

'I'll file a complaint!' he shrieked. 'They'll hear about this in Kitega!'

'I'm willing to pay for your lousy beans.'

He stopped ranting and stared at me avidly. 'My price?'

'The legal price. Not one franc more.'

'You're cheating me,' he said bitterly. Then, turning to the crowd, he appealed to their sympathies. 'Those *bazungu*!' he shouted. 'Those *white* men! They beat us! They steal from us! They think they can get away with anything they want, just because we are *black*!'

The plump shopkeepers of Butana nodded sympathetically, but the emaciated Bamosso hooted derisively.

'You can talk as much as you want,' I told the angry *évolués*, 'but you're still going to sell those beans at the legal price—all of you.'

They did. I paid the big Tutsi for his burst sack, and the Bamosso bought the rest. When the frustrated profiteers pedalled away, they were still complaining bitterly about 'white men's injustice'.

*   *   *

In Bururi that night I made an important decision. I had to get some high-protein food into the starving people of the South Mosso without wasting a minute, and I knew how to do it. Shooting was relatively slow and ineffective and obviously out of the question in an area denuded of game. There was only one logical source of food—fish—and only one rapid, grand-scale method of fishing. So I unlocked the territorial warehouse and loaded the Studebaker with axes, machetes, a fifty-foot roll of

Bickford fuse-cord, detonators, and a massive wooden box containing fifty hundred-gramme sticks of gelatine dynamite.

Dynamite fishing was, of course, prohibited by law throughout the Congo and Ruanda-Urundi, and I usually followed those conservationist principles. But now human lives were at stake, the fate of fish seemed trivial and the law altogether irrelevant. I left a note at the Territorial Office, explaining vaguely that I was going on safari to the south. Then I drove rapidly towards the great escarpment between Bururi and Nyanza-Lac, a little trading-centre near the southern border of Ruanda-Urundi, heading for Lake Tanganyika.

I was travelling in the right direction for fish. With a total of 233 species, including those of the surface, the depths, and the shore, Lake Tanganyika possesses the richest, most diversified collection of fresh-water fish in the world. At this moment I was particularly interested in just one of those species: *Stolothrissa tanganicae*, a herring-like fish about two or three inches long which the Arabs called *kashua'a*, the Barundi called *agahuza*, and the Congolese called *ndagala*. Exceptionally rich in protein, calcium and phosphates, the *ndagala* travel in dense shoals that make them ideal prey for the dynamite fishermen.

The natives also fished for *ndagala*, but using an entirely different method. On moonless nights they paddled out in their dug-out canoes known as *mashua*, armed with fifteen-foot torches of false bamboo, and big mallets, with which they beat on the hulls. Lured by the unusual sights and sounds, the fish came to investigate, only to be scooped up by the hundreds in the fishermen's landing-nets.

I had several times witnessed that operation near Mwekarago Cove, about twelve miles south of Nyanza-Lac, near the Tanganyika border. Here there had been an incredible profusion of the silvery herring-like fish—and an impressive number of crocodiles, which sometimes bothered the native night fishermen, snapping voraciously at the nets. Secluded Mwekarago Cove, with its vast schools of *ndagala*, was the logical scene of operations for my clandestine 'Fish Safari'.

I settled down for the night in the *gîte d'étape*. Very early next morning I hired four pirogues and six native fishermen in a little village about ten miles to the south. The men were members of the Bagoma tribe who had emigrated originally from the northeast part of Katanga on the other side of the lake. We left the boats at the village and I drove the six of them two miles farther down the wretched little dirt road—that had once led to Kigoma across the Tanganyika border—to where an old trail branched off west through the bush.

The trail was so heavily overgrown that I had to send my six helpers ahead with axes and machetes to cut back the bush. Slowly, as they slashed a passage for us, the Studebaker and I crawled towards Lake Tanganyika; after carving a green tunnel for about three miles, we came to a dead stop. The trail petered out in a dense grove of trees, and we could not force our home-made highway any farther towards the lake; it would have been a major project to carve out space in which to turn the truck round. We hacked our way another mile along a small footpath and reached the beach of Mwekarago Cove, a curved expanse of white sand overgrown with creeping lianas. We inspected the fishing-site briefly, returned to the truck, drove in reverse for three miles and then headed for the Bagoma village.

When we arrived I sent the fishermen to their boats, with instructions to leave at once for the cove, and negotiated with the chief to hire a number of porters. Within a few minutes the back of my truck was packed with most of the young adults in the village—fifteen muscular men and women armed with tightly-woven baskets; each would hold about forty pounds of *ndagala*—and I headed for the trail. By the time I led the long caravan of porters on to the beach, the fishermen had already arrived.

The crowd of natives watched from a respectful distance as I prepared my charges. First I taped two parallel sticks of dynamite together, spiralling the tape up and down the length of the sticks to augment the force of the blast. That operation finished, I attached a detonator to a one-foot length of Bickford fuse-cord and crimped the hollow end on to the cord with my teeth. After peeling back the heavy waxed paper at the end of one stick, I took an old pencil, poked a little tunnel in the gelatinous explosive, and dropped the detonator into position, pressed the sticky gelatine around the fuse-cord, pushed the paper back into place and taped the joint securely.

After preparing four of these double-charges from eight sticks of dynamite, I packed them into a waterproof metal case, stowed it in the largest pirogue and paddled away from the shore; my six helpers followed in the three remaining boats. We moved slowly through the water, watching closely for shadows beneath the surface that might reveal large schools of fish. About two hundred feet offshore I decided to drop the first charge.

The fishermen grouped their three pirogues in a rough triangle around mine, about a hundred feet away. Holding the two sticks of dynamite in my right hand, I fired the fuse with a cigarette-lighter in my left, waited about three seconds to make sure the fuse had caught and tossed the charge into the water about twenty feet away. It sank slowly and exploded with a muffled boom at a depth of some fifteen feet.

A few seconds later a cloud of stunned, silvery fish floated to the surface, and the six helpers started to scoop them up in their nets, turning frequently to stare at some crocodiles lurking in the background. Several of the big reptiles had tried to invade our fishing circle, only to make an abrupt U-turn when the dynamite exploded. Now, on the fringes of the circle, the baby crocodiles were starting a spirited gymkhana with the fish while the adults watched condescendingly. Simultaneously, half a dozen big white pelicans dived at the surface of the water, greedily snatching at the *ndagala*. One young crocodile lunged repeatedly at the confident birds, but was much too slow and awkward to catch them.[1]

After a second blast, and with about twelve hundred pounds of fish in the three collecting pirogues, we paddled to shore and unloaded. An hour later I dropped two more charges, we collected another thousand pounds of fish and by early evening the truck had been loaded well beyond capacity with a ton and a quarter of life-giving *ndagala*. I paid the porters, warned them to be ready for work at 5.30 next morning, chose two to come with me as helpers and sent the rest back on foot.

[1] Older crocodiles are scarcely more efficient, for these animals are handicapped by anatomical peculiarities which severely limit the seizing ability of their ferocious-looking jaws and make real mastication impossible. The rib-like processes of their cervical vertebrae prevent them from turning their heads to the side; their tongues are fastened completely to the bottom part of their mouths and are virtually useless for manipulating food; their lower jaws are immobile, and although powerful muscles enable them to close their upper jaws with tremendous force, the muscles that *open* the mouth are so weak that a crocodile can be muzzled with a piece of twine. For these reasons, the crocodile is primarily a scavenger and not, as he is so often represented, a predator. Crocodiles certainly engulf and digest an appalling number of African natives every year; but in almost every case human carelessness is involved, usually because someone fell asleep near the water's edge. After the unwary native has been tucked away to putrefy in the crocodile's underwater larder, many sermons are preached about the animal's rapacity. One might as well denounce a train for running over a man lying down on the permanent way.

I shall never forget the expression on the faces of those emaciated people when the truck reached Butana. Their mouths fell open, they took a few steps forward and stared with wondering eyes at the silver-glinting *ndagala* heaped high in the truck. Then the mouths tightened, the eyes dropped, and they started to turn away.

'What's the matter?' I called out in Kirundi.

My answer came from Munduve, the *évolué* clerk in charge of the market. 'They have no money to buy your fish.'

'You think I want to *sell* the fish? And *they* think so?'

'Of course. Isn't that why you chased the men with the beans? So that people would have to buy from you?'

For a moment I was speechless, then with great self-control I answered, 'I don't want to sell them, Munduve. I've brought these fish from the great lake to *give* them to the Bamosso.'

'Give them?' he repeated, apparently shocked. 'That isn't good business, *Bwana*.'

I lost patience completely. 'Free fish!' I shouted. 'Free fish for the Bamosso!'

The natives stared without comprehension.

'Spread the word to all of the *itongo*!' I urged them. 'Tell the people that the head of every family who comes here with his identification book will receive five kilos of fish. But make sure they understand that they must have the books, and tell them to bring baskets. Go quickly, and you'll all be able to eat dinner tonight.'

Suddenly, explosively, the long-delayed reaction came. '*Agahuza!*' the starving men shouted—'Fish!' '*Agahuza!*' they screamed, running in every direction. '*Agahuza! Agahuza!*'

In almost any other part of Ruanda-Urundi my announcement would have met with an entirely different reception, for the majority of the Batutsi, and even some Bahutu, would prefer death to eating fish. Fortunately, the people of the Mosso were, like the Batwa, free of those troublesome taboos. Within moments the big drums boomed an insistent call that would bring messengers from the surrounding hills to find out what was going on in Butana. In the Congo, among tribes like the Lokele, Bambole and many others, drum-language could have told the whole story; but here the *ingoma* served as a siren rather than a bush-telephone.

I stationed two helpers on top of the truck, right in the midst of the precious *ndagala*, each equipped with a five-kilo aluminium pot, under orders to distribute a measured quantity of fish only to those natives who had previously submitted their ID books to the market clerk's scrutiny. This was a very necessary precaution, since otherwise several members of each family would undoubtedly try to claim the five-kilo ration; some might get away with twenty-five kilos of fish while others, arriving late, would receive none. Trouble, perhaps even rioting, would surely follow.

Munduve, the market clerk, took his new job quite seriously and settled down at a table complete with rubber stamp, pad, fountain pen and bottle of ink stoppered by a baby corncob, and a thirty-centimetre ruler—an impressive display, since his only function was to check the books, making certain that their bearers came from the famine area, and stamp each one with a large '5'. In the background, two husky *Chefferie* policemen in dark blue *kaniki* uniforms stood by to ensure an orderly distribution.

I turned down most of my first prospective customers, since they lived near the market-place and were obviously healthy. To them, the owners of small shops, the famine had meant real prosperity. They went off angrily, threatening to lodge complaints against me. Eventually the people started streaming in from the hills—wave after wave of gaunt little Bamosso, and a long line started to form behind Munduve's table.

Some presented him with books that looked more like lace than paper: the precious documents had been attacked by termites. When he received the first of those ravaged books, the pompous little clerk called out to me in disgust, '*Bwana*, do these people get fish?'

'They certainly do. Just stamp the paper instead of the holes.'

The long line of Bamosso started to move forward, only to halt again when the clerk's table became the centre of a furious argument. 'Look at this!' Munduve complained petulantly, pointing to a one-inch scrap of singed paper held by an angry young native. 'He says it's a book!'

'My hut burned down,' the man insisted. 'I lost all my things, even my book, but I found this piece in the ashes.'

'Stamp it!' I told Munduve.

A few minutes later one of the *polici* rushed up, dragging a skinny old man by the arm. 'I caught him trying to sell his fish. For two bottles of beer!'

'It's my fish!' shouted the old man. 'I'll do whatever I want with it—trade it, sell it or even throw it away!'

That was too much. '*Inyana y'imbgwa!*' I roared in Kirundi, 'You son of a bitch! You have a family waiting to eat that fish! What will happen to them if you sell it for beer? What will happen to you?'

'He insulted me!' the old man shrieked. 'He called me a son of a bitch! All the *bazungu* are like that. They hate us and try to keep us down!'

The policeman was going to clout the insolent Mumosso on the side of the head, but I caught the blue-clad arm. 'Let him go,' I said disgustedly, and the aggrieved victim of paternalist injustice hurried off, fuming, his basket of *ndagala* still balanced on his head. That particular ration of fish, I feel sure, was converted into beer the moment he got out of sight.

*   *   *

Despite such small incidents, the first three days of the great Fish Safari were an unqualified success. After the initial distribution in Butana, I managed to improve the organization to the point where we could make two trips a day with morning and afternoon blasting sessions at Mwekarago Cove. By the afternoon of the fourth day, 24 October 1955, we had brought more than seven tons of fish to a thousand starving families in the *Chefferie* of South Mosso, and the famine was conquered.

Only six sticks of the original fifty of dynamite remained. I decided to use them that afternoon, and bring the great Fish Safari to a quiet, successful end. After the late morning distribution in the Mosso I drove west towards Lake Tanganyika, stopping briefly at Nyanza-Lac to take on petrol. Judging from the position of the sun, it must have been a little before three o'clock when I stood up in my pirogue, about three hundred feet offshore at Mwekarago Cove, ready to drop the last three charges.

I lit the first one and tossed it overboard. It sank slowly, but there was no explosion. Apparently the fuse was defective; this hadn't happened during any of the twenty-two previous drops. Now only four sticks were left, two double-charges. '*Nom de Dieu!*' I cursed to myself. 'The next one had better go off!'

I touched the flame of my lighter to the fuse and waited for the spark and the familiar crackling noise, but nothing happened. Two or three seconds passed while the little yellow flame licked at the fuse. Then, instead of a spark, there was a rapid abnormal *hiss-s-s-s-s*. Immediately, I started to toss the charge into the lake, but too late. The two sticks of dynamite exploded in my right hand.

There was a vast, shattering moment of mindless oblivion. Suddenly, inexplicably, I found myself dazed and gasping for breath while my feet instinctively trod water and my thoughts whirled in complete confusion. *What happened? I must have fallen out of the boat. But how could I? No, the dynamite must have exploded. But how could that be? I didn't hear anything, and I'm not hurt . . . I don't feel any pain . . . But why can't I see? . . . Why can't I see?*

Desperately, I tried to rub my eyes with the back of my right hand, but for some reason couldn't manage to do it. I tried again and felt something sharp rake over my eyebrows—something sharp, what the hell could it be? I ducked my head, hoping the water might restore my vision. The simple manœuvre worked, washing away the blood that had streamed down into my left eye. The right eye was apparently blind. Still, I felt immense relief being able to see at all. Then I remembered the trouble I had trying to rub my eyes—something sharp—and raised my right arm out of the water. It ended just above the wrist in two jagged bones and some tattered frills of skin.

I stared incomprehendingly at the mutilated stump. There was no blood, and the white, macerated flesh looked like the skin of a plucked chicken. Abruptly, I realized what I was looking at and grew savagely angry. *Merde!* I thought. *I've lost my hand!*

Now I began to feel pain, a terrible burning pain that raged over my face, neck, chest, arms and hands. My *hands*? The right one was still full of fire, though it no longer existed. In the left the pain was even more frightful—if I still had it. That thought really shocked me! I raised my left arm out of the water and the hand was still there. The thumb and the first two fingers were badly injured; they were split open longitudinally like burst sausages, and the bones of my forefinger gleamed whitely through torn skin, but the hand was still there.

Another thought, and I reached down to pass the mangled fingers over my belly, half-expecting to find dangling coils of intestine; nothing seemed to be wrong. Instinctively, I explored a little farther down; intact, undamaged. I felt overwhelming relief and relaxed for an instant, still treading water. Suddenly, I became aware of a strange new sensation in the stump of my right arm.

Only a few seconds before, the severed wrist had been a dead-white colour; now it spurted jets of bright red arterial blood. Immediately, I flexed the limb as hard as I could, and pressed the flat inner surface of the stump against the upper part of my chest, squeezing the radial and ulnar arteries against my rib-cage, thereby slowing the pulsing stream to a trickle.

Then, for the first time, I looked round and tried to find the pirogues. Until then I must have been unconsciously expecting to be caught by the back and hauled up into one of the dug-outs. Now I saw my own pirogue floating about twenty feet away, upside down and completely useless, and the other boats, manned by the six Bagoma fishermen, moving rapidly in the opposite direction, away from Mwekarago Cove. Frightened by the prospect of being involved in a white man's death, my helpers were deserting me, paddling furiously towards their lakeside village farther north.

I stared at them with brief, futile rage. Then suddenly I spotted two greenish-grey snouts about a hundred feet away, moving towards me rapidly, their ridged, scaly backs carving a wrinkled wake through the water.

That shocked me into action. I struck out towards land in an awkward left-handed Australian crawl, keeping my flexed, mutilated right arm pressed tightly against my ribs. The pain was atrocious, but I rejected it, just as I rejected the inexorable logic of my situation. I knew that even if I reached shore, I was a mile from my truck. If I reached the truck, I was three miles from the road. If I reached the road, where was I? Alone, terribly hurt, in the middle of nowhere. Everything proved, conclusively, that I was going to die, yet, irrationally, I was determined to live.

I was still a hundred feet from shore when the crocodiles caught up with me. The two big ones I had spotted first were almost at my heels; as I turned my head, I saw five more approaching from my blind right side. I'd swum in crocodile-infested waters before, so knew what to do. I changed the angle of my body, assuming an almost vertical position in the water as I kept moving towards the shore with a clumsy, one-handed dog-paddle. This made it extremely difficult for the big reptiles to seize me, the anatomy of their jaws, skull and neck prevents their turning their heads sideways and forces them to seize their intended prey on a horizontal plane.

Now I moved towards the shore more slowly, splashing as violently as possible. Undismayed, two more crocodiles came towards me on the left. One was an enormous beast about twenty feet long, almost as large as a native pirogue, who shot forward like a ridged green torpedo; an instant later I heard a hollow *clack* at my rear, the sound of his jaws as they snapped shut where I had been only a fraction of a second before.

Instinctively, I moved to the right, where his five colleagues waited. Another *clack* sounded near my right shoulder and I felt a crocodile pass behind me, his scutes scraping my back and tearing off the remnants of my shirt. Appalled, I sped up, summoning my final reserves of strength. Then, unbelievably, my feet touched bottom. I swam the last few yards with a heart that seemed to be bursting, and staggered out of the water, leaving a fan-shaped flotilla of frustrated crocodiles behind.

I desperately wanted to rest, but forced myself to walk a safe distance from the shore, then my knees buckled and I sat down hard, among the empty baskets my native crew had abandoned. They had all gone, porters as well as fishermen. I was alone.

The stump of my wrist still trickled blood, and I realized that I'd have to make a tourniquet, but from what? My shirt was gone, along with my shoes and Aussie-style hat, and my khaki shorts were reduced to incredible tatters. But my brown cotton socks were intact. Using my injured left hand and my teeth, I managed to tie a sock round the upper part of my right arm; this was quite ineffective. I took the other and knotted it just above my right elbow, with only a slightly better result. I picked up a piece of liana and wound it tightly around my arm. The bleeding stopped—until the liana broke. I tried again; the second liana broke.

Finally, only a few feet away and half-hidden by the creeping lianas, I spotted a short length of rope, a fragment of an old fishing-net, some eighteen inches long with a little loop at one end. I passed the free end into the loop, slipped it over my arm and tightened it. Then I took one of the socks, wadded it into a hard ball and stuffed it under the rope where it would press against the brachial artery. The final touch was a small stick wedged under the rope on the dorsal side of the arm. The bleeding slowed to a negligible ooze.

Afterwards, I was able for the first time, using my two sound fingers, to make a systematic survey of the other damage. There was no way of telling how badly my right eye was injured, but the entire right side of my face was an expanse of burned lacerations, which had already clotted; but blood was still trickling from a long, superficial slash on the top of my head apparently made by the detonator. My jaw and neck were badly torn. A big flap of skin hung down on my collarbone, and blood from the large shallow wound seeped down my chest; I pushed the skin back into place and it adhered, at least partially.

The rest of my injuries consisted of innumerable minor lacerations covering my arms and the right side of my chest. The worst damage sustained, apart from my missing right hand, was undoubtedly the condition of my left: only the ring-finger and little finger were intact; I could see that I might lose the first three fingers and perhaps the entire hand.

I watched some waterfowl flying overhead. They seemed strangely silent. Then I realized that I was almost completely deaf. I had heard the drum-like *clack* of the crocodiles' jaws, but I couldn't hear the birds; I soon discovered I couldn't hear my own voice unless I came close to shouting.

What sort of future lay ahead, if I survived? No hands, one eye, deaf, a scarred face—it was an appalling vision, but I was determined, whatever the difficulty, no matter how impossible the challenge, to go on leading a fully active life. So I forced myself to ignore the future and concentrate on the immediate present.

That I was alive at all was far more than I could have possibly expected. After all, the charge of high-grade dynamite which had exploded in my right hand was capable, if strategically placed, of destroying a twelve-storey building. It was only the complete instability of my position, standing up in a shaky canoe, that had saved me; even dynamite has to work against some resistance. Then, after the blast had hurled me into the water, my continued consciousness and endurance were undoubtedly due to my being in top physical condition; I was big, rugged and only twenty-eight years old, toughened by seven arduous years in the Central African bush country—a hard man to kill, even with dynamite.

I knew I could never be the same man again, but I refused to accept the idea that I might somehow be *less*. My life was in my own hands—or rather, in my two unwounded fingers. With that in mind, I struggled to my feet, ready to start my mile-long walk towards the waiting truck. I rose, swayed and nearly fell to the ground, feeling unbelievable pain and weakness in every part of my body. I closed my eyes for a moment, trying to adjust to the pain. It would have been so terribly easy never to open them again.

The walk was interminable. I took step after step after step through a narrow green tunnel of apparently unchanging bush, and every step was a separate act of will, a triumph over my desperately injured body. A hundred, five hundred, a thousand, two thousand torturing steps . . . and then, with a feeling almost of disbelief, I saw a small light blue patch, the front of my truck.

I climbed into the cab, slowly and very awkwardly, and slid behind the familiar steering-wheel. It was an immense relief to be off my feet. I knew that the worst physical exertion was past and felt a surge of new confidence and an even stronger determination to survive. Then I caught sight of myself in the driving-mirror. A strange and terrible face stared back, but I examined it with more curiosity than emotion.

The entire right side was encrusted with coagulated blood, the skin was pocked everywhere with peculiar little holes. The right eye was swollen shut but appeared to be intact. Both eyebrows were scored with long horizontal cuts: I had inflicted them myself with the naked bones of my arm. The big flap of skin, loosened during the long walk from the beach, hung down on my collarbone, and I could see quite clearly the injuries to the right side of my jaw and neck. A large muscle was exposed, probably the sternocleidomastoideus, partially surrounded by a layer of fat, mottled heavily with blood still oozing from the wound; it was as red as a raw steak. A white network of nerves, apparently part of the cervical plexus, ran through the lacerated area.

The whole thing was an unexpected anatomy lesson, and I didn't especially enjoy it. Nervously I pushed the skin into place once again, patting at it with my two sound fingers. As I did, I began to feel a new pain in my truncated right arm: it felt hot and terribly swollen. The tourniquet, of course; I had to loosen it. In my condition, the one-mile walk must have taken at least half an hour. The stump had been oozing slightly, but still, there had been almost no circulation.

I pulled out the four-inch wooden stick, intending to release the pressure for less than a second, but my injured left hand fumbled and I dropped it. My wrist started to spurt and I lunged for the stick, whipping my arm up to press it against my ribs. The blood splashed in a bright arc on to the windscreen and dashboard. I found the stick and jammed it into place; the pulsing stream slowed to a tiny trickle.

I was furious at having wasted those precious cubic centimetres of blood: it brought me a shade closer to the danger of lapsing into shock. I knew that the adult male averages eighty millimetres of blood per kilo of body weight, and so, at my weight, I should have had close to ten litres an instant before the explosion. Men have been known to lose up to 35 per cent of their blood volume before reaching a state of clinical shock, and for me that theoretical limit meant three and a half litres of blood. By now, as nearly as I could guess, I had lost two or perhaps even three of them.

I rummaged through the glove compartment until I found a clean handkerchief and a strong rubber band. I wrapped the handkerchief carefully around my mutilated wrist and fixed it into place with the elastic, hoping that the cloth might help clot the raw surface of the wound and keep it as clean as possible. Then, feeling a little better, I decided that I was ready to start out on the three-mile journey to the road.

The ignition key was still in the dashboard. I turned it, hit the starter button and the engine, to my intense relief, roared into life at once. I put the truck in reverse, reaching around the wheel to pull the gearshift lever into position with my two working fingers. Then, as I started to move backwards, I turned my head to the left to check my direction. When I did that, the tortured skin of my throat tore loose again, and I had to stop to tuck it into position. A moment later, I was travelling backwards, trying to hold my head rigid as I watched the driving-mirror with my left eye.

Three miles in reverse on a dark jungle trail, snaking my way around tree trunks . . . and then there was blue sky and brilliant sunlight. I was back at the dusty road that petered out to the south at the Tanganyika border and led north to the trading-centre of Nyanza-Lac.

I paused for a moment to relieve the pressure of my impro-vised tourniquet, and the handkerchief covering the stump of wrist swelled like a blood-red balloon. Then I turned the truck round, excited by at last being able to go forward. I shifted into second, skipping the lowest gear, gathered speed and shoved the lever down into third with my right elbow. The needle reached fifty, and I felt better than I had since the moment of the blast. I was finally on my way . . . but where?

My ultimate destination, I knew, had to be the Rodhain Hos-pital in Usumbura, at the northern tip of Lake Tanganyika. It was the only place where I could find qualified medical aid to keep me alive and to save my eye and my precious left hand.

Usumbura was eighty miles from Nyanza-Lac. A smooth, easy road, running along the eastern shore of Lake Tanganyika, led to it but according to the last reports I had heard in Kitega, two bridges were down near where it crossed the Ruzibazi and the Karonge Rivers. Farther to the south, between Nyanza-Lac and Mutambara, the territorial public works department was taking advantage of the resultant lack of traffic to repair some of its own shaky wooden bridges. The only crossing I could really count on was the metal Bailey bridge over the River Nyengwe, about five miles north of Nyanza-Lac. Beyond that point, the condition of the bridges was pure conjecture.

The only alternative route was a two-hundred-mile circuit winding through Makamba, Bururi, Ruzira and Kisozi before reaching Usa. It was almost a scenic railway, with more sharp curves and dangerous escarpments than any other road of comparable length in all of Central Africa. Starting at an altitude of 2,534 feet near Lake Tanganyika, it swings out in a big arc to the east, climbing almost a thousand feet a mile to a peak of 5,578 feet, and it dives only to climb again to over 7,000 feet at Kitaba; then it descends to 3,000 feet, rising after a series of wild undulations to 7,240 feet at Majejuru, about thirty miles east of Usa. Finally it spirals dizzily towards the capital city and Lake Tanganyika nearly five thousand feet below.

There was a serious complication at the summit of Majejuru. After that point, the road was too narrow and precipitous for two cars to pass each other, so the next eighteen miles, ending at Buhonga, were 'one-way', sectioned off by a system of barriers. Cars travelling west in the evening had to reach Majejuru by nine o'clock, at which time, punctually, the barrier was closed and no traffic could pass towards Usa until eight-thirty next morning.

The time limit made it a gamble, but one less dangerous than the lakeside road, with its series of questionable bridges. Yet I had to accept the fact that this serpentine route through two hundred miles of mountains, difficult enough in ordinary circumstances, was obviously impossible for anyone in my physical condition. I would have to find help.

I thought of Nyanza-Lac, only a few minutes away. A Greek trader there, who might have been able to drive me, was convalescing from a severe illness, his nervous wife would have been worse than useless. The Arab, like most of his compatriots, didn't drive. Any of the native population would, like the fishermen and porters, have been appalled at the very idea of being involved. But if I by-passed Nyanza-Lac, the nearest place where I could count on finding European aid was the Catholic Mission of the White Fathers of Makamba, thirty-six miles to to the east at the end of the great escarpment.

There was no other alternative, so, when I reached the cross-roads a moment later, I turned east without hesitation. I would have to chance the escarpment.

The Studebaker and I had travelled over this same road a dozen times in the past four days, but under somewhat different conditions—loaded beyond capacity with a ton or more of *ndagala* and with myself operating normally. Now the truck was empty, although it still stank of fish, and I was having the utmost difficulty taking those spectacular curves with two fingers, elbows and forearms and trying to keep up maximum speed without going over the side. Holding and turning the wheel through all of those sudden changes of direction was extremely painful, especially since I felt a mounting sense of pressure in the stump. As I descended to the vast grassy plains on the other side of the escarpment I stopped to loosen the tourniquet.

Judging from the sun's position, it must have been about 5.30, so there were three and a half hours left before the nine o'clock barrier closed at Majejuru, more than a hundred miles ahead. Nine o'clock was in every sense my deadline.

I drove on to Makamba at top speed. When I reached my destination, turning off into the long driveway leading to a cluster of imposing red-brick buildings, I felt almost at peace. Here, among the White Fathers, I was sure to find someone to take me to Usa. I pulled to a stop and tried to get out of the truck. It was difficult: I was pasted to the seat by a layer of dried blood. I was shocked by the terrible weakness I felt the moment I tried to walk, and I leaned against the bonnet, gasping a little, trying to overcome waves of vertigo. Then a 'boy' came running up, a sturdy little Muhutu native in a dark-blue apron. He stopped short, petrified at the unexpected vision of a towering white man, nearly naked, atrociously mutilated, and crusted from head to foot with coagulated blood.

'*Padri iko wapi?*' I asked, 'Where is the Father?'

He swallowed several times, licked his lips nervously and managed to stammer an answer. The words were inaudible.

'*Mi hapana sikia, sema ile tuzamisha,*' I said anxiously, 'I can't hear you. Say it louder!'

'*Padri Robert peke yake. Padri ingine yote iko ku safari,*' the boy repeated, 'Father Robert is here alone. The others are all on safari.' Then he backed away slowly.

I walked over to the massive wooden door of the refectory. I banged on it with the side of my right foot. Nobody answered. I banged again, a moment passed, and a white-robed priest opened the door, a slender man whom I had never seen here before. He stared at me in horror, his eyes widened, he tried to speak, but the words never passed his lips. He buckled and slid towards the ground. Instinctively, I reached out to catch him with my right hand, and took most of his weight on the stump of my right wrist. The pain was unbelievable. I fought it for a long moment, while I nearly bit through my lower lip. Then I poked at the fallen priest and called his name. There was no answer.

'Is no one else here?' I asked the trembling native.

'*Hapana! Hapana!*, No!'

My time was too precious for me to try and revive the priest who in any case would probably have proved a bad driver, so I told the frightened 'boy' to throw water on him, and staggered back to the truck. Each step took enormous, sickening effort, but once again I felt relief the moment I sat down. I loosened the tourniquet and rested very briefly. Then I set off at top speed towards the northwest.

Now that Makamba had failed me, I had to try to reach Bururi, about forty miles away. This stretch of road was relatively easy, but I felt much weaker since the incident at the Mission, and the pain was increasing. My whole body burned with it; paradoxically I was beginning to feel terribly cold. The sun was almost at the horizon, the temperature was falling rapidly and soon there would be a typically chilly Burundi night, which alone might be enough to finish me off. As a last torment, I began to feel incredible thirst. I cursed myself for not having taken a drink at the Mission. Then I tried to forget about it and concentrate on the road. It took me three-quarters of an hour to reach Bururi, just as the last remnants of sunset were fading from the western sky. I felt tremendously happy when I saw the familiar little headquarters and the *zamu*, the native night-watchman, dozing on the front steps. Here in Bururi were three people whom I knew I could trust to make the rest of the long drive to Usa—my boss the Territorial Administrator; Dr. Stack the Sector Veterinarian; or Jacques Dandier, one of the Territorial Agents. Any of those three, I knew, would remain calm and dependable and had enough driving skill to reach the Majejuru barrier by nine.

I stopped in front of the little brick building, but it took only a moment to find that Bururi was as hopeless as Makamba: all three men I had counted on were away on safari. The only European in the area was the *Chef de Poste*—a sort of chief bookkeeper at the Bururi headquarters, who was a rookie, newly arrived from Belgium.

I drove to his home, and tried to slide out from behind the wheel. Once again I was glued into position by my own blood. The steering-wheel, windscreen, dashboard, upholstery and floorboards all were smeared with it. It looked as though a pint bottle of blood had exploded inside the cab. I pulled loose from the cushions with a faint crackling noise, climbed down shakily and lurched towards the front door. I felt like a man walking under water.

I knocked on the door with the side of my foot. When it opened, I thought the *Chef de Poste* was about to follow Rather Robert's example. He seemed so close to fainting at the sight of me that I knew at once he wasn't my man. Of course he volunteered to take me to Usumbura and was astonished when I turned him down. What he said confirmed my instinctive decision, especially when he disclosed that he had only just learned to drive.

Nine o'clock and a closed barrier were coming closer and closer. There was no more time to waste in enlisting help from fainting priests or novice drivers. I would finish the drive alone. I would race towards Majejuru, negotiate the horrible curves of Burundi's worst one-way road, and not stop again until I reached the Rodhain Hospital in Usumbura.

*   *   *

Before leaving Bururi I drank five or six glasses of water but refused cognac, since I didn't know how much blood I had lost, but felt sure that even a small amount of alcohol would dull my senses dangerously. The water was wonderfully refreshing. I gulped it down quickly and then asked for, and received, three very precious things from the frightened but helpful *Chef de Poste*: a khaki blanket to drape over my shoulders, a pair of woollen socks for my chilled feet, and a cushion to support my back. The cushion made me feel a trifle more comfortable as I hunched forward to steer with my forearms and elbows.

When I started the engine again, turned on the headlights and left Bururi, it was a little past seven o'clock—I had less than two hours left and eighty miles to go. For the first twenty-three miles the road was easy, but after the Kato crossroads, it became rougher every moment. Near Ruzira, I was riding a roller-coaster on an up-and-down escarpment snaking through the dry golden hills.

Every laboured heartbeat filled me with new pain as I swung the truck round those interminable bends. The stump of my wrist and my mangled left hand throbbed with indescribable deep-seated agony. My face burned and the skin felt as though it had cracked into a thousand bloody fragments. The cold air bit into my naked throat with its loose flap of lacerated skin.

Several times I felt myself starting to fall into a stupor and fought it by singing and reciting classical French poetry. This kept me awake, but tortured my wounded throat. Soon I was hoarser than ever and inconceivably thirsty. Not only my throat but my whole body seemed to cry out for water.

After more than seventy miles of thirst, cold and endless pain, I saw the side-road leading to the agricultural research station at Kisozi. That meant I was approaching the Kitega-Usumbura crossroads at Nyakarago, only ten miles from the nine o'clock barrier. *What time was it now?* I had no way of knowing, but I felt sure it must have been well past 8.30. Perhaps I was already too late. . . . I pushed the throttle to the floor, and the truck shot forward at sixty miles an hour, a dangerous speed on this road. The landscape shot backwards in a green haze of banana plantations, and in less than five minutes I saw the crossroads loom ahead.

I slowed down and started to swing into the left turn. Then, at the last moment, I became aware of a truck on my blind right side, a big lorry, heavily laden with produce, racing down the road from Kitega. I swung the wheel to the left, missing him by inches. The Studebaker skidded crazily and I hung on to the wheel with my two sound fingers, fighting for control. I rocketed off the road, skimmed past a huge Grevillea tree, ricocheted to the opposite shoulder and finally bounced back on to the road, miraculously still pointed in the right direction.

My fingers were bleeding after that session with the steering-wheel, and I was shaken by the close call. But I speeded up again, feeling a strange mixture of relief and anxiety. The fact that a heavily loaded vegetable truck was travelling at that speed meant only one thing: he was trying to get to the barrier at Majejuru; it wasn't nine o'clock yet, and I still had a chance to live.

I caught up with him. I hovered at his tail in the cloud of dust from his wheels. I started to pass and then fell back; the road at this point was a series of blind curves. I sounded my horn again and again, but he refused to pull over. There was very little traffic here, but there was still a chance that a car might be coming towards me round the bend, and if I tried for maximum speed on these curves, I might have trouble holding the road. But the big truck ahead was slowing me down by fifteen or twenty miles an hour. That could cost five minutes in the race to Majejuru, five minutes that could save my life.

I swung left, with my accelerator down to the floor. But the curve was sharper than I thought: the Studebaker skidded and nearly went off on the shoulder again. I clawed at the wheel with my bleeding hand and swung back to the right, almost too far. Then the big truck was behind me, and I was headed for Majejuru.

No clock could have measured those last ten miles to the barrier; what seemed an endless hour of motion must have lasted only eight or nine minutes. For the first time since the blast, I could forget the pain completely. My whole conscious thought was fixed on one inexorable vision: a native guard placing a heavy padlock on a red-and-white-striped wooden barrier across the road, and setting off on his motor-cycle for his nightly inspection of the eighteen-mile strip to Buhonga.

I covered the remaining distance in an agony of doubt. Then I swung round the last curve and saw the native guard coming down from his hut on the hill, his motor-cycle waiting on the shoulder, and the red-and-white arm of the barrier still pointing to heaven. I drove past it, stopped about thirty feet beyond, loosened the tourniquet for a second, and watched as the khaki-clad native reached the bottom of the hill. The striped wooden arm fell and the padlock clicked into place—behind me. Now the barrier would remain closed for nearly twelve hours. The big vegetable truck would arrive in a few minutes and the driver would probably explode into futile Swahili curses. I'd nearly wrecked the Studebaker trying to pass him, but had I been cautious I would never have made it.

I still had some way to go. Usa was less than thirty miles away but it was down five thousand feet of curves spiralling to the lake in great hairpin bends, surfaced with crushed red laterite making it terribly easy to slip and plunge over the side into the jagged ravines two or three thousand feet below. Many good drivers, even after years in Burundi, were reluctant to cover the first eighteen-mile stretch, the notorious one-way road. I had always enjoyed the trip, conscious of my own skill in handling a car or a truck, but this time I felt my heart pound through my wounds, and began the long descent with the gravest misgivings.

With two fingers, elbows and forearms, I hung to the wheel, peering through the gathering mist with one eye that was dazed with pain. The mist deepened—or was it the pain?—and I felt myself slipping away, sinking to the bottom of the lake and a beautiful, easy oblivion. The lake? Of course, I was in the lake and the whole agonizing drive was only a dream. If I closed my eyes, I knew that I would awaken. 'I am awake!' I shouted. '*I am* awake! And I won't close my eyes, I swear it!'

As I drove, I felt myself growing weaker and weaker. I was very close now to the absolute limit of my endurance. Then, suddenly, a pair of elegant bushbuck loomed up in my headlights. I braked, stopped and stared at them with a sort of pantheistic emotion. They were so beautiful, so innocent and so completely unaware of my own agony. They were wonder, and youth, and above all life, everything I was fighting to hold. They stared back with huge, incredulous eyes, then leaped to the side and vanished into the bush.

I started moving again, but now I felt stronger in spite of my pain and exhaustion. Without consciously meaning to, I began singing an old Scout song I had learned twenty years before as a child in Belgium:

> *Compagnon, voici la route*
> *Qui s'élance vers le ciel;*
> *En toi fais silence, écoute*
> *Son impérieux appel . . .*

> *Route fière, de lumière,*
> *Route des forts!*
> *Nous te suivrons jusqu'a la mort,*
> *Sainte route d'effort!*

I was determined that, whatever the song said, my road wasn't going to end in death, but I went on singing those same stubborn words all the way to Buhonga, where I halted long enough to loosen the tourniquet for the last time. The severed ends of the blood vessels had probably clotted, since there was only a brief trickle of blood from my wrist. I felt terribly weak, at the point of fainting, but forced myself on. I had come down four thousand feet: Usumbura lay seven hundred feet below and only twelve miles away.

Those last twelve miles were an unbroken succession of smooth curves. The road itself was far less dangerous, but the mist was thicker and I had to look out for other traffic. After four or five miles, the mist cleared and I caught my first glimpse of Usumbura, a shower of golden lights next to the moonlit waves of Lake Tanganyika. It seemed an impossibly beautiful vision. Then I saw another vision: a petrol-gauge that registered empty.

I was outraged. It was too stupid, too meaningless to lose everything now. I refused to believe the possibility existed, and kept my eyes fixed on the road and the glorious lights of Usa, trying to ignore the ominous needle pointing steadily to the letter 'E'. I drove on, conscious of every tenth of a mile registering on the speedometer. Then, with a feeling of incredulous relief, I saw the metal bridge across the Muha River at the southern edge of Usa. The Studebaker and I rattled over and a moment later turned into the Avenue de la Limite, a name which was all too apt.

I drove another mile, stopped the truck in front of the Rodhain Hospital and turned off the engine. I sat in the cab for a moment, staring at the crusted wheel, the dashboard, the streaks of dried blood on the windshield. I found it almost impossible to believe that the journey was over. Then I struggled to get out of the cab and nearly fell to the ground. I swayed and caught the handle of the door with my two good fingers. I stayed there, trembling, trying not to buckle and fall.

The *infirmier de service*, a tall native in a white blouse, saw me standing clutching at the door. His jaw dropped and he started to run towards me, Then he rushed back into the hospital, shouting for the doctors and nurses, calling for a wheeled stretcher. When I saw him next, a moment later, he was pushing the stretcher, and I was already in the main hall, walking along very slowly but without touching the walls. Something inside me rebelled at the thought of being carried into hospital. I wanted to finish my trip as I'd started it, *alone*, and under my own power.

The tall native caught at my left elbow, trying to help. I pushed him aside impatiently. 'I can walk!'

At that moment, the white Sister on night-duty came along the corridor. She stopped, shocked by the unexpected vision of a dead man walking. Then she whirled on the native medical assistant. 'Why aren't you helping him?' she cried angrily.

'Leave him alone, Sister. I need no help.'

She stared at me with obvious disbelief. 'Where did you come from? Who brought you here?'

'Nyanza-Lac. I drove here myself.'

'*You drove?* But that's eighty miles!'

'No. Two hundred. I came the long way round, through Makamba and Bururi.'

She nodded, apparently trying to humour me, then rushed down the corridor and whispered anxiously to an approaching doctor. He was successively astonished, clinically curious and extremely concerned. However, I continued to walk—under the eyes of a growing crowd—and to refuse any aid. I had to do so. I was conscious of the strange drama I had lived, and I wanted to play the last scene to the end, and with style.

I pushed my way through a swinging door into the treatment room, and the doctor moved quickly towards the opposite end where another door opened into the operating theatre. He planted himself before it, with arms outstretched, obviously intent on preventing any violation of his sterile domain. I looked round, resentful but terribly weary, and saw a high metal bed covered with a clean sheet. I lurched towards it and with a last dizzying burst of effort managed to climb on to it and lie down. Then I closed my eyes and didn't open them again for the next two days. 24 October 1955 had finally ended.

11

A Magic Chicken

Inuma ntigira ngo hu gu gu, igira ngo ha uguha—'The turtle-dove doesn't say "Give! Give!" but "Give to him who gives to you!"'

KIRUNDI PROVERB

FOR at least twelve hours after my strange arrival the medical staff of Rodhain Hospital, headed by its Director and Chief Surgeon, Dr. Albert Lodewyckx, worked over my battered, unconscious body with all the dedicated skill they could command. For the next day and a half I lay somewhere in limbo, between life and death.

As I awakened, my first sensation was pain: a deep burning pain which never left me for the next two weeks. From the waist up, my body seemed almost to be on fire, especially the stump of my right arm where the burning alternated with spasms like electrical shocks. My ears felt as though they were filled with water and ached abominably. My right eye was covered with gauze and when my left eye blinked open the assembled doctors and nurses appeared through a thick but gradually dissipating fog.

They questioned me intently, trying to determine whether an explosion only a few feet away from my head might have seriously damaged my brain. I answered lucidly, in spite of the pain and the heavy bandages swathing my face, jaw and neck. After five minutes of questions and answers, the doctors were satisfied that—for better, for worse!—my mental capacities were unchanged. I myself derived a little satisfaction on finding that my left hand—every finger of it—was still with me, and that my right forearm was long enough to be useful; it ended only two inches above the wrist. I hadn't expected to keep so much of it.

Later I was moved to a large, brilliantly sunny private room, deposited in a new bed and placed in the custody of a five-foot, white-robed and white-coiffed angel with a worn birdlike face, gentle hands and the determination of a well-meaning female Napoleon: Sœur Marie-Ghislaine de l'Enfant Jésus. It was immediately obvious that she was not only bent on healing me but on organizing and disciplining me, physically, mentally and spiritually. Of course, it was all for my own good. And, of course, she never succeeded.

She insisted that I rest, but I watched attentively as she changed the dressings on my left hand. The thumb and first two fingers looked like a botched embroidery lesson: everything was sewed together with wavering lines of black surgical thread and covered with a dark patina of dried blood. 'Are you going to do the right side now?' I asked as she rebandaged my fingers. 'I'd like to get a good look at that arm.'

'No, Monsieur Hallet. I have instructions not to touch it for the next two days. Now I'm going to dress your face, so you'll have to stop talking.'

As she worked, Sœur Marie-Ghislaine told me all about our first meeting—in the operating theatre. While the doctors were busy with my more serious wounds, she had been delegated to wash my face and scrub it with a stiff brush, a technique supposed to help stimulate the recovery of the damaged tissues, during which she had removed from each of a multitude of curious little holes a small fragment of bone—pieces of my erstwhile right hand. One of the doctors had excavated from my neck muscles a chain of three silver links, part of an identification bracelet I had worn since I was twelve. The rest of it must have been at the bottom of Lake Tanganyika.

When she had finished dressing my face the Sister swabbed the blood and sera out of my leaking ears. It was exquisitely painful. The right eardrum had been obliterated and the delicate bones of the middle and inner ear crushed; and I was completely deaf on that side. The left eardrum was badly perforated, but the hearing loss eventually subsided to about fifty per cent.

The rest of the day passed in a haze of pain which continued even after the doctor gave me two injections of morphine. The pain seemed greater in hospital than it had been on the day of the explosion. During the long, demanding trip I had kept moving almost constantly. I had been through hell, but hell is full of distractions; a sick-bed is not.

That night it was impossible to sleep. My body burned and my mind, half-stupefied by narcotics, shuttled back and forth from the Mosso to Lake Tanganyika or drove desperately towards the nine o'clock barrier at Majejuru. Then I started to think nostalgically about my missing right hand and visualized its eight carpals, five metacarpals and fourteen phalanges, twenty-seven little bones which were now in heaven together with the proximal ends of my radius and ulna. I made a quick calculation and decided I still had 179 bones left.

Next morning my doctor examined my stiff, swollen left hand and tried to seem cheerful. After a great deal of hemming and hawing, he spoke frankly: the thumb was in fair condition, but the index and middle fingers looked far from promising. I would keep them, but probably would never again be able to use them fully. Only time would give me the answer.

That day, with less morphine in my system, I tried to give some serious thought to my future. How would I ever again shoot a bow and arrow? Or hold a shield in one hand and a spear in the other, as I had when I killed my Masai lion? Or thump out messages on the talking drums? Or paddle a pirogue, tie knots, climb trees? How would I dazzle the natives with deft sleight-of-hand or ride my big new *Sarolea* motor-cycle?

At that point I had to smile. I hadn't even thought of the more essential details of everyday life, such as writing, eating with a knife and fork, or using a rotary tin-opener, so much less important did they seem to me than the demands of life in the African bush.

Had I lost my left hand instead of my right the problems would have been similar, but on a far less demanding scale. The right had been strong and skilful; the left was comparatively weak and almost untrained. Now I would have to teach that unused, badly injured left hand to assume the functions of both; it wouldn't be easy.

Two famous precedents sprang to mind; Nelson, who lost his right arm at Santa Cruz but went on to his greatest triumphs, and Goetz von Berlichingen, whose right hand was blown off at the Siege of Landshut, after which he became, if anything, bolder, more adventurous and endearingly wicked than ever.

The Siege of Santa Cruz, the Siege of Landshut, the Siege of Lake Tanganyika—I laughed at the overblown phrase but enjoyed the comparison. Each of my historic precedents had lost his *right* hand, so that they had had to struggle against the acute, built-in polarization of body and mind which results, for most of the human race, in overwhelming right-hand dominance. To lose either hand is a serious blow; to lose the dominant hand is a major physiological disaster. Yet, after much thought, I decided that was what I preferred: it presented a much greater challenge.

* * *

On the fourth morning I was allowed visitors. The first guest, as might be expected, was an official investigator from the local Provincial Headquarters. Considering I had not only broken the law but blown it to smithereens, I braced myself for the worst, but he proved extremely kind and solicitous, questioning me in detail about the Mosso famine and my Fish Safari. Then he left, went off to conduct official inquiries at Nyanza-Lac and the Bagoma fishing village.

Many friends and acquaintances followed, most of whom seemed to expect to find me sobbing bitterly, in the style of Hollywood movie heroes, that I would have preferred death to amputation. I really could not oblige them with this reaction since I was too happy to be alive and too curious to see what I could make of the future to feel either bitter or humble. This worried some of my friends, who thought I should take my own suffering more seriously. One colleague, I remember, insisted on referring in hushed tones to what he called 'my tragedy'. My reply was unprintable.

My father arrived from Kisenyi that afternoon, pale and haggard after leaving a sick-bed of his own. He had been convalescing from a mild heart attack, and when he first entered my room I thought he was going to have another. While he had been told the details of my accident, the reality was almost too much. But when I greeted him with my customary insolence he smiled bleakly and began to relax, and we had a wonderful hour together.

The next day's assortment of guests included a complete surprise. 'You have a native visitor,' Sœur Marie-Ghislaine announced, with a strangely intriguing smile. 'Do you want to see him?'

'A native?' I was baffled. Most of my native friends hailed from Kisenyi or southern Urundi; I could think of no one here in Usumbura, unless, perhaps, my blood bride Ndagizye had

hitch-hiked all the way to the hospital. 'Is he tall and skinny?'
I asked nervously. 'A real Mututsi with a hooked nose?'

'No, the very opposite. Do you want to see him?'

'Of course! Send him in!'

She went to the door, smiled and beckoned. My visitor
proved to be a half-naked little Mumosso, with a dirty white
rooster dangling head downwards from his hand. He stood there
speechless, obviously terrified at the sight of my mummy-like
bandages.

'*Bwakeye!*' I called to him, a cheeerful Kirundi 'Hello'.

His reaction was unexpected. He stammered a few words I
couldn't hear, threw the rooster on to my bed, and ran out of
the room.

'*Gwino! Gwino!*' I shouted, 'Come back!' while the rooster,
whose legs were tied, squawked hysterically and flapped through
my bedding. 'Sœur Marie! Please bring him back!'

She succeeded in stopping him after a little race down the
corridor and marched him back to my room. He was very
reluctant to talk, but after much coaxing finally explained his
surprising gesture.

'My name is Mwerodike,' he said shyly, 'and I come from
Bigunzo Hill. That is not far from Butana. I am very poor, but
am the only man on Bigunzo Hill who still owns a chicken. The
others ate all their birds when the famine started to kill us.'

'Why didn't you eat this one?'

'Because it is a magic chicken, *Bwana*.'

'What do you mean?'

'I had a lot of bad luck last year, so I went to see my *umufumu*. He told me that he needed an egg, and I brought him one
laid by this chicken's favourite wife. The magician looked inside
and said that the father of the house would always be healthy as
long as the father of the egg stayed alive. *I* am the father of the
house, so I made sure nobody ate *this* chicken, no matter how
hungry we were. Now I want to give him to you.'

'Why?'

'I have nothing else to give, *Bwana Ale*, and I feel that I must
give you something. You gave *me* two rations of fish, and it
kept my family alive. Then Chief Kigoma told us what happened
to you and I couldn't forget about it, no matter how hard I
tried. So I walked for four days to bring you this chicken. I hope
you will eat it, just as I ate your fish.'

'But what will happen to you if the chicken dies?'

'If the rooster is killed by an accident far from his own home,' he explained knowingly, 'the evil spirits won't bother me. And if you eat him, it will be just like an accident. Anyway, I don't trust that *umufumu* any more. His magic didn't help us when we were starving. Yours must be much stronger.'

He paused, hauled the chicken out from under the bed where it had finally subsided, and held it out with a beseeching gesture. 'If I were *Imana*,' he said gravely, 'I would give you back your hand. But I am not God, I am just a poor Mumosso, and this is all I have. Please eat my chicken, *Bwana Ale*! He is old and tough, but if you have him cooked in peanut oil, he will taste very good and make you feel strong.'

I was deeply moved. In more than seven years of working with Central African natives, this was the first time I had seen an action inspired by sincere gratitude. I knew many missionaries and government workers who were bitter and disillusioned because they had not seen a single example after thirty or forty years of dedicated work. Most had come to Africa with the altruistic desire to see only good in its natives, but after years of frustration and repeated failures, of trying to help people unable or unwilling to help themselves, many of them had come to dislike or even to hate the Africans for their indolence, fatalism and maddening insincerity. Most whites failed to realize that the natives were capable of sincere loyalties, but only to members of their own clan or, more rarely, tribe, never to anything as alien and unfathomable as the white man. My new friend Mwerodike was an incredible exception.

'I shall eat your chicken with joy!' I told the ragged little Mumosso. 'The Sister will take him to the kitchen, and he will be cooked in peanut oil, just as you say.'

Mwerodike rushed forward and took my bandaged hand gently between both of his. I noticed then that his lips were dry and terribly cracked, so I asked the Sister to bring him some water. He drank four glasses without a pause.

'Are you hungry?' I asked.

'Yes. It took four days to get here, and I had no money. Once I managed to steal some corn along the way. Then I asked for food from some Bahutu working in a cotton-field. They called me names and threw two rotten bananas in my face. I ate them and they weren't so bad.'

'Sœur Marie-Ghislaine, can you bring him some food?'

'Certainly. I'll fetch something hot.'

As she left, rooster in hand, Mwerodike looked very sad, and I knew what a sacrifice it represented.

'Your chicken will cure me,' I said consolingly. 'From that one bird I shall regain all my lost strength! Even to look at it has made me feel stronger!'

'I will tell everyone in the Mosso about my magic chicken, *Bwana Ale.* They will talk of nothing else from Butana to Ruyigi.'

'How are they, Mwerodike? Has the government food come to them yet?'

'Not yet. Just before I left, we got a message from Chief Kigoma. He said the beans would come in four or five days.'

'What about you? You won't get back in time.'

'I may miss my beans, *Bwana,* but I just had to come.'

I was so deeply impressed by his artless sincerity that I had to show Mwerodike my own gratitude. I decided to do so hand-somely. 'You may not get the beans,' I assured him, 'but I am going to give you something much better, the most beautiful present in the world.'

'What can it be, *Bwana?*'

'A cow.'

Poor Mwerodike nearly expired with shock. His eyes rolled upwards, his knees buckled, he shook like a man stricken with tertian malaria. '*Urakoze!*' he screamed wildly. '*Urakoze! URAKOZE NEZA!*'

It was probably the loudest Kirundi 'Thank you' in the history of Usumbura. It startled Sœur Marie-Ghislaine, who was just coming through the door with a plate of steaming corned beef and potatoes. It must have been five minutes before Mwerodike calmed down enough to consider eating. Then he tore into the food ravenously while I dictated an important letter to my nurse.

It was addressed to François Mortier, a close friend with a cattle ranch in the hills about eight miles from Usa. François had visited me only the day before and had urged me, when I was back on my feet, to stay with him as long as I liked. 'I'll kill a young steer,' he said, 'and you can eat bloody steaks until you're strong as a bull again.' This was the letter I sent him, with my name painfully inked in at the bottom:

My dear François,

Thank you for your generous offer of a sacrificial bull. However, I shall really be much happier if you let the animal live and give it to Mwerodike, a native of the Mosso, who is the bearer of this letter. Come to think of it, you'd better let him have a heifer instead of a bull—a good-looking heifer which will throw many calves—and I'll even be willing to pay you. Mwerodike has been very generous with me and I want to reward him. Perhaps if he works hard enough, he can re-establish cattle-breeding in his part of the Mosso. *Un grand merci!*

JEAN-PIERRE

PS. This letter is definitely *not* a joke!

Mwerodike returned next day, trailing after a puzzled François Mortier, to whom I told the whole story of my valiant sympathizer and his magic chicken, which he enjoyed enormously, but raised an objection. 'Look, if you're really serious about setting him up in the cattle business, I must point out that you've forgotten a small matter: he'll need two—one of each kind—a cow and a bull. Remember?'

'That might speed things up.'

François grinned. 'I was going to kill a bull for you—free; now you've offered to pay me. Why don't the two of us get together and give him a cow and a bull? You can pay me for one of them, whenever you have some spare money, and I'll contribute the other.'

'That's a deal!' I said briskly. Then I asked Mwerodike in Kirundi, 'Would you like a bull as well as a cow? Can you handle two cattle all the way home?'

'What? What did you say, *Bwana*?'

'A young bull and a heifer. We are each giving you a cow.'

Mwerodike stared in stark disbelief, and then launched into a wild salvo of formal appreciation such as I have never heard before or since. '*Urakoze!*' he cried ecstatically. '*Uragize neza! Wampaye! Urakarama! Urakagira Imana!*', 'May you be thanked! You have done well! May you be blessed! May God be with you!'

'*Ndashimye,*' I answered simply. 'You are welcome.'

'I will build a special kraal for my cattle and name them in your honour! They will be called The Gift of *Bwana Ale*.'

'Soon you will be a *Bwana*, Mwerodike. Many people will want to serve you, just to be near your cattle.'

'*Ego! Ego!* I will be like a Mututsi and have many boys!'

'Be good to them, Mwerodike.'

'*Ego! Ego!*' he answered, still dazed with shock. Then he followed François from the room, looking like a man about to fall *up* through the notorious hole in the floor of heaven . . . the Tutsi heaven replete with beautiful cows.

In the days that followed I heard much about Mwerodike's return trip to the Mosso. Reports of his progress filtered back to Usumbura via the native grapevine, and everyone in western Burundi knew of his journey. It took him more than a week to herd his two cattle from Usumbura to Butana, since he stopped to tell his story to virtually everyone he met. Soon, most of the native population were busy coining proverbs about 'a chicken for a hand and two cattle for a chicken'. Mwerodike became an overnight celebrity, in spite of his Mosso origin which usually brought nothing but contempt from the class-conscious Batutsi and Bahutu. Everyone offered him food along the way, and he drank so much free beer that he practically staggered all the way home. He was the happiest man in Burundi.

I may add that when I returned to the Butana area for a brief visit in 1959, I found that my Mumosso protégé had taken full advantage of his working capital. He had a big hemispherical Tutsi hut, a large kraal and a small hut for his 'staff', two men working for bed and board plus the promise of a future calf. He had repudiated his faithful former wife and acquired a new one, a very young girl whose dowry he had paid with the promise of another calf, and had sired three and a half children in four years. The cow and the bull hadn't kept pace, having produced only two calves, both heifers. Mwerodike himself had changed greatly. His speech was pompous as he gave his 'boys' their orders, and strutted about his kraal in a loud red jacket with a Tutsi pipe in his hand. He was rich, but no longer happy, since he spent most of his time worrying lest some envious neighbour poison his cows.

*   *   *

After a fortnight of boredom, insomnia and severe pain I could no longer tolerate the enforced idleness of life in a hospital bed. For a while I tried to keep busy reading, dictating letters, scandalizing my visitors, and scrawling primitive ABC's with my stiff, bandaged fingers. Then I discovered the pleasures of crime.

That meant violating the doctor's orders and slipping out of bed whenever Sœur Marie-Ghislaine left the room. During these furtive interludes I walked up and down, practised easy setting-up exercises on the floor and peered dismally out of the window. On the morning of my twentieth day in hospital I coerced François Mortier, who had come to see me, into aiding and abetting a far graver breach of the rules.

'I've got to get out of this place,' I told him, 'and you're going to help me. If I can't escape for at least an hour or two, they'll have to transfer me to an asylum.'

'But where do you want to go?'

'Anywhere! All I want to do is take my truck on a drive into the bush, walk about, and sniff some fresh air. That isn't much to ask, is it?'

'But Jean-Pierre, do you think we can get away with it?'

'Of course we can! Buy me a shirt and some *kapitula* and collect my truck from the Old East garage. Bring it round to the rear entrance at one o'clock. Lunch will be finished by then and Sœur Marie-Ghislaine won't look into my room for some time. Keep the engine running if I'm a few minutes late.'

François left, looking as furtive as though we were planning a bank robbery instead of a little drive; I felt equally guilty when I tiptoed down the corridor in pyjamas. Once I had to hide in a broom cupboard while two white-robed Sisters sailed majestically down the hall. Then I shot out through the back door and found François in my truck, a cap pulled down over his eyes so that he looked like a cross between Humphrey Bogart and Fernandel.

'Move over!' I ordered. 'I want to drive.'

'Are you sure that you can?'

I glared at him disgustedly. 'How the hell do you think I got here from Mwekarago Cove?'

'Oh. All right.'

We drove off in a hurry. Then I pulled the truck to the side of the road and changed my clothes inside the cab. 'Something's wrong with these *kapitula*,' I complained. 'Look at them, they'll fall down if I stand up!'

'Jean-Pierre,' said François patiently, 'you may not realize it, but you must have lost nearly two stone.'

'I have discovered a new wonder diet: blow off your right hand and exercise vigorously for two hundred miles; then try to survive hospital cooking for three weeks. It works every time!'

François cackled happily. I grinned back, hit the throttle, and headed for the Uvira road. As soon as I reached the highway I went up to seventy and broke into a medley of my favourite songs. I began 'Route Fière . . .' but stopped abruptly when I noticed traces of dried blood in the groove round the horn button; the upholstery had been cleaned and there was a new floor-mat, but there were still some little souvenirs of my blood-drenched odyssey.

We crossed the two branches of the Ruzizi River and passed over the border into the Congo. Just before Uvira, I turned left on a sandy little trail leading to a deserted beach on the shore of Lake Tanganyika. We parked, climbed out of the cab and went for a walk. The air was delightfully fresh and the water looked incredibly inviting, until I spotted two long wakes about a hundred feet out, and two large cruising crocodiles.

'*Comment ça va, mes copains?*' I shouted at them amiably, 'How goes it, pals?'

'Are you all right?' my friend said, peering at me intently.

'Certainly. I'm just paying my respects to some old friends.'

'Those vicious brutes? Why, the damned things tried to kill you!'

'At least they didn't want to make a wallet out of me or a pair of lady's shoes. All they wanted to do was eat me—that seems reasonable enough.'

François snorted indignantly. I answered him by sitting down on the sand and delivering a long discourse on ecology in general and the necessity of crocodiles in particular. It was one of my favourite crusades, since all-out attacks on the crocodile population had already caused serious damage to some of the Congo's rivers and lakes, also, surprisingly, to its people.

Professional hunters killed the giant reptiles for their valuable hides, and on one unfortunate occasion many years before, the Government had even encouraged organized slaughter along the Semliki River south of Lake Albert. Its intention was to free the natives from a persistent nuisance, but the near-extermination of local crocodiles had unexpected consequences. The large carnivorous fish, on which the departed crocodiles had formerly preyed, multiplied without restraint and decimated the smaller herbivorous fish population on which the Bahamba, Bambale and other local tribes had subsisted. The natives missed a few fatal encounters with crocodiles' jaws, but their main food source was nearly destroyed. Even today, the ecology of the lower Semliki River has not recovered from that drastic imbalance.

After about half an hour of my classic crocodile monologue, François finally managed to break in. 'Don't you think we ought to get back to Usa?' he asked. 'Sœur Marie-Ghislaine may be looking for you.'

I had to agree. I drove the twenty-one miles back in less than twenty minutes. Then, just before I sneaked back through the *Entrée des Artistes*, I gave my parting instructions. 'Two days from now, François. Be here with the truck at nine in the morning. You know where I want to go!' I extracted his promise, sneaked back to my room, hid my baggy new *kapitula* and shirt under the mattress. Sœur Marie-Ghislaine looked in about ten minutes later.

'Did you have a nice nap like I told you to?' she inquired, a trifle officiously.

'No, Sister. I couldn't sleep, so I sneaked out and drove my truck to Uvira.'

'Monsieur Hallet, how can you keep a straight face when you say things like that? For a moment, I almost took you seriously.'

*   *   *

When the doctor made his daily eight o'clock visit two mornings later, I was impatient for him to be gone. François would be here with my truck within the hour, and I was planning to drive eighty miles down the shore of Lake Tanganyika. The bridges were back in commission and the direct route was open to a very familiar spot: Mwekarago Cove.

'You're looking very well,' the doctor informed me. 'You've made so much progress that I'll let you get out of bed.'

'I'm happy to hear that.'

'You can walk round the room, but you'll have to take it easy, of course, and you can sit in that chair by the window.'

'That's wonderful!' I said dutifully. Then I couldn't resist adding, 'How about my going out to get some fresh air? I feel like doing some driving.'

'Driving? You mean *yourself*?'

'Yes, just a little trip along the street, something like that. My hand's much stronger now: I can even wiggle the two bad fingers.'

'You don't realize how weak you are. I'm afraid it's out of the question.'

He departed, with a patronizing little sigh, and a few minutes later Sœur Marie-Ghislaine made a great fuss over assisting my first official steps. Then she installed me and an old copy of *Paris-Match* in the chair by the window and ordered me to stay put. I had to conserve my strength.

The moment the good Sister left I jumped into my *kapitula*, ran a comb through my hair and crept along the corridor.

François was waiting with the truck, and we drove to a friend's house in Usa, where I had a lovely non-hospital breakfast: four eggs, half a pound of bacon and a whole tray of toast. Then I took off, alone, on the long trip back to Mwekarago Cove.

Several times along the way I stopped to chat with passing natives. The results were intriguing, for most of them had seen Mwerodike and his two cows in the course of his drunken trip back to the Mosso, and had been deeply impressed with his story. 'Do you know any other white man who has lost a hand?' one Muhutu asked me. 'If I can find one, I will be happy to give him a chicken.'

A few miles north of Nyanza-Lac, I stopped at Mugozarika, a large village where I lunched on bananas and peanuts, and bought two old *likembe* for my collection—small musical instruments consisting of thin metal strips set over a bridge on a wooden sounding-board known elsewhere as *sansas* or 'thumb-pianos'. Then I drove directly to the village of the Bagoma fishermen who had left me to die.

I pulled into the clearing near the *baraza*, where they all gathered at midday to laze about and talk about fish (and occasionally women). Most of them recognized the truck the moment they saw it, and two of my Fish Safari colleagues shot to their feet, obviously ready to start running. The rest lay on the ground, terrified by the sight of my bandages and my missing hand. Then, as if they had all felt a seismic shock, they jumped to their feet.

'*Jambo, Bwana!*' said the *kapita*, with a sickly smile.

I stared at him without speaking.

'I feel very bad that my men left you in the water,' he volunteered nervously, 'but they told me you were dead.'

'You *were* dead!' one of them burst out. 'Now you must be a *muzimu!*'

'If I am a ghost, then you are a wet chicken! You ran away like miserable cowards without even trying to help! Now, could a ghost tell you that?'

'Maybe.'

'They brought me proof,' the *kapita* insisted. 'They picked up your hat from the water, and they had a piece of your shiny little bracelet.'

'My ID bracelet? How could they find *that*? It was on my right wrist!'

'It was *mayele, Bwana*. Magic! They found it in one of the

boats. The big wind from the dynamite must have blown it there.'

I told him to bring the things to me, and a moment later I was reunited with my old Aussie campaign hat and the remains of the bracelet. The crown of the hat had been scarred by the detonator and several pieces of bone from my pulverized hand were embedded in the brim. The bracelet consisted of a single link attached to the nameplate, on which, although it was scratched and battered, my name was still perfectly legible.

'They brought these things,' the *kapita* explained, 'and told me what happened. We talked about it for a long time. Then I took my bicycle and went to Mwekarago Cove. I saw lots of big bloody footsteps on the beach and the trail, but no body and no truck. I couldn't understand it.'

'Are you mad at us, *Bwana*?' one asked.

'No, just disgusted. I thought we were friends. Then you abandoned me. Now you don't even look pleased to see me. Aren't you glad that I'm still alive?'

'*Ndio, Bwana!*' they all chorused. They said it very loudly, but the words had a hollow ring.

'Are you really sincere?'

'*Ndio! Ndio!*'

'Then how about a little trip back to Mwekarago Cove?'

Without hesitation the whole group jumped into the back of the truck, while the *kapita* took the place of honour beside me. Almost immediately they started to sing the same tune they had sung twenty-two days before, during our explosive trip to the lake. We reached the turn-off and I snaked the truck through the three-mile tunnel in the bush. Then we made the one-mile walk to the beach. At the end of it, I felt so weak that I had to sit down, almost at the same spot where I had made a tourniquet after my unexpected swim.

I rested for a few minutes until I noticed a dark object about two hundred feet away. I walked over to investigate it and discovered one of my shoes, washed up on the shore. 'I'll give twenty francs to the man who can find the other shoe!' I announced, and the natives searched for it eagerly. One man brought me a blood-stained fragment of cloth that must have come from my shirt, and I bought it for ten francs. Nobody found the other shoe, but they did turn up several odd objects, and the *kapita*'s young son tried to sell me a battered bicycle tyre as a souvenir of my accident.

When I questioned them about their memories of the accident

the results were just what I might have expected: they told me that I had exploded and subsequently died in the water. Then the *kapita* asked a question of his own: '*Bwana*, tell us how the truck disappeared and you got to Usa. A man came from the Government and asked us lots of questions. He said that you drove to Usa by yourself, but we didn't really believe him.'

'He was right.'

'*We na tumia mayele nguvu!*' the *kapita* said softly, 'You must have used powerful magic!'

'*Mayele!*' they all murmured. '*Mayele!*'

This interpretation of my ordeal certainly didn't please me, but I knew better than to argue with them about *mayele*. The idea that the white man employs a strange magic of his own is almost universal among Central African natives. So I smiled mysteriously and let it go at that.

I drove back to the Rodhain Hospital in high spirits. But when I sneaked in through the back door it was to find the Sister waiting in my room, with a steely glint in her eyes.

'Where did you get those clothes, Monsieur Hallet?' she demanded.

'From a charitable friend.'

'And where have you been all day?'

'I've been making some anthropological studies.'

The little nun shook her head sadly. 'You won't last long at this rate, Monsieur Hallet. You may not realize it, but there's such a thing as too much dedication, even to good works.'

*   *   *

A couple of days later I received wonderfully exciting news. Towards the beginning of November, I had dictated an imposing collection of letters to my long-suffering nurse, addressed to the Belgian Ambassador in Washington, the American Consul at Léopoldville, the U.S. Department of State, and President Eisenhower. I had conceived an ambitious plan for my immediate future, but to carry it out I needed official co-operation from the governments of the United States, Belgium, the Congo and Ruanda-Urundi.

Considering the humanitarian motives of the Fish Safari, the Belgian Colonial Government had decided not only to overlook its illegal nature but to classify my explosion officially as an accident at work. This assured me of government backing for my staggering medical expenses, but meant I would have to receive orthopaedic treatment and 'rehabilitation' at the Brugmann Hospital in Brussels.

I revolted immediately at this idea for I knew the European attitude towards physical handicaps and wanted no part of it. I had seen one of those Old World 'rehabilitation centres' before I came to Africa, when I was studying at the Sorbonne and supporting myself by driving a Paris taxi. It was a sombre, dismal place where cringing people received an inadequate re-education while trying to hide from public view. They were convinced of their inferiority and afraid to shock the unwritten conformist code of the average bourgeois Frenchman or Belgian, which seemed to demand that anything 'abnormal' had to be hidden away to avoid scandalizing the community.

I felt sure that the New World would be different. Since my accident friends had told me not only of the amazing level of American medical technology but of Americans' wonderfully casual attitude towards people who had suffered accidents or crippling diseases. In America, they said, there were many vigorous and active people who went to school, held jobs and even engaged in sports, in spite of amputation, paralysis or other physical handicap. Nobody found it bizarre or shocking that they wanted to live full, exciting lives. There, I knew, I could benefit from the latest developments in the orthopaedic field, in a stimulating atmosphere, and take advantage of American plastic surgery to repair some of my scars. I wouldn't have been bothered by a clean, dramatic slash, like a Heidelberg duelling scar, but I disliked the unpleasant patches of puckered skin on the side of my face, jaw, neck and chest. I felt sufficiently marked with a missing right hand—there was no point in overdoing it.

The Belgian Embassy in Washington now wrote to say it was making arrangements with the U.S. State Department to secure my admission for free treatment at the famous Walter Reed Army Hospital. The American Government was ready to make this wonderfully generous gesture, even though the Walter Reed facilities were usually reserved for military and diplomatic personnel. There was, however, a slight hitch; before I could accept the treatment I must obtain the approval of the Belgian Minister of Foreign Affairs, who would have to be approached through the Minister of Colonies, who in turn would have to receive a request from the Governor-General of the Congo, who would have to be advised of my situation by the Governor of Ruanda-Urundi.

My departure from standard operating procedure obviously was going to bury three nations in paper.

I started things going by writing to Jean-Paul Harroy, Governor of Ruanda-Urundi, who was most gracious and sympathetic and did his best to rush the matter through. Nevertheless, the question of my American journey dragged on for weeks, as did my enforced stay at Rodhain Hospital, and I was not finally released until 23 December, two months after the accident.

Since my whole status was up in the air until the matter of rehabilitation had been settled, I asked the Government to find me some suitable work in the interim. They accepted, but their idea of 'suitable work' proved very odd. I was sent off to the hot, humid Ruzizi plains—the 'steam-bath' of Ruanda-Urundi —to make an agricultural survey.

It would have been difficult enough for anyone in perfect health. For me, it was excruciating. From seven in the morning until four in the afternoon, I walked from one native field to the next with a clip board in my hand. I questioned the natives and then, leaning the clip board on the stump of my right arm, scrawled the various names and acreages of cotton, manioc and sweet potatoes. I had regained partial use of my first two fingers, but writing was still difficult and very painful (as it remains today). Ironically, it made both hands hurt, the missing one more than the other.

The temperature rarely dropped below a hundred degrees and I was drenched with sweat after the first half-hour. The bandages were gone by now, but I still wore a stump-sock to protect my right arm. It was always soaked with sweat, and the arm underneath pained me atrociously.

I realized I must have received this extraordinarily unsuitable assignment because of petty administrative intrigues within the Agricultural Service. Someone's nose was out of joint, either because I hadn't been prosecuted for my illegal use of dynamite, or because of the publicity I had received in the local press, or perhaps simply because they were determined to prove that a 'handicapped' man couldn't perform a 'normal' man's job.

Its sheer impossibility meant I must do it better than anyone else. So I struggled through my daily rounds in the Ruzizi steam-bath and succeeded in flooding the Agricultural Service with a series of detailed graphs, maps and statistical reports whose preparation with my left hand had cost me unspeakable suffering to prepare during the evenings. Then, after more than a month of such purgatory, I received a message from heaven.

The long chain of important officials had finally reacted in series. The governments of Belgium, the Congo and Ruanda-Urundi would all permit me to make my American journey.

Within a week I flew to Brussels, where I spent a few days of preliminaries with various administrative departments, including some important financial arrangements with the Fonds Colonial des Invalidités. Then I visited the United States Embassy, where I was given a special visa of unlimited duration. Finally, on 20 February 1956, I boarded an air-liner and set out on a journey that was to take me through every state of the most civilized, chromium-plated, asphalt-paved, push-button-operated and wonderfully exciting jungle in the world: the United States of America.

In Washington, with the approval of the U.S. State Department and the Secretary of the Army, the Belgian Embassy conferred on me the temporary rank of Military Attaché, which qualified me for admission to the Walter Reed Army Hospital. There, after a month of painstaking examinations, plastic surgery, treatments, fittings and adjustments, America literally gave me a hand—the Army Prosthetic Research Laboratory (APRL) Hook and Hand.

It was a remarkable collection of modern apparatus. An articulated metal hand or a shiny steel hook could be snapped into a laminated plastic socket, which had been moulded on to fit the stump of my arm and was held in position by a heavy leather strap encircling my biceps and a webbed harness stretching across my back to my left shoulder. A steel cable anchored to the middle of the harness extended along my back and arm to the end of the socket, where it connected to the control mechanism of the hook or the hand. Thus, when I flexed my back and shoulder muscles the cable opened or closed the prehensile device.

The artificial hand was encased in a plastic 'cosmetic glove' that simulated to some extent the appearance of real flesh; it was ugly, repulsive and comparatively awkward. In contrast, the hook was a clean, efficient, surprisingly versatile mechanism, stronger and in some respects more dependable than a real hand. I learned very quickly to use the gadget with precision and finesse, but after I'd played with it for a short time, I decided to discard it.

The reason was very simple: I'd already discovered that I

could do anything I wanted to without the aid of prosthetic equipment. Using a little ingenuity, patience and determination, it was quite possible for me to solve every problem with my left hand, my right forearm and my teeth. There was no need to burden myself with a Heath Robinson contraption, even if it worked. On the contrary, it would create a definite disadvantage, especially when I returned to the tropical climate of Central Africa, where the irritating harness would be a torture, and among whose primitive peoples the piratical-looking hook would inspire only fear and repulsion.

In every respect, I felt certain that I would be not only more natural and at ease without the artificial replacements, but considerably more agile and efficient. After all, if a bird can construct such a remarkable piece of architecture as a nest using only its beak, a man can certainly accomplish as much with five fingers.

So having reached that decision, I packed up my prosthetic gear and decided to forgo the one-month course of rehabilitation training generously offered by the Walter Reed Hospital, and I embarked instead on a rehabilitation programme of my own which was far more difficult and demanding. I bought a new 8-millimetre movie camera and a used Chevrolet convertible, stepped on the gas and began a meandering seven-month safari through the United States, Canada and Mexico—during which I drove over twenty thousand one-handed miles and lectured about the Africans, wrote articles about the Americans and put together a three-hour Kodachrome movie about my adventures in the New World.

I fell in love with America, and when I returned to Belgium after nine months of skyscrapers, freeways, swimming-pools, deserts, giant sequoias, cowboys, Indians, prairies, canyons—and above all, 175,000,000 friendly, energetic, broadminded and good-hearted people—everything European seemed very small and unprogressive. I was already planning to settle some day in America, but had no suspicion of the strange circumstances which were to send me back to the United States only four years later.

Instead, I looked forward eagerly to resuming my work in the Congo and Ruanda-Urundi, in spite of red tape and some government opposition. The Fonds Colonial des Invalidités had already ruled that I had 'undergone a permanent depreciation of 79 per cent in working capacity', which grim statistic included 65 per cent for the loss of my right hand, 11·1 per cent for partial deafness, and 3·25 per cent for *douleurs névritiques*, the acute, persistent pain in the stump of my right wrist. From an official point of view, I was less than 21 per cent of a man.

I was determined to show how very far from the truth that estimate was, but before I could do so I had to convince a Medical Commission of the Belgian Colonial Government that I was fit for continued African service. I knew and disagreed with what they would expect in the way of 'rehabilitation', but since I was scarcely in a position to argue, I put aside my personal feelings, got out my prosthetic gear and turned up for the examination armed with my spectacular APRL hook and hand. I gave a dazzling demonstration and the doctors—who had obviously never seen anything like it—unanimously approved my return to active service. Afterwards, I packed the artificial hand, hook, socket and harness away in the bottom of my suitcase and never wore them again.

A few days later, to my vast satisfaction, I was instructed to report to the Administrative Headquarters of the Congo's Kivu Province. I flew directly to Bukavu, where I received an assignment to the territory of Masisi, a bush post about forty miles west of Lake Kivu. Next day I bought yet another Chevy truck, paid a quick visit to my family in Kisenyi, and set out on the short drive to Masisi, full of optimistic confidence.

I needed it. The major part of my new duties was to run a re-afforestation project among the local Bahunde and Banianga natives, a massive planting of eucalyptus trees on steep hills and cliffs with an average gradient of over 45 per cent. It was extremely difficult to climb and work on those treacherous slopes with only one hand, and my difficulties were increased by frequent bouts of vertigo—another souvenir of the dynamite explosion, for the blast had damaged the delicate organs of equilibrium located within the inner ear.

I took several minor tumbles and then a really serious rolling fall of more than a hundred feet, in which the stump of my arm was badly bruised and the persistent pain flared into real agony. I kept working until the Sector Doctor ordered me to hospital at Goma, where examination disclosed that a thick plexiform neuroma had developed on the radial side of the stump, necessitating surgical intervention. So, to my complete disgust, I found myself again on the operating table, only fifteen days after returning to active service.

The operation was apparently successful, but the pain continued to torture me during my brief convalescence. In addition,

I had a much smaller but very annoying physical problem. The healed wounds on my jaw, neck and chest were still giving me trouble, in spite of the plastic surgery. Keloid scar tissue had formed, particularly around the site of the deeper wounds on my jaw, and the skin was extremely irritable, especially when I tried to shave. The solution was simple: I gave up shaving and grew a full, bushy, old-fashioned beard. Soon it acquired considerable status: it became my personal equivalent of the peacock's tail, the cat's whiskers or the bull elephant's tusks.

While convalescing, I wrote a series of eloquent requests for a transfer from the impossible working conditions at Masisi, and waited glumly for the answers, expecting my application, as usual, to stagnate in murky official channels. For once I was agreeably surprised: on 5 December 1956 I was told my transfer had gone through with unprecedented speed and I was being assigned to a new post, Mbau.

I read the short telegram three times, jumped out of my hospital bed, kissed the nurses good-bye and headed for my waiting truck. The bandaged stump of my arm wasn't completely healed, but I was too excited to care. After eight years in the service of the Belgian Colonial Government, I was finally headed in the right direction. Mbau was twelve miles north of Beni, on the southeastern fringe of the great Ituri Forest, and its population included some scattered outposts of the oldest, smallest, most elusive of all human races—the Bambuti pygmies.

12

I Attack a Leopard!

Nta wukina n'ingwe—'Nobody plays games with a leopard.'

KIVU AND RWANDA PROVERB

MOST of my time at Mbau in the Territory of Beni was spent among the local negro tribes rather than with the pygmies. The Colonial Government, I soon discovered, wasn't really interested in the Bambuti, apparently because it hadn't found a way to fit these wary, primitive nomads into the framework of the Plan Décennal. Officially the pygmies were ignored, and the Territorial Administrator of Beni, with whom I skirmished briefly at our first meeting, concentrated all his attention on the health, welfare and economic progress of the Batangi, Bambuba, Batalinga and other sub-tribes of the complex Banande group.

My part of the Plan Décennal involved supervising the agricultural activities of forty thousand Banande who had to be badgered into cultivating their own cash crops of cotton, coffee *robusta* and *Elaeis* palm-nuts, as well as such life-sustaining staples as manioc and sweet potatoes. I had made some tentative plans for sneaking the pygmies into that rigid agenda, but during the first few weeks I was almost constantly on safari, surveying every part of the sector. Then something happened about thirty-five miles east of Mbau which nearly brought all my plans to an abrupt end. I had an intimate encounter with a large and very shrewd specimen of Africa's most dangerous animal—the leopard.

Any meeting with a leopard is, of course, extremely uncommon. The beautiful, elusive cats generally confine themselves to hunting small game or occasionally invading the fringes of a native village to grab a dog, a child or an unwary woman. Leopards rarely attack a full-grown male native, and an attack on a white man is almost unheard of. Like the other cats, great and small, the leopard preys only on victims he knows and understands, humans or beasts who are part of his customary landscape.

The white man is obviously an alien. His clothing, his speech, even the way he moves, everything about him is unusual and therefore, to the mind of the cat, dangerous. The leopard or the lion generally will not attack him unless seriously provoked, usually with a bullet. For that matter, even when an enraged lion starts to charge a white hunter who has shot and wounded him, he will sometimes veer aside at the last moment and attack a native gun-bearer instead. In that way the animal feels more sure of himself.

When unusual circumstances pit a leopard and a man against each other at close quarters, the cat almost invariably wins, since he has not only the advantage of fangs and claws—eighteen razor-sharp talons—but pound for pound he is the world's strongest animal, capable of carrying three times his own weight into the trees where he customarily hangs his kill. It *is* possible, of course, for the man to triumph, as did Carl Akeley, the great American naturalist, sculptor and explorer, who was attacked by a wounded leopard on his first expedition to Africa in 1896.

Akeley's encounter differed in many important respects from mine. His leopard, an eighty-pound female, rushed him after he had broken her foot and creased her neck with two rifle bullets; she mauled him badly, chewing his right arm from shoulder to wrist, before he succeeded in knifing her. My leopard, a seven-foot, one hundred and twenty-pound male, hadn't been touched by bullet, spear or any other weapon; his strength and faculties were unimpaired, yet he failed to inflict any wounds during half an hour's hand-to-paw battle, even though he enjoyed an unusual added advantage—he had one more paw than I had. The explanation of these seemingly incredible statements is that, unlike Carl Akeley or anyone else, I attacked the leopard.

*   *   *

We had broken camp near Kamango at 7.30 on the morning of that fateful day in January 1957, deep in the Watalinga bush country between the Semliki River and the northwestern edge of the Ruwenzori massif. My caravan of sixteen Banande porters, *moniteurs* and policemen walked in single file through heavy bush towards the village of Muregeta. Our headman, the tallest and strongest native in the group, chopped away with his machete, clearing the overgrown trail for the heavily laden porters; I brought up the rear.

After a two-hour march, just as the bush was thinning out a little, I heard a terrible scream from the head of the column. At first I thought the porters were fighting, but as the men ahead of me hastily dropped their loads and bolted into the bush, I knew it was far more serious. I raced forward and found the second porter down on his belly, half-buried under the weight of a furious leopard.

The giant cat slashed at the screaming Munande's shoulders with his dragon-like front talons, while his hind legs furiously raked the muscles of the man's calves and thighs. Within seconds I knew the leopard would go for the neck, and then it would be over.

I had neither gun nor knife. The stump of my right arm was still tender from the operation at Goma five weeks before. There was no time for me to do any thinking or planning, yet it was impossible to stand there and watch a man die; to see him, passive as only an African can be, surrendering to an atrocious death without even attempting to struggle, and hear his piercing, monotonous cries as the arrogant cat tore at his flesh. It was intolerable.

Moved and guided by instinct alone, I jumped on to the leopard's back. Confidently mauling his native victim, he was completely unprepared for rear attack—one in his own style. As I seized him, he tried to turn and confront me. We rolled sideways, freeing the Nande porter, who had enough strength left to stagger to his feet and run, shrieking into the bush, blood streaming from his torn back and thighs.

In that first moment of surprise, I had to establish the hold I maintained throughout the coming battle. Passing my arms under the leopard's forequarters from behind, I forced his front legs forward and apart. Since members of the cat family, unlike ourselves, have no strengthening collarbones, it was possible for me partially to dislocate his shoulder joints, so that I could press the upper end of the humerus in each of the animal's forelegs against his neck. It was a choke-hold that forced the leopard's head, with its terrible battery of teeth, into relative immobility against my chest, with the roof of his skull just beneath my chin. Fortunately, the stump of my forearm was long enough to hook around the leopard's right front leg, and the trained muscles of my upper arm and shoulder were still in reasonably good condition. I locked the hold by gripping my right elbow with my left hand, thus putting his front end out of commission.

But I was far more concerned about the rear part of his body. The leopard's hind legs are his most efficient and terrible weapons: he uses them to tear the bowels from his victim's abdomen. So, while establishing my grip on his forequarters, I simultaneously took a scissors hold with my legs on the leopard's hind limbs, forcing them stiffly and widely apart.

When I felt that enormous cat in my arms, I realized how much I had underestimated him. It was like trying to contain a living hurricane of nerves, tendons and muscles. His four feet clawed wildly, and I knew that I would be a dead man if I lost for an instant the vice-like grip of my arms or legs. I prayed that one of the natives might have enough presence of mind and courage to drop me a knife, but there was no one in sight.

'*Kisu! Kisu!*' I called, 'A knife! A knife!'

Nobody answered.

The leopard surged—and I forgot about the knife. I tightened the grip of my arms, forcing his shoulders even more deeply into the sides of his neck, and shifted my hands so that I could squeeze his throat. Then I tried, with all my strength, to strangle him. He coughed and seemed to show some signs of weakening, but when I had to relax the pressure, just a little, I felt a new wave of power sweep through those amazing muscles and tendons. I realized then that I could never master him with my body alone.

'*Kisu! Kisu!*' I called again. '*KISU!*'

Again no answer.

All I could do was try to maintain my hold, hoping at least to tire him. I knew that I would have no chance at all if I released him. Unlike the lion, who will turn away when a battle proves unusually difficult, a leopard is very persistent, and never stops fighting until his opponent is disembowelled and completely lifeless. So we rolled over and over together, now on the trail, now in the bush, now back on the trail again. Although I outweighed him by a factor of two to one, he tossed my 18 stone about as though I were a mere toy.

My heart pounded with sickening force, and the pain in my groin grew almost unbearable as the sharp ridge of the leopard's spine dug into my genitals. By now my legs, back and shoulders were slashed and bleeding—not from the leopard's claws but

[Photo René Hürner]

THE SHOP'S PREMIER DANSEUR, MUREKEYE

[Photo René Hürner]

THE AUTHOR'S PERSONAL WITCH DOCTOR, KAMENDE

PLAYING WITH A LION
The Author with Simba, who is starting to lose his temper.

from the thorn bushes we tangled with during the struggle. Once, as the cat twisted convulsively, I struck my back with stunning force against a tree trunk; it might just as easily have been my head.

We fought on, neither of us able to gain more than a momentary advantage, for what must have been nearly twenty minutes. It was an eternity of force and motion, an endless nightmare permeated through and through with the rank odour of the giant cat, with the deep moan of his constant coughing and choking, and the nauseating slobber of his spittle on my forearms, face and clothing.

Finally, almost at the limit of my endurance, I saw the caravan's headman standing on the path. He was very far away, perhaps a hundred feet ahead, and held in his outstretched hand an enormous knife. I knew it was much too large and clumsy for the job—but it was a knife!

'*Tupa!*' I shouted, 'Throw it!'

He was too frightened to come a single step closer. Instead, he threw the knife from where he stood, a hundred feet up the trail. When it flashed in a bright arc through the air, I knew it would never reach me. I watched its trajectory with desperately straining eyes, knowing that I dared not lose sight of it for an instant. It landed twenty feet away.

Twenty interminable feet. My only hope was to wrestle the big fighting cat closer and closer to the knife, a procedure that took six or seven minutes of hectic, frustrating manœuvres. Then, less than three feet away and almost exhausted with the long struggle to force the leopard towards the weapon, I took a terrible but necessary chance.

Freeing my hand, I held the upper part of his body with the stump of my right arm alone, pinning him against the ground so that his left foreleg was caught under him. Then, stretching as far as I could, I strained to reach the knife—and finally succeeded in catching it by the very tip of the blade. Had I failed, I would have had no second chance. As I caught the knife, the leopard nearly broke free, and it took an agonizing effort to regain my hold around his left foreleg and neck. Meanwhile, I had to shift my fingers so that I could grip the knife by the handle instead of by its blade.

I waited a minute, covered with blood and sweat, breathing the bitter odour of the leopard's breath, almost dizzy with the pain pounding through my stump. Then I gathered all my strength for the final effort.

Knowing the chance I had to take, I relinquished my prized grip on the leopard's throat to explore his chest with my fingers. Feeling his sternum and ribs, I determined as closely as I could the approximate position of his heart. Slowly, carefully, I brought the tip of the knife into place between two of his ribs. Then, bracing the handle against the ground, I tried to turn the writhing leopard so that the weight of his own body would force the blade into his flesh.

The knife slipped, and I nearly lost it. The great cat leaped in my arms and it was only by a terrible effort that I prevented him from breaking loose. I tried again, and this time the knife slipped sideways as the leopard moved convulsively and I just missed stabbing myself in the chest. I could feel the cold metal of the huge blade slide across my ribs, and the hilt caught in the khaki fabric of my shirt. It was only with some difficulty that I managed to pull it loose.

Desperate, exhausted, I tried again. This time, turning sideways on top of the leopard, I managed to force the knife into his chest. The one-foot blade sank almost to the hilt. Even as he made a final tremendous effort, which was nearly fatal to me, I saw the blood spurt back along the handle of the knife, and I realized with a tired and terrible joy that I had reached his heart. Yet I still had to maintain my relentless grip. His heart transfixed by that massive knife, the leopard's convulsive dying struggle lasted at least another three or four minutes. Then it was over. I released his body, strangely limp and motionless, and lay on the ground, trembling, trying to regain my breath.

*   *   *

When I sat up, after a minute or two, I was disgusted to see my Banande porters starting to emerge from the bush. Some were scrambling down from trees where they had taken refuge. The headman, who had been the bravest among them, called excitedly, '*Chui na kufa!*', 'The leopard is dead!' All the others joined in this chorus with him, but still hung back, making very sure that he was *really* dead before approaching the bloody spot where he lay.

Finally, there was an ecstatic scene round the animal's corpse. Several Banande fell on their knees. '*Mungu yangu!*', 'My God!' cried one, stretching his arms towards the sky; '*Mama yangu!*', 'My mother!' shouted some of the others. One little native stood quietly, staring first at the leopard and then at me. 'Kill leopard—one hand—one knife,' he kept muttering, shaking his head in bewilderment.

I was happy to think how smoothly the rest of this trip would go. On every safari, much time is wasted arguing and haggling with the natives over innumerable details, and I knew these Banande would never again question any order of mine. Like most other Africans, they were far more impressed by physical strength and power than by virtue, devotion or any other moral quality. 'Bwana Mukubwa', the great or powerful master, was still their ideal; 'Bwana Muzuri', the 'nice' or 'kind' master, generally meant 'weak' or 'stupid'.

I asked the headman what had happened to the leopard's victim.

'He ran into the bush and went towards Muregeta. He was still crying, Bwana. Nafikili ye iko na kuya pumbavu, he must have lost his mind.'

'Perhaps you all lost your minds,' I said sharply. 'Either that or you are cowards.' I pointed to the boxes and bundles they had dropped on the ground. 'Now we shall finish our safari and take the leopard with us.'

Smiling rather sheepishly, the headman cut a stick eight feet long. Then with some *kekele*, or rattan string, the leopard was tied to the stick by his paws, slung up like a pig for the slaughter. But the burden dropped by the leopard's victim, a wooden box full of books, had to be considered, as well as the leopard. There was no way to take both.

'Leave the box by the side of the trail,' I ordered. 'After we reach the village, one of you must come back for it. Now, you men,' I gestured at two of the shamefaced Banande, 'you managed to climb higher than anyone else. For that, you may have the privilege of carrying the leopard besides your regular burdens.'

A new excitement awaited us at Muregeta. My wounded porter was lying on the ground, surrounded by the entire population of the village. The local medicine man had gone into action, dropping leaf-juice in the man's wounds while pronouncing magical spells. The injured native, convulsed with spasms of hysteria, didn't even recognize me.

'Abari, abari?' I asked him, 'How do you feel?'

He sobbed and made meaningless gestures with his hands. 'Pumbavu,' I thought, 'he's gone mad, just as the headman said.' I left him to the ministrations of the medicine man, who seemed to be accomplishing some good as far as his body was concerned.

It was only at that point that I started to worry about my own body. Although the leopard had never succeeded in reaching me with his teeth or claws, there were at least twenty major scratches from thorn bushes on my back, sides and legs. My elbows were completely raw from their constant abrasion against the ground, and the stump of my forearm trembled with pain.

I asked a second medicine man to help me take care of my troubles. This young fellow was the old one's nephew, a sort of bush 'intern' eager to impress me with his knowledge. When he started ransacking his pharmacopoiea, I presented him with some of my own magic preparations, alcohol, ether and mercurochrome, which he stared at in amazement. Then I explained the use of bandages and adhesive tape, leaving him entirely dumbfounded. Finally, fearing infection, I shot some penicillin into my right arm; my new-found physician could not believe his eyes.

The leopard's victim remained permanently deranged. I took him to the American Inland Mission at Oicha, where my friend Dr. Carl Becker was unable to help him.

                              *   *   *

For months afterwards the natives of North Kivu told and re-told the story of my leopard fight, with many exaggerations and embroideries, until almost every village had its own version. Some were almost unrecognizable, even to me. Meanwhile, as an even more touching demonstration of their feelings, the Banande accepted me as a tribal brother. When an account of the event filtered down to my Balega friends in South Kivu, a symbolic ivory talisman was presented to me, in March 1960, by the Bwamé Secret Society of Maniema which ten years earlier had permitted me to become its first white member.

This carving, which the Balega call Master of the Leopard, was made about seventy-five years ago for one of their tribesmen who killed a leopard with his spear as it tried to leap upon him. After his death his senior male descendant was entitled to wear the emblem, but when his only grandson died without male issue, it was returned to the safe keeping of the Society. When my old friend the A-Tumba-Kindi presented me with the carving, he announced that since I was the only living member who had killed a leopard in single combat, I was the sole heir to the talisman, which I would be privileged to pass on to my male descendants.

This beautiful object, which I still wear hung round my neck, is fashioned in the precise shape of a leopard's fang. On its concave side, where the ivory is pale amber with age and wear, is carved the traditional stylized mask of the Bwamé Society, a strange, simple, mouthless face which seems lost in deep thought. To this day, living in 'civilized' surroundings, it is my only adornment. I never wear rings, cuff-links or a watch, and never even carry a wallet. My sole ornament is and will always remain this worn little ivory carving.

13

A 6 ft. 5 in. Pygmy Candidate

> *Utrum pygmaei sint homines?*—'Are pygmies men?'
>
> ALBERTUS MAGNUS
> thirteenth-century scholastic philosopher
> [His answer was 'No.']

'WHY don't you ask a man to do it? I'm only a pygmy.'

I stared at the sullen little brown man who had just uttered those words. I had asked him to help me by holding a stick I was driving into the ground to mark off the corner of a new *Elaeis* palm plantation near the western end of Mbau. It had been a simple request, but his reply shocked me.

'Whoever told you that you aren't a man?' I asked.

'Everybody knows it. The negroes treat us like slaves, they make us work hard and pay us off with bananas and a few drinks of *pombe*. The white people think we are monkeys, all they like to do is watch us dance or climb trees. Nobody cares about us or writes down our names in little books as they do for the negroes.'

'If the white people give you identification books with your names written down in them, you may have to pay taxes just like the rest of the natives—'

'*Ndio, Bwana!*' he cried eagerly. 'That's what we want! To pay taxes and go to jail!'

'You want to go to jail?'

'If we steal sweet potatoes or bananas from a negro's plantation, nobody bothers to punish us. They don't put a chimpanzee in jail when *he* takes a piece of fruit. People say we are monkeys because we have no books and no taxes. Perhaps if we had them, we could be men.'

220

'You have to pay taxes with money,' I told the excited pygmy. 'That means you'll have to go to work for yourselves. Now, if I gave you tools and seed, would you use them?'

He looked shocked. 'Pygmies don't plant things,' he explained. 'We don't know how.'

'What if I teach you? Would you be willing to learn?'

'I don't know, *Bwana*. I just don't know. We want money, but we don't want to work.'

*   *   *

That night, in my house at Mbau, I thought of his words and the underlying problem; the heartbreaking predicament of over a hundred human beings, living in poverty, ignorance, filth and disease at Ebikeba, a sedentary Bambuti encampment tied by bonds of feudal servitude to the negro villages of Mbau. Tragically, the people of Ebikeba were far more representative of the Congo's pygmies than the band of free forest nomads I had visited seven years before.

Situated only two miles away from the large clay-wattled houses and productive green fields of the nearest Batangi village, the pygmy establishment smelled like an open cesspool and looked like a primitive Central African version of our 'civilized' slums. It consisted of several dozen crude hemispherical huts, scattered over three irregular clearings at the edge of the dense forest, bearing little resemblance to the carefully imbricated *mangungu*-leaf dwellings I remembered so well. Instead, the sagging frameworks were thatched unevenly with sorghum straw and withered banana leaves whose curled edges left innumerable chinks for the wind and the rain. Some of the huts had pathetic little doors put together from old packing crates, complete with advertising slogans; the dirt floors were a stew of mud after every rain. Flies, fleas, rats and worms infested the interior of the huts, attracted by the ever-growing heaps of garbage, detritus and human excrement which littered the edge of the clearing.

The occupants of those stinking hovels were mostly frustrated bachelors and old or barren women. The Batangi negroes had bought most of the healthy young girls and taken them to their own villages; as a result the pygmy population was decreasing at an ominous rate, and it was obvious that within a generation or two Ebikeba would come to an end.

The same sordid little tragedy was repeating itself throughout the Ituri Forest. Formerly the pygmies had lived as free nomads, moving from place to place every two or three weeks and building new *mangungu*-leaf huts at each temporary encampment, a way of life which had profound advantages for a people physiologically and psychologically adapted to the deep forest and, of course, totally ignorant of elementary hygiene. Now, at least 80 per cent of the pygmies had abandoned their old ways to settle down in what they called *pa*, sedentary camps like Ebikeba, more or less closely attached to the villages of their negro overlords. As a result, they were succumbing in terrifying numbers to ills they had never encountered before—sunstroke, heat prostration, pulmonary congestion, pneumonia, tuberculosis, syphilis, yaws, gonorrhea and even leprosy. Thus, a people who probably numbered over a million only two or three hundred years ago, had been reduced to a mere twenty thousand survivors struggling to eke out a precarious living in forty thousand square miles of the Ituri Forest and headed directly towards extinction.

The Belgian Colonial Government's answer to this desperate problem had been well-intentioned but unrealistic. 'We shall leave the pygmies untouched,' the Administration had declared, 'free to follow their traditional way of life in the virgin forest they love so well, and to which they are, in every respect, completely and perfectly adapted.'

So, unlike all the other peoples of the Congo, the pygmies had never been included in a census, given identification books or subjected to the capitation tax levied on every able-bodied native adult. This tax, the equivalent of £2–£3 a year, constitutes official acknowledgement that a man was both mature and capable of work. Most young boys were impatient to get their book and start paying tax, just as a few proud old men liked to go on paying in order to feel younger and stronger; natives between these two extremes resented the tax, and usually tried to evade it.

Exemption was of course intended for the pygmies' benefit, but the effect was to deprive them of their status and their feeling of responsibility. Still worse, the Government had placed them beyond the legal code which governed all other inhabitants of the Congo, black and white alike. Instead, responsibility for their criminal acts—mostly theft and murder—was assigned to their negro overlords, who were frequently hauled off to jail for their servants' misdeeds. As a crowning touch, the Government actually permitted the pygmies to establish themselves in the Albert National Park (mainly in the Semliki Sector), where they were allowed to kill protected animals as though they were themselves part of the fauna.

The hordes of tourists who visited the fringes of the pygmy country apparently had the same idea, and doled out peanuts and sweets from paper-bags as though they were feeding monkeys at the zoo. Sometimes they threw the tempting morsels on the ground and enjoyed watching the hungry people scrambling desperately for them. Once I saw a man throw a handful of salt from the window of his car and crank away at his movie camera while the salt-starved pygmies got down on their hands and knees to lick the precious grains from the soil.

Other movie-minded tourists offered the wide-eyed little men spectacular gifts—a cheap watch, a pen, a cigarette-lighter—to climb into the trees and leap from one branch to the next; two young men from Ebikeba had been permanently crippled and one had died as a direct result. Still others, presumably trying to produce a filmed record of the 'real' Africa to impress their friends at home, tried to bribe the shocked, incredulous pygmies into removing their *ficus*-bark loincloths and making love under the recording eye of the camera.

Here at Mbau, where the pygmy encampment of Ebikeba was situated extremely close to the road, the tourists' influence was especially conspicuous. As professional beggars, the pygmies had grown more indolent, arrogant and irresponsible than ever, and their old feudal ties with the Batangi tribesmen were starting to break down. The negroes demanded wild game or menial work in exchange for their beer and bananas, and the pygmies preferred to solicit along the road or ask charity from the nearby establishment of Little Sisters of Jesus, a well-meaning but practically ineffectual missionary order.

That was the irony of the situation: most of the whites who came into contact with the pygmies—missionaries, tourists and government officials alike—had basically good intentions, but had managed to make a bad situation worse. Deeper in the forest the Bambuti had at least the status of serfs; here at Ebikeba and other camps close to the road, they had lost all human dignity. How was it to be restored to them?

I realized that any valid working approach to the problem would require an intensive personal knowledge of Bambuti psychology, habits and customs—far more than I could ever acquire from the spoiled people of Ebikeba. Many of them had forgotten or never even learned Ki-Efe—their own dialect of Kimbuti, the strange, little-known pygmy language—and the majority had been so badly corrupted by outside influences that little of their traditional culture remained. Obviously the only useful source of information would be the few remaining bands of free pygmies in the interior of the Grand Forest.

There was only one way to gain their confidence and learn what I needed to know—to walk into the forest, alone, and seek out those elusive, unspoiled Bambuti. It was certainly a far-fetched idea for a 6 ft. 5 in. candidate with a white skin, shaggy beard and amputated arm to try to learn their beliefs and customs, participate in their rituals, share their life and be one of them, a pygmy myself among other pygmies.

As a first step I wrote to the Provincial Agriculture Service, which had already approved my first tentative work among the Bambuti, notifying them that I intended to leave on a long safari to visit the free nomads of the interior; a few days later they gave me *carte blanche* for the project, thus leaving only one obstacle in my path: the Territorial Administrator of Beni.

As usual, I was having A.T. trouble, and for the usual reasons. My new boss, a fanatical Fleming from Antwerp, whom I shall call 'Vermeulen', had one overriding objective in life: the advancement of his career. According to his narrow viewpoint that meant scrupulous devotion to the minutest details of the Plan Décennal, as though it had been handed down from Mount Sinai rather than Brussels, and almost complete indifference to the traditional native cultures of the Congo, especially the pygmies. He was stiff, arrogant and set in his ways, and naturally any really unusual project such as I proposed was anathema to a man of his stamp.

'I don't approve of the trip,' Vermeulen told me flatly.

'You know how bad conditions are with the pygmies. Something has to be done.'

'Your concern should be the Banande plantations. Their crops are important and the schedules must be observed. I therefore *order* you to leave those damned pygmies alone and restrict your activities to coffee, palm trees and cotton.'

'If that's your attitude, then there's no point in discussing it. I'm leaving tomorrow.'

'You're looking for trouble, Monsieur Hallet!'

'From you? Don't you think I'll have enough trouble where I'm going?'

'If you continue to defy my authority,' he said, 'I can promise that you'll find more trouble in Beni than you ever will in the forest.'

'I'll take my chances with both,' I said bluntly. Then I turned and walked away.

Next morning I locked the doors of my square house at Mbau, with its whitewashed brick walls and red-tiled roof, unlocked the cages in the back yard, released my six pets—a baboon, two monkeys, a pangolin, a spitting cobra and a Gaboon viper—and stood there for a moment, watching them scamper, shuffle and slither into the nearby bush. Then I checked the left-hand pocket of my *kapitula*, the only one I habitually used, to make sure it was empty. I wanted to take absolutely nothing with me.

Gun, camera, knife, helmet, insignia, watch, matches and money . . . there was no reason for any of those things. They weren't a part of the forest and its hidden life. If my experiences among the pygmies were to be valid *in terms of their own existence*, I would have to share their struggle without relying on any props from the outside world.

I remembered what a Masai elder had said five years before : 'If I had pockets, I would need money and other foolish things to put in them. Then I would really start to have problems. I would have to go to work, like the Kikuyu or the Wakamba, to make that money, and little by little I would turn into a slave. But, as you can plainly see,' he threw back his calico robe, revealing his lean, naked old body, 'I have no pockets . . . and I have no problems.'

Now my pockets were empty, and I was leaving the banal details of civilized life behind me to face the oldest and most basic problems of mankind : the struggle for survival against the raw elements of nature. The forest lay before me, a dark, tangled labyrinth full of provocative questions. They had to be answered, and so I simply walked in.

*   *   *

My first goal was the Muhekuva encampment directly west of Mbau, which was home to a semi-sedentary band of pygmies only a little less spoiled than those of Ebikeba. I hoped that the people here might be able to direct or guide me towards one of the elusive groups in the interior. That was the plan, but when I arrived at Muhekuva, after a difficult two-hour trip through dense bush, I found the camp deserted except for a few old women and two children. The men were hunting and the younger women were off on one of their daily scavenger-hunts for vegetables, edible insects and fruit.

I spent a long, impatient day waiting for their return. When the noisy band of hunters returned at sunset, I was delighted to find among them two young boys whom I had befriended at Ebikeba. Yoma and Ebu were very quick, friendly and honest, and spoke excellent Kingwana. During the past few weeks I had taught them to identify and print all the letters of the alphabet, a convincing proof, as far as I was concerned, that the mental capacity of the 'unteachable' pygmies had been completely underestimated.

I waited until the campfire had been laid and all of the pygmies were ranged around it and then tried to explain my plan. 'I want to go into the heart of the forest,' I told them in Kingwana, 'to live with Bambuti who still follow the old ways.'

'That is a very hard thing to do,' one of the men answered, scratching his neck in bewilderment. 'Almost all of the bands are tied to the negroes. You know that.'

'But there *are* a few free pygmies left. Can you take me to them?'

'No. Some have met bad white men and now are afraid of all the *wazungu*. If they saw you on their hunting trails, they would kill you. Other bands have never even seen a white man. They would think you a savage ape with a bleached skin, or maybe even the *lulu* monster. They would kill you too.'

'The *lulu* monster?' I was intrigued. 'What is that?' I asked. 'Do I look like it at all?'

'A little. The *lulu* monster is supposed to be as tall as a tree and as wide as a negro's house. He is fiercer than *Kituri*, the giant snake monster, and more powerful than *Piobo*, the elephant monster who loves to kill men. Sometimes he roars like a motor-car!'

'Where does he live?'

'He isn't really alive any more, but still, we're not sure. Once, a long time ago, he ate everyone in the world, except for one pregnant pygmy woman. She escaped and hid herself away in the deepest part of the forest. Then, when her time came, the baby talked to her from the bottom of her belly; he told her he didn't want to come out from the usual place and that she was not to be surprised, whatever happened. Then he was born—out of a little hole under his mother's big toe. What's more, he was full-grown, clever, brave and knew how to handle a spear. He asked his mother where the rest of the people were, and she told him how the *lulu* monster had killed all the pygmies in the forest.

"Then I will kill *him* to take revenge," her son said, and he went to look for the monster. "*Lulu odi avie!*" he called, again and again, "*Lulu, killer of men!*" but it took a long time for the monster to come, because he thought he had eaten everyone in the world. Then he rushed through the forest, roaring like a tornado, breaking down the big trees, and opened his mouth to swallow the pygmy hero. That was his great mistake! The pygmy hurled his spear into the blood-red hole, as big as a house, and killed him. Then he cut off the monster's head, opened up his belly with the spear-blade—and all the pygmies crawled out through the hole and marched back into their forest. That happened a long time ago, but some people think that the *lulu* monster is still alive.'

'It is a wonderful story,' I said smoothly, 'but I feel sure that no one will really mistake me for the *lulu* monster. I may be big, but I couldn't fit even a single pygmy into my belly. Anyway, I'm willing to gamble on it. I'm dead-set on going deeper into the forest until I meet the free, wild Bambuti.'

Ebu looked up at me intently. 'Why? Why do you want to do this thing?'

'I want to help the pygmies. All of them. But I can do nothing until I learn to understand them.'

Ebu turned to Yoma, the other boy from Ebikeba, and spoke to him in rapid, staccato Kimbuti. Then they lowered their eyes and refused to look at me again.

'Won't any of you help?' I asked the circle of silent pygmies. 'It is for your people that I want to do this, not for my own.'

'If you will travel like a real white man,' one said slowly, 'we will come with you.'

'How does a real white man travel?'

'With guns, tents and lots of boys. With soldiers to protect him.'

'How can I live with the free Bambuti—with guns, tents and soldiers?'

'It is too dangerous. You'll be killed and *we'll* get the blame for it.'

A general murmur of agreement seemed to end the discussion. The pygmies of the Muhekuva camp were obviously frightened by the whole idea, but they were very kind. They shared their small meal with me and let me sleep in one of their huts, a real *mangungu* beehive about seven feet in diameter. It was a minor problem the next morning extricating myself from that tiny hut. When I finally managed it and stood up, stretching and scratching in the dawn, I found Yoma sitting nearby, watching me intently.

'I've thought about it, *Bwana*,' he said, 'and I will go with you. But first you must go back to Mbau and get some trade goods to give to the wild pygmies. And a gun.'

'No. I don't intend to buy their friendship, and I won't kill people with a gun, even to protect myself. If you don't want to come with me, then I'm going ahead by myself.'

As I left the encampment, in front of the last hut at the edge of the clearing, I saw Ebu, squatting on the ground with his chin on his fist. I looked at him and he lowered his eyes. I waited a minute and nothing happened. I turned and walked into the forest, and ten minutes later I heard running footsteps behind me. It was Ebu.

'*Bwana! Bwana!*' he called excitedly. 'I've changed my mind! I'm coming with you!'

'Why?'

'After you left, I talked with Yoma. He told me what you said. I can't let you go alone, *Bapa*. I'm coming with you.'

I looked down at the earnest pygmy boy, deeply moved by his simple words, especially the significant word *Bapa*, 'father'; the boy had used the affectionate term of respect.

We smiled at each other and my new-found guide took the lead, bow in hand, a full quiver on his shoulder, passing easily through tangled spots where I had to bend double. We set out in the direction of another pygmy outpost about an hour's walk to the northwest, but when we arrived at the little clearing, we found only a collection of weather-beaten abandoned huts. These pygmies had obviously moved on.

'Which direction shall we take now, Ebu?'

'There are free pygmies at Ebuya, but they are very wild, *Bapa*!'

'How far away?'

'*Pale!*' the boy answered, pointing to the west. '*Pale!*'

That word reminded me of Mulume, my first guide in the Ituri. *Pale*—it might be ten miles, fifty, a hundred. We walked north. We walked endlessly. We paused along the way to pick some fruit and gather a few mushrooms which we ate raw after washing them in a little stream. Ebu devoured some caterpillars, picked off the bark of a tree, but I didn't feel enough of a gourmet to join in this experiment, so I contented myself with chewing a few stems of *umnyoka*, a sugary kind of liana.

We walked until the end of the day, and still there was no

sign of a pygmy encampment. Finally, after the trail petered
out in a slippery bog, we decided to camp for the night. We
travelled a little farther to escape from the dank, swampy area,
and when we reached solid ground again, Ebu announced that
he would build a hut.

I helped him, of course, and he was amazed to see that I knew
all the different phases of pygmy house construction. We made a
fire, which Ebu started by friction in the traditional way, and
kept it burning all night as a little precaution against prowling
leopards. Each time I got up I put some more sticks of wood on
the fire—and I got up often. My mattress, consisting of a few
large *mangungu* leaves, was supremely uncomfortable; my
pillow, a small piece of half-rotten tree trunk cushioned with
leaves, was even worse.

We left very early next morning and walked steadily for about
three hours. Then Ebu stopped abruptly, turned and hurried
back to me, his eyes full of fear. 'Look!' he whispered, pointing
with his finger. 'There! But don't go near it!'

I advanced very cautiously and found a little stick about three
feet high thrust into the ground in the middle of the trail. The
upper end was wedged into a split twig forming a narrow open
triangle at the top.

'Don't touch it!' Ebu warned me again. 'That is the way the
wild pygmies mark their hunting grounds. Anyone who steps
over that stick will find big trouble!'

'If we don't hunt, there's no reason for them to attack us.
Come on, Ebu!'

'No. I can't cross that sign. But I'll build a hut here and wait
for you—if you come back.'

On that ominous note, I entered the forbidden territory alone.
I walked for about half an hour, watching the bush on either
side of the trail, ready at any moment to dodge a poisoned arrow
or an elephant-spear. Suddenly I saw three pygmies, a tough-
looking old man and two younger companions, walking very
slowly in my direction. They stopped about fifty feet away and
stared at me.

All were armed with the traditional two-and-a-half-foot Bambuti bows and lightweight, poorly-feathered arrows, weapons
which the pygmies used with remarkable accuracy at distances
of up to twenty feet. At thirty feet they often missed a small
target, at forty they sometimes failed to hit a tree of two-foot
diameter, and at fifty their shots usually went wide of the mark.
When they hunted the forest antelope or other small game, they

stalked it with dogs, tried to encircle it and generally succeeded only when the fleeing animal passed within their twenty-foot range. I was, of course, a much larger target than a *mboloko*, but considering the fifty-foot gulf that lay between us, I was relatively safe.

'*We kwenda wapi?*' the leader asked me in bad Kingwana. 'Where-you-go?'

'I want to visit your camp.'

'*Hapana!*' he said brusquely.

'*Sababu gani?*', 'Why not?'

The answer was a very long, rapid string of Kimbuti words which were completely lost on me. Trying to understand him better, I took a few steps in his direction and, simultaneously, I saw all three pygmies raise and cock their bows. *They're only trying to frighten me*, I thought, moving forward again. *They have no reason to kill me* . . . And just at that moment an arrow flashed by only a few inches from my left shoulder.

That stopped me in my tracks. '*Sababu gani?*' I repeated.

'*Hapana!*' the old man shouted. '*Hapana!*' Then, to punctuate that last decisive 'No', he shot again.

This time I saw the arrow coming. Leaping to the side to avoid it, I just missed intersecting the trajectory of two other arrows fired by the younger men; one struck the ground near my left foot and the other passed through the right leg of my *kapitula*. I tore the arrow out of the khaki fabric and saw that the wooden tip was covered with a film of fresh poison. The argument was extremely convincing.

I took several steps backwards, feeling instinctively that it would be dangerous to turn. There were no more arrows. Instead, the three pygmies shouted at me in Kimbuti, a torrent of angry words that were obvious threats. After ten backward steps, I decided that it was safe to turn and retreat with dignity. The moment I did, two arrows flew by on either side of my body. I did another about-face and they stopped shooting; but with every backward step I took, the three pygmies took a step forward.

The ludicrous slow-motion chase went on for about ten minutes until I finally broke and made a run for it in the direction of the little pygmy signpost, the red light of the forest. Apparently satisfied that I was leaving their domain, they didn't bother to follow. A few minutes later, when I reached the spot where I had left Ebu, I found the first crude framework of a hut but no sign of the boy himself. I waited. Half an hour later

I was astonished when not only Ebu, but Yoma as well, rushed up the trail towards me, bursting with excitement.

'*Bapa!* You are alive!' Ebu exclaimed. 'I saw the arrows. I was terribly afraid!'

'*You* saw the arrows? I don't understand.'

'After you crossed the sign, *Bapa*. Yoma came a few minutes later and I told him to wait here. Then I went after you. I was afraid, of course, but I just had to do it. I followed you down the trail, and when the three wild pygmies came, I hid in the bushes on the side. I saw them shooting arrows at you and I ran away! Then I came back here and told Yoma what happened. He said, "We'd better go back to Ebikeba. If *Bapa* is dead, we can't help him. If he's alive, he'll keep on looking for trouble." So we started to go back—'

'You make me sound very bad,' Yoma broke in, 'and *I* was the first to say "Let's go back anyhow!"'

I tried to soothe them. 'Let's build a fire. Then we can all calm down and discuss what to do.'

Once the three of us were huddled around a comforting little fire, there seemed to be nothing to discuss. Ebu and Yoma were violently against taking a single step into the forbidden territory and the hidden encampment, which was probably no more than two miles away. Being pygmies themselves, they certainly could have approached without too much risk and tried to explain my friendly intentions; but they didn't volunteer, although it must have occurred to them, and I refused to suggest it myself. Finally, after much argument, we agreed that I would go first and my two friends would follow about fifty feet behind. Then, when the wild pygmies challenged me again, Yoma and Ebu could shout Kimbuti explanations from a position of relative safety.

We slept very badly that night, squeezed together in our hastily completed hut, and set out again next morning shortly after sunrise. I walked first, as planned, about twenty steps ahead; moving very warily behind me were first Ebu and then Yoma, who was slightly taller. Everything seemed normal, but after only five minutes I heard an unusual noise in the bush, which I thought at first was a small antelope or a monkey, expecting that the pygmies would confront me openly as they had done the day before.

I took a few more steps; the noise increased on both sides of the trail. I stopped, and at that precise moment I saw the face of a pygmy, almost completely hidden in the heavy green bush, about forty-five feet away. I looked round more carefully and I saw an arm holding a bow, and just above it, another face. Evidently the people of Ebuya had decided to waste no more time on conversation.

'Come back!' my two friends shouted at me. 'Come back!'

Unfortunately, there was no way I could. As every second crept by, I saw more faces, more bows and several gleaming elephant-spears. I felt certain that they would shoot whether I moved forward or backwards. So I stood in my tracks, motionless, hoping to impress them with an air of calm resolve. A full minute must have passed, while the half-hidden faces in the bush watched me silently. Then a sharp cry, obviously an order, cut through the quiet air, followed by an incredible number of arrows from both sides of the trail. I tried to leap aside, but there were arrows everywhere, and I was certainly a large enough target.

Two found the mark. The first, an arrow with a three-inch iron point, embedded itself in my right calf. It was painful enough but I didn't worry about it, since I knew that the pygmies used metal points for hunting antelope, and never poisoned them. The other arrow, which lodged itself in my right shin about halfway between knee and ankle, was the type used for hunting monkeys and birds. The wooden tip was wet with fresh poison, and almost immediately I felt a strong burning sensation in the wound.

I stood there, shocked, staring at the two arrows embedded side by side in my right leg, their shafts sticking out to form a rough right angle. I knew how lethal Bambuti poisons are, a sentence of slow death, but still I refused to accept the idea that I was going to die. I looked at the band of pygmies, waiting with bows cocked, ready to shoot again, and I spoke to them in Kingwana: 'I came here to help you . . . to protect you . . . to keep you alive.'

Yoma and Ebu interrupted me, calling frantically in Kimbuti from their position twenty steps away. The people of Ebuya answered them angrily with some complicated Kimbuti verbiage of their own. I waited, trying to remain impassive in spite of the pain. 'Ebu!' I called out during a lull in the Kimbuti storm. 'What are they saying?'

'I told them you're a good man. That I know you. That you never beat anyone. They don't want to believe me, *Bapa*! They keep saying that you're an enemy and that you must die!'

I thought about that for a moment and then I decided on a

new strategy. It was entirely possible that the same people who manufactured the poison might be in possession of the antidote. 'Ebu,' I said finally, 'tell them these words for me in Kimbuti: "I want to help. If you want to be helped, keep me alive. If you don't, kill me all the way."'

The boy shouted a salvo of excited words. The people listened, considered and started to argue with each other. Then the same old man who had led the attack stepped forward, brandishing his loaded bow. '*Mi ua we*,' he said in bad Kingwana, 'Me-kill-you.' Apparently my strategy had backfired, but suddenly, just as he uttered those words, Ebu and Yoma ran towards us until they were only ten steps away, raising their own weapons to threaten the pygmy elder.

'Drop your bows!' I shouted at them. '*Now!*'

They hesitated, completely confused.

'Drop them!' I repeated. 'You can't help me like this—and I don't want you to die with me.'

Reluctantly, they dropped the weapons to the ground and I waited for the final arrow. Instead, to my astonishment, the old man lowered his own bow with an emphatic gesture, apparently impressed by my unexpected actions. He peered at me and I looked back at him steadily. His eyes shifted and he stared at the stump of my right wrist. Turning to Yoma, he said something in Kimbuti. 'He wants to know how that happened,' the boy explained to me.

Hastily, I tried to simplify the long, complicated story. 'Tell him that I tried to get fish with dynamite for some people who were dying of hunger and there was a big explosion.'

'He doesn't know what dynamite is, *Bapa*. I'll tell him you were struck by lightning when you were taking the fish.'

'All right, but hurry up!'

Yoma translated and the old pygmy stared at my arm with even greater curiosity. Then he asked another question.

'He wants to know if the tribe you stole the fish for are white like you.'

'I didn't steal the fish—oh, never mind, Yoma. Tell him that they were black like him.'

A moment later, another question. 'Are they tall black men, that tribe?'

'No. Tell him they are a kind of pygmy called Bamosso, who live far away. They are taller than the Bambuti but much smaller than the negroes. Tell him that I will try to help his people just as I helped the Bamosso.'

Another rapid Kimbuti exchange while my leg throbbed and trembled.

'He doesn't know if they want the help, *Bapa*. He says that they don't like to eat fish like those fake Bamosso pygmies—'

Nom de Dieu! I thought to myself desperately. I'll be dead by the time they stop talking about fish!

'—but he admits that they've made a mistake. One of the men from Ebikeba came this way not long ago and said you were talking about putting all the Bambuti to work and making us pay the taxes. He was afraid that you wanted to take pygmies for slaves.'

'Slaves! Did you explain what a mad idea that was?'

'Yes, *Bapa*. We told him, and he says that he's sorry. Still, he doesn't know what he can do to help you. That arrow was poisoned with the juice of the *kago* vine . . . it may take a few hours, but you will certainly die.'

With those words my two young friends, deeply moved, abandoned their last vestiges of caution and ran to my side. Ebu pulled out the arrows while I grimaced with that sudden new wave of pain. He stared at the poisoned arrow in his hand, seeming to realize for the first time exactly what it meant. Then he raised his big imploring eyes to the old pygmy and pleaded with him in Kimbuti, a long speech ending with three intelligible words, '*Bapa-nda-Bambuti.*'

I felt an odd thrill when he said that, in spite of my pain and apprehension. The boy had just called me, literally, 'The Father of the Pygmies'. Unfortunately, however, the pygmies were about to become not only orphans but patricides—unless they did something damned quick.

While the talk went on, they gradually drew closer into a tight, curious circle round us, arguing the question stubbornly. Finally, a very old man walked up to me and took a good look at my leg, prodding at the skin surrounding the arrow wounds. He spoke briefly to the leader of the band, they scratched at the napes of their necks for a moment, and then turned to confer with Yoma.

'That old man's name is Mutuke,' the boy said excitedly, 'and he says that there is a chance to save you. There is no plant that fights against the poison, but he knows how to do it. Sit down on the ground, *Bapa*, and he will begin.'

I seated myself in the middle of the trail and immediately felt much better—or at least, less worse. Mutuke took a very sharp arrow point and made a slash about half an inch deep across the poisoned wound on my shin. He cut again, forming a cross, and peered gravely at the results. Apparently it wasn't bleeding enough to satisfy him, because he picked at it again and again until the blood streamed freely over my leg. Next he borrowed a hide belt from one of the bystanders and made a tourniquet around the upper part of my thigh, knotting it tightly into place. He gestured at me, and obediently, I lay down flat on my back, and he poked again with his arrow point, forcing even more blood to flow.

The entire procedure was quite rational, obviously intended to minimize the absorption of poison from the wounded area by the rest of my body. Yet I felt certain that this simple technique would scarcely be adequate since I knew that the poison of the *kago* vine, an exotic member of the milkweed family, was extremely powerful and killed by its effect on the nervous system. It was only because I had received a relatively small dose in one of my extremities that its action had slowed down.

A moment later Mutuke turned to Yoma and spoke briefly.

'He says that you must go to the camp,' the boy explained. 'He can't do the big stuff here.'

I staggered to my feet, wondering what 'big stuff' Mutuke had in mind. It was a long, agonizing walk through dense bush; it probably took about twenty minutes and I left little spatters of blood on the trail. The whole thing gave me a strange sensation of the *déjà vu*: I might almost have been back at Mwekarago Cove on the long walk to my truck.

When I finally arrived at the camp, to the big-eyed astonishment of Ebuya's women and children, I was exhausted. I tried to sit down and virtually fell to the ground, but stubbornly I pulled myself up on my elbows and took a look at the injured leg. It wasn't too encouraging. The entire area surrounding the wound was reddening gradually, and the vein above, swollen and coagulated, stood out like a bas-relief. Mutuke bent down over me and palpated the leg, following the course of the swollen vein with his swift little fingers. With a small piece of charcoal he drew a line at the upper limit of the coagulation, and then raised the right side of my *kapitula* and tightened the tourniquet which had become loose during the long walk. Less than a minute had passed, but when he finished fussing with the tourniquet and turned back to the wound, the line of coagulation had already advanced upwards about half an inch.

The old pygmy looked horrified when he saw that, but when he realized I was watching him, he turned to me at once with a forced, reassuring smile—the doctor's classic bedside smile. Then he spoke to Yoma.

'He wants to cut your leg, *Bapa*, there—' the boy pointed to my thigh.

'How large a cut will he make?' I asked, thinking of the 'big stuff' Mutuke had mentioned before.

'He says that he may not cut it all the way off.'

That explanation really jarred me. 'Look, Yoma,' I said nervously, 'I've already lost my right hand, and I think that's quite enough. Tell Mutuke to leave me alone.'

'But he says you'll die, *Bapa*, if he can't cut your leg!'

'Yoma, talk to Mutuke. Try and find out *exactly* what he wants to do and tell me *exactly* what he says, every word of it.'

There was another conference. Finally Yoma explained, 'He says that he'll cut very slowly. He promises that he won't cut any more than he has to, and he'll definitely try not to cut it all the way off.'

It was a grim proposition, but I really didn't have any choice. Either I gambled the leg or I died: it was as simple as that. 'Tell him to go ahead with it,' I said abruptly.

Mutuke called an order to a waiting helper, and a few minutes later the man returned with the surgical instrument, a massive, shiny blade about eighteen inches long, the business end of an elephant-spear. Slowly, with the silent absorption of a connoisseur, he tested both edges of the blade with his dirty thumb. When he almost cut himself on one of them, his worn features relaxed in a slight smile of satisfaction which was replaced almost at once by an air of stern determination.

I felt somewhat reassured when the old man called for water. I assumed that he was going to wash his hands or perhaps even to give me a drink. Then I saw the foul, stinking water that was carried on to the scene in a cracked pot and watched glumly as Mutuke took an old piece of corncob, dipped it in the water and rolled it in some dry soil. He rubbed the spear-blade energetically with the filthy cob, especially near the tip, and afterwards rinsed the blade, patting at it with his fingers. The water dripped on to the ground—water that was almost black from the touch of his hands.

'Ask him to wash his hands,' I told Yoma anxiously. 'Tell him to use soap, if he has any.'

'He doesn't know about soap, *Bapa*. And he doesn't understand why you want him to wash. But he says he'll do it anyway.'

Smiling broadly as he tried to humour me, Mutuke rubbed his little hands several times in the same foul water and dried them on a piece of *ficus*-bark cloth. A moment later, he presented the cloth to my two friends, who used it to sponge the sweat off my forehead. Then Mutuke raised the huge blade and, simultaneously, Yoma and Ebu each put a hand on one of my shoulders. I shook myself nervously, not wanting to be held, and they stared at me with their eyes full of concern. So, I relented, allowing Yoma to hold my head while Ebu grasped my hand, and I waited for the pygmy operation without benefit of anaesthesia to begin.

Mutuke himself was getting terribly nervous by now, perhaps at the prospect of having to cut my alien white skin. Perspiring heavily, he looked around with irritation at the crowd of curious women and children, barked a quick order, and they backed obediently away. Then, as his helper pulled my *kapitula* away from the site of the operation, Mutuke plunged the point of the spear-blade into my right groin.

I ground my teeth together as he turned the knife sideways, sawing at the upper part of my thigh as though it were a tough steak. I felt the blade go very deep and I shuddered. This part of the body—possibly because of its proximity to the genital organs—must be exceptionally sensitive. The pain had a remarkably penetrating, nerve-racking quality, one of the worst sensations I have ever experienced. Gasping, I tried to sit up; Yoma pulled me back by the hair.

Relentless, Mutuke plunged the point of the spear-blade deeper and sawed at the flesh again. Several times I felt a small geyser of blood spurting across my thigh when he cut a minor artery, carefully avoiding the main trunk. Then I felt the blade grate across the upper end of my thigh bone. It was agonizing, but I grimly refused to lose consciousness, and I watched through a haze of pain while Mutuke severed what appeared to be my right femoral vein and massaged my leg upwards, apparently trying to expel the rest of the poisoned blood. A moment later, he pressed the two sides of the huge wound together, holding his hands flat against the skin.

The old man muttered something in Kimbuti. 'He says that he won't cut any more,' Ebu explained with obvious relief.

Mutuke's method of closing a surgical wound was almost as painful as his manner of inflicting it. He massaged the skin on either side of the gaping crevice, held the two edges together even more closely, and shook the whole thing vigorously. That was bad enough, but his helper brought him a pile of brownish-grey swamp salt and I learned that the worst was yet to come. Mutuke relaxed his grip on the wound and let it bleed freely. He waited a moment before pouring the salt over the entire area, using the back of his hand to mix it with the blood into a thick paste. Then, using both hands, he pulled apart the two lips of flesh, which had already begun to adhere a little, and the salty mixture penetrated deep into the wound.

That little demonstration of Bambuti antisepsis was even more painful than the operation itself. My whole body went rigid with shock and I ground my teeth so violently that I chipped two of them. It was unbelievably difficult, but I managed to see it through without making any outcry, so my old pride remained intact even if the rest of me wasn't. Mutuke pressed the wound closed again and issued another order to his helper.

'What does he want now?' I asked Ebu nervously.

'He's asking for leaves, *Bapa*. To put on the wound like a bandage.'

I sighed with relief, only to find myself twitching again as Mutuke thoughtfully put the remaining salt in the arrow wounds. It hurt, but the pain was certainly less than what had gone before. My pygmy M.D. waited patiently until his helper arrived with a pile of dry leaves and an open gourd of water. Wetting the smaller leaves, he pasted them directly on the wound, laid several large strips of plantain leaves over them, and as a finishing touch wrapped the whole thing with a double layer of bark cloth and tied the complicated bandage in place with some rattan string.

Finally Mutuke released the tourniquet enough to allow some fresh blood into the leg, stepped back and stared critically at his handiwork. I thanked him weakly in Kingwana, but the old pygmy walked away without answering and sat down in front of his hut to smoke a pipe, without even bothering to wash my blood off his hands.

'How do you feel?' Yoma asked me anxiously.

'Terrible. I wish I had somewhere to rest. I don't feel comfortable lying here on the ground in the middle of the camp.'

'Do you want a hut, *Bapa*?'

'No, I have to stay here. It won't do me any good to be moved.'

Ebu smiled knowingly. 'That's no problem, *Bapa*. We'll tell the women to build a house around you.'

Weak as I was, I laughed to see the practical genius of my pygmy friends. Within half an hour, I found myself watching with febrile admiration as several old ladies briskly started to construct the traditional wooden framework over my prostrate form. I lay there, feeling like a tropical version of Gulliver, as the green *mangungu* leaves gradually walled me in, row after row after row. . . .

I slept fitfully during the afternoon as my fever continued to rise. By evening I knew that my temperature was dangerously high and I was beginning to worry. Then Mutuke paid a house-call, bringing with him a gourdful of evil-looking liquid. It was some kind of root extract with a very bitter taste, and I gagged as I drank it, but my temperature started to fall and I felt perceptibly better. I paid a little more attention now to the loud *brouhaha* which had been going on outside my hut for the past few hours and wondered what the pygmies were up to. I found out a little later when my two young friends scrambled through the three-foot entrance.

'We had a wonderful time!' Ebu told me. 'The people of Ebuya discussed everything that has happened today. They talked and argued and tried to work out what you are and what you are trying to do. At first, some of them still said you were trying to take us for slaves. Others said they were wrong, that you were *avi musoi*—'

'That means *pumbavu*,' Yoma said apologetically. 'Mad.'

'Mutuke was angry when he heard that. He said you were just as brave as any pygmy when he cut you. And Mwenua, the old man who wanted to kill you, said you were almost as bold as the Bambuti themselves. They talked a lot more and finally decided that you are just a man, like the rest of us. So, you can stay here at Ebuya and be a pygmy for as long as you like.'

It was a wonderfully touching and ironic tribute. I had come, perhaps a trifle pompously, with the intention of proving to the pygmies that they were men, only to find that I had first to prove my own right to the title. For the Bambuti, manhood was measured, above all, by raw courage, and in this they resembled the splendid Masai; but they were obviously unique among African people in considering a certain measure of insolence— the style of a strutting bluejay—to be the unmistakable mark of a man.

According to those standards, I was definitely a pygmy, and according to my own very similar notions, the pygmies were certainly men.

14

To be a Part of the Living World ...

> 'God! Stop the rain! Stop the wind! The big trees
> will crush your frightened children below! God, tell
> the wind to go home!'
>
> BAMBUTI PRAYER

AT sunrise, after a long, uncomfortable night, I was awakened
by the pygmies' customary morning chatter. Yoma and Ebu
brought news that the men of Ebuya were setting out on a
special hunt to bring meat for my convalescence. The two boys
kept me company all the morning, patient and helpful, as I tried
to enlarge my limited stock of Kimbuti words. At midday
Mutuke arrived and examined the big leafy bandage on my
thigh. He peered critically at the surrounding skin and spoke a
few words to Yoma.

'It looks pretty good,' the boy explained. 'He'll put some fresh
leaves on the wound in two or three days. Meanwhile, he says
that you should be quiet and not start jumping about.'

For once, there was no danger that I would disobey the doctor's orders. I felt more like a wet *mangungu* leaf than an acro-
bat.

At sunset, when the hunters returned, I had a strange but
strengthening meal: wild bananas, turtle flesh and several
delicious slices of horned viper. There was no red meat, since the
people had been camping here for several weeks and game—
especially the dwarf antelope—was growing scarce. Soon they
would have to abandon camp and move on to another site a few
miles away within the Ebuya sector of the forest, but exactly
when depended on how long it would take my wounded leg to
recover sufficiently for the long trek.

240

That was a difficult question to answer. I was certain that Mutuke's elephant-spear scalpel had sliced through the three inner abductor thigh muscles, the femoral vein and several branches of the saphenic nerve. I wasn't at all sure that the leg would ever recover completely from damage of that sort.

I worried about it for three days, while Yoma and Ebu entertained me with Kimbuti lessons and all of the local gossip. Then Mutuke finally decided to change the dressing. He removed the layers of leaves, clucking briskly as he threw them aside; the wound was covered by a crust of dried blood, but underneath the edges were evenly joined, there was little inflammation, and cicatrization had already begun. Mutuke dampened some long narrow *matungulu* leaves and wrapped them round the area without further treatment.

After this I felt much more optimistic and really began to enjoy myself, even though I couldn't jump about. The men of the camp paid me little visits throughout the day, bringing fresh water and fruit, and all started to call me *Bapa*, something I enjoyed more than their material attention.

After more than a week in my hut, I managed to hitch my way out, stretch and take a few steps. It was reassuring but quite painful, and it was another week before I could manage to get round the camp and walk to the nearby spring, a distance of some three hundred feet. There I took a bath, without benefit of soap, and tried to launder my filthy *kapitula*. This proved impossible, the stiff, blood-spattered khaki shorts came to pieces when I beat them on the rocks. My shirt was already gone: I'd cut it into strips and made crude puttees to support my wounded shin and protect my legs from the thorn bush.

The civilized world seemed a distant illusion by now, compared to the vivid realities of the forest. I knew neither the day of the week nor the date of the month, and I had only a vague notion of where the Ebuya camp was located. Maps and clocks were a fading dream, no more real to me than monthly reports, A.T.s, motor-cars or money.

I realized that while I could not join the men in their hunting, I must find a place in their daily life; for the time being I was prepared to go gardening with their wives. We dug for tuberous roots like *aveto* and *apa*, *kitsombi*, a kind of wild potato with long, skinny rhizomes that looked like withered asparagus, *mokode* (wild manioc leaves), forest onions, and collected a wide variety of mushrooms, including one called *tabororokua*, which grew only on decaying wood, another with a funny little red hat known as *ihi*, and a very large variety, *bogbolita*, which was really delicious.

Grasshoppers, worms, beetle larvae, snails, frogs, small snakes, caterpillars, molluscs, crayfish, elegant little grey mice— they all went into our baskets and, ultimately, our stomachs. Initially it took some effort to face a dinner of simmered worms wrapped in *mokode* leaves, grilled mushrooms and caterpillars, or roast bananas garnished with snails. But, after all, while Europeans or Americans may be completely horrified at the idea of eating a fat, juicy caterpillar, Africans feel exactly the same about Camembert cheese. So I often hesitated, trying to approach my dinner like a real pygmy, and finally I ploughed into these frightful concoctions, only eventually to find myself actually enjoying some of them. Apparently, the old maxim is still true: there is no sauce like hunger.

Sometimes we had game—mostly antelope and monkeys, with occasional porcupine, aardvark or hyrax, but on the whole, our diet consisted of starchy vegetables supplemented by what fastidious people call 'vermin'. In the past, before the Bambuti acquired iron weapons from the neighbouring negro tribes, they had probably eaten no game to speak of. They had been, as the eminent anthropologist Paul Schebesta called it, 'a people of insectivores', subsisting on creatures containing at least twice as much animal protein as the finest red meat.

The pygmies were conditioned by ages of evolution to tolerate and even to thrive on their peculiar bill of fare. Unfortunately I was not, and for a while my life among the Bambuti consisted of one stomach-ache after another. Some of their vegetables and fruit had an extremely high acid content; in others, the physiological irritants were unknown to me. About a week after I started making daily rounds with the women, we gathered a big crop of attractive-looking fruit, delicate green in colour with a thick peel and soft gelatine-like flesh; I liked it so much that I ate six of the seemingly innocent little fruit, only to spend the next two days retching my regrets.

We searched for food and ate it; that was the major part of our lives. Still, the people of Ebuya found time for evening dances, endless conversation and vigorous games, such as hide-and-seek, tug-of-war and a primitive version of volleyball played with a bundle of dry leaves tied with lianas. Above all there was a wonderfully good-natured atmosphere around the camp, unlike any negro village in the Congo.

Food was becoming increasingly scarce, and so, after I had

spent about a month at Ebuya and had almost completely recovered from my wounds, the people decided to move. Two young men were sent out to scout the adjacent terrain. They returned next morning with wide grins and a word that galvanized the entire population: *mako*. It meant 'termites', and Yoma explained that the scouts had found a series of nearly mature nests somewhere to the west of our present location.

At once the women gathered up their simple household goods, a few chipped pots and four or five crude wooden stools, and were ready to go. The men carried only their weapons, but took a few minutes to round up their four silent yet very friendly dogs. Then we simply walked off, single file, into the forest, leaving our houses behind us: twenty-nine hungry pygmies (including myself) headed for a new home.

We had gone about four miles along the half-obliterated trail before we saw the first termitarium. It was a roughly conical, brownish-coloured mound about three feet high formed of earth particles cemented together with the insects' saliva, and as hard as sun-baked adobe. According to the scouts, there were at least twenty nests within the immediate area.

We made a new camp in a nearby clearing; the men hacked with their spear blades at a few badly placed saplings, and then vanished into the bush to gather wood for the huts, while the women and I collected large quantities of *mangungu* leaves. We were all ravenous, but there was nothing to eat except a few handfuls of nuts we'd picked up on the way.

The women spent the rest of that day building new huts; early next morning, hungrier than ever, we started to make preparations for the expected feast of *mako*. The men cleared the bush away from round the nests and dug circular ditches round them, while their wives built flat roofs of sticks, lianas and leaves over the termitaria. The whole set-up was obviously intended to function as a trap, but it was two days until, at twilight, the first mature winged insects finally emerged on their nuptial flight and the half-starved people of Ebuya sprang into action.

There were hot coals ready, and each family built a smoky fire of leaves at the base of its own nest. Soon, termites emerged in hundreds and thousands—robust Ituri termites nearly an inch long and correspondingly fat. They flew vertically, collided with the unexpected ceilings and shattered their fragile wings. Then, as the mutilated insects crawled along the ground, they fell into the shallow ditches and were grabbed by our eager hands.

Men, women, children, all of us snatched up the writhing *mako* and dropped them into deep, closely-woven wicker baskets. Most of the hungry people stuffed raw termites into their mouths as they worked, but I decided to wait. Yoma, Ebu and I were sharing a nest together, and when our own particular tenants had all taken flight and crash-landed, we must have had six or seven pounds of the big brown insects to share among us. We grilled them over hot coals, half a dozen at a time, skewered on long pointed sticks. A few minutes later, the two boys started eating, with a look on their faces of addled ecstasy—eyes half-closed, and grease dripping from the corners of their mouths. I understood perfectly how they felt when I took my first bite of toasted termite. It was rather like lobster, with a strong sugges-tion of snail and a faint hint of mushroom—a crisp little nugget with a wonderfully succulent centre. I ate hundreds of those fat, beautiful termites and loved every one of them. Even more important, they loved me and let themselves be digested with selfless devotion.

Other nests matured, we shifted operations, and more ter-mites flew, crashed and perished. By the end of this hectic, four-day gourmet orgy, I was such an enthusiastic convert that I was even eating them raw, along with my fellow pygmies. Then the last nest was empty, and we returned to our normal hit-or-miss diet.

Although I may seem to have been spending all my time either gathering or eating food, I managed to work in some practical ethnology on the side. My intimate daily contacts with the people of Ebuya gave me a unique opportunity to absorb the style of Bambuti culture. Every casual conversation or incident around the camp revealed new facets of their habits and cus-toms, and even such seemingly trivial activities as playing *mali* with Yoma and Ebu enabled me to gauge their perception, judgement and capacity for learning. In odd moments I taught them some simple drill and gymnastic exercises, testing their physical abilities. My instructions were always in French rather than Kingwana or Kimbuti, for I wanted to discourage rela-tions with the negroes, to impress any Europeans whom Mwenua's band might meet in future and to impress the pygmies themselves with pride and confidence in the fact that they could actually learn to speak the *wazungu*'s mysterious language.

Starting with Yoma and Ebu I taught the 'unteachable' pyg-mies how to count, and within weeks nearly every man in the camp could count to a hundred. I told my friends some fables of La Fontaine, explaining that Maître Renard was a smart dog with a pointed nose and a shaggy tail, and Monsieur le Corbeau was a small, shiny black parrot with a straight yellow beak; of course, the object of their contention wasn't a high-smelling piece of *fromage* but a savoury turtle-egg—the prime delicacy of the Ituri Forest. (In that respect, I submit, my version was an improvement on the original, since a fox and a crow would undoubtedly find a turtle-egg more intriguing than even the finest Roquefort or Port-salut.) Then I taught them old French tunes like *Au Clair de la Lune* and *Frère Jacques*, and soon the people of Ebuya were going about their work whistling and singing them—a touching but almost surrealistic development.

They mastered everything I offered them, with a few exceptions such as French nasal sounds and the Gallic 'u', both of which they found as difficult as most Americans and British seem to. If I had a supply of paper and pencils or chalk and a blackboard, reading and writing, I was sure, would present no major difficulties for the Bambuti, although many authorities had long considered this to be impossible.

This was only one of the general misconceptions concerning my much-maligned fellow pygmies. There was a whole gamut of others, even more important, which had been accepted as axiomatic by the world at large. Even some of the so-called scholarly anthropologists had joined in the general chorus: according to them the Bambuti had neither religion, ethics nor morals, and no racial, cultural or linguistic autonomy; they were simply 'degenerate negroes'.

Nearly every simple-minded tourist who visits Central Africa helps to reinforce that disgusting myth, coming away babbling about the Congo's 'vicious, filthy little dwarfs' who so pitifully contrast with the tall, immaculate 'Noble Giants' of Rwanda—the Batutsi!—only a few hundred miles away. The whole situation was particularly ironic since my pygmy friends had proved in many respects the most profoundly moral and religious people on the African continent.

They were completely free from the craving for social status that drives the Batutsi to collect cows as a symbol of wealth and power, and leads the Bantu of the Congo to acquire many wives. The Bambuti's simple goal in life was to have a large family, and their only social status lay in their children, whom they not only loved extravagantly but initiated into the merciless life of the forest. Monogamy was a strict rule among them, and the pygmy wife enjoyed more freedom and equality in her rôle than any of her African sisters, perhaps a trifle too much, to judge from several shrewish old ladies at Ebuya.

Adultery and incest are rare and universally despised among the Bambuti; homosexuality and all forms of perversion virtually unknown; unlike most negro tribes in which even very small children play at intercourse, the pygmies practically never have sexual relations before reaching puberty, the boys at the age of eleven or twelve, the girls at ten or sometimes even earlier. (One fifteen-year-old girl at Muhekuva had five young children, none of them twins, and another baby on the way. At Ebikeba I saw a happily married eight-year-old with newly budding breasts who was obviously pregnant.)

Most old-fashioned pygmy marriages had a strong element of convenience, since they practised the betrothal system called in Swahili *kichwa na kichwa*, 'head for head'. Before the negroes began buying their women, each wandering *parentèle* or band of families exchanged its marriageable girl for the daughter of another band, providing a healthy circulation of genes throughout the forest. Even then there was considerable freedom of choice and often what might almost be described as romance.

To the men, the prime feminine virtues were fertility and food-gathering ability. Young girls, on the other hand, dreamed of landing a husband who was not only strong, clever and courageous but the best hunter and dancer in the band. Some of them overdid it, like Muroke, one of the better-looking girls at Ebuya, who was still unmarried although she must have been almost fourteen. Poor Muroke was the favourite target of Mwenua's wit, and whenever the pygmy elder saw her, he made sarcastic remarks which she tried to shrug off.

'There have been other women like her,' he told me one day in very awkward Kingwana. 'They think they are too good for the rest of us and waste their time dreaming. They always come to grief, just like the foolish *abeke*.'

That puzzled me. I knew that *abeke* is the Kimbuti word for the elephant-shrew, an aberrant member of the insectivore order which looks like a big kangaroo-rat with a sizeable trunk. 'What do you mean?' I asked.

'Little Miss Abeke,' he said, 'lived in the forest a long time ago. She was good-looking but terribly conceited, just like that one! All the animals wanted to marry Abeke, but she was so pleased with herself she turned them all down. One by one she insulted the wild pig, the antelope, and even the beautiful okapi. Then the elephant came to her hut, touched trunks with

EIGHT FACES OF A CHIMP
Sophie in some of her varied moods.

PIERROT, VENUS AND JEAN-PIERRE
Pierrot, an African black rhino with his two friends,
the Author and Venus.

her, and asked for her hand in marriage. "At last I have found someone worthy of me!" foolish Abeke told her mother. "He is the strongest and most handsome creature in the world!" "Are you mad?" the mother asked. "He's as big as a house, he'll kill you without even knowing it." "He loves me!" Abeke said, with a stupid little smile, "and I love him! Nothing will ever change my mind.'"

Mwenua paused after delivering that classic dialogue between the elephant-shrew and her mother. His manner had been wonderfully mincing, but now his tone changed.

'The elephant made love to Abeke *all night*,' he declaimed dramatically. 'She never stopped giggling and screaming with joy, but later, when the sun came up, the hut was completely silent. There was no sign of Abeke. Her poor elephant husband didn't know what to think, until he looked down and found her —ground into the floor of the hut, as flat as a *mangungu* leaf. Abeke was dead! The elephant ran away horrified when he saw what had happened, and the wise old mother was so stricken with grief that all she could say was "I told you so."

'That's what happens,' Mwenua concluded sagely, 'when women get big ideas. Trouble!'

I was inclined to agree, especially since his weird little fairy tale might have had personal applications. A love affair between an 8,000-pound elephant and a one-pound elephant-shrew was only a little more absurd than a romance between an eighteen-stone ethnologist and a six-stone girl pygmy.

A few days later I received another startling insight into the pygmy-style war between the sexes when Mwenua told me quite a different kind of story. It happened at twilight, shortly after the old man had returned from the hunt, overjoyed with the day's bag, two turtles and a monkey. He was sitting on a stool near the entrance to his hut, contentedly watching his wife struggle across the clearing with a heavy load of firewood.

'It is good to be a man,' he remarked, 'and to know that God is on our side.'

'On your side?' I repeated. 'Why?'

'He is still punishing woman,' Mwenua explained, 'for leading man into sin.'

This theme sounded very familiar, but as the pygmy elder went on, I saw even stranger echoes of Genesis in the heart of the Ituri.

'God made the first man and woman,' he said, 'and put them into the forest. They had no problems: there was so much food that all they had to do was bend down and pick it up. God told them they would live for ever, and He let them do whatever they wanted except for only one little thing. He said that they shouldn't pick the fruit of the *tahu* tree.

'The man never bothered with the tree after that, but the woman thought about it all the time. Then, when she got big with a baby, she decided that she simply must eat that fruit and no other. She told the man to pick it for her, and of course he said, "No, God doesn't want us to." When she heard that, she started to argue and cry and scream and call her husband bad names. So, just to stop the noise, he picked a fruit from the *tahu* tree. He even peeled it for her. They ate the *tahu* fruit together and hid the peel under a pile of leaves.

'But God was very clever: he sent a big wind to blow away the leaves! He saw the peel and he became terribly angry. He came and stood in front of the woman and said, "You broke your promise to me! And you pulled that poor man into sin! Now I'm going to punish you: both of you will find out what it is to work hard and be sick and die. But you, woman, since you made the trouble first, you will suffer the most. Your babies will hurt you when they come, and you will always have to work for the man you betrayed."

'And that is why God is on *our* side,' Mwenua ended smugly, 'and still against woman.'

'What does God look like,' I asked, 'and what is His name?'

'His name is Toré, and he is wonderfully big, white and hairy —a little like you—but he is a very old man. He sits in the sky and his long beard hangs down to the earth; when he shakes it big winds blow and trees fall down. Sometimes he kills wicked men with a bolt of lightning and sometimes he sends a leopard. That is what happens to any pygmy who tells lies, or steals or plays about with another man's wife.'

I found this last part rather hard to swallow. The pygmies' sexual morality was impeccable, but lying and stealing were two of their favourite pastimes and usually regarded very lightly. If Toré really decided to crack down on such minor infractions, the old gentleman would run out of lightning and leopards long before he ran out of sinners.

'Those things are bad enough,' Mwenua continued, 'but God has a much more terrible punishment for the really big crimes that men do. He closes the forest, the game disappears, the plants shrivel and die.'

'What are the big crimes?'

'To be cruel to children or old people. To be unfair dividing the meat. To waste food: the man who does that insults God!'
He was right.

In future, I was to hear many different names and descriptions of the deity in other parts of the forest, until it seemed almost that every camp had its own peculiar theology. Kalisia, Arebati, Asobe, Mugu, Masupa, Epilipili, Muri-Muri—these are only a few of God's manifold names. According to some pygmies he is a solemn old man who lives in the moon; others were sure he is very much like a pygmy himself and dwells in a vast tree. Still others thought of him as an immense being whose eyes light the world and whose voice is the terrible thunder. His sacred beast is the chameleon, which everyone admired and protected; his magic tree was the *ti'i*, which some pygmies believed had borne the first men like fruit; and the warning sign of his rage was the rainbow, which sent them into hiding, terrified.

At first I thought the Bambuti had a whole pantheon, but three main avatars of the deity eventually emerged from that tangled Ituri chaos: *God the Creator*, *God of the Forest*, and *God of the Hunt*—three divine beings who were somehow one, or one vital force, which the pygmies called *megbe*—taking three different forms in order to animate every living thing with God's will and essence.

'If Toré died,' as Mwenua put it, in his crude but moving Kingwana, 'then we would all die with him.'

This was the faith of the pygmy, differing completely from the animistic fear that ruled the life of the Bantu negroes, for whom every object—a stone, a tree, an antelope or a man—has its own separate spirit, an inner self or *anima* which lives on even after death. Most of these are hostile, especially the spirits of the dead who wander round their natal villages, hounding the living with incessant demands. The pygmies are free from those nagging ghosts because they do not share in that most persistent of all primitive beliefs, the survival of the soul, which lingers on even in our civilized Christian religions. Unlike the Bantu they understand that death can occur from natural causes rather than witchcraft, and so there are no sorcerers or 'black magicians' among them. Until they came into contact with the negroes, they had no amulets, talismans, ordeals or sacrifices, but instead moved each day through the wonderful world of *megbe*—a world entirely permeated with God; unlike any other tribe in the Congo, they prayed to him.

I remember vividly the first time I heard and understood a

Kimbuti prayer. We were once again moving to another part of
Ebuya, when we were caught by a sudden thunderstorm. The
giant trees swayed like saplings, huge branches crashed to the
mossy floor, the lightning flashed with blinding intensity, rain
cascaded down from foliage a hundred feet high on to our
dripping heads. My twenty-eight pygmy companions stared up
towards the hidden sky, then, between the crescendos of thunder,
I heard Mwenua's voice, pleading with his God.

'Toré!' the old man cried. 'Stop the rain! Stop the wind!
The big trees will crush your frightened children below! Toré,
tell the wind to go home!'

Four or five men joined him, adding their voices to the prayer.
Toré must have heard all of them . . . since the storm stopped
with dramatic abruptness a few minutes later (as they very
frequently do). That evening, at our new home, I was talking
with Mwenua at the campfire after most of the people had gone
to sleep in their brand-new huts. Only four or five men were
left round the fire, which was burning very low. Mwenua threw
on a few sticks of damp wood; they crackled and smoked until
the yellow flames burst out among them.

The light and warmth were immensely comforting and I wondered how the pygmies had ever managed to get along without
them. 'Is there any story,' I asked Mwenua dreamily, 'that tells
how you got fire from the negroes?'

'From the negroes!' he repeated angrily. 'We didn't get fire
from *them*. We got it from the chimpanzees.'

'*They* knew how to do it?'

'Yes, the *cheko* knew how. Once they used to talk and live in
huts just as people do, and they were much brighter than anyone else in the forest—even us. We watched their beautiful fires
and asked them to give us a little flame. They said, "No, it is
our secret and nobody else will ever share it." We were jealous
of them for a long time until a clever pygmy figured out what to
do. He waited until the grown-up chimpanzees were all busy
working in their banana groves. Then he put on a *milumba* with
a very long tail in the back and entered their village.

'He sat down by the fire and talked to the *cheko* children,
very sweetly, and gradually sneaked the tail of his *milumba*
closer and closer to the flames. Then, when the tip caught fire,
he ran back to his own people just as fast as he could. Afterwards, when the big *cheko* came home and their children told
them what happened, they rushed to the pygmy camp. They
found a nice warm fire burning in front of every hut! That

made them so angry that they never talked to people again. They left their houses and fields behind them, and ran away into the forest.'

'But, Mwenua, where did the negroes get fire?'

'They stole it from us. They weren't clever enough to trick the *cheko* as we did! Why, those negroes were so stupid that we had to teach them how to make babies—they didn't even know how to do that!'

'Come, Mwenua, this time you're going too far!'

'No, *Bapa*, we really did! You see, God had three children, two boys and a girl. One brother was a pygmy and the other was a negro—'

'Wait a minute,' I interrupted. 'What about the story of the *tahu* tree? And the first man and woman? How do you make the two stories fit together?'

'I don't know, but they're both true. Anyway, God loved His pygmy child and talked to him all the time until he became very clever. But God never talked to the negro. He was so simple-minded that he came to his pygmy brother one day and said, "What shall I do with our sister? She has a bad wound, and she bleeds every time another moon comes into the sky. I tried to help her: I put medicine and leaves on the wound, but it did no good."

'Then the pygmy laughed so hard that he nearly burst. God had told him all about that wound. So he went to his sister and made lots of babies. Afterwards, he took her to the other brother and explained how to make her stop bleeding. The negro learned, very slowly, until he could make babies too, but not as many as we do!'

It was a proud, ludicrous boast, and of course there was no way that it could ever be refuted, unlike the fire-myth, which was obviously an exact reversal of the truth. What the old man's stories and his incidental remarks emphasized was the deep-seated antagonism between pygmy and negro, and the resentment the smaller race felt at their subordinate position in the life of the forest.

The free people of Ebuya had taught me what it meant to be a part of the living world, and that was uniquely valuable knowledge. I would have been content to continue living among them for many more months, but there was an urgent, desperate problem elsewhere, as I had always known, but almost forgotten—the plight of the 'marginal men', caught between two discordant cultures and dying of attrition, at Ebikeba, and all the places like it, where the pygmies had lost their ancestral world without finding another.

*   *   *

I left Mwenua's band next morning and headed north with my two young companions. We fought our way through dense, almost impenetrable bush for five or six hours until we reached the big bend of the Ituri River, a sluggish arc of beige-grey water about 150 feet wide. During the next week we travelled northeast along the river's tangled, winding shore, visiting four Bambuba villages on our way, where the negroes lived by a mixture of farming and fishing. Each of them had its complement of pygmy hunters about five hundred feet back in the forest. Eventually we came within a few miles of Erengeti, near the northern border of the Kivu Province, and doubled back slowly towards the south, stopping at twelve sedentary pygmy camps.

The perimeter of our journey formed a great inverted triangle of forest whose base was the Ituri River on the north, and whose sides, converging at Beni, were formed by the road to Mambasa on the west and the road to Irumu on the east. That triangle contained some five hundred square miles of forest and about three thousand of the southern Efe, almost one-tenth of the entire race. Among them, apart from Mwenua's people at Ebuya, there were only two or three bands of free nomads; the rest, the vast majority of North Kivu's pygmies, were virtually the property of the Banande negroes.

Along the eastern edge of the triangle I saw, spoke and lived with at least two thousand of those broken, dependent people; gradually I began to assemble the myriad bits and pieces of the Ituris' unrecorded human history which had led up to the present-day tragedy. It was true, as various authorities had so often proclaimed, that the pygmies were almost perfectly adapted to life in the virgin forest. But the forest was no longer virgin.

The perfect biological balance of the pygmies' ancestral home had been violated three or four hundred years before, when wave after wave of invading Nilo-Hamites had swept down from the north, driving the Bantu and Sudanese tribes of the adjoining regions to refuge in the Ituri. The negroes brought with them a galaxy of wonders acquired from very early contacts with more advanced peoples; the pygmies, whose own culture had never even reached the Stone Age, were dazzled to behold such miracles as man-made fire, beer, bananas, tobacco, iron weapons, domesticated animals and elaborate 'magic' rituals.

Ironically, the negroes' own cultural poverty had once been virtually complete. Domesticated animals, useful plants and most of the economic techniques which form the basis of modern tribal life had originated elsewhere: dogs, cattle, goats, sheep, pigs and fowl were all borrowed from Asia and Europe; metal-working was probably acquired through contacts with the Arabs and the Egyptians (who also contributed circumcision and some of the other rituals). From Central and South America came the two most important staple foods of Africa today—manioc, which was brought by the Portuguese about 1600, and 'mealies', maize or Indian corn, which came by way of Spain; as well as sweet potatoes, white potatoes, peanuts, tobacco, red peppers, guavas, pineapples, cinchona and coca. India contributed sorghum, beans and eleusine, and southeast Asia was the source of the vital banana, plus rice, millet, sugar cane, soybeans, Cajun peas, citrus fruits, mangoes, cotton, tea and black pepper. Coconut palms and the breadfruit tree originated in Oceania, and the papaya came from Mexico.

Just about the only important edible plants native to negro Africa were taro and yams. How the natives had lived in that state of chronic privation, especially on the bare savannahs, is almost impossible to imagine. The present type of village organization and activity was certainly out of the question, and the severe shortage of animal and vegetable food must have been a prime factor in the origin and establishment of cannibalism.

Using all their acquired cultural advantages to awe and dominate the Bambuti, the newcomers had relied heavily on magic. They realized that the smaller race lacked such mysterious, complicated rituals as circumcision, wedding and funeral rites, and so, gradually, they bound the pygmies in a sticky web of Bantu hocus-pocus, adding a few bizarre touches designed expressly to intrigue their unsophisticated victims.

Above all, the negroes created a special secret society whose patron was supposed to be Toré—God Himself—and whose sacred symbol was the *lusomba,* a long wooden trumpet. Originally called *Molimo* (and still known under that title farther west in the forest), the society was renamed the 'League of Toré', a clever device intended to make it mean even more to the pygmies. As with most Bantu secret societies, no women, children or non-initiates were permitted to violate the sanctity of the meeting place. Only members—*kare* or blood-brothers who had been initiated by the strange set of ceremonies called the *nkumbi*—were entitled to participate in the ritual mysteries.

The *nkumbi* was performed every five or six years, whenever there was a large enough crop of young boys to warrant the extensive preparations. Each pair of candidates consisted of a 7 to 9-year-old pygmy and a 9 to 12-year-old negro, carefully chosen to emphasize their differences in size and power. They were dressed in shaggy hemp skirts like ballet tutus and painted with white clay on half of the face and one leg, with a few geometric designs on the chest. Then the boys squatted in an irregular circle while an old negro sorcerer intoned magical formulae to ready the pygmy-negro pairs for the ritual surgery. At the precise moment of each simultaneous circumcision and mingling of blood, there was a cacophonic play of horns, bells and drums—a scene not easily forgotten by wounded, frightened children—after which there was a solemn procession of the new blood-brothers and a long, impassioned speech from the sorcerer.

He told the boys that they were now bound together for life, more strongly than if they had been born from the same womb. If the negro went to war against another tribe, his *kare* pygmy was supposed to fight at his side. If the negro was murdered by one of his enemies, the pygmy was obliged not only to revenge the killing but to bury his blood-brother and cry over the grave for several days; it was much simpler if the pygmy died: his partner had only to bury him, without benefit of crocodile tears.

Most important of all—and the real reason why the negroes had cooked up the entire stage-play—the pygmy boys were told that they would receive iron arrow points from their *kare*, who urged them to hunt bigger and bigger game: from the dwarf antelope to the large bongo, from the bongo to the red buffalo, and from the buffalo to the biggest game of all, the elephant. In return the negroes would be entitled to virtually all the pygmies' hunting bag, a lifetime supply of the most precious commodity in protein-starved Africa: meat.

That was the beginning of the infamous pygmy-negro 'social contract', which had reduced the wily, resourceful little people of the forest to increasing dependence. More than any other operating factor the Toré Secret Society and the associated *nkumbi* had bound the Bambuti to their new overlords in a relationship strongly reminiscent of a medieval feudal system, with indolent lords and subjugated serfs.

In time the pygmies grew to depend on iron blades for their hunting; they learned to count on the negro's bananas as the most basic element in their diet; they craved the negro's beer, salt and tobacco. Gradually the *nkumbi* ceremony and the Toré Secret Society started to fade away, for they were no longer needed. The pygmies were caught fast by their new customs, habits and desires and needs. Then, towards the close of the nineteenth century, the situation took a turn for the worse when the white man invaded the Grand Forest. He brought with him two diseases far more damaging to the human ecology of the Ituri than the syphilis, leprosy and yaws transmitted by the negroes. They were called trade goods and money.

Now it was the negroes, confronted by the fascinating gim-cracks of a more advanced material culture, who found that they had new desires and needs for cigarettes, patent-leather shoes, alarm clocks, plastic jewellery, bottled beer and mismatched articles of cheap Western clothing. For this they needed money and it did not take them long to realize what a wonderful money-making device they had in the pygmies.

The large antelope for which the Bambuti hunter received thirty francs' worth of bananas could be sold for two or three hundred francs by his feudal lord. The elephant the pygmies were urged to kill, often at the cost of several lives, was a lucra-tive mountain of meat which the negro bosses could peddle for five to ten thousand francs in exchange for the inevitable stalk of bananas, the tempting pots of beer and some scraps of the elephant's entrails and flesh. So their demands grew more and more exacting: now they were eager for meat not only as food, but as something which could be sold and turned into *francs Congolais*.

The negroes made a large profit from these transactions with the pygmy hunters and simultaneously took advantage of another great bargain: pygmy women at bargain rates. My Balese guide Mulume had made that very clear to me seven years before; why pay a large cash dowry for a woman of your own kind when you can buy a pygmy girl for a dog, a chicken and a spear-blade? The pygmy is hard-working and extremely fertile, she makes a satisfying second or third wife, as well as a useful servant to do most of the real household work. But, above all, she represents a great saving in money, allowing a man to get more and more nice things for himself, perhaps even a bicycle, a radio, or a sewing machine.

Inevitably the pygmies themselves fell prey to the lure of the white man's money and trade goods. They loitered round the ugly little *magazini* that mushroomed up in the forest and gaped at prodigies like bread, dried fish, cigarettes, cotton cloth,

aluminium pots and plastic braces. Here was food un-
connected with the soil and garments which could be worn
without first being pounded out of tree bark. Here were miracles
more exciting than negro ritual magic: shiny bracelets that
ticked, boxes with music inside and little metal cases that made
fire at the flick of one finger. Here was the promise of an easy,
wonderful, dream-like life, beyond the hard realities of the
forest.

So the pygmy men were eager to sell their daughters, the
pygmy girls were eager to be sold, the negroes were eager to
buy—all driven in various degrees by the desire for wealth,
goods, ease, and in the case of the negroes, social status.

The end-result of that whole three-hundred-year process
could be found in such stinking sedentary camps as Ebikeba,
Makumbo, Ngadi, Ngite, Mambafika and a dozen others in
North Kivu, where the pygmies lived short, bitter, frustrated,
disease-ridden lives, surrendering their freedom, their labour
and their women to the negroes in a process which many anthropologists, with unconscious irony, complacently refer to as
symbiosis.

*   *   *

My most vivid experience during my long journey, one revealing the ugliest aspects of the situation, happened near the pygmy
camp of Mbuteka in the Efilonge sector of the forest, in the
northeast corner of my triangle, ten miles from the Ituri River.
Here I took part in one of those strange events which have
been the subject of so much speculation—a pygmy elephant
hunt.

I had been on three previous hunts, but had never before seen
the climactic phase of the operations, since it is almost impossible for a white man, or even a negro, to keep pace with
Bambuti hunters who can pass swiftly and silently through
inextricable bush. The fourth time, near the Mbuteka camp, the
bush was rather thinner, I was a trifle faster and I saw the
whole thing.

The hunt started with all twelve members of the party observing a strange ritual, originally devised by the ubiquitous
League of Toré. A tall and wizened pygmy elder named Mate-
leka held a squawking chicken, which represented a small fortune
to the Bambuti, since they raise no fowl themselves, but barter
or steal birds from the negroes, over their piled-up spears, cut
off its head and sprinkled the blood over the blades. He touched

each hunter's right arm with the bird's bloody neck and placed the body among the spears, where we could see it flapping through aimless convulsions before it was finally still.

The old man stared at the bird and gestured with his soiled little forefinger. 'The neck points that way!' he cried. 'So you must travel in that direction!'

We set out towards the east. Quite soon we wandered from the ordained course as the hunters searched for traces of the elephant, but no one seemed in the least worried about this. Soon Yoma, Ebu and I found ourselves forming a sort of rear-guard, a separate little party tracking the hunters through the bush. The thorns were maddening, even though I had wrapped my legs in new bark-cloth puttees to keep the damage to a minimum.

We fell further behind, and I sent Ebu ahead to serve as a liaison between the hunting party and myself. Ordinarily, it would not have been necessary for Bambuti hunters generally make so much noise they are easy to locate. But an elephant hunt is a very different proposition: the silence was absolute and unnatural, the longest I have ever heard in all my experience with the pygmies.

We must have walked for four or five hours before the hunters finally came to a halt and we caught up. I was covered with sweat, dirt and an infinite number of tiny, irritating leaves; my battered shoes, with their sixth pair of home-made antelope-hide soles, were threatening to give way completely; as usual I was terribly hungry. The hunters of Mbuteka munched away on some bananas and cooked meat they had carried along with them, and Yoma produced our own little *posho*, a handful of mushrooms and nuts. I chewed my share slowly, wishing there were ten times more of it.

'How does it look?' I asked one of the hunters.

'We've heard elephant sounds, but we need *bwa*. We've sent Kibondo ahead to look for it.'

A moment later Kibondo materialized from the bush, a grin on his face and a pile of *bwa* in his hand. My new friends beamed at the sight like hard-luck miners entering El Dorado, and they all rushed into the bush while the boys and I tagged after them. When we caught up again we saw twelve earnest pygmies conscientiously plastering each other from a fifteen-pound heap of spherical, light-brown turds. They coated their bodies heavily, patting gobs of the stinking elephant *bwa* on to each other's chests, backs and thighs.

Two pairs of big, questioning eyes turned slowly in my direction. Yoma and Ebu were obviously wondering if this was the point at which 'Bapa-nda-Bambuti' left off and Monsieur Hallet, the Agronomist from Mbau, took over. The prospect wasn't appealing, but I wanted to see the climax of the hunt and had no intention of prejudicing it with my alien aroma. 'What are you waiting for?' I said. 'Do you think I'm afraid of a little *bwa*?'

The boys hesitated, then they grinned and started to work; soon they developed real enthusiasm for the grand-scale plastering project. *Bwa* came at me from every direction, and several of the sticky projectiles caught me smack in the beard. By the time Yoma and Ebu had finished with me I looked remarkably like an abstract modern painting, perhaps a Jackson Pollack, featuring an irregularly mottled white and golden-brown background ornamented with random touches of seeds, fibres, leaves and little twigs. I watched critically while the boys plastered each other with a much quicker and less complete coating and then we hurried on after the hunters.

They were in the bush again, moving more slowly with wary precaution. They stopped after only ten minutes, and as we joined them made emphatic gestures to be quiet. I stared at them and then, to my complete surprise, saw a large expanse of grey-skinned elephant rump jutting out from the bush a hundred feet ahead.

Now the group of hunters progressed even more slowly. Two men on the left and two on the right angled off, detaching themselves from the main body of eight Bambuti. Then a single pygmy advanced from the centre. He was the *Tebe*, the hunter who would have the honour and danger of leading the attack. Thirty feet behind him the seven remaining hunters fanned out, leaving about ten feet between every man.

With infinite caution and stealth the hunters closed the gap between themselves and the unsuspecting animal, which was gradually coming more and more into view. The great beast, an old male with rather puny tusks, was intent on his meal, ravaging an uprooted mimosa tree and chewing noisily on the leaves, twigs and bark. Suddenly, as he pulled at the branches, there was a deep rumble like the distant sound of thunder—borborygmus, the sound made by his enormous, inefficient gut as it tried to digest a previous meal.

At the very last, when the *Tebe* crept soundlessly up behind him, he took alarm and started to turn. Simultaneously the pygmy thrust his spear, with incredible force, into the region of the bladder. Shrieking with rage and pain, the elephant whipped round, thrusting out with his tusks. The *Tebe* leaped to the side and the four pygmies of the advance guard immediately rushed forward to sink their own spears into the animal's belly and flanks. A few seconds later the main body of hunters closed in like a swarm of angry bees.

The elephant stampeded wildly through the undergrowth, lashing out from side to side at his tormentors. More and more spears pierced him as the hunters, completely caught up in the passion of the kill, seemed to throw aside the last vestige of caution. Soon the elephant found it almost impossible to move. With every step he took, the protruding shafts of the spears caught in the bush, twisting the weapons deep in his entrails. Nearly insane with agony he paused in confusion, only to receive the last and most terrible wound of all: a spear-thrust into the upper portion of the extremely sensitive trunk.

He lunged in the direction of his last tormentor, while the hunters pulled at the loops of bowel hanging from his belly. Then, finally, it was over. The elephant fell to his knees, convulsed with maniacal spasms. His legs flailed, his bowels emptied, he rolled over on to his side, his great head rose and smashed to the ground. At last he died—that immense, wise, beautiful creature—in a stinking miasma of pain and blank bewilderment.

Immediately, the pygmies started a victory dance, forming a circle around the mountainous corpse. A shrill, tentative, tuneless music rose into the air as they blew on their *segbe*, wooden hunting whistles with a much more piercing note than their dance-flutes called *malinga*. I was immensely relieved, as I counted, to see that there were twelve pygmies dancing: it had been an exceptionally lucky hunt, with not a man killed or seriously wounded. As for minor injuries, that was impossible to say. They were all so completely bespattered with elephant blood and dung that their own blood would scarcely show.

The tuneless music grew stronger and the hunters pranced round their dead prey in an endless, bloody circle. Then, abruptly, everything stopped. Out from the bush came three Bambuba negroes, with elephant-spears in their hands. It was immediately obvious that the masters had come to claim their property. Not a word was spoken. Evidently both sides knew their position well enough from past experience. One of the Bambuba took up a guard position beside the corpse while the other two vanished into the bush, heading for their village. They were going to call their *duku*, their relatives, to carry away the tusks and the meat.

As the solitary Mumbuba leaned on his spear and watched, the band of pygmy hunters re-formed their circle around the elephant's stinking corpse. Round and round they danced for at least half an hour, piping their monotonous notes on the *segbe*. Then the circle broke and the hunters marched in single file on top of the carcass, and then again formed up in a circle as the last man descended from the huge, bloody head.

They repeated this grotesque saraband with minor variations for an hour, when a long caravan of Bambuba negroes arrived, men, women and children, all carrying large empty wicker baskets except for three who were lugging some spindly stalks of bananas and a big pot of *pombe*—the pygmies' reward.

The negro *kapita* called out to the circle of dancing Bambuti. They stopped. He made an imperious gesture. The pygmies gathered up their spears and handed them back to their legal owners. In return, each received a machete to cut up the corpse. Later, of course, the machetes would also have to be returned to the masters. Then the *kapita* gave the signal to start cutting.

The elephant's belly was laid open. Some of the pygmies got right inside the body cavity, hacking as they went. Others crouched on the animal's flanks, carving off huge chunks of meat which they heaved towards the waiting baskets. I turned aside, sickened, and walked away from that nightmarish scene. It wasn't the insupportable stench or the ugly butchery that filled me with so much revulsion; it was the complete degradation of my friends. I knew what risks they had taken—ninety-pound men attacking a five-ton elephant with borrowed spears. I knew what courage and tenacity the prolonged attack had involved. Now I saw them deprived of dignity and will, moving like bloody little puppets under the direction of their arrogant negro masters.

At that moment I realized that I could wait no longer. There were many gaps in my knowledge and experience yet to be filled, but the time was past for passive study and observation. It was no longer enough to be a part of the living world, not when that world was dying. I had to *do* something about it.

15

'An Ethnological Revolution'

> 'Thus, by a peaceful revolution, a new life is opening
> for the oldest people in Africa, who have remained,
> curiously enough, the most primitive and the most
> neglected of all.'
>
> GOVERNMENT-GENERAL OF THE BELGIAN
> CONGO, Léopoldville, 2 May 1958

FREEDOM for the Bambuti—the words came, irresistibly, to my mind. But words cannot be planted or eaten, and they cannot bring freedom where there is no social and economic base for it. The Government had itself spoken those same ringing words, without facing the underlying realities, and the situation in the Ituri had grown steadily worse.

There could be no return to the crude, uncomplicated innocence of the past, for the Bambuti had tasted the negro's bananas and the white man's apple of knowledge as well as the fruit of the *tahu* tree. Now their traditional way of life was dying, and in its place negro and white had offered the pygmies two different substitute versions of economic dependence. Ironically, the *matabish* and charity of the white man had proved even more degrading than the feudal mastery of the negro.

The pygmies needed neither masters nor alms-givers but *teachers*—dogged, practical, unsentimental teachers to guide them. They needed their own economy, a brand-new way of life shaped to their psychological and physiological requirements. They needed recognition of their usefulness and dignity as human beings. In short, they needed a social revolution—and they needed it *now*.

* * *

Two days after the elephant hunt Yoma and Ebu returned to camp with a blood-spotted, dark-brown *mboloko*. The little antelope would have made an appetizing meal for the three of us, but we lunched on caterpillars and raw mushrooms, and then I sent the boys on a one-day walk to Erengeti, with instructions to sell the meat at the local *magazini* and use the money to buy paper, envelopes and a ballpoint pen.

They were baffled by this and asked me to go with them, but I had to refuse. The half-civilized roadside village of Erengeti wasn't prepared for the sight which had already shocked the negro tribesmen of the bush: a Belgian administrative official dressed in a *ficus*-bark loincloth, a *segbe* hunting whistle and tattered, disreputable leggings.

When the boys came back, the entire pygmy population of the camp gathered round to watch me covering sheet after sheet of clean white paper with my alien hieroglyphics. By sunset I had a beautiful case of left-handed writer's cramp but had completed three long and important letters.

The first was addressed to AGRIPRO, the Provincial Service of Agriculture at Bukavu, and explained that it was entirely feasible to persuade the sedentary pygmies of Kivu to take up a new way of life, away from the highways and the negro villages, back in the forest where they belonged. At a series of carefully planned *paysannats*, agricultural colonies, they could be taught to cultivate crops systematically, to build comfortable wattle-and-daub huts and to practise adequate sanitation. Eventually there could be schools. I asked AGRIPRO to finance my new programme or at the very least to make an initial grant for the purchase of axes, machetes and hoes so that we could get started.

The second letter was directed to Father Paul Schebesta, the noted anthropologist in care of the Institut Royal Colonial Belge. This noted anthropologist, unquestionably the foremost academic authority on the pygmies, had made expeditions to the Ituri in 1929, 1934 and 1950, had spent altogether more than two years in the forest and had recorded many facets of Bambuti culture with remarkable perception and detail. Yet during the entire twenty years of his work, he had issued no call for definite action. Now I spoke of my deep concern for the survival of the Bambuti and the programme I was planning on their behalf and asked if he would use his recognized authority to help me.

(Father Schebesta never answered me directly, but in August 1957 he published an appeal on behalf of the pygmies as an epilogue to his book *Vier Fahrten zu den Ituri-Pygmäen*. He proposed the major elements of my programme, without mentioning me, and ended with the words: 'The question involves the racial survival of the pygmy Bambuti.')

The third letter, addressed to Vermeulen, the A.T. at Beni, concerned the action I intended to take and included a copy of my financial request to AGRIPRO. Then I added a little note which eventually brought me more trouble than a whole quiverful of poisoned Bambuti arrows. Had I realized what a furore my words would create among the high ecclesiastical dignitaries of Kivu, I might have been tempted to mine and smelt iron ore to make my own axes, hoes and machetes; it would have been easier and far less noisy.

The note merely read: 'Can you try to persuade the FBI to switch the 100,000-franc budget which has been used by the Petites Sœurs for so many years without appreciable results to a positive, substantial programme?'

The FBI—the 'Fonds du Bien-Être Indigène'—was the Belgian Colonial Government's 'Native Welfare Fund', whose 100,000-franc budget was an annual grant that was being frittered away on a sort of sentimental relief programme for the roadside pygmies of Mbau. Each year's money was channelled through the Mission of Beni to a zealous religious order called the Petites Sœurs de Jésus.

The Little Sisters used the funds to distribute trilby hats, shirts and *kapitula* to the pygmy men, *kitenge* robes, or at least bras, to the women, and knitted caps, sweaters and booties to the infants. According to classic missionary traditions clothing was supposed to make pygmies more decent and moral; instead it was constantly damp and dirty in the Grand Forest's moist heat and the real effect, as in Polynesia and many other parts of the world, was simply to increase the incidence of pulmonary disorders. At intervals the Little Sisters distributed tinned food, cigarettes and a few rakes, hoes and machetes—with entirely predictable results. The uneven dole of food made the spoiled pygmies of Mbau less self-sufficient than ever; they grew increasingly more expectant, dissatisfied and resentful; as for the tools, it was pointless to give out hoes or machetes without first providing stout axes to clear away the heavier bush, and a rake, a tool never traditionally used by any Bantu tribe in the Congo, is far more suitable for tending Belgian flower-beds than for coping with the equatorial forest's ferocious vegetation. The few pygmies who received these shiny, brand-new tools had no inclination to use them and no understanding of the basic facts of agriculture; they did not even know how to plant a seed. So they never bothered to cut handles for the hoe blades, but rushed, invariably, to trade the tools to the negro villagers for a few drinks of *pombe*.

Thus, ironically, the missionaries' efforts had succeeded only in further debauching the pygmies, under the aegis of the Belgian Colonial Government and at its direct expense.

I finished the last letter, sealed all three, and sent them via Yoma and Ebu to the village of Kakola, where the Nande *kapita* would dispatch a runner to the *Chef de Poste* at Mbau, who would forward the letters to AGRIPRO headquarters at Bukavu, the Institut Royal Colonial Belge in Brussels and the A.T. at Beni. Any replies would come, as I had requested, to *Poste Détachée* at Mbau. When my two young companions returned from their all-day postal safari, we headed slowly towards the south, stopping to visit each band of sedentary pygmies living near the western edge of the road to Mbau.

Three weeks later, when we were ten miles north of Mbau, I sent Yoma ahead to look for letters. He returned with one from AGRIPRO approving my vast programme for more than a thousand sedentary pygmies living in the Territory of Beni and granting me five thousand francs (less than £35) to start with.

Yoma, Ebu and I walked on to Mbau and when we arrived, after a hard four-hour trip, I had to sneak into my own house. It was that damned *milumba* again: I didn't want to give the local Batangi tribesmen an opportunity to laugh at my scandalous pygmy costume. The key was where I had left it, hidden under a big stone near the door; everything inside seemed to be in good order.

I took a quick bath in cold water laced with Dettol antiseptic coloured almost brown with rust from the metal storage drums in which it had stood unused for many months. Over the angry scratches on my arms, legs and chest I daubed long red lines of mercurochrome which made me look like a hydrographic map of the Congo. Only when I put on a fresh khaki shirt and *kapitula* did I realize how much weight I had lost—three and a half stone—during my months as an *évolué* pygmy.

Then my Chevy truck refused to start. The battery had completely run down, and I had to get a push from a Greek planter passing by in a van. At first the engine wouldn't turn over, but it coughed into life after half a mile and I drove the remaining twelve miles to Beni at high speed. I left the truck, with the motor running, opposite the Territorial Office and walked inside for a talk with the A.T.

Vermeulen stared at me coldly. 'So, you're still alive. I received that letter you sent from your pygmy jungle, but I couldn't take it seriously.'

'AGRIPRO did. They've approved my programme and they've allotted a small budget. . . .' I held out the letter from Bukavu. 'I've come to pick up my five thousand francs.'

Vermeulen was outraged. 'Who do they think they are?' he stormed. 'By giving you that ridiculous token grant, they're only encouraging you to go on with your pygmy fantasies. What's more, haven't you ever heard of the Plan Décennal? You're supposed to take care of the Territory's industrial crops. That means coffee, palms and cotton, and *not* pygmies.'

'I'm certainly aware of it: you've said it often enough. But this situation is desperate. If we don't take some kind of action, the Bambuti will be extinct within two generations—'

'Why do you have to complicate my life with pygmies?' he interrupted. 'Let them alone, Monsieur Hallet! Let those little beasts roam about in their forest. That's all they're good for.'

I forced myself to be calm. 'Just give me the five thousand francs, Monsieur Vermeulen. There's nothing else to discuss—'

The A.T. had to comply with AGRIPRO's authorization, and the bookkeeper gave me the money. On my way out I paused for a parting shot: 'I'll start the programme at Mbau, and I'll keep an eye on the Nande plantations while I'm doing it. So you don't have to worry about the Plan Décennal; it won't collapse because I'm trying to do something for the pygmies.'

'Look, Monsieur Hallet, I have enough trouble as it is. Don't make life impossible for me! Especially now, just when I'm going on six months' leave.'

'*Bon voyage!*' I said dryly. 'If you don't bother me, I won't bother you.'

At the Greek store I had to haggle for a while with the owner, Pericles Dimitrios Milingos, a clever, heavy-set mulatto, before I got what I wanted at a reasonable price: twenty axes, twenty machetes and forty stout hoe blades. I took my change in a few kilos of dried fish, some potatoes and a package of salt. Then I filled up the truck with petrol and bought a new battery.

Back in Mbau, twenty minutes later, Yoma and Ebu gobbled the fish and ate salt as though it were candy, and built a fire in my back yard to roast the potatoes. I went exploring in the pantry and turned up some tins of Vienna sausages, mushroom soup, corned beef and delicious Hawaiian pineapple. I attacked them all with my traditional one-handed method: using a beer-can opener, I punched each lid repeatedly until it was transformed into an artistic metal star. The contents vanished very quickly, and I went outside to help the boys eat their potatoes.

I tried to explain my plan to them. 'The Bambuti are going to have a new life,' I told them, 'and it will start here at Mbau, in your own camp of Ebikeba. The three kinship groups from the three little clearings will all join together, move farther away from the road, and set up one big camp back in the forest. But it will be a different kind of camp, with green fields and beautiful *pisé* huts, where the women will be happy to live, and the babies won't sicken and die.'

The boys stared at me sceptically. '*Bapa*,' Yoma said gravely, 'it sounds good but it won't work. We don't know how to make plants grow or how to build houses.'

'You can learn, and I'm going to teach you. Now listen carefully: I want you both to go back to Ebikeba and tell the people that I'm coming to see them in the morning. Explain what I've told you, and say that there must be a big meeting to talk about the new plan. Try to have all the men on hand.'

'We'll try,' Yoma said dubiously, 'but I don't think they'll like it.'

He was right. When I visited Ebikeba the next morning, I found the general reaction to what the boys had said was not so much scepticism as outright fear. I went first to Kikwetu, the largest of the three clearings where the pygmies lived and the one closest to the road. There were twenty men in this *parentèle*, or group of families, but only five or six showed up for the promised discussion. None of them seemed to have any enthusiasm. At Batikina, the second clearing, there were only a few women and children; the ten men of the *parentèle* were nowhere in sight, and at Bapo, the remaining sector, it was the same story.

'Talk to them again,' I said to Yoma and Ebu. 'Try to make them see what the new kind of camp will mean, how it will help them and make their lives easier. Tell them I will come again tomorrow, just after sunrise, and *show* them how it will really work.'

Early next morning eighteen men were waiting for me. Though still sceptical, they were curious to see my demonstration. 'From now on,' I told the circle of silent, uneasy pygmies, 'you

will be completely independent of the negroes, under my own
protection. All of you will receive an ID book, but you will not
have to pay taxes until you start to make money—'

'Make money?' one of the men repeated. 'How will we do
that?'

'The money will come later. First you have to feed yourselves, and I'm going to show you a better way to do it. I have
fine new tools waiting for you: half the people will get axes, the
other half machetes. Later, when the land is ready for it, everyone will get a hoe to turn over the soil. Those tools will belong
to *you*.'

Several men smiled; I knew what they had in mind—trading
my tools for beer as they had the Little Sisters' gifts.

'A monkey doesn't know what to do with a hoe,' I said emphatically, 'and the Banande say you are monkeys. They laugh
at you when you trade them good tools for a few little drinks of
pombe. Then they take the tools and use them, as men do, to
make food come out of the ground.'

They stared at me.

'I've brought just one hoe with me today, but you will be
able to *see* its wonderful power.' I walked to the side of the
clearing and marked off a three-foot square of ground between
two of the dilapidated little huts. 'Take the hoe,' I ordered
Ebu, 'and turn over the ground.'

He obeyed, the crowd watching expectantly.

'Bring a lot of small sticks,' I said to two men. 'Fetch me
mangungu leaves,' I told an old woman.

They were baffled—almost spellbound—by these strange preparations, but asked no questions and waited silently for the
next scene in this mysterious little drama. I stared at them
intently; then, with a magician's grandiose gesture, reached into
the left-hand pocket of my baggy *kapitula* and pulled out—not
a rabbit, but a single ear of multicoloured Indian corn. I held
it at arm's-length, smiled at it ostentatiously and gave it to Ebu.
'Take every kernel off the cob,' I told him. 'Do it very carefully,
and put all the seeds together on one of the leaves.'

Ebu stripped the cob while the people stared with increasing
puzzlement at the bright mosaic of seeds on the shiny, dark-
green *mangungu* leaf.

'Look!' I said softly, passing my fingers through the heap.
'There are hundreds of them! More than any man in Ebikeba
can count!' Then, with one finger, I pushed a much smaller pile
to the side. 'Here are ten seeds, and every single one of them

can make a heap like the big one. Ten seeds will not fill a man's belly, all of us know that. If he eats them, he can hardly tell the difference. But if he plants them in the ground and takes good care of them, those ten little seeds can fill his belly for a long time.'

Ceremoniously I placed the kernels of corn two inches deep and about a foot apart in the fresh, upturned earth. Then I set up the little sticks as a protective barrier. 'Each time you have an ear of corn,' I explained, 'don't eat it all. Save ten little seeds for the ground, and you will *always* have corn to eat. A chimpanzee doesn't know that, he just picks nuts and fruit from the trees. Only a man can use his brains to get more food from the earth with less trouble. Now, if you really want to be men, and not the Banande's monkeys or servants, I'll give you the chance to *prove* it.'

Four and a half months later the people of Ebikeba saw the direct results of that first tiny planting: eight seeds had germinated and there were fifteen ears of corn. We stripped them and had a large pile that must have contained at least five thousand seeds. I put ten of the seeds on a separate *mangungo* leaf. 'That is what you get,' I said, pointing with a wide gesture to the five thousand seeds, 'from this,' pointing to the ten kernels.

No one could argue with plain facts like that, an astonishing 500 to 1 ratio, but at this stage, when the original ten seeds were still fresh in the ground, the pygmies were far from convinced. They seemed to resent the chimpanzee comparison, as I had hoped they would; but when I finished, they simply stared blankly, first at me and then at each other. I had to repeat the whole thing several times before I felt that they really got the point, and then they argued the question back and forth for more than three hours. They were still hard at it when I left Ebikeba to check the negro plantations south of Mbau.

Early next morning Ebu knocked at my door. '*Bapa*,' he said, 'we've talked a lot more about the new kind of camp. The people really liked your corn story, but they asked me a whole lot of questions. Maybe, if you come back today, they will be willing to start.'

'You mean they agree?' I asked incredulously. 'All of them?'

'No, not all of them. Still, I expect they will do it anyway. But when you go back, don't even ask if they're willing. If you say too much, they'll think that they're doing you a favour. Just go there, they'll know why you're coming.'

I went to Ebikeba an hour later, with two Nande porters to

carry the axes and machetes. I found waiting for me thirty-five pygmies, nearly all the men and older boys from the three *parentèles*. I took them down the little trail that led from the Kikwetu clearing back into the forest, and after half an hour's walk decided on a wide stretch of ground without any swampy spots, where there were relatively few sizeable trees and a little less thorn bush than usual. It was the right place for the first *paysannat pygméen*, an agricultural colony where free Bambuti, for the first time in the long history of their race, would clear land, plant crops and harvest the fruit of their labours.

* * *

It took three weeks to measure and carve out of the forest a rectangle two hundred yards long by a hundred yards wide. On this site we built temporary huts, and a group of pygmies, varying daily in number between fifteen and forty, hacked away with their axes and machetes at the inextricable mass of tangled trunks, branches and lianas. The rest of the men hunted, while the women and children gathered food to keep us all going. Finally, on the morning of the twenty-second day, the major part of the job was over: we had cut down, uprooted, chopped up and burned practically all of the vegetation from a chunk of forest the size of a soccer field. Only the largest tree stumps remained, fallen trunks too big or too green to be burned and a heavy débris of twigs, branches and leaves.

The five-acre rectangle was divided by boundary stakes into forty roughly equal homesteads in which each family would be responsible for finally clearing and preparing its own land; a homestead consisted of five fields, small enough not to overwhelm the pygmies by the magnitude of their task, but of sufficient size to yield a substantial crop. Once they mastered the basic principles of agriculture on these model fields, the limits of the *paysannat* could be extended indefinitely into the forest.

Four of the fields would be cultivated systematically, with rotation of crops, to yield a steady succession of beans, peanuts, corn, bananas and manioc. The fifth, on the outer edge of the rectangle, was reserved for the family's permanent wattle-and-daub hut, a few sweet-potato patches and a surrounding banana grove for both fruit and shade.

The whole thing was starkly logical and adapted in every detail to suit the pygmies' psychology and understanding.

Now I made a plan of the new *paysannat* and filled in the names of the men whose families would occupy each domain.

There were thirty-six of them, leaving four vacancies. I felt certain that new pygmy candidates would come to fill them as soon as the project really got going, but I was taken completely by surprise when I was approached by a group of white candidates who wanted to join my new colony—none other than the Little Sisters of Jesus.

Most of the missionaries in the Congo, even the Catholics, disapproved of this strange religious order, but the Little Sisters had been invited to Kivu six years before by the Assumptionist Bishop of Beni, apparently to give the impression that some good works were being accomplished among the pygmies. But since this particular sect's vocation lies midway between the contemplative and the apostolic life, outside the province of action, things never went beyond an impression. The Little Sisters are supposed to bring a message of Christian charity and friendship, a benevolent 'presence' to the wretched of the earth, by living among them without attempting to aid them in any substantial way but simply by sharing their poverty, misery and squalor. Most of the Petites Sœurs de Jésus du Père de Foucauld came from wealthy, refined, and often noble families, in which respect they resembled their founder, the Vicomte Charles Eugène de Foucauld, a rich, spoiled French aristocrat born in 1858 who spent his youth as a dissolute hussar. Repenting his sins at twenty-eight, the young viscount entered the Church; but as Trappist Brother Marie-Albéric he found the stark monastic life insufficiently austere to satisfy his massive guilt-complex. So he journeyed to the Holy Land, bent on 'the total rejection of all human dignity' and 'a deliberate quest for abjection'.

Dressed in a tattered striped *gandhura* Brother Charles of Jesus, as he now called himself, roamed the streets of Nazareth gathering dung for the garden of the Clarist Sisters and rejoiced when street urchins jeered and stoned him. He was looking for martyrdom. As he himself wrote a few months after coming to Nazareth: 'Imagine that you should die a martyr, divested of everything, lying naked on the ground, unrecognizable, bloodied and riddled with wounds, tortured and violently slain, and wish that it might be today.'

Brother Charles finally found the fate he so desperately craved on 1 December 1916, when he was murdered by raiding Muslims at Tamanrasset, in Algeria. During his lifetime he had failed to make a single convert, but after his death his strange, tormented principles were revived by three new religious orders:

the Little Brothers of Jesus, the Little Sisters of the Sacred Heart,
and the Little Sisters of Jesus (founded in 1939).

In their own personal quest for abjection Father de Foucauld's
spiritual descendants here at Mbau had established their settlement on the edge of the forest, within easy walking distance of
the old pygmy camp at Ebikeba. Their numbers varied, but
three or four were generally in residence, headed not by a
Mother Superior but simply a *Responsable*.

For six long years this little group of zealous, idealistic women,
clad in blue-grey robes and coifed with dark blue scarfs, had
shared the pygmies' life—though themselves maintaining two
cars and living in large, comfortable *pisé* huts with conical
grass roofs whose repair cost at least three thousand francs a
year.

The pygmies called the whole strange set-up '*Pa-nda-Petisher*'
(their own version of Petites Sœurs) and were always coming
begging for scraps. The Batangi negroes had a much harsher
name for it; baffled by the spectacle of European women trying
to live a poor imitation of primitive life, they spoke contemptuously of '*Bikira Masikini*', which can be translated as either
'Miserable Sisters' or 'Broken-Down Nuns'.

Tourists who flocked to Mbau searching for pygmies got a
quite different impression: they saw the round huts with their
picturesque but impracticable roofs (more costly, in the long run,
than the finest Roman tile!) and watched the Little Sisters
meditating in their rustic chapel, sweeping their yard with a
palm-leaf broom or dandling an orphaned Bambuti baby. They
found the whole scene very touching, and most of them contributed generously to the nuns' good works, while they gave
the pygmies a small coin or a handful of peanuts.

Thus, six long years had passed for the Petites Sœurs of
Mbau—until I launched the new programme at Ebikeba. Now
the *Responsable*, Sœur Jeanne-Mariette de Jésus, accompanied
by one of her fellow sisters, paid me a visit and made the
startling announcement that the nuns wanted to move in and
live with my pygmies. They would set a good example, she
explained, by tilling the soil themselves and building their own
pisé hut. One Sister would always be present at the *paysannat*,
on a rotation basis, to convey their customary message of
friendship and comfort.

Knowing the background and principles of their order, I
didn't like the idea, but there was no point in antagonizing the
Church any more than necessary. So I accepted their strange

'presence' and assigned a set of five fields at the southeastern end of the rectangle to this handful of European women deliberately seeking abjection at the same place where more than a hundred African pygmies were looking for human dignity.

A few days later I brought some sacks of peanuts and beans from Mbau for the first planting, and distributed seed to all families whose fields had been cleared and hoed. With only three exceptions, all newcomers who had taken the last vacant places, the pygmies were ready and waiting. They rushed to work immediately, anxious to get their share of the seed. There was only one set of fields which hadn't been cleared, that of the Little Sisters.

On 9 May 1957, the day when the Bambuti planted their first seeds in the soil of the new Ebikeba, I decided to make my first official statement about the results of my programme: I wrote a long letter to the A.T., discussing the creation of the *paysannat*: its rationale, its goals, its problems. My answer came on 20 May, an official communication from Beni that praised my initiative and promised aid for my project. Needless to say, the signature wasn't 'Vermeulen'. Instead, the name inscribed beneath those encouraging words was André de Maere d'Aertrycke, the Interim Administrator during Vermeulen's vacation.

At Beni next day André de Maere and I discussed the project in every detail. He was so impressed with the initial results that he gave me *carte blanche* for the next six months, in spite of Vermeulen's past opposition. As to what we would both do when the A.T. returned—well, we decided to worry about that when we had to.

André's official *carte blanche* was quite reassuring; especially since I had acted on it in advance. After writing my letter to Beni on 9 May, I had stripped the Territorial Depot of its available tools, solicited more from the nearby European plantations and borrowed back from the pygmies some of my original axes and machetes. Then, with a truckful of tools, I drove north to start a second *paysannat* at Erengeti.

This time it was much easier. Yoma and a husky, very bright boy named Kalingama came with me to tell what they had seen with their own eyes and accomplished with their own hands. We gave the people facts rather than theories, and their reaction was almost overwhelming: 'If Ebikeba can do it, then we can, too.'

A day later they were starting to hack their own *paysannat* out of the forest, while I went on to Kasana, five miles away, and told another group about what had been happening at Ebikeba and Erengeti. They were excited and anxious to prove to their fellow pygmies that they could do just as well as larger, more civilized camps. I used the same technique at Kakola, Liva and Kisiki—and a growing wave of enthusiasm started to sweep through North Kivu. By the time I got down to Oicha, so many pygmies had joined in that I ran out of tools, but even that didn't stop them; determined to have their own *paysannat*, the Bambuti from the camp southwest of Oicha attacked the bush with their elephant-spears.

When André de Maere gave me his official blessing in Beni, I had already established five more *paysannats*. A month later, on 20 June, there were fifteen, in varying stages of progress, from Ngite where the great trees were still being felled, to Ebikeba where the fields were green with fresh new shoots of manioc, corn, beans and bananas, and the first *pisé* huts were under construction.

I rushed to and fro among them, distributing tools, seed, encouragement, orders and advice. For a while I felt rather like the legendary pygmy Prometheus running like hell with his tail on fire—not to one camp but to fifteen. Between sunrise and sunset I was constantly on the move. There wasn't time for regular meals, so I took my food as I found it: bananas, peanuts, snails, or whatever was on hand. Then in the evenings I returned to Ebikeba and plotted campaign strategy with the help of my pygmy friends. At night my mind was so busy running over the next day's activities that I hardly slept, and when I did, I cleared bush, planted seeds, and gave pygmy pep-talks in my dreams.

For a while there were no serious problems, aside from the chronic shortage of funds. Then trouble began to brew with the Banande negroes. At Ebikeba the feudal bonds linking the pygmies to the Batangi villages had already been badly frayed; further north the Bambuba and Banisanza sub-tribes held a much tighter rein, and now they saw their authority slip away as their former subjects grew not only more economically independent, but increasingly self-assured and even insolent. Furthermore, since the negroes, according to the Administration's policy, were legally responsible for the pygmies' acts, their position was becoming more and more difficult.

I talked to most of the important Nande *kapita* as I travelled among the *paysannats*, trying to convince them that the profits of their traditional 'social contract' were decreasing wherever the pygmies lived near the road, and that an end to the old feudal system would not only relieve them of their legal responsibility but prevent the Bambuti from raiding their crops.

On 20 June, after my propaganda had more than a month to sink in, I again discussed matters with André de Maere. I recommended that the Territorial Administration of Beni convoke a council of negro chiefs and Bambuti elders, obtain their agreement and issue an official 'Emancipation Proclamation' for the pygmies.

Six days later, on 26 June 1957, the oldest, most primitive and most neglected people in Africa were formally liberated from the bonds of feudal dependence: the negro chiefs renounced their status as lords and masters, and the Administration granted full civil rights and responsibilities to the pygmies. There would be no more of that false and disgusting 'symbiosis' in the Territory of Beni, and the old question, 'Are pygmies men?' had finally been answered—with a decisive Yes.

It was a great date in the history of the Belgian Congo, the date of an event far more important than the discovery of a river or mountain range: it was the discovery of human dignity and human rights where they had been most lacking.

To celebrate, I added two more *paysannats* northeast of Mbau —Naiti and Mambafika—and a little later Ngadi, near Beni, at the southern limit of Bambuti territory. That made eighteen *paysannats* with 353 families, a total of nearly a thousand pygmies taking part in the great revolution.

*   *   *

The next four months were wonderfully exciting. I whizzed faster and faster round the eighteen *paysannats*, teaching my people how to dig septic holes, plant manioc slips, forge arrow points, build tables and chairs for their new *pisé* huts and rustic cradles for their babies, put salt in their cooking instead of eating it separately, take soap and water baths and wash their *milumba* at least once a week, build barbecue spits, and above all, to stay away from the negro villages and the tourists.

Their response was tremendous.

At Liva a man named Mwedore, who had finished planting his crops and building his hut, remembered my metal-working demonstrations. He decided to set up shop as a blacksmith, the first professional smith in the history of his race, and made a forge, using one iron rail for a hammer and another for an anvil, with a bellows of carved wood and antelope skin. He succeeded, and soon there were one or two aspiring smiths in every one of my colonies.

At Erengeti a band of wild pygmies from the bush attached themselves to the *paysannat* and cleared an acre of forest on their own, where they planted a grove of bananas.

At Kisiki most of the men made a ceremonial gesture to confirm their new freedom: they returned their elephant-spears to the former Nande masters. The negroes were furious and tried to chase them out of the village, but as one pygmy told me with new-found pride, 'We didn't run away: we *walked* out.' The same gesture was made at several other *paysannats*, and in some cases, where the negroes had been more domineering, the pygmies gave *me* the spears to avoid a direct confrontation and eventually I had several dozen stacked in my garage.

At Naiti, northeast of Mbau, where the new *paysannat* lay at the end of a long and very difficult trail, the pygmies gave me one of the biggest presents, and surprises, of my life: they built a Bambuti version of a government *gîte d'étape* to encourage my overnight stays—a thatched rectangular hut, amazingly soundly constructed. Later I found they had actually hired a Nande adviser as a sort of Bush Building Inspector, paying for his services with a leg of *mboloko*. It was not only a touching gesture, but an enterprising project which only a few months before would never have entered their heads.

At Ebikeba five new families had moved in at the southern end of the rectangle. Entirely on their own initiative they had migrated from Muhekuva, cleared bush, put in boundary stakes and sown crops. Here, at the charter headquarters of the *paysannats pygméens*, the crops were the farthest advanced. Every field was beautifully, vividly, productively green, and every *pisé* hut was completed, with only one exception: the débris-littered uncultivated fields of the Little Sisters and the shaky partial framework of their half-hearted house.

By now it was mid-October and my biggest problem was money. Up to this point, the project had been financed by AGRIPRO'S original £35, plus whatever material I could beg or borrow from the wealthier European planters, padded out by sizeable chunks of my own monthly salary. It wasn't enough. More funds had to be found, not only to provide tools and seed for the long list of *paysannats* but for temporary rations to help keep them going until crop production increased.

There was a very simple way, I realized, to solve our financial problems: the same tourists who had given the pygmies a trifling *matabish* could, if handled correctly, become their chief source of revenue.

For a fixed fee, perhaps two hundred francs per car, the pygmies could demonstrate their dances, archery and wood-craft at a custom-made camp of shaggy *mangungu* huts close to the highway at Mbau; different families from Ebikeba would be rotated daily to avoid overexposure of any particular group. The entire camp, with an attached curio shop, could be run by an experienced negro *kapita*.

The tourists could pass through Mbau and get an educational dose of Bambuti culture, while the pygmies would be spared the indignities of uncontrolled contact. Simultaneously, the entire *paysannat* programme would at last find financial backing.

It was beautifully logical, and once again André de Maere gave it official sanction. Together we set up 'La Caisse Communautaire des Bambuti'—a pygmy Community Chest—to handle the expected revenue from tourist fees, contributions and sales of curios and refreshments. Since there was no current revenue, I made the first contribution, £70, about half a month's salary, to buy the needed material and supplies.

We all started work immediately on the new project: a dozen old ladies from Ebikeba built the *mangungu* huts, a crew of hired Nande labourers built the curio shop and a round *pisé* Rest Room (especially designed for female tourists), and I built, one-handed, a loquacious rustic billboard advertising 'The Only Accessible Pygmy Camp'. There was another sign at the entrance, smaller but very prominent: 'The Administration insists that all visitors respect the human dignity of the pygmies at all times.'

The entire establishment was finished in five days, and we opened for business on 20 October 1957. We were a smashing success.

Once they knew there was an easily accessible, organized camp, the tourists stopped hunting pygmies on the road and came to Mbau instead. We gave them a much fairer and more informative picture of forest life, and to my great satisfaction the visitors treated my people with friendly respect. Then social scientists, missionaries, foreign dignitaries and highly placed Belgian officials began to arrive, and all of them, especially those who went farther into the forest to see the *paysannat*, were full of praise for what was being done.

Now, with money pouring into the Pygmy Community Chest (at an average rate of about £7 a day) and all eighteen *paysannats* making steady progress, I decided to devote more time to education. I had bought a big blackboard and sixty slates in Beni for the initial experiments and held open-air classes at Ebikeba. Working with several new methods of my own, I had taught classes of twenty-five to thirty men and boys the basic principles of reading, writing and simple arithmetic. I used peg boards with large movable wooden numbers to illustrate problems in addition and subtraction, and devised a strange but very effective technique for teaching the alphabet. Each letter became the focal point of its own model sentence, which the pupils acted out with real gusto.

'*Lave la lame!*' one boy would order another, holding out a soiled blade; '*Je lave la lame*,' the second boy would answer, as he actually washed it clean. '*Je tue la tortue*', and they banged solemnly on a turtle's empty carapace; '*Je mange la mangue*', and they ate a juicy mango. Naturally everyone's favourite exercise turned out to be '*Je bois la bière*'—to the point where I substituted '*Je brise la branche*'. Branch-breaking proved more conducive to classroom discipline than beer-drinking.

The method was slow and often very involved, but it held their attention, stimulated their curiosity and gave them the opportunity to indulge their very strongly developed mimetic sense. I devised several others and then, having seen both their capacity for learning and their enthusiasm, decided to build my first real classroom. It was a monumental *pisé* structure, almost as large as the great Mangbetu houses near Paulis: fifty by thirty feet, with large windows and a straw-thatched peaked roof, eighteen feet high at the ridgepole. My twenty-five pupils and I built the whole thing in a fortnight.

We cleared a large field for recreation, and in one corner I set up a miniature *paysannat* with plots only five metres square, to teach the children the principles of agriculture. It was a failure. They were much happier playing soccer or practising military drills while they sang the latest Bambuti folk songs: 'Sur le Pont d'Avignon', 'Alouette' and 'Route Fière'.

As a crowning touch, I established a small pygmy police force, based at Ebikeba with occasional tours of duty at the other *paysannats*. Ironically, that made my people feel much more 'civilized' while it helped to keep things running on an orderly basis. I chose eight of the strongest and most trustworthy pygmies I could find, taught them precise military drills and dressed them in custom-made uniforms (sewn by a Nande tailor who worked at Molingos' store). The new *kapitula*, jackets and overseas caps were not made from the blue *kaniki* worn by the negro *polici*, but from cotton cloth dyed a wonderful bright red. Immediately, most of the men at Ebikeba and the other *paysannats* wanted red uniforms of their own, and I had a hard time explaining that the clothing was only a symbol of special authority. As a whole, they were certainly much healthier and better off unclothed.

*   *   *

Thus, by the end of November 1957 my ten kernels of corn had sprouted into eighteen productive *paysannats*, an 'Emancipation Proclamation', a tourist organization, an experimental school, soccer teams, blacksmiths and even a pygmy Police Force. In less than a year I had made my impossible, revolutionary dream come true for nearly a thousand Efe pygmies at the southeastern edge of the Grand Forest. Now I was filled with even more ambitious plans to improve and expand my whole programme and was completely unaware of the ruthless storm heading towards the pygmies' brave new world.

16

A Giant Pygmy Campaign

> 'In revolutions everything is forgotten. The benefits
> you confer today are forgotten tomorrow. The side
> once changed, gratitude, friendship, parentage, every
> tie vanishes, and all that is sought is self-interest.'
>
> NAPOLEON at St. Helena, 25 July 1816

On 30 November 1957, Maurice Vermeulen, Territorial Administrator of Beni, returned from his long vacation in Europe and paid an unofficial visit to Mbau.

He was greeted by an unexpected phenomenon which had sprung into being during his absence: the green fields, neat huts and contented, hard-working people of the new Ebikeba. It must have seemed to him almost like a mirage. He explored the *paysannat*, looking for me, until two red-clad pygmy policemen marched up and directed him to the school. He followed the three-hundred-yard trail through the forest and came into the big *pisé* classroom just as thirty pygmies held up their slates, eager to show me that $12 \times 23 = 276$.

The A.T. stared blankly at that astonishing vision before he finally broke into a smile. Then he congratulated me on the success of my work, in spite of his former opposition, and in his first flush of dazed enthusiasm wrote a tribute in my 'Golden Book', a log-book I kept for visitors' comments: 'Very happy and grateful for these inspired results obtained in such a short space of time. All my thanks to Monsieur Hallet for his devotion.'

Vermeulen's warm glow of gratitude cooled very quickly, as soon as he realized what the pygmies' revolution meant to him *personally*. My programme had already attracted tremendous

279

interest in the Press, and the 'Golden Book' of Ebikeba had been signed by the Belgian Provincial Governors, the National Council of Switzerland, the Superintendent of Uganda, the Inspector of Economic Affairs from Bukavu, the Personnel Committee of Kivu, the Belgian National Defence Commission, the Director of the Native Welfare Fund (F.B.I.) and the African Inland Mission of Oicha (American Protestant medical missionaries).

They all praised the programme and myself enthusiastically, but there was nowhere any mention of the name 'Vermeulen'. This was only natural: apart from the A.T.'s original discouraging attitude towards the project, he hadn't even been on the African continent when my pygmies and I had hacked our clearings out of the forest and sown our revolutionary seeds. But now he was back, and throughout the Kivu Province the two words he heard most frequently were pygmies and Hallet. His nose went farther and farther out of joint every day.

Meanwhile, the Little Sisters of Father Foucauld had been doing some hard thinking of their own. 'No visible result was ever obtained by these courageous pioneers,' André de Maere had written in an official report, 'but that was not their mission.' To put it more bluntly, the nuns had spent six years and about £3,500 of government funds in Mbau and accomplished practically nothing. Then along came Hallet, and in less than a year, with a 'ridiculous token grant', a new life had been launched for a thousand sedentary pygmies.

Simple comparison showed the futility of their efforts. The Little Sisters knew it, and they were deeply concerned—about their 100,000-franc grant they received every year from the Native Welfare Fund. The Fund's Director had visited Ebikeba and put on record his good wishes 'for the complete success' of my work. If the grant were shifted from the religious organization to the *paysannat* programme, as I had originally requested, the Little Sisters would find themselves without government funds for their expenses. Then they might *really* start to share the pygmies' poverty—and that was unthinkable.

So, during December, while the people of Ebikeba were harvesting their first bananas, late corn and second bean crop, the Little Sisters of Father Foucauld and the A.T. were brooding separately over their waning prestige. When they put their heads together, they came up with some startling results.

The Little Sisters told Vermeulen that the pygmies were giving 'immoral and degrading exhibitions' at my new tourist camp—

they were *dancing*! The nuns apparently regarded these 'exhibitions', the same traditional dances which the pygmies had performed for thousands of years, as more shameful than begging on the road, stealing, or selling their daughters to negroes—previous 'exhibitions' which the Little Sisters had done nothing to discourage.

The A.T. had no great liking for the Foucauld sect but was aware of what tremendous power the Catholic Missions have always had in the Congo, and had not only his career but his ego to consider. Now he saw an opportunity to advance both by supporting the Little Sisters' sanctimonious censure of dancing.

So, on 2 January 1958, I received a little New Year's Greeting from Vermeulen: an official order to abstain from all activities of a non-agricultural nature, especially those which he described as 'touristic' and 'Barnumesque'. Then he demanded that I turn over the funds of the pygmy Community Chest and produce the books for his inspection. The implications were outrageous.

I sent Vermeulen the whole thing—cash, ledgers and a big stack of receipted bills for tools, seed and rations. There was only one outstanding debt, but I pointed out that the pygmies would never have to pay it: the Community Chest owed me roughly £175 for money advanced from my salary.

Less than a week later, on 8 January, I received an important visit from Luc Otto, an official of INEAC, the Belgian Congo's National Institute for Agronomic Studies, whose headquarters at Yangambi comprised the largest scientific research centre on the African continent. Ironically, while the Little Sisters of Father Foucauld were fretting over the pygmies' 'immoral' dances and the A.T. was checking the receipts for red beans and dried fish, Luc Otto made the following statement:

> The gigantic work undertaken here by Monsieur Hallet is the result not only of patient and thankless effort, but of action in which educational, social and, above all, human implications are all combined.
>
> The *paysannats* which have been brought about on his idealistic initiative are admirably conceived in sympathy with the spirit and the understanding of the pygmies who, only a few years ago—or rather, a few months ago—were still so primitive, so neglected and, unfortunately, so despised.
>
> The concept of these *paysannats* is, from an agricultural point of view, a well-directed and rational first step towards permitting the pygmies who have become sedentary to live

entirely from the fruits of their own labour, to be completely free and independent, and at last to believe themselves a part of human society—as men, and not as poor creatures exposed to exploitation, hunger, sickness and finally, as all the anthropologists have claimed, to 'the inevitable disappearance of this race'.

One must pay homage to this exceptional work, which I believe to be unique in the world, even more since it is joined with a tourist organization which is making Mbau an undoubted attraction as far as both folklore and ethnology are concerned, while the tourists themselves are contributing effectively to the pygmies' sound and rapid evolution.

This organization assures that the pygmies derive maximum benefit from tourism while preserving their dignity, whereas formerly they received no advantage from this 'necessary evil', and used to be displayed to the public only as freaks or local curiosities whose only attraction was to be found in their racial primitiveness.

It is also thanks to this organization that Monsieur Hallet has been able, not without difficulty, to distribute to them what they needed to make them independent (tools and seeds), to permit them to live more humanly (beds, covers and utensils) and to instruct their children in schools constructed by and for themselves in the heart of the virgin forest where they live. It would be appropriate for Monsieur Hallet to be supported morally and effectively in this noble enterprise, not only for the salutary evolution of the Bambuti pygmies, but also for the good name of the 'Civilizing Work' which the Belgian Administration pursues in Africa.

Entrusted with an official mission by the Direction Générale of INEAC at Yangambi, I particularly wish to bring this exceptional work to the attention of my Institute, which has always been deeply concerned not only with material evolution but also with the social and moral well-being of the native population of our colony.

In conclusion I affirm that the Government can be proud of such a representative who, on his own initiative, has known how to undertake this high humanitarian task with such devotion.   *Mission Direction Générale Est-Congo*
                                OTTO Luc   INEAC, Yangambi

Every one of those generous words was a mortal blow to the A.T.'s aching ego, and growing interest from the Congolese

Press did nothing to soothe his feelings. He simmered slowly for more than a week; then, when I tried to discuss the situation with him on 18 January, boiled over.

'If you say that damned word pygmy again,' the A.T. snarled, 'I'll throw you out of my office!'

'Pygmy . . . PYGMY . . . PYGMY!' I answered, in a cool, defiant crescendo.

He gripped the edge of his desk until his knuckles whitened, but didn't make a move.

'What are you waiting for, Vermeulen? If you put your hands on me, I'll have to defend myself, and I'll probably kill you.'

We stared at each other until the A.T. blinked and lowered his eyes. Then I stalked out of his office with slow, deliberate contempt.

Vermeulen's answer came eight days later—in my absence. I left for Stanleyville to have some major repairs done to my truck, and as soon as I was well out of range the A.T. of Beni set out courageously, armed with a sledgehammer. He used it to demolish, personally, the rustic billboard I had made to advertise 'The Only Accessible Pygmy Camp'. The scene was described to me later by a dozen men from the crowd of more than twenty pygmies and negroes who had looked on, appalled, while he wielded his hammer.

'*Bwana Ale* will be very angry when he sees that,' several had remarked innocently.

That was too much for the A.T., who thundered, '*I'm* the boss around here!' Then, in a paroxysm of rage, he spewed out, in front of twenty native witnesses, some incredible words: '*Bwana Mundevu iko masikini!*, Bwana Beard is only a cripple! *Ye iko mukono moya bule!*, He has only one hand!'

Next day, still taking advantage of my absence, Vermeulen went to Ebikeba and skinned my pygmy Police Force. While the people of the *paysannat* watched him, completely puzzled, the A.T. ordered the eight members of the élite squad to strip off their uniforms and left them, utterly humiliated, in their bark-cloth *milumba*. Their proud red uniforms were hauled off and put under lock and key in the Territorial Office, in spite of the fact that they were the legal property of the pygmies, purchased with two thousand francs from their own Community Chest.

When I returned to Mbau next day, I was shocked to find an idle, dispirited Ebikeba. '*Bwana Commandant* smashed your sign,' a doleful policeman reported, 'then he made us take off our clothes. Afterwards, he told all the people that they don't have to work any more. Now they don't know what to do.'

Infuriated, I headed for the Territorial Office, looking for Vermeulen. He wasn't there. Instead, I found André de Maere, his assistant, who was obviously very unhappy but powerless to do anything about the recent turn of events. André commiserated with me and then told me, with obvious embarrassment, of the latest administrative order. It was another shock, but it helped me to understand recent developments. Vermeulen's actions had been those of a man driven into a jealous rage, but there had been an element of cunning calculation as well.

Elisabeth, the Queen Mother of Belgium, was coming to Mbau the very next day and was to make an unexpected royal visit to the pygmies. By destroying the sign and denuding Ebikeba's Police Force, the A.T. was trying to cover up the more obvious traces of my influence and to avoid any embarrassing questions. His latest order, as I learned from André de Maere, followed logically: I was strictly forbidden to show my face at Ebikeba during the royal visit.

Thus, on 28 January 1958, the A.T. proudly displayed the new world of Ebikeba to the Queen Mother of Belgium, and congratulated the Little Sisters of Father Foucauld whose patient, tireless work had made it all possible. Ironically, there still remained one unfinished hut and one set of littered, uncultivated fields at the *paysannat*—those of the Little Sisters.

Only one discordant note marred the festivities: Queen Elisabeth asked to see a pygmy dance, although no dances were on the programme and the nuns tried to explain that they considered such 'exhibitions' indecent and degrading. The dignified, serene, eighty-two-year-old monarch insisted. The people of Ebikeba danced.

On 29 January, less than twenty-four hours after the A.T. had proudly displayed Ebikeba to Belgian royalty, he switched tactics with a dazzling display of illogic. He wrote to the Governor of Kivu that my *paysannats* were 'concentration camps' in which oppressed pygmies were working at forced labour. Then he delivered a little Kingwana speech at Ebikeba, officially 'liberating' the slaves. Afterwards, he sent negro policemen to the other *paysannats* to make the same emphatic, almost menacing gesture.

Most of the pygmies abandoned their new huts and fled into the forest. The rest wandered around the *paysannats* with hangdog expressions, completely confused and bewildered. I spent the following week trying to reassure those who remained and persuade the others to return. Vermeulen was relatively quiet, but on 5 February there was an unforeseen development.

Inforcongo, the official Information Service of the Government General at Léopoldville, devoted a complete issue, Number 346, of its *Pages Congolaises* to what it called 'An Ethnological Revolution'. The article began, 'The news, at first, seemed unbelievable to those who know the Ituri and its native populations: the pygmies are cultivating the soil! The little men of the Grand Forest have left the hunt for the furrow and the seed . . . In the territory of Beni (District of North Kivu), at Mbau, under the direction of an agronomist, Monsieur J. P. Hallet, the pygmies are trying their hand at agriculture.' It went on to describe the long history of feudal servitude, now a part of the pygmies' past, and the 'Emancipation Proclamation' which I had obtained on 26 June 1957. It spoke enthusiastically of the tourist establishment, the pygmy Community Chest and even of the shocking dances, all of which Monsieur Hallet had undertaken on his own initiative to keep the *paysannat* programme going.

'Thus, by a peaceful revolution,' *Inforcongo* concluded, 'a new life is opening up for the oldest people in Africa who, curiously enough, have remained the most primitive and neglected of all . . . The true friends of the pygmies can only rejoice in such a promising material and spiritual transformation.'

Tragically, the Government General's proud announcement came just as I was trying to salvage the remains of that revolution from chaos—the chaos into which its own local administration had thrown it.

Vermeulen reacted violently to this issue of *Pages Congolaises* —since his name hadn't been mentioned. Immediately, he ordered a special investigation of all the *paysannats* to make sure, as he said, that I really had eighteen of them. It took André de Maere two full days, 6 and 7 February, to tour my colonies and prepare his exhaustive report: a detailed statistical breakdown of the men, women, children, huts, hoes, axes, machetes, and land measured, cleared or planted at Erengeti, Kasana, Lisosiseni, Kakola I, Kakola II, Liva, Kisiki, Matombo, Oicha, Tenambo Bandepola, Tenambo II, Mambafika, Naiti, Ebikeba, Sikwaila, Makumbo, Ngite and Ngadi . . . exactly eighteen *paysannats*.

This immense mass of irrefutable statistics kept Vermeulen quiet for nearly three weeks while I managed to patch up some of the damage at the *paysannats*. Then, on 28 February, the situation burst wide open when a front-page article appeared in the daily newspaper *Centre-Afrique* under the headline, '*What's Going On at Mbau?*'

It described the pygmies' precarious situation, and the lack of any real concern on the part of the Government, the scholarly anthropologists or the Little Sisters of Jesus. Then *Centre-Afrique* went on:

At this point, our man intervened: a certain J. P. Hallet (the son of the painter), an agronomist in the Government service. Hallet, the son, is a big, bearded character built like an oversized wardrobe: well over six feet in height. A particular trait: his right hand is missing as the result of an accident. Other characteristic traits: he has a practical nature, overflowing with initiative, generous to a fault, and the ambition to make himself useful.

He has defects as well: a big mouth, direct manners and a complete refusal to conform. But he gets things done: in less than a year and with a grant of only 5,000 francs from the Provincial Service of Agriculture, this devil of a man has succeeded in doing what no one else ever did before him: he has made farmers out of the pygmies.

The article went on to describe the creation and success of the *paysannats* and the tourist establishment. Then it got down to business, describing the A.T.'s demolition activities with my sign, the ban on pygmy dances and the ensuing loss of revenue to the pygmy Community Chest.

The reason? [*Centre-Afrique* demanded.] Nobody seems to know the real story. Is it jealousy, and *whose*? Is Hallet's initiative incompatible with the presence in the parish of the Little Sisters of Jesus? Are pygmy dances immoral? Has Hallet embezzled the pygmies' funds? We know, in any case, that the local Chamber of Commerce has just protested unanimously at the closing of the tourist establishment. Explanations have been demanded from the authorities by the *colons* of Butembo.

Those who have had the opportunity to become acquainted with and to appreciate Hallet's efforts, and who were happy to see his tourist establishment flourish—all to the profit of the pygmies—are asking why this dynamic servant of the Colony's initiative has thus been sabotaged.

Editor's Note: We ourselves are putting that question to the provincial authorities.

Vermeulen hit the roof when he saw that article. He couldn't afford to have *any* questions asked. Then, on 1 March, before he had a chance to calm down, he was attacked from three directions at once.

La Presse Africaine came out with an article entitled '*Pygmées, Cultures et Rififi*'. They told the story of the ethnological revolution, criticized the 'hostile attitude of a certain functionary' and ended with the solemn warning: 'Today the situation is such that the hard-won agricultural programme is being dangerously compromised in the *paysannats* . . . Thus, the most remarkable social achievement in recent years is being menaced.'

A very popular and sophisticated weekly magazine called *Pourquoi-Pas?—Congo* came out with a strange little fable called 'The Friend of the Pygmies': 'Once upon a time, there was at Mbau a sort of good giant called "Hallet". Although he had lost his right hand during the course of his work, he was a wonderful teacher and had a passionate interest in certain little men called Bambuti whom he showed how to cultivate the land. . . .' It went on to describe my programme in glowing terms.

Both of these articles rocked the A.T., but the greatest blow of all was a letter he received on 1 March from the Governor of Kivu, announcing that the Provincial Administration had chosen to revise its 'synthetic evaluation' of my work from *Bon* to *Très Bon*. The significance of this gesture needs some explanation. All government employees in the Congo were graded once a year by their immediate superiors into five categories: *Médiocre—Assez Bon—Bon—Très Bon—Élite*. My immediate superior, Vermeulen, had officially decided that I was *Bon*. Now the Kivu Personnel Committee and the Governor, acting together, had overruled his decision with a much more complimentary *Très Bon*, which in the circumstances amounted to a stinging slap in the A.T.'s face.

On the following day, while Vermeulen was still vibrating from the effects of that triple blow, I made what came to be known in Government circles as Hallet's Notorious February[1] Report. It was a five-page document opening, innocuously enough, with a statistical analysis of the month's weather, followed by a review of the industrial crops which confirmed that all went well with the 71,799 *Elaeis* palms and 214,913 coffee trees of Beni's Plan Décennal. Then, towards the bottom of the first page, I launched into the subject of the *paysannats pygméens*, and devoted the rest of the report to it exclusively.

[1] It was in fact dated 2 March 1958.

I discussed André de Maere's exhaustive survey of the *paysannats* and provided an even more detailed statistical breakdown of my own. Then I commented on a fact which de Maere himself had noted briefly but had hesitated to describe in detail. 'At Ebikeba near Mbau,' I wrote, 'there is only one house which has not been completed and one neglected parcel of land (that of the Little Sisters of Jesus who installed themselves there to show a good example of "Work"!) Results: the pygmies have raised themselves to the status of agriculturists—very satisfactory!—while the European women have achieved the reverse (living in *mangungu* huts and using the forest for the same necessities [sanitation] as untaught pygmies). Scarcely an edifying example, at least from a temporal point of view.'

Coming to the A.T. I described in detail, and without mincing any words, the incredible sequence of his actions from the very beginning of our conflict. He had, I wrote, employed 'Draconian measures' and been guilty of 'spectacular vandalism' in 'an attempt to demonstrate his superiority, his authority and his power . . . at a terrible price'.

I described exactly what that price had meant to the pygmies: abandoning the *paysannats*, emptying the schools, returning to a life of sickness, danger, thieving and semi-slavery. I cited the example of Ngite, formerly one of the finest of my colonies, where the pygmies had demolished their new *pisé* huts in a gesture of frustrated despair before they fled to the Albert National Park for an orgy of carnage among the protected animals.

We all know [I wrote] that the pygmy problem is especially complex and requires a profound study of their relevant psychology and customs. For more than a year, I have applied myself to studying this problem and gaining the pygmies' confidence and understanding. Now I can use the same patience and perseverance which were necessary to bring this project into being, to reintegrate progressively all those pygmies who, troubled and frightened by the recent events, have fled into the forest to become even more primitive than they originally were.

But I cannot repair these grave errors [I concluded] unless I am given entire *responsibility, confidence and freedom of action*, all of which are essential to reach positive results in a problem as delicate as this.

I turned this report in to Vermeulen; far from being disturbed, he smiled with satisfaction. Evidently he thought I had finally overreached myself. He forwarded it to the office of the District Commissioner in Goma, who in turn passed the document to the Governor in Bukavu before it finally reached its destination with AGRIPRO's office in the same city. At every stage of its journey through Kivu my February Report evoked spirited discussion but no immediate results.

Meanwhile, back in Mbau, I was spending my days travelling among the *paysannats*, trying to save what was left of them, while I worked in the evenings on a long, detailed appeal: *The Pygmies: Will They at Last be Able to Enter a Civilization which Respects the Dignity and the Liberty of the Human Being?* I sent copies to the Fonds Colonial, the Belgian Minister of Colonies, the Governor-General of the Congo, King Baudouin and Pope Pius XII.

The future of an entire human race was at stake, as I stated urgently, but I failed to arouse the moral indignation or even the curiosity of those highly placed dignitaries. The only answer I received was from the Fonds Colonial, which tried to help by relaying the appeal to the Inspector of Colonies in Brussels—where nothing was ever done about it.

Weeks passed, while I went on working and waiting. Then I received an entirely different kind of answer: the Native Welfare Fund sent me a carbon copy of the latest 100,000-franc grant they had made to the Little Sisters of Father Foucauld. I read it with a feeling of weary outrage. 'A new experiment for the benefit of the pygmies is now in the process of realization in the Territory of Beni. It implies the collaboration of the Little Sisters of Jesus, the Mission of Beni, and the Administrative Authority.' Now the religious group was using the *paysannat* programme, which it had helped to sabotage, as a tool to prise more money out of the Government. Worse still, the money would be used with the same utter futility as in the past. This was obvious from the specifications of their budget.

Under the heading *To Provide the Pygmies with Priority Tools and Products*, the initial category was *Clothing*. The nuns demanded funds to buy a hundred bonnets for new-born babies, five hundred frocks for children aged from two to ten, five hundred *kapitula* and five hundred shirts for the men, and five hundred metres—a quarter of a mile—of cloth to provide dresses for the women. They were obviously intent on clothing *all* the pygmies—to hide their shameful human bodies, no matter how many of them succumbed as a result to pulmonary congestion, pneumonia or other respiratory ailments.

Under the same category, *Clothing*, the Little Sisters specified three hundred sets of knitting needles and twenty kilos of wool, to implement their plan to persuade the pygmy women to take up knitting and make woollen sweaters, an idea almost comparable to the crackpot schemes of Jonathan Swift's Laputan professors (who busied themselves trying to trap sunshine in bottled cucumbers), especially since wool, with its pronounced hygroscopic properties, is perhaps the least suitable of all materials to use in a dank, dripping equatorial forest. The Little Sisters' arithmetic was, incidentally, almost equally at fault: twenty kilos of wool were just about enough to make sixty pygmy-sized sweaters, but here they were asking for three hundred pairs of knitting needles; but of course this numerical discrepancy had no real significance since none of the knitting needles would ever be put to any use by the pygmies, unless perhaps they converted them into chopsticks.

In the *Food* category, the Little Sisters mentioned a thousand kilos of sugar and only a hundred kilos of beans. This 10 to 1 ratio of tooth-rotting sugar to high-protein beans is entirely representative of their saccharine thinking: the pygmies *liked* sugar, and so the nuns gave it to them, regardless of the results.

Under *Tools*, a hundred rakes and a hundred spades were listed—all quite useless in the Central African milieu—as well as a hundred hoes and machetes, which might have done some good if most of the pygmies had not already abandoned the *paysannats*; as usual, no axes were requested.

Under *Miscellaneous*, the budget's final category, the Little Sisters demanded funds to purchase pencils, notebooks, slates and styluses. This was totally pointless since there were now almost no pygmies left in my schools, and the nuns were quite incapable of making any educational efforts of their own; none of them knew more than two or three words of Kimbuti, and most spoke only pidgeon-Swahili. Moreover the guiding principles of their order conflicted with any action as positive as teaching: they were merely supposed to convey their ineffable 'presence' of friendship.

The whole tragi-comic document was especially galling to me for the simple reason that the pygmies would in fact receive only token quantities of the clothing, food and tools. Judging by the pattern of the past six years, most of the money would either end in the massive metal safe at the Beni Mission, or be squandered on the expensive needs of the poverty-seeking Little Sisters.

After I had studied the document, I drove to the nuns' picturesque establishment near Mbau and told them bluntly what I thought of their budget. I suggested that before soliciting money for work, they should do some themselves on their neglected parcel of land—a far more useful activity than bothering hard-working pygmy women with knitting needles or babies' bonnets.

My call on the Little Sisters had major repercussions. They complained to the Bishop of Beni, and he instructed them to report the matter to Vermeulen. They did, and the A.T. swung into action, confident that this latest incident had given him enough moral rope to hang me. So, on 9 April 1958, exactly eleven months after the first seeds of revolution had been planted in the soil of Ebikeba, the Territorial Administrator of Beni took official disciplinary action. I was charged, on four separate counts, with having:

(1) in my February Report made 'disrespectful remarks about the missionary work accomplished by the Little Sisters of Father Foucauld';

(2) on the same occasion delivered comments which constituted a 'grave and extravagant insubordination towards my immediate superior';

(3) 'given false statistics in an official report' concerning the amount of land under cultivation at the eighteen *paysannats*;

(4) forbidden the pygmies to hunt and—most fantastic assertion of all—'forced them to dance for the tourists'.

There was no mention of Vermeulen's former hint that I had embezzled money from the pygmy Community Chest. I was grateful, at least, for that.

My answer was a massive typewritten document entitled *Justifications Relatives aux Fautes Disciplinaires*, in which I demolished, step by step, the A.T.'s four allegations.

My remarks concerning the Little Sisters of Father Foucauld had, I explained, been far from disrespectful. I had simply dealt with them on the level they were allegedly trying to reach: as pygmies. If Mungalulu or Bulahimu, their next-door neighbours at Ebikeba, had neglected to work their land, finish their huts or follow elementary rules of camp sanitation, they would have been forced to leave the *paysannat*. The nuns, on the other hand, had not only persisted in their lazy, inefficient course, but on several occasions demanded help from their neighbours. 'Do we *have* to help them?' Bulahimu had asked me. My answer had been, 'No, every family here does its own work.'

Consciously or otherwise, the Little Sisters had sought privilege at Ebikeba, which not only violated the democratic rules of the *paysannat* but conflicted sharply with the stated aims of their order: 'to live like the poor, renouncing the exterior dignity which confers social rank', 'to put the accent on poverty, humility, even abjection and the total rejection of all human dignity', and 'to shed the attitude of technical superiority and unconscious pride too often common to the white race'. It was very strange, I concluded, that a religious order seeking humility and even martyrdom should be so sensitive to 'disrespectful remarks'.

I disposed of the other charges equally firmly—what the A.T. called 'grave insubordination' resulted inevitably from Vermeulen's treating the whole important question of the pygmies' racial survival as a personal vendetta. As for the 'false statistics', the A.T., deliberately or otherwise, had confused the total area of the *paysannats* with the area actually seeded and producing at any one time. The charge that I had forbidden the pygmies to hunt showed how little Vermeulen really understood of their *modus vivendi*. On several occasions I had actually *urged* them to go hunting—to get some vital animal protein into their diet, and had encouraged them to make their own arrow points. But I had always insisted that their new agricultural crops come first: the cultivated fields represented a steady, sure source of food, while hunting was always a gamble. Two days of hard, concentrated effort by ten or twenty men might result in one small *mboloko* . . . or nothing at all.

The ludicrous charge of forcing the pygmies to dance for the tourists was easiest of all to refute. Not only had dancing always been part of the pygmies' traditional life, as with any other Central African people, but my tourist establishment at Mbau had been approved in every detail, including the dances, by the District Commissioner of North Kivu, the Director of the Native Welfare Fund, the Provincial Head of the Native Labour Commission and, unofficially, by the Queen Mother of Belgium.

*   *   *

Vermeulen sent the entire file, including my defence, to the District Commissioner at Goma. There was no immediate reaction, but I knew one was coming. I had officially criticized both my direct chief and a Catholic religious order, and even made statements to the Press about both. Something was bound to happen, either to Vermeulen or to me. The higher authorities simply couldn't afford any further scandal.

Letters poured in from every part of the Congo, hundreds of compassionate letters urging me to keep up my courage and try to continue my work with the pygmies. Many of them criticized the Little Sisters of Jesus for the rôle they had played, and among them there was one from R. Piron, a prominent lawyer and publisher, who wrote that, concerning the Foucauld sect, 'I cannot conceive of a more perverse degradation of our civilized ideals.' Then Piron did a very thorough job on Vermeulen in the May 1958 issue of *Europe-Afrique*, under the headline '*The Scandal of Mbau*':

> Certain functionaries have not yet learned that the Golden Rule of the Administration consists of futile paperwork. Such a one is Monsieur J. P. Hallet, the agronomist of Beni. Situated in the neighbourhood of the pygmies, he decided that these little people deserved as much attention as the neighbouring Bantu tribes . . .

He went on to describe the *paysannat* programme, its success and the series of disasters which had overtaken it at the hands of the A.T. Vermeulen's acts of 'spectacular demolition' were described in detail, and their tragic results:

> Since March, Monsieur Hallet stands before the ruins of his civilizing work. The *paysannats* have been abandoned by 90 per cent of the new farmers. The schools are virtually empty. The Bambuti sell their tools and eat their seed. Once again, they are engulfing themselves in the pitiless forest to take up an even more unequal struggle against hunger, sickness and death. Thus, the most ancient race in the Congo is being sentenced to extinction. Such was the decision of the all-powerful and benevolent Administration.

On 26 April I received a telegram from AGRIPRO headquarters at Bukavu, promoting me to 'Principal Agronomist' with an increase in salary. On 28 April this was confirmed by the Governor's office. Then, on 2 May I had a third official message: acting in accordance with orders from the Governor-General of the Congo at Léopoldville, the Governor of Kivu announced my transfer to Katako Kombe in the Province of Kasai.

The situation was clear: anxious to end the controversy and

scandal in Kivu, the Governor-General of the Congo had solved the problem by 'kicking me upstairs'. I was to be given a pat on the head, in the form of a raise and promotion, and hustled five hundred miles off to a post in Kasai, thus giving things a chance to cool down in the Province of Kivu. The fate of the *paysannat* programme and the racial survival of the pygmies were obviously of minor importance compared to administrative decorum.

My answer was simple: I sent a telegram to the Governor of Kivu, informing him I wasn't going to Katako Kombe or anywhere else. I preferred to stay downstairs with my pygmies.

In return, the Governor merely confirmed the transfer—with emphasis—and a gloating Vermeulen wrote out an order evicting me from my house.

I drove to Bukavu and made a personal appeal to the Governor. He was sympathetic, but told me that he had to take his own orders from Léopoldville. He urged me to submit and accept the transfer to Kasai. Then, when things had calmed down, he suggested that I could once again approach the higher authorities—more diplomatically—concerning the possibilities of a new programme for the pygmies.

I knew how futile it was. If the Administration didn't realize the gravity of the question now, while the issues were strong and alive, things were unlikely to change in some indeterminate future. The whole question of the pygmies' racial survival would be filed away and forgotten.

'Are you certain,' I asked the Governor of Kivu, 'that there is no way I can continue my programme?'

'I'm sorry to say that there isn't.'

'Then I quit. I'll leave the Administration and do the job on my own.'

                    *   *   *

I spent the next week saying temporary farewells to my eighteen *paysannats*, putting my papers in order and writing the final report of my ten-year career in the service of the Belgian Colonial Government. On 30 May 1958, the day it came to an end, I received a special-delivery letter from the Governor of Kivu.

It expressed not only his sincere regrets concerning my decision but his appreciation for my 'devoted and exceptional contributions to the great work of bringing civilization to the Congo'.

17

An Arena without a Circus

'De l'audace, encore de l'audace, toujours de l'audace!'
DANTON'S SPEECH in the French Legislative
Assembly, 2 September 1792

ON 1 June 1958, when I started out on my own, my assets included ten years of working experience in a profession now closed to me, a seven-ton collection of African artifacts which I vowed never to sell, the equivalent of £4 10s. in cash and a sick Chevrolet truck. Prospects for employment outside the Government were extremely slim, but I wasn't worried about finding a job. As a matter of fact, I wasn't even looking for one: I was determined to go into business for myself, though at that stage I had no suspicion that I was about to become Central Africa's first self-taught, one-handed lion-tamer.

At first I ran into a series of catastrophes, starting when Vermeulen gave me a touching send-off from the territory. While preparing to leave, I had stored my personal belongings and part of my huge collection in the government depot at Beni. The A.T., feigning ignorance of my intentions, made out an official order dispatching all my things by truck to Katako Kombe in Kasai. His action left me with only the clothes I was wearing, and the dismal knowledge that several tons of historic African art treasures, hastily piled into tin trunks and cardboard boxes, were bouncing away on an unplanned five-hundred-mile journey which most of the native pottery, delicately carved wooden pipes and other fragile objects would probably not survive.

I lodged a volcanic complaint at Provincial Headquarters in Bukavu, demanded reshipment and threatened a lawsuit against the Central Government of the Congo. When I drove back north and tried to establish myself in Beni, Vermeulen's long arm reached out again.

The owner of Le Vieux Manguier, a local hotel, was interested in my plans to salvage the *paysannats*. We decided to go into partnership, redecorate his place, set up a small museum and curio shop and build a model pygmy camp nearby. In short, the Old Mango Tree was to become a new and improved version of the defunct tourist establishment at Mbau, my partner and I would divide the profits, and I would devote most of my 25 per cent share to the pygmies.

After more than a month of hard work, when we were just about ready to open, my partner had a visit from Vermeulen and some strongly worded hints from the Mission of Beni. To put it more bluntly, he was intimidated, under threats of boycott and continual harassment, into abandoning our plans. He blamed *me* for the fiasco, presented a bill for twenty-five thousand francs, and confiscated against repayment both the stock-in-trade of the curio shop (which I had purchased on credit from the Nande craftsmen of the Beni area) and the contents of the museum (some fine collection pieces I had brought from my parents' home in Kisenyi).

Now I was not only broke but deeply in debt, with my collection divided between Katako Kombe, Beni and Kisenyi. Just then, when it seemed that the situation couldn't get any worse, there was a loud metallic snap as the Chevy's left rear axle broke. I was stranded, a few miles from Beni, without a franc to my name.

I sat in the cab and thought things out until I reached a painful but realistic decision. The A.T. and the religious group would undoubtedly sabotage any efforts I made to go into business in the Territory of Beni. Without money the *paysannats* could not be revived; if I simply went back to live among the pygmies, I could gather mushrooms and *mangungu* leaves for years, but there would be nothing really concrete I could do for them.

I walked to Ngadi, nearest of the *paysannats*, and stared at the abandoned huts and unweeded fields. I talked with a few unhappy old people who remained and left a message for the rest: 'Tell them that I'll be back, but it may be a long time . . .' Then I walked two miles back to the Route de la Beauté and hitch-hiked 245 miles to Kisenyi.

The latest developments appalled my father and both my parents urged me to beg forgiveness, and a job, from the

Government. I listened to their frantic harangues while I devoured three *biftecks-frites*, said 'No' and then retreated from the family storm to go for a lonely walk along the Avenue des Palmiers which runs beside Lake Kivu.

I passed many private villas as I ambled towards the north, until I reached the block which was bordered on either end by the Palm Beach Hotel and the Hôtel Beau Séjour. Then I stopped to stare at a real historic monument, the oldest building in Kisenyi, a massive, abandoned adobe skeleton without doors or windows that dated back to 1915 when the Germans still ruled Ruanda-Urundi. Directly opposite the main beach, between two large hotels and in the tourist centre of Kisenyi, was obviously the ideal location for a business.

I worked all night, drawing up plans to remodel the old building to house my business in the front with living-quarters in the rear, and next morning I swung into action. I started talking shortly after sunrise; when I finally stopped, at about midnight, I had succeeded, completely on credit, in renting the building (for £35 a month), hiring a crew of native workmen from a contractor friend and ordering timber, cement, steel, glass, electrical wiring, paint, plaster, varnish, furniture, office supplies and other essential items. No banks were involved, no one charged me interest and I offered no security. The people of Kisenyi and Goma knew me and trusted my word.

The work began, and a week later I got a lift back to Beni, where I had my truck repaired (on credit) and obtained (still on credit!) more than £700 worth of ivory and ebony carvings from the Nande craftsmen, who were willing to trust me with that huge stock of goods—representing several months' labour—even though I still owed them for the curios locked up at the Old Mango Tree.

Three hectic, backbreaking weeks later, on 15 August 1958, the Central Africa Curio Shop opened its doors to the public. The old building, completely remodelled, was decorated in a lavish, exotic style with an eye-catching façade. The big square columns along the *baraza* were adorned with stylized paintings by Jean-Pierre Hallet (generally admired, but mildly criticized by my father); the staircase, made from sections of palm trunk, was bordered by a constantly changing display of elephant tusks, wooden statues, leopard skins, baskets and drums; the path leading to the Avenue des Palmiers was carpeted with grass mats, lined with ornamental plants and flanked by two impressive seven-foot wooden statues from Kasai. The shop held an incredible variety of carvings, weapons, artifacts and curios of all kinds, and on the walls were some of the finest collection pieces I still had left in Kisenyi. It was like walking into an organized jungle of African art.

The staff of the shop was as exotic as its décor. Besides several of the inevitable 'boys' and *moke* (the 'boys'' own 'boys') I had three spectacular employees: a wild Hutu 'witch doctor', a tall Tutsi drummer and a lithe, elegant *Ntore* dancer.

Murekeye, the dancer, was an easygoing young Mututsi, tall, with a wide, engaging smile. I made a special trip to the Nyundo Catholic Mission to buy him the beautiful uniform and *umugara* headdress manufactured by the industrious White Sisters for the government-sponsored dancers of Kisenyi, but the first time he put them on I nearly had a fit—he had supplemented the costume with an athletic undershirt, white tennis shoes and a Belga cigarette. Murekeye explained he was trying to be civilized. It took me an hour, arguing in Kinyarwanda, to impress upon him that his new job (at five hundred francs a month) depended on his being picturesque rather than progressive. He heaved a deep sigh, took off his underwear and ground out his cigarette, all in the name of art.

In contrast, my cadaverous, unsmiling drummer, Johanni Serukenyinkware, was a Mututsi of the old school, a forty-five-year-old bulwark of classic Rwanda traditions, dignified, aloof, fantastically arrogant—a 6 ft. 2 in. pillar of pure gall in a blindingly white toga, with a long pipe clenched in his jaw and his head shaved except for the *amasunza*—two long crescents of hair. He drank like a fish.

Serukenyinkware had formerly been a sub-chief near Nyanza and served for a time as Royal Instructor to the dancers of Charles Rudahigwa Mutara III, thirty-ninth *Mwami* of Rwanda. Gradually, because of his perennial drinking, feuding and political intrigues, he had lost his influence, his job and his cattle. This left him in an awkward position, since he had the usual Tutsi horror of manual work and a great love for giving orders. So he had consented to join my staff at £5 a month, much more than he had ever received from the King of Rwanda.

Kamende, the 'witch doctor', was a stocky, extremely intelligent Hutu medicine man from the hills northeast of Kisenyi whom I had met several years before. When I first got the idea of equipping the Central Africa Curio Shop with an *umufumu* of its own, I drove, walked and climbed to his *itongo*, perched like an eagle's nest at the top of a steep cliff. Inside it was almost like a chemist's shop, crammed with mysterious bones, organs, talismans, amulets and magic paraphernalia dangling on strings from the roof, or lying on the floor packed in little banana-leaf bundles.

Kamende made a pretty good living in the hills, supporting three wives and five children by his pastoral labours as a combined doctor, druggist, psycho-analyst and fortune-teller, but he was eager to come and work for me. He looked forward to the excitement of his new job, and his salary, and knew it would increase his prestige to be a white man's official 'witch doctor'.

So Kamende came to the Central Africa Curio Shop—a wonderfully weird-looking character in a goatskin skirt overlapped with dangling civet-cat pelts and a trellis of strings dripping serval tails and spiralling pennants of otter skin wound around his chest; dancing bells were on his ankles, massive ivory bracelets on his wrists, a string of beads and *kaki*-nuts round his neck and magic antelope horns at either side. The whole costume was topped off by one of three flamboyant headdresses donned by the *umufumu* in strict daily rotation: a gorilla scalp, a helmet of antelope skin crowned with hornbill feathers and a big casque made from the feathers of thirteen different birds.

The dancer, the drummer and the medicine man were an integral and important part of my new business. Murekeye performed in the front yard to attract tourists, while Serukenyinkware, stationed near the front door, pounded on his Tutsi drums. Kamende wandered about in his bells, skins and alternating headdresses, dancing or singing, looking mysterious and telling fortunes with his *imbehe y'inzuzu*—a Rwanda divining board.

When no tourists were in sight the two Batutsi usually played *igisoro* on the veranda or Serukenyinkware plucked his *inanga* and sang petulant nasal ballads. Kamende amused himself during slack periods by giving advice to passing natives on any and all problems relating to health, love, money, cattle, agriculture or 'white man trouble'. (His advice was generally quite sound.) Then, when a car or a bus pulled up, or tourists came strolling down the Avenue des Palmiers, the trio launched into their repertoire of dancing, drumming and witch-doctoring.

Whenever a tourist entered the shop Serukenyinkware beat ceremonially on the biggest drum; this gave the visitor a thrill and brought me running in from the back yard.

On our first day of business, the big drum never stopped booming. At closing time, when I added up the receipts, I was stunned to find we had taken in 32,783 francs, more than £230.

From then on the shop was open every day, including weekends and holidays, from ten in the morning until midnight. The big drum kept booming . . . and I averaged about £30 a day. By the end of the first month's operation, I was able to repay the Nande craftsmen of Beni, settle the bill at the Old Mango Tree and repossess my confiscated collection.

This proved, when the rest of it finally arrived from Katako Kombe, to be in wretched shape. The Government sent an official appraiser, I hired one of my own and the two of them spent an entire day opening cases and trunks. Many precious pieces had been damaged beyond repair and virtually nothing was left of the native pottery. The appraisers decided on 75,000 francs (£540) total damages and I presented a bill in that amount to the Government. They tried to haggle but I refused to compromise and finally, under threat of lawsuit, they paid up in full. A satisfactory feature of the proceedings was that the A.T. of Beni was held financially responsible, so the money came out of Vermeulen's pocket.

I used it to pay off most of my creditors in Kisenyi, enlarge my stocks and expand my native payroll. Murekeye had been complaining to me for some time that he couldn't give a really good performance alone, so I hired three more *Ntore* dancers to leap and stomp about with him in the front yard. A Nande ivory carver and an ebonist joined the staff a few days later, followed by a carpenter, a packer, and a strange old man named Tureko who functioned as dancer and clown. His specialities were acting the rôle of client in fortune-telling demonstrations —with all the tragic gestures of a silent-movie actor—and taking part in mock fencing matches with Kamende and the dancers.

For the next month the boom at the Central Africa Curio Shop continued and my main problem was to keep the peace between the arrogant Serukenyinkware and the Tutsi *corps de ballet*. He was always ordering the dancers about as though they were children, with limp, effete gestures of his long, elegant hands. They resented it, and tempers boiled over several times a day. Kamende was very diplomatic and tried to keep everyone happy, but it was a hopeless task, even for a witch doctor. I myself kept planning a return visit to my pygmies, but was always putting it off for fear that the whole complex, crazy Kisenyi establishment would fly apart if I went away.

Then a much more serious problem developed. A wealthy Fleming from Goma bought the building next door, between us and the Hôtel Beau Séjour, redecorated it, and opened for business, selling the same type of merchandise—at half the price—in a building so similar to the Central Africa Curio Shop that it looked like an annexe. He even tried to steal Serukenyinkware away from me for a raise of a dollar a week, but the Mututsi turned him down; he was far too happy fomenting intrigues among my staff to consider making a change.

My unprincipled competitor's cut-rate prices were obviously losing money, but he was well-heeled enough to take the loss until he had driven me out of business. The answer was not to start a price war, which would have been suicidal, but to make my own establishment even more alluring to the tourists. So I installed loudspeakers which diffused exotic music across the Avenue des Palmiers: tape-recordings of Kamende singing, shaking his bells and playing the *likembe*, and Serukenyinkware crooning Tutsi cow-poems to the accompaniment of a wailing *inanga*. As further new attraction, I built a large aviary next to the shop, and filled it with orioles, finches, parakeets and other colourful birds. Then, optimistically, I cleared more space for parking.

Unfortunately, it wasn't good enough. The tourists were using my big new car park, listening to my music, looking at my dancers and my birds, admiring my drummer and enjoying my witch doctor's equilibrations. But when it came to *buying*, too many of them went next door where the prices were so much lower.

My receipts diminished, and I knew I had to find a new approach to the problem. I did some hard thinking and concluded the logical answer was a back yard full of intriguing animals accessible only to those tourists who found their way into my good graces. It was five hundred miles to the nearest public zoo: my idea of a private one would draw tourists like a warm, furry magnet. At the same time I would have a good excuse to surround myself with animals, something I had wanted ever since I built my 'Garden of Eden' back in Bururi.

As soon as I made the decision I put my new carpenter to work building cages and advertised in the local papers: 'ANIMALS WANTED, FOR PRIVATE ZOO: Contact J.-P. Hallet, Box 90, Kisenyi.' The responses during the next month yielded five young antelope, twenty-one monkeys, three baboons, a big male chimpanzee (which I christened Joseph), two pangolins and a sleepy-looking potto, two bottle-sucking lion cubs, two pythons, one Gaboon viper, one black mamba, one spitting

cobra and eight *umusambi*—the emblem of Rwanda's Royal
Family—crested cranes who stalked proudly round my back
yard like feathered Batutsi.

While I was about it, I managed to acquire nearly a thousand
small seed-eating birds: serin finches, ring-necked doves, orioles,
mouse birds, weaver birds, widow birds and bright red Bengali
birds, most of which I bought from the natives at two francs
each. My carpenter built a huge circular aviary, twelve feet in
diameter with a conical roof fifteen feet high, and we placed it
opposite the big cage where my horde of monkeys screamed at
each other and practised gymnastics.

I was still working out the final disposition of other new cages
when a startling telegram came in from Luberizi, a Congolese
village about two hundred miles to the southwest. It read,
'FULL-GROWN LION FOR SALE. MALE. FIVE THOU-
SAND FRANCS. ARE YOU INTERESTED?'

A full-grown lion . . . That would be a wonderful attraction
for the Central Africa Curio Shop. But a caged lion is not as
interesting as all that, since it spends most of its time lying down
and looks like a fat, sleepy cat in need of a haircut. Now a
performing lion is a different matter entirely: a huge, ferocious
cat trained to do difficult tricks in a big arena is the most
exciting creature in the world. How could the tourist trade of
Ruanda-Urundi miss the opportunity to see a performing lion
in a country without a single circus, carnival or zoo?

I sent off an answering wire at once—'SOLD AT FIVE
THOUSAND, PLEASE DELIVER.' Then I drove three miles
to the foundry in Goma and ordered a dozen interlocking sections of iron bars twelve feet high by five feet long that could be
assembled into a twenty-foot back-yard arena. Now I was
thoroughly committed: I was going to train a lion.

Afterwards, when I lunched at the Hôtel des Grands Lacs in
Goma, I thought over the new project while I waited for a dozen
escargots de Bourgogne and a steak. My actions might have
been inspired by business reasons, but to be perfectly honest,
ever since I was a boy I had been dreaming about training lions.
After seeing a few circus performances in Belgium, I had been
completely fascinated by them and overawed by their trainers—
romantic figures in Hussar uniforms, leopard skins or English
riding-breeches, who cracked whips and fired pistols to answer
the roars of angry defiance.

I realized how naïve I was, compared to those circus professionals, in spite of my Masai lion-spearing adventure and some

casual encounters in Africa's national parks. Virtually all circus lion-tamers had learned their profession from a master trainer, a seasoned expert with practical knowledge of how lions behave in captivity and a bagful of clever techniques based on many years of working experience.

The apprentice trainer listened to his master's patient explanations and followed his every step, movement and gesture for weeks or even months. When he found himself alone in the arena for the first time, it was always with relatively gentle animals already trained in an established routine. His teacher stood outside the bars, delivering rapid-fire instructions, and a small army of helpers waited with steel forks, guns, ammonia-sprays and electrified goads, ready to rescue him if serious trouble developed.

Under these conditions any man with guts and presence of mind could usually learn how to posture heroically and crack his whip at the right moment while a group of cats performed the routine learned from the real hero, the backstage 'breaker' of the lion act. In effect, the man rather than the cats was trained, taught to push the right buttons to operate the animals' previously conditioned responses—while displaying the proper air of domineering courage.

Most American circus stars fell into that category: they were 'lion operators' rather than lion-tamers or trainers. But in Europe, especially in Germany and Switzerland, many of the great performers had been men of stature who, with a true understanding and love of animals, insisted on breaking and training their own acts. Roman Proske and Alfred Court were among those bona fide heroes, as well as Captain Albert Schneider, who had actually worked in an arena with a hundred lions.

I would have to cope with only *one* lion, but at the moment this seemed more than enough, since I was not only totally ignorant of conventional lion-taming techniques but alone and one-handed, and, according to a plan I had just made, I would face the lion with neither gun nor whip. The decision was less rash than it seems: like any other so-called 'wild' animal, the lion is not the cruel, savage murderer we like to pretend, but simply a creature shaped by evolutionary forces to perform certain functions: to observe, stalk, seize, kill and devour his destined prey. He makes his living in this way, and no cruelty or ferocity is involved, only an empty belly and the process of filling it. We may not realize that fact, but the zebra and antelope do. They graze with impunity a few yards away from the peaceful spendour of a well-fed lion, only to be slaughtered by a 'white hunter', 'sportsman' or native poacher.

The important difference is that humans select the finest, strongest, most impressive-looking animals for trophies, while the lion usually succeeds in capturing only the weak, the slow or the sickly. Often, a complete herd of zebra or gnu escapes the epidemic spread of disease simply because a lion has liquidated a single contaminated animal, and in areas where lions (or leopards) have been exterminated the health and vigour of the herbivores usually declines. Thus the lion's kills actually aid the species he feeds on, and over the long range of time he maintains the biological health of his prey by acting as an agent of their natural selection.

If the 'wild' lion is to be plucked from his rolling savannah and placed in a cage, his prime emotional and physiological requirements will not change. He will still want to feel that he has his own territorial domain and will still need large quantities of raw meat. If his life in captivity meets those demands, the satisfied lion will generally have no more object in murdering a man than he did in killing a strolling antelope. As a matter of fact he will have less. The man will soon become the most important thing in the lion's life—his only friend, companion and playmate, and their joint sessions in the arena will be his major source of exercise and diversion. Gradually, mutual confidence will grow between them until the lion and the man are really friends.

*   *   *

When I got back to Kisenyi another telegram was waiting for me. I ripped it open, worried that someone else might have bought my lion, but the problem proved only a minor one. 'CANNOT DELIVER,' read the telegram, 'COME AND GET HIM YOURSELF.'

Next morning, leaving Kamende and André in charge of the shop, I jumped into the old Chevy, crossed the Congolese border two miles away and raced around the western shore of Lake Kivu, headed for my lion waiting two hundred miles to the south. It was shortly before noon when, at Luberizi, I met the animal's owner, Yorigu Poulious, who led me to his back yard where a chain-link cage contained an enormous, very aggressive lion. The moment he saw us he roared with incredible fury, hurled himself against the heavy wire mesh and then turned aside with majestic contempt. 'He was such a sweet little baby,' Poulious reminisced. 'You should have seen him four years ago when I bought him from a game-farm in Kenya. He was such a gentle cub he even used to let me clip his claws. Now look at him: four hundred pounds of pure meanness!'

'He's beautiful.'

'Simba may be beautiful,' Poulious warned me, 'but he's a real devil!'

For the rest of the day Simba seemed determined to live up to his reputation. The Greek planter and I spent eight hours trying to bribe, threaten, trick or cajole the wary lion into a small metal box—the transportation cage he'd arrived in as a cub. During these frenzied proceedings, Poulious ripped his velveteen trousers, skinned his knees and just missed having a nervous breakdown. I managed to catch my hand in the sliding door of the small cage and just missed tearing off four of my remaining five fingers. The whole hand was badly bruised, but fortunately, there was no lasting damage.

Next morning Simba succumbed to the lure of a raw chicken and we trapped him in the box. I drove back in high spirits, with a bandaged hand and a furious lion. Five hours later, in Kisenyi, the entire staff of the shop watched nervously as the roaring metal box was unloaded. Of them all, only Kamende had ever seen a lion. This may seem strange, but it is typical of the situation in the Congo and Ruanda-Urundi, where more than half the natives, those living outside 'lion areas', have not only never seen one but actually have no idea what a lion looks like.

Kamende's encounter had been with a dead lion; he had travelled ten miles to buy its whiskers and claws for his wonder-working pharmacopoeia. Now the *umufumu* offered me the benefit of his wide knowledge and experience. 'I will make a special amulet for you,' he said eagerly. 'The claw of an eagle and the bone of a Mutwa, rolled up in a dog's placenta and wrapped in banana bark! That will protect you from harm!'

André rolled his eyes at Kamende and expressed his own opinion: the lion was *Shetani* himself, a Swahili version of Satan. As for Serukenyinkware, I heard him whispering in Kinyarwanda to the stupefied dancers, 'The master's gone mad. This great *ntare* will kill him and we'll all be out of a job!'

As we assembled in the back-yard arena, the tension increased. Everyone watched solemnly as the metal box was fastened to the small chute-door and the two gates were slipped. Simba inched his way out of his cramped prison and shot across the arena like a golden tornado. The *Ntore* dancers leaped backwards, in an entirely new choreographic movement, and Kamende rattled off a string of choice magic incantations.

When I came closer, Simba leaped against the bars with an infernal roar. Then he noticed the basin of water I had left for him in the arena; he drank every drop and it seemed to soothe him. He paced back and forth more quietly, decided to sit, stared at all of us for a minute and finally lay down with his forepaws stretched out in front of him.

As soon as I saw the lion relatively quiet, I had only one idea in my mind: to open the large gate, step in, and see what would happen. But something told me this might be a mistake—and a fatal one. His nervous temperament, the long, uncomfortable ride in the metal box, the shock of a completely new environment—these were certainly not the best conditions for our first encounter. 'Tomorrow morning,' I announced loudly, 'I will step into Simba's cage. Tell all your friends and family to come and watch!'

Again there was general consternation followed by whispered comments in several languages about the condition of my mental health. I ignored them and stalked back into the house with a regal, untroubled air. 'Tomorrow morning', I had said; tomorrow morning it would have to be. Now, for the second time, I had committed myself publicly: I would have to keep it. That was the best possible antidote to the weakening poison of fear.

I dreamed about lions that night and woke up next morning at 6.30, knowing that I would have to translate my newly formed theories about lion-training into immediate action. 'Be calm and determined!' I told myself, as I ate my breakfast omelet. 'Make every action decisive! Never leave the lion with a feeling of superiority! And never take more than one step backwards!'

From the kitchen window I could see at least fifty natives in the arena waiting to see me make good my boast or, as most of them probably expected, die trying.

My omelet tasted more like wood-pulp than anything else, but I forced myself to finish it. Then I went out, holding the heavy kitchen chair in my bruised and bandaged hand, and with a broomstick tucked under my arm. When I appeared the natives buzzed with excitement.

Simba was running nervously to and fro, glaring at the

crowd. I watched him for a moment. I laid my stick down on the ground, with one end just beyond the bars. Then, when he reached the opposite side of the arena twenty feet away, I opened the gate, shoved the chair inside and closed the gate again quickly. The lion whirled and stared in astonishment. I waited outside, observing his reaction.

The natives stopped chattering. The silence was absolute. Suddenly there was a jangle of sound as Kamende, arriving late to confirm his high social status, entered the scene. He gave me an eloquent, melancholy smile, as though of regret at having to disturb me in one of my last moments. Unfortunately, he hadn't delivered the promised amulet: he had the claw and the placenta, but he had run into difficulties obtaining fresh Batwa bones.

When the lion reached the far side again, I made my move. I opened the gate and entered the arena with two decisive steps. The iron door swung back on its heavy springs and the massive latch clicked into position behind me. Simba and I were together at last.

The lion's first reaction was surprise, followed by intense curiosity. He stood there, staring at me, for about ten seconds. Then he lowered his haunches, preparing to spring. According to my theories it was essential at this point to put him on the defensive, so I caught up the chair, held it in front of me and took a couple of steps in his direction. The lion didn't move, but his hindquarters swayed slowly and his attitude was precisely like that of a huge domestic cat about to spring at a strange bearded bird.

'Simba! Simba! Simba!' I shouted at him in a commanding tone of voice.

His hindquarters stopped moving. He came out of his crouch and started to walk slowly towards me. After he had taken three steps, I brandished the chair and thundered 'Stop!'

I had already decided that English was more suitable than French for lion-taming. To my intense surprise, the lion actually stopped and stared at me with indecision. 'S-e-e-mba,' I crooned, trying to show him I wasn't really angry, 'S-e-e-emba. . . .'

He listened, motionless, but I didn't like the look in his eyes. Quickly I consulted my general principles and came up with an excellent maxim: Go after the lion if you don't want the lion to go after you! And I remembered that an experienced game-capturer had told me lions, like horses and some other animals, have to be approached from the left side.

So, growling loudly, I charged him on the left, as prescribed. He didn't move an inch. Instead, for the first time since I had entered the arena, he saluted me with a tremendous, aggressive roar. Determined to prove my point, I moved even closer. 'Go!' I shouted. 'Go back!'

Simba sat down on the spot. Then, rearing up, he swiped with his two forepaws at the legs of the chair, caught one of them with the claws of his right foot—an amazing grip I couldn't shake off—and a second later, hooked the other leg with his left, pulling the chair, and me along with it, in his direction.

Following the basic principles of intimidation, I shouted at him, trying to demonstrate my authority. Again Simba ignored me. The chair was definitely under his control and I was merely attached to the other end. I didn't like that at all, and so I pulled at the chair stubbornly. One huge paw let go, and I felt a brief sensation of triumph. Then he swiped with it again, catching the seat of the chair less than a foot away from my hand.

A thrill of terror swept over the native audience. The crowd moaned and I heard Kamende shrieking magical formulae. I am sure they all felt it was only a matter of seconds until the lion seized and devoured me before their eyes.

Simba's next move was to catch one of the chair legs with his teeth. As he chewed it, he must have bitten either his lips or his tongue, because he flew into a passion against the chair. I had a very strong impulse to give it to him and make a quick departure in the opposite direction—if possible. But I stayed there, holding the chair only a few inches away from his claws. Then I tried a new trick: I eased my grip on the chair. Feeling it slacken, Simba released his claws in order to take a better hold. At that instant, I jerked the chair away from him, the bitten leg sliding out from behind his teeth.

Pleased with the success of this simple manœuvre, I permitted myself a step backwards, while Simba stared at the chair, meditating revenge. I thought about that: after all, the lion hadn't been nearly as aggressive as I expected . . . he was much angrier with the chair than he was with me . . . and my bruised hand was getting very tired holding the damned thing.

I reached my decision, took another step backwards and threw the chair to the opposite side of the arena.

As I expected, Simba leaped on it and tore it to pieces. Meanwhile, I grabbed the broom handle and stood waiting quietly with the five-foot stick in my hand. When the lion finally looked up from the pile of splintered wood, he stared at me, his head held high, as if to ask, 'What are *you* doing here?' I knew that I had to answer his question.

So I charged him again, on his left side and three-quarters to the rear. This time it actually worked: Simba ran away. I chased him, shouting 'Go! Go!' and the two of us went around the perimeter of the arena three times. Then I stopped. Simba stopped. He sat down and stared at me with baffled golden eyes. I stood opposite him, holding the stick to one side.

'You see,' I told him softly, 'I trust you. The chair is gone, and very soon I shall drop the stick if you don't like it.'

Slowly I lowered myself into a squatting position only four feet away, so that I could look directly into his eyes. Simba raised one big paw, as if to slap me. But he hadn't shot his claws, and he drew the foot back without following through. That gesture made me feel so confident that I lowered the stick gradually and at last put it down on the ground beside me. Simba didn't move.

I remained in that position for several minutes, squatting in front of the seated lion while we looked steadily at each other— becoming friends, as I hoped. But I knew that wasn't enough: I had to *prove* my friendship to him. So, very slowly, only an inch or so at a time, I moved my feet in his direction until I reduced the space between us to about two feet. At that distance, and in the squatting position I still maintained, Simba would have no trouble in seizing me. But I had the very strong instinctive feeling that he wouldn't attack a man who offered him such an unusual proof of confidence and peaceful intentions.

Then the lion did something completely unexpected. Moving his head forward, he sniffed at my face from a distance of less than a foot, and without moving a paw. It was a gesture of friendly curiosity and I knew that I had to follow suit. I moved my own face closer and closer, very slowly, until our two noses touched.

Simba growled—a low, gentle growl. Then he saluted my nose, cheeks and beard with his long rough tongue. I enjoyed it enormously, even though it felt as though my face were being sandpapered. Almost unconsciously, I raised my bandaged hand, touched his neck and started to scratch him. He seemed to like it and he continued to lavish large abrasive kisses on my face while I moved my hand through the coarse tangled hair of his mane. Then he turned his head in the direction of my left arm.

I thought he merely wanted to wash a new part of my anatomy, but when his nose was half an inch away from my good arm, he simply opened his mouth and started to engulf it. I didn't move. I knew that if I pulled the arm away his natural reaction would be to seize it, and our new-found friendship would come to a bloody end. Instead, I kept scratching his neck while he moved his open mouth around the arm very carefully —as though he were trying to avoid hurting me with his huge canines.

Slowly, Simba closed his mouth. I waited, apprehensive but motionless. As soon as he felt the flesh squeeze between his teeth he slackened his jaws but still kept the arm imprisoned between his fangs. Then he opened his mouth a trifle wider and moved an inch or two farther down towards my hand, chewing delicately at the new site of operations.

I shot a quick look towards the natives, worried that they might start screaming again. Fortunately, they were too frightened to utter a word. Their faces showed every shade of emotion: they were convinced the lion was eating my arm.

I was convinced that Simba was only trying to demonstrate affection, so I tried to remain completely relaxed while he chewed his way down to my wrist. Then, when he reached my hand, he felt something with an alien texture—the bandage— and one of his huge fangs caught in the gauze. I refused to panic. Instead, I turned my hand gradually until the bandage came free. Simba opened his mouth wider, and very slowly I withdrew the precious fingers. For a moment the lion turned his great head from side to side with his mouth still open. Then, abruptly, he closed his jaws and sniffed at my face again. This time, when he drew his head back, I rose to my feet at last. Simba did the same and obviously very happy, he rubbed against my legs like a quarter-ton house-cat.

A few seconds later his mood changed and he sprang to the side. I sprang with him, reasoning that the lion needed more than affection: he wanted to play. He paused for a moment and approached me again, but this time, instead of rubbing against my legs, he gave me a little bite just above the left knee. It was really more of a nibble than a bite, performed with the same exquisite care as his pinch on my arm. He watched carefully for my reaction and seemed quite pleased that I hadn't resented his gesture. We played for a little while longer, and then, after almost an hour in the arena, I stepped out and closed the gate behind me.

CONGOLESE SCULPTURE

Ten of the 5,000 specimens in the Author's collection.
(*Top left*) Lega mask of type used in ritual of Bwame Secret Society.
(*Right centre*) A Bakuba sorcerer's divining *itombwa*.

NATIVE POACHERS AND THEIR VICTIMS

(*Left*) Waliangulu poachers in eastern Kenya fire poisoned arrows, dance round the body of an elephant they have killed for ivory, and feast on meat from its trunk.

(*Right*) Zebras killed by poisoned arrows and wire slip nooses.
(*Centre*) An eland strangled by wire.

Immediately, the natives exploded in an hysterical demonstration of their pent-up emotions. '*Bwana Simba!*' my carpenter saluted me with obvious awe. 'Master of the Lion!' He touched my left arm, still wet with the animal's saliva, that showed no broken skin but only a small bruise near the elbow. He stared at my face, reddened by the huge abrasive tongue.

'*Iko mayele ya Mungu!*' Kamende said knowingly. 'It is the magic of God!'

'*Mungu* had nothing to do with it,' I retorted. 'It was strictly between Simba and me.'

'*Mayele!*' he insisted. 'It was magic!'

'*Mayele!*' fifty native voices echoed . . . and I argued no longer. The word *mayele* is generally used throughout Central Africa to designate any baffling phenomena which have no connection with traditional native magic. An aeroplane, a camera, a radio—any device that is beyond local limits of comprehension—is immediately labelled *mayele wa wazungu*, 'the magic of the white man'. Other objects and events, more elemental and mysterious (without obvious pushbuttons or batteries), are called *mayele ya Mungu*, 'the magic of God'.

So, *Mungu* got all the credit for taming the lion—for a few days. Then my people stopped talking about *mayele*: the first session in the arena had been a 'miracle', but after three or four more they grew blasé and didn't even bother to look.

*   *   *

A week later I finally managed to escape to North Kivu for a long visit to my pygmies. Everything in Kisenyi had more or less settled down—as much as it ever would—and I had found a reliable European to handle sales in my absence. As for the rest, Kamende would manage the 'show business', André and my new clerk Lunduka would attend to the practical details of the ménage and the gardener, Mugerero, would be responsible for the care and feeding of the animals. Serukenyinkware would, of course, be very busy pretending that he had charge of *everything*.

I drove the 245 miles from Kisenyi to Beni with a truckful of peanuts, beans, salt, soap, dried fish, axes, machetes and hoes; but when I reached Ngadi, the southernmost *paysannat*, I found no one there to receive them. It was completely abandoned, and the Ituri was rapidly taking back the great rectangle which twelve pygmy families had struggled to clear. As I walked among rows of stunted manioc, half-hidden by invading weeds,

and went into hut after hut still containing the crude furniture
I had taught them to make, I felt almost physically ill at the
tragic futility of the whole scene.

Afterwards I went to the former pygmy camp near the negro
village, expecting to find at least some of them re-established
under servile conditions, but that, too, had been abandoned.
According to the local Nande *kapita*, the people of Ngadi had
refused to return to the old life under his tribe's domination,
and had gone instead deep into the forest to resume their
ancestors' free nomadic ways. The negroes had seen them from
time to time, but the pygmies refused to have any real traffic
with them.

Hearing that, I realized that Ngadi was neither tragic nor
futile: the *paysannat* was dead but its people had learned what it
meant to be free men and they had left the old feudal servitude
behind them. Now, back in the heart of the forest, they had
reverted to a more primitive state, but at least they had escaped
from the diseases and dangers of their former 'symbiosis'. They
would keep their women—and survive.

At Ebikeba, it was a somewhat different story. Most of the
people had fled from this oldest and most advanced *paysannat*,
but thirteen families remained, stubbornly working their land.
Some had even extended their homesteads to four or five times
the original size, taking over the abandoned fields of their
neighbours. All boundary lines had been obliterated, the entire
system was disorganized and the crops were planted in straggling clumps and irregular rows—yet the incredible fact remained: the pygmies were still working the land at Ebikeba, the
one *paysannat* where they had been most fully exposed to the
crude intimidation of the administrative storm.

I asked Kalingama, formerly my best pupil at the school,
what he knew of the twenty-six families who had fled. Like the
people of Ngadi, most of them had turned in frustrated revulsion
to the depths of the forest. The eight members of the defunct
pygmy Police Force had been among the most bitter, unable to
forget their public humiliation. Yoma and Ebu, who were away
hunting, had remained and had been a powerful influence on the
others. Yoma was particularly good, Kalingama told me
proudly, at leading raids to steal seed and young banana trees
from the negroes to help them keep up their crops.

Vermeulen simply ignored the remains of the *paysannat*, but
the Little Sisters of Father Foucauld were still being a nuisance.
They had given up any pretext of coming to live at Ebikeba,

and yet, according to Kalingama, still harassed the pygmies whenever they found them dancing, either for tourists or simply for their own pleasure. I looked everywhere for some sign of the charitable 'necessities' the nuns were supposed to have bought with their 100,000-franc grant, but nowhere in Ebikeba could I find a single gardening rake, baby bonnet or plastic knitting needle.

North of Mbau, the situation at the rest of the *paysannats* was roughly similar. The more sensitive pygmies had fled, leaving a hard core of stubborn determined little people. At the extreme northern limit, where they had been least exposed to the controversy, things seemed almost normal. When I arrived at Kakola, they were whitewashing the *pisé* walls of their huts—inside and out, as I had taught them—and at Erengeti, where nearly all the original families remained, things were in better shape than at any of the other *paysannats*, but still, the old revolutionary spirit was gone and things were starting to run down.

I travelled among them for nearly three weeks, distributed fresh supplies and gave them whatever advice and encouragement I could. Then I had to leave—but this time I took a little bit of the Ituri Forest with me. My people at Oicha had captured a tiny female chimpanzee, only two or three months old, and one of the women had suckled it at her breast to keep it alive. Now they gave it to me as a parting present, and I drove the tiny ape, which I christened Sophie, back to Kisenyi in a big wicker basket.

This demanding, emotional baby primate kept us all in a state of constant upheaval. She hated being caged or left alone, so I put a rope around her waist and tied her to one of the trees in the back yard. She never stopped screaming, fussing and having fits until I turned her loose. Immediately she gravitated towards Kamende, fascinated by his dangling, rattling paraphernalia, and spent most of her time following the 'witch doctor' around, when she wasn't in the kitchen having a bottle or trying to beg tomatoes and bread from André.

Except for these two and Mugerero, the animal-keeper, Sophie feared and disliked the rest of my native help, probably because they teased her whenever I wasn't looking. As for Simba, I thought the baby chimp would die of fright the first time she saw him and heard him roar. She gave the arena a wide berth for more than a week; then, growing bolder, she came closer to the bars and started to tease the lion, just as the natives teased her, making incredibly grotesque faces and gestures just beyond the range of his claws. Once, while he was asleep close to the edge of the arena, she managed to grab his tail. He woke up with a start, leaped against the bars in berserk fury and Sophie shot backwards screaming for pity as though it was she who had been ill done by.

Two other primates used to watch the lion-chimpanzee conflict from their own stations about twenty feet away: a big, morose silver monkey about ten years old, the size of a half-grown chimp, who lived in a large cage by himself, and Kikihibu, an owl monkey, who was tied out under a huge *ficus* tree. Both were very tough customers and would have decimated the community monkey cage if given a chance. As it was the twenty members of my simian community had trouble enough in the form of Jeune-Homme, a strong, clever, year-old baboon who had made himself boss of the cage. He knocked his companions off the rope swings with calculated abandon whenever he wanted to play, and at feeding time always wound up with the choicest morsels of carrots and corn.

The monkeys were shrewd, noisy and fascinating, the antelope and crested cranes were wonderfully elegant, and all the other animals had peculiar, intriguing characteristics of their own. But the centre of interest—and the big challenge—was always the iron arena.

Until now the only thing I had accomplished with Simba had been to step in with him on a dozen occasions, demonstrate my friendly intentions and step out again without having been mauled or eaten in the process. During those encounters I had tried to study his different moods and reactions, to observe and remember which of his little characteristics belonged particularly to him and not merely to lions in general. Now I intended to take the next big step: to train Simba to obey my commands and to learn some 'show business' tricks.

We were fairly good friends by now, and I felt that the lion actually looked forward to seeing me every day. The big danger, as we embarked on the training, would be to place too much faith in that friendship. No matter how much understanding or even love may exist between a lion and his partner, the element of danger is always present. Even a well-fed, well-adjusted lion has his peevish moods, just as we do—without intending to kill, he may decide to administer a little rebuke for some real or fancied grievance, or simply because he has a sore spot on his tail. A rebuke from more than four hundred pounds of peevish lion can have a lasting corrective effect—since he can crack a man's neck with one blow of his paw.

The danger is almost as great when a perfectly happy lion decides to show his goodwill. Even our small domestic cats will scratch, and scratch hard, when carried away by a wild, playful mood. A lion likes to play too, but if his razor-sharp claws enter the trainer's flesh and he sees blood streaming from the long gashes, his mood may change quickly from jest to earnest.

All lions are dangerous, popular myths to the contrary notwithstanding. People claim that performing lions are overfed to make them less ferocious, but that is nonsense: a lion who has eaten too much, too recently, has no intention of sitting on a pedestal or jumping through a hoop. All he wants to do is to lie down, preferably with his feet in the air, for a long languid nap; not even a whip will change his mind about that. Others maintain that trained lions have been de-clawed, de-fanged and equipped with false teeth, but that, too, is entirely absurd: without claws a lion would lose most of the agility he needs to perform; without teeth he would gradually starve to death, and even a clawless, toothless lion would be more than able to kill a man—to crush a skull with one blow of his massive paw or crack a neck in his toothless but powerful jaws.

For all these reasons, danger is always present when men and lions meet. The *intensity* of that danger depends on two things: the individual lion and the individual man.

*   *   *

On the day that Simba's real training began I entered the arena with a very definite goal: I was going to teach him to sit, to stand and to lie down on command, and to acquaint him with the tools of his new trade: the pedestals.

Teaching him to sit was the first step, and a few little experiments yielded a very simple method. If I approached Simba and held my hand over his head, his reaction was always the same: it offended his dignity and so he sat down, simply to bring his head to a higher level. If I left my hand in position, he reared up and tried to catch it with his forepaws. Once he almost succeeded, and from that moment on I used a four-foot wooden baton. When I removed it, he remained seated—he was comfortable and there was no real reason to get up.

To make him lie down from a sitting position, I traced a line on the ground leading away from his nose or tapped the earth about three feet in front of him. Intrigued, he stretched out on his belly, reaching forward with his paws to investigate the mystery—a movement which later became a conditioned reflex —and from that position he was relatively easily made to roll over: I tapped the ground a couple of feet from his left side, and playfully he rolled over trying to catch the stick. After repeated practice he was making three or four consecutive turns, and eventually I was able to cue him with a movement of my hand.

To make Simba stand up I took a quick step to his left and slightly to the rear. That alerted him and he rose immediately to his feet.

I made him practise all these elementary manœuvres for about half an hour. Then I introduced him to the pedestals: two sets of weighted wooden stands, 2 ft. and 4 ft. high and 2 ft. in diameter, which had been sitting idly at the edge of the arena for a couple of days while Simba got used to the sight of them. He had sniffed suspiciously, and pushed one a few inches with his paw but then, finding nothing of any great interest, he had decided to ignore them.

Now I shoved one of the two-foot pedestals into the centre of the arena—the lion eyed it warily. 'Simba, UP!' I ordered, tapping the centre of the wooden stand with my stick. He came closer and watched the moving baton, but made no attempt to mount. I moved to his left rear and tapped again, crowding him as much as I dared. Finally, with a baffled expression, he jumped up and stood there, looking rather foolish and ill-at-ease. I raised my stick over his head, he sat down and at once seemed much happier and more secure.

To make him stand up again I tried several methods and soon found the most effective was to walk towards his rear with an intriguing, mysterious air. The lion immediately became curious, scrambled to his feet and turned to watch me. Observing that reaction, I continued to walk round the pedestal, the lion continued to turn. After three circuits I reversed and Simba reversed with me.

It was a wonderful beginning, and I left the arena convinced that the roaring devil in the metal box had become not merely a friend but a willing, relatively well-behaved pupil. Of course, nothing I had done up to this point involved teaching the lion a trick or 'imposing my will' on him; instead, I had merely taken advantage of his natural gestures and built-in psychological reactions. I knew that the next phases of his training would become increasingly difficult, as I introduced him to situations and actions farther removed from his own instinctive behaviour.

That became obvious a day later, when I tried to make Simba mount one of the four-foot pedestals. It took more than an hour of persuasion before he finally agreed to ascend the taller pedestal from the smaller one; then, when he landed, he sprang off immediately, and it took another hour of hard work to make him repeat the trick. Again he refused to stay on the taller pedestal, but this time when he sprang to the floor he lay down on his side and refused to budge. He was obviously nervous, tired and disgusted with the whole thing.

The trying two-hour session had involved more moral friction between the two of us than real physical action: otherwise I could never have worked him so long. A lion, designed for rapid bursts of power and not for a steady output, is almost completely exhausted after fifteen or twenty minutes of continuous exercise. In nature, he makes a kill every four or five days, eats as much as a hundred pounds of meat at a sitting and spends most of his spare time snoring under a cassia tree. Compared to a cheetah or a leopard the lion is overweight, indolent and virtually sedentary. Still, he is much more amiable and easy to teach than the nervous leopard and much happier in close captivity than the lean, active cheetah.

Simba obviously needed a stronger motive than curiosity and the desire to play if his innate laziness were to be overcome. So, when I stepped into the arena on the third day of his training, my pockets were loaded with meat—for a lion the strongest motive in the world. Simba had had a raw chicken as a snack the evening before, but now it was ten in the morning, the usual time for his big meal of the day: fifteen pounds of meat—goat, mutton or beef—plus half a dozen eggs in a gallon of milk. He was extremely hungry and much more active and nervous than usual.

He growled peevishly when I urged him on to the smaller pedestal. Then, as soon as he looked aside for a few seconds, I took a one-inch piece of meat out of my pocket and skewered it on the sharpened tip of my stick. I waved the bait in front of his nose and moved it away quickly, dropping the cube of meat on top of the four-foot pedestal. The results were dramatic.

What two hours of moral persuasion had failed to accomplish the day before happened in less than two seconds; Simba jumped to the taller pedestal without hesitation, snatched up the little chunk of flesh, bolted it down and stood there uneasily, looking around for more. I dropped another cube of meat on the shorter pedestal and he jumped back at once. I repeated the gesture a dozen times, and the lion jumped steadily from one pedestal to the other until I ran out of meat. Then, when I tapped with the naked stick, he looked confused but decided to jump anyway. He repeated the trick five or six times, at which point, since he was obviously tiring, I decided to call it a day.

When we started our next training session and I tried him without the meat, Simba stared at the stick and refused to act, apparently having forgotten the association of ideas linking the pedestal or the stick with a juicy reward. So I sneaked a little meat out of my pocket—and we were in business again. First we went through a series of the jumps he had already learned, and gradually I increased the distance between the two pedestals to six feet. Then I made a change in the routine: instead of using a 4 ft. and a 2 ft. pedestal I used the two taller ones. It didn't bother Simba in the least; in fact, he definitely seemed to prefer moving between two spots on the same level.

The sight of my beautiful lion leaping so confidently inspired me to a new and dangerous idea. Simba's trips between the two pedestals would be much more exciting if he passed over an interesting object in the centre—me. Gradually, with each consecutive leap, I came closer and closer. I had no meat left by now and knew I couldn't wait much longer. Finally, I crouched down directly between the two tall pedestals and gestured with my stick. Simba didn't even pause to consider the new object: he sprang without hesitation and sailed over my head.

We repeated the trick twice, and I left the arena, exultant. Now, for the first time, my lion and I had actually performed *together*. I was no longer an aloof instructor; instead, after only four days I was becoming his partner. My ambition soared, a glorious vision came to mind: Simba, majestic and fearless, leaping through a circle of fire which I held aloft from my position between the two pedestals.

It took thirteen consecutive days of patient, excruciating work to turn that vision into reality, but it was worth it.

I started by obtaining a three-foot iron hoop from the foundry at Goma, and getting my carpenter to build two wooden stands to hold it in place. I spent the next three days persuading and bribing Simba to jump through the hoop, until, with perfect technique, he was able to leap seven feet between the two tall pedestals, passing through the supported ring in the centre. Then, on the fourth day, I substituted myself for the hoop-stand, crouching in the centre and holding the iron circle at a height of about six feet.

The trick worked perfectly and we spent the next two days repeating it. Then, to prepare Simba for the big shock, I wound the iron hoop with spirals of white cotton and wired them into place, leaving a bare spot of about thirty inches for my hand-grip. To avoid frightening him with the white cloth and to accustom his nose to the smell of fuel, I soaked the cotton with crankcase oil. The first time Simba saw and smelled the trans-formed hoop, he would have nothing to do with it. We spent almost an hour arguing until he finally agreed to accept a large bribe and sail through the stinking circle. The next day he was much more co-operative, making most of his leaps without bait. Then, on the ninth day of hoop-training, I was ready to introduce Simba to fire.

It was only a tiny petrol flame at the very top of the hoop, but he was outraged. He jumped down from his pedestal each time I lighted the flame, and once, infuriated, he decided to charge me. I stopped him with the hoop itself and the frighten-ing two-inch flame.

At that point, I knew the whole process had to be started all over again: the small pedestals, the tall pedestals, the hoop-stand, and big chunks of meat for every jump. But even with that patient re-education, it took two more days before Simba would leap through a hoop—which I held to the side at arm's length—with about six inches of fire along the rim. It was only on the thirteenth day that Simba and I succeeded together in accomplishing something that established professionals would have considered impossible: a full-grown lion, with less than a month of actual training, was making a seven-foot leap, six feet above the ground, through a complete arc of fire which I held overhead.

As soon as Simba performed the trick regularly without a reward of meat I began to enlarge his repertoire. I taught him to stand on a barrel and roll it round the arena, a feat he mastered in four days, but we ran into difficulties when I stationed my carpenter next to the arena with a gramophone and some records of Strauss waltzes, and tried to teach the lion to dance with his paws on my shoulders. He lacked a strong sense of musical rhythm and the forced *pas de deux* seemed to annoy him. He kept stepping on my feet, which ruined a good pair of shoes, puffing his rank breath into my face, and dripping saliva on to my beard and shirt. Finally, we both grew so bitter and disgusted with the whole thing that I put aside the dancing project temporarily and decided to concentrate on a far more demanding, but less intimate, trick.

To sit up and beg, completely without support, is undoubtedly one of the hardest feats for a lion, or any other great cat, to perform. The animal is not constructed to hold such a posture and his dorsal muscles must be strengthened slowly and progressively until he can do it. Professional trainers estimate that only one lion in five can master the trick, and for that reason it is rarely seen in circus performances.

The odds were slim but I had confidence in Simba. What I didn't realize was that to teach him this trick, which looks relatively simple, would take more than twice as long as the spectacular flaming hoop and would put me in far greater danger than the dance.

I spent the first ten days trying to make Simba sit by holding a piece of meat over his head on the tip of a long stick. It was good exercise for him, but that was all. He reared up, caught the meat and came down again without even considering a brief pause. Since this approach didn't seem too promising, I gave Simba a day off and thought about the problem. Then I presented him with some muscle-building apparatus: a lion's gymnasium consisting of a heavy metal pipe driven into the ground beside one of the pedestals, a wooden pole inserted into the pipe, and a wooden crosspiece fixed in place with angle-irons at the very top of the pole. The bribe would be placed on top of the crosspiece.

It looked good, but after a few experiments I found that every time I put a chunk of meat on the top, Simba reared up, picked it off and came down again just as before. So I changed my tactics, skewering the meat on the tip of my stick and holding it very high and a little forward. That had the desired effect: the lion actually rested his paws on the support while he manœuvred for the meat, keeping his back very straight in the process. I was encouraged, but the moment I let him catch it, he sprang off the pedestal instead of merely sitting down.

He repeated that performance without improvement for several days, until I further refined the system. I found a long flexible pole, put a very large piece of meat at the tip and planted it in the ground just ahead of the pedestal. The lion clutched his crosspiece and peered up at that tantalizing vision until he seemed almost hypnotized. Meanwhile, I stood on his left, trying to look as large and impressive as possible while I threatened him with my forefinger and repeated the words, 'Stay there, Simba! Stay there!'

For the next ten days he stared at different chunks of meat that swayed over his head on the end of the pole. He didn't particularly enjoy this phase of the operation, but he was far more fortunate than those few circus lions who have mastered the trick: their trainers force them to rear up and hold the difficult posture by means of repeated thrusts with an electric goad.

On the tenth day, the accident happened—one of the few really close calls that I've had in all of my dealings with 'big game' animals.

Simba had grown tired and disgusted with the elusive mirage of meat. He decided to jump down on the left side, where I was standing, but I raised my hand and shouted 'Stop!' Sulkily, he returned to his position. Then his eyes roved in the opposite direction and I knew he was going to jump. Quickly I ran to his right—but not quickly enough. The lion was already launched, our bodies collided and down we crashed.

I was pinned on my back with well over four hundred pounds of lion on my front. He lay on top of me, a warm, rank-smelling sphinx, a huge paw on each of my shoulders and the rear part of his body on my legs. He looked confused, nervous and slightly menacing. I didn't move a muscle. Instead, I widened my eyes and stared at him while I crooned his name, 'S-e-e-mba, S-e-e-mba, S-e-e-e-m-mba . . .' He stared back without crooning, brought his head very close, and I felt his rancid breath on my nose while his claws pricked my shoulders.

That really worried me, for I knew that if he once shot those claws into my skin, even without malice, there was only one way he could free them: by pulling them through my flesh; the mechanisms which operate a lion's paw leave no other method.

'Relax!' I told myself. 'Make him think we're playing together, don't resist him or he'll decide it's a fight. Relax!'

At that moment André wandered into the back yard to give the silver monkey a carrot. He glanced casually towards the arena, looked again and churned himself into a frenzy. '*Bwana na kufa!*' he shrieked wildly, 'The boss is dead!' He ran towards the house, eager to spread the tragic news. '*Simba na kula Bwana!*' he cried, expanding on the theme, 'Simba is eating the boss!'

Remarkably, the lion chose to ignore that loud suggestion.

Instead, he decided to kiss me—big rugged schlupps that drenched my beard and smelt awful. I decided it might be wise to return his affection, so raised my hand and scratched him gently on the chest. Once again, I felt his claws prick my shoulders, playfully but a little harder than the first time, and I began to feel really desperate. I pictured André returning with a crew of screaming dancers, and I knew what effect the noise and confusion would have on Simba and consequently on me.

I struggled to raise one shoulder and the lion merely pressed down harder. I scratched his chest and tried to push him aside. I might just as well have attempted to move the Great Sphinx he resembled: Simba didn't budge. Instead, he opened his mouth and chewed delicately on the upper part of my arm. Then his attention shifted to my khaki 'safari shirt' and the cloth strap on the left shoulder.

A button cracked and one end of the flap came loose. That really intrigued him. He shifted position to investigate more closely and somehow managed to put his left paw squarely in the centre of my face, claws resting directly over my eyes. Now the situation was becoming really impossible: I was starting to suffocate and I knew the lion would grow excited while he played with the scrap of cloth . . . and shoot his claws. Simultaneously, I heard what sounded like a small riot converging on the back yard.

I felt the lion's claws tickle my eyelids and this helped me reach a quick decision. I brought my arm up from beneath until my hand rested beside his incredibly massive and solidly planted left foreleg. I knew that any attempt to push the big paw off my face had to be executed with rapid, abrupt finesse; otherwise, the claws would shoot and tear as his foot slid over my flesh. Then, again, even if I were quick enough and emerged intact Simba might interpret the movement as hostile and decide to fight.

Action was terribly dangerous, but at this point, with an hysterical crowd approaching, inaction was even worse. So, abruptly, with all my strength, I slapped the leg to the side.

To my vast relief, Simba didn't even seem annoyed: he was completely preoccupied with the stubborn piece of cloth. Instead, he simply lumbered to his feet and moved a little towards the left, giving me my first real chance to escape; I took full advantage of it. While Simba worked on my shoulder-strap, I unbuttoned my shirt to give him a little more slack, and then slowly pulled my short right arm out of its sleeve. Simba tugged at the cloth and this actually helped me as I slipped my left arm and hand out of the other sleeve. The lion backed up, shaking his head furiously with my shirt in his mouth, and I got to my feet—after five nerve-racking minutes that had seemed more like five hours.

All seventeen members of my native crew were standing round the arena, staring open-mouthed at the scene. They had arrived just in time to witness my escape. I gestured at the lion and the shirt. I threw my shoulders back and raised my head high, showing off a little for their benefit and curious to see how they would react. The answer was quick and very deflating: Serukenyinkware looked indifferent and stalked off in silence, while Kamende grinned, shrugged and spoke one infuriating word. The others echoed his judgement and wandered back to their work, reassuring each other that my little ordeal was simply another outbreak of . . . *mayele*!

I turned my attention back to the lion. Just to keep him from getting any fancy ideas for the future, I made a point of driving him away from the tatters of my shirt. I spoke very roughly and menaced him with the little stick, unusual tactics which made him anxious to please me. Then I put him through one of his pedestal routines, to restore a more normal atmosphere, patted him on the head, and left the arena.

Afterwards, I went into the house and inspected my shoulder. Parts of it were almost purple with subcutaneous haemorrhage, but the skin hadn't been broken. I peered at my face in the bedroom mirror and found only one tiny nick on the left eyelid. Then, as I turned towards the window, I saw something extraordinary: my lion, alone in the arena, was sitting up on his pedestal, his paws on the crosspiece, begging beside an empty stick.

Perhaps he did it because he was hungry or even because he wanted, somehow, to please me, but I think Simba had discovered, after a month of hard work on the difficult trick, that he really enjoyed it. A week later, he was sitting up to beg for his meat, completely without support, for as long as five seconds. After another week, he stayed in position for fifteen to twenty seconds and performed the trick without any reward. By the end of the month, he was holding the pose for a full half-minute with neither meat nor stick but only an upward movement of my finger.

Now I had the spectacular climax for our act, as well as some of the major tricks, and so I started to fill out and perfect the routine. It went slowly, since I interrupted the training for another visit to the pygmies in North Kivu, a few business trips to Nairobi, Kampala and Mombasa, and many quick drives to Bukavu where I was setting up a branch of the Central Africa Curio Shop.

I was also trying to spend more time with my father, who had suffered several minor heart attacks during the past six months and had been forced to curtail all his former activities—a very trying state of affairs for a man of his mercurial temperament and fierce, almost obsessive will to work. I shall never forget the wonderful evening I spent with him on 17 April 1959. He spoke eloquently of life, philosophy and art with the same keen, rebellious spirit he had always shown and the same quick changes of mood. Then, next morning, he suffered a massive coronary attack and died.

Thus, André Hallet, a Walloon born in Liège on 26 March 1890, had come to the end of his long pilgrimage—sixty-nine years later—in Kisenyi, Ruanda-Urundi. As a struggling young artist he had left the grey Belgian skies behind to follow the sun to Provence, Naples, Capri and Sicily, eager to flood his impressionist canvas with light. Then he found the great burning equatorial sun of the Congo, its wild, fantastic landscapes and its warm, exciting people.

Among the hundreds of accolades he had received during his lifetime, perhaps the finest tribute came from Adolphe Hardy, the renowned Belgian poet and art critic (who was also my godfather), who said, 'To the eyes of those who can see, to the hearts of those who can feel, to the minds of those who can think, André Hallet reveals himself and stands forward as an artist of the first rank, exceptionally gifted with unique originality and a rare genius. . . .'

The legacy of that genius could be found in more than *five thousand* magnificent paintings created during the past half-century. Since 1925, when he was only thirty-five, *Autumn Landscape* and *A Bend of the River Dyle* have been hanging in the Louvre in Paris, and the leading museums in Brussels, Marseilles, Liège, Louvain, Tournai, Ottawa, Belgrade, Kovno and New York treasure his paintings. His canvases had been displayed at more than fifty exhibitions, including the World's Fairs in London and Brussels, and he had often been compared to Van Gogh, Cézanne and Monet.

King Leopold of the Belgians had acquired two André Hallets and the Queen Mother Elisabeth owned *Lake Kivu—*

Kisenyi. The Bank of the Belgian Congo had five wonderful scenes including *The Market at Usumbura*; his *Sun Setting at Wangata* was displayed in the Ministry of Colonies and the Government General of the Congo was the possessor of his *The Valley of the Mpozo* and *Falls of the River Rutshuru*. Even the designs for the ten- and twenty-franc Congolese banknotes were his work.

Now my father was dead, but his works were a living testimony to his force and genius. What Paul Gauguin had been to Tahiti, André Hallet was to the Congo.

18

Tembo

> 'There is no creature among al the Beastes of the
> world which hath so great and ample a demonstra-
> tion of the power and wisedom of almighty God as
> the Elephant.'
>
> EDWARD TOPSELL, *The Historie of*
> *Foure-Footed Beastes* (1607)

THE first twelve animals I acquired during May 1959 were
plump, lively, rabbit-sized bundles of soft brown fur, with
pointed snouts, small round ears, stubby tails, dorsal scent-
glands, rodent-like front teeth and molars like rhino. *Procavia*
(*Dendrohyrax*) *arborea adolfi-friederici* lived highly unconven-
tional lives in the equatorial forest, sleeping all day in hollow
trunks and browsing at night on leaves and green twigs, screaming with a weird cry like the rasp of grinding gears and scuttling
through the great trees on sturdy feet equipped with naked
climbing pads and elegant little hoofs.

Great hordes of the strange little creatures—hyraxes, the
world's only arboreal ungulates—had abandoned their ancestral
trees and installed themselves on the lava fields of the Virunga
volcanoes. There, like a few related Syrian, Ethiopian and South
African species, they nested under rock piles in large colonies,
posting sentinels to warn them of oncoming danger while they
basked in the sun or foraged for wild sorrel at night. Unfortunately, their sentinels were useless against the slip-noose traps
of the pygmoid Batwa hunters, who sold the captured animals
at twenty-five francs each, for their fur.

I bought twelve and installed them, temporarily, at the bottom of the big aviary, where they paid no attention to the aerial

bombardments of almost fifteen hundred birds and the comments of my visitors. Virtually all of the tourists thought they were rodents, whether they called them 'rock rabbits', 'klipdas', 'damans', 'dassies' or 'coneys'.

The next two animals I adopted in May were the paradoxical hyraxes' closest living relations, *uku* to the pygmies, *inzovu* to the Batutsi, *ol-tome* to the Masai, and *tembo* to all Swahili-speaking peoples of Africa. Elephants. How and why I acquired the two great *tembo*, and what happened when I marched them four hundred miles through the Congo, is a long, often bizarre story.

* * *

It all began when I left Kisenyi for another visit to the pygmies, drove north to gather Mangbetu artifacts for my collection and decided to make a stop at Epulu, in the heart of the Ituri, where the Government maintains an okapi trapping station, a small zoo and a training camp for forest elephants.

The sixteen docile, hard-working animals I saw at Epulu disproved all the established popular myths concerning the savage, unteachable nature of the African *tembo*. People repeat endlessly that only the Indian species can be trained, forgetting that the most notorious trained elephants in history were the thirty-seven African animals which Hannibal pitted against the legions of Rome.

About sixty years earlier Ptolemy Philadelphus, Egypt's most intellectual, sophisticated and dissolute pharaoh, had established a station for capturing elephants on the shore of the Red Sea, and the Egyptians were the first to train *Loxodonta africana cyclotis*, the smaller, forest-loving variety of the great *tembo*, then living all along the southern edge of the Sahara. During the palmy days of the Roman Empire the training of African elephants reached an incredible peak: according to reputable authors such as Seneca, Pliny and Dion, they performed as gladiators, acrobats, dancers, comedians and tightrope artists; the most dazzling performance of all, recorded by Suetonius, was that of an intrepid *tembo* who walked up a slanting tightrope to the top of the Circus Maximus and down again.

Here in the Congo taming and training the *Loxodonta africana cyclotis* variety was undertaken in 1899, for the first time since the fall of the Roman Empire, as a pet project of Leopold II. Convinced that the forest elephants of the Ituri would make useful draft animals, the King put Major Laplume in charge of stations established at Kira Vunga, Api and Gangala na Bodio in the northeast Congo and imported *cornacs,* experienced Indian trainers, to educate the first animals and impart the secrets of their art to crews of Congolese natives.

Four- or five-year-old calves were stalked, chased, captured and put into training for ten months. Their *cornacs* sang traditional Hindu songs while they rubbed the young *tembo* down and plied them with titbits such as sugar cane, sweet potatoes, pineapple and bananas. Only when the calves had absorbed enough music and delicacies to make them amiable and co-operative were they taught to kneel and rise on command and to allow a man to mount and ride on their backs, while they walked, attached by leg-chains to a fully-trained elephant 'monitor'.

The *hawkus* or elephant goad was used to tap them lightly or to make gestures, but no elephant was ever really struck. They were handled with extreme patience and kindness, not simply for humanitarian reasons but because, as with most other animals, force produces only an illusion of control. The graves of six would-be African *cornacs* at the Api station were mute testimony to the folly of trying to bully an elephant with blows.

When the young *tembo* reached the end of their ten-month taming period, their real education started. They were taught, by means of kindness, persuasion and bribery, to haul loads, pull ploughs, uproot small trees and carry away débris. Over a period of five to six years, the work-load was gradually increased until the fully trained elephant could haul about nine hundred pounds and work four to six hours a day, usually in the morning to avoid exposing a forest animal to dangerous doses of sunlight. It was impracticable to work them longer, since in order to stay alive the elephants had to spend an average of sixteen hours a day eating.

The trained forest *tembo* of the Congo proved fully as intelligent and reliable as their Indian colleagues, but the economics of the system were basically unsound: the lengthy education produced a draught animal of seriously limited capacity but with an enormous appetite. Modern technological developments in transport and agriculture made the working elephant obsolete. None the less training continued at Gangala na Bodio, near the Garamba National Park, and at Epulu in the Ituri. Some of the educated animals were destined for zoos and circuses, the rest remained in their home country as occasional farmhands and, of course, as a great tourist attraction.

I watched the native *cornacs* put them through their paces, then strolled over the iron bridge across the Epulu River and revisited the small zoo with its collection of red buffalo, warthog, monkeys and okapi, those primitive, forest-dwelling relatives of the savannah's giraffes.

During all my time in the Ituri, I had only twice encountered okapi: each time all I had seen was merely a striped rear disappearing into the bush. At Epulu I could observe at close range at least twenty of Africa's rarest and most elusive mammals, a herd of bongo-sized, purplish-brown animals with white-striped haunches, huge pink and grey ears that never stopped moving, and long, protractile, almost circular tongues which they reversed over their narrow yellow cheeks to chase away the flies from their ears.

I watched them browse, pace and amble around their big kraal. Then I walked over to the newly built motel-style Domaine des Okapis where I got into chance conversation with a burly forester named Devos. He told me he had bought two full-grown, fully trained female elephants and hired two former government *cornacs*, hoping to use them in his logging operations, but soon found the elephants created more problems than they solved and ate more than they hauled. He was eager to sell them, but no one in the district wanted to buy his seven-and-a-half-ton problem.

'Now if you own a private zoo—' Devos began, trying to look casual.

'I can't keep two elephants in Kisenyi. I haven't enough room, and I'd spend a fortune trying to feed them.'

'—I could let you have Bella and Venus for only twenty thousand francs,' he concluded. 'It's a wonderful bargain!'

Two trained *tembo* for £140 was an extremely reasonable price. If I could acquire some land not too far from Kisenyi, I could install the elephants there and gradually add other large animals. Then I could send whole busloads of tourists from the Central Africa Curio Shop to my new private game park. The idea was very attractive, but almost impossible, since Epulu is four hundred miles from Kisenyi.

To transport the two *tembo* by truck was out of the question: even if I could find an eight-ton flatbed truck with a wooden superstructure tall enough, the load would make it top-heavy and the rig would probably tip over somewhere along the hairpin bends of the Mitumba Mountains and the Kabasha Escarpment, if it ever got so far. It was much more likely that the elephants, unaccustomed to close confinement, would become so upset that they would demolish the wooden top of the truck and pitch over the side.

'Why don't you take a look at them?' the forester suggested. 'They're very nice animals, perfectly trained, with beautiful dispositions.'

Devos took me to his logging station and almost at once I fell in love with two very refined ladies named Bella and Venus. Bella, the larger and apparently dominant one, was a magnificent four-ton female with shapely four-foot tusks. Venus was a trifle shorter and weighed about half a ton less: she had stubby foot-long tusks and a slightly petulant expression. (The females of the Indian elephant lack tusks, one of the many ways in which *Elephas maximus* differs and falls short of the superlative African species.)

Before long I had beaten Devos down to £100 for the pair and hired their *cornacs*. It might be impossible to move them by truck, but I saw no reason why I should not, like a latter-day Hannibal, march the two *tembo* across the Grand Forest and the challenging Alps of the Kabasha Escarpment.

My *cornacs* were a pair of diminutive Balese brothers named Bodeko and Bokwe. Bodeko did most of the talking, and I listened with growing pleasure: he showed more interest and sympathetic understanding of animals than most Congolese feel for their wives and families. Obviously, the natives who worked at the Epulu station received as much education as their elephants.

'Bella is much more intelligent than my brother's *tembo*,' said the round-faced, big-eyed *cornac*. 'She tells the little one what to do. You can see how they talk to each other—with their ears and their trunks.'

'Venus is clever too,' Bokwe protested.

'Venus is always hungry,' sighed his brother. 'She eats more than the big one and still doesn't get enough! She fusses all the time and always wants to be loved and petted. She lets my Bella do all the hard work, and then tries to take the credit for it!'

'Bella doesn't seem to mind,' I remarked.

'Of course not, *Bwana*. Bella has such a big heart that she loves Venus in spite of everything. They are like two sisters. If you ever sold one of them, I think they would both die.'

'I won't, so you needn't worry about it, Bodeko. Anyway, we have a much more immediate problem on our hands—the big safari. As I see it, we can do those four hundred miles in seven or eight days. You and Bokwe can make a long march with the elephants every morning, let them take it easy and have a big meal about noon, and another long march until sunset. Then you can find a nice green grove where they can forage during the night and tie them out with their chains. All right?'

'But *Bwana*! We don't know how to get to Kisenyi! We've never been there!'

'We're only going a little past Rutshuru; I think I can find some nice land there for the new elephant park. And I'm going to be with you all the way: I'll drive ahead to the big towns to let them know we're coming, and I'll make sure you take all the right crossroads. There's absolutely nothing to worry about.'

* * *

The two little brothers and their enormous mounts were ready to start at 6.30 next morning. Bodeko sat in the centre of Bella's back on a small round cushion of braided leaves, holding his *hawkus* in one hand and in the other a rope which encircled the elephant's massive body just behind the front legs. Bokwe, mounted on Venus, carried his own *hawkus* and all their extra equipment: a spear, a club and a large *kitenge* knapsack.

'*Endelea!*' I called, 'Let's get going!' My *cornacs* relayed the signal by drumming on top of the elephants' heads with their naked feet, and the two great *tembo* lumbered down the road, Bella first and Venus about ten feet behind. For about fifteen minutes I drove abreast of them at five miles an hour, encouraged by the calm, orderly air of the whole procession. Then I sped ahead to the first good-sized town on our route, Mambasa, thirty miles to the east.

Before visiting the A.T. of Mambasa to announce that two mobile traffic hazards were headed in his direction, I stoked up on breakfast at the Hôtel des Pygmées. It was a wise move, since I never like arguing on an empty stomach.

'W-w-what?!?!' he sputtered furiously. 'What kind of authorization do you have, Monsieur Hallet?'

'I didn't know I needed one. Is there any law against moving two elephants from one territory to the next?'

The A.T. dived into a large dark-green book, *Législation du Congo Belge et du Ruanda-Urundi*, and thumbed through several hundred pages of small print before he lost patience and slammed it shut. Apparently, the founding fathers of the Congo hadn't bothered to discourse on the legal aspects of elephant marching, so the A.T. had no power to interfere. Instead, he held a quick conference with his two white officers and a worried native chief of police, who summoned his force of twelve blue-clad *polici* by beating on a drum. '*Tuliza!*' he shouted excitedly, as soon as they arrived, 'Keep calm!' All twelve immediately started to panic, and I heard loud Swahili cries of 'What's happened?' 'Who's fighting?' 'Who's dead?'

'*Tembo mbili iko na kuya,*' he explained, 'Two elephants are coming.'

'*Wapi? Wapi?*' they shouted, 'Where?'

'*Apa ku Mambasa. Kati kati ya posta.*'

'Mambasa? The two *tembo* are coming here? But the poor *bashenzi* will panic!'

'They are trained *tembo*,' I explained, 'and they won't hurt anyone. Tell the people to stay at the side of the street when the elephants pass, slow down the traffic at the crossroads, and make sure the dogs are tied up—if they bark and run around under their feet, the *tembo* will become nervous. They might even stampede.'

'*Ndio, Bwana! Ndio!*' the twelve *polici* cried, and rushed off in every direction.

My elephants toiled down the road to Mambasa for the next few hours while I passed the time at the Hôtel des Pygmées, chatting with a group of American tourists who had motored up from South Africa. It was fascinating to see how many apparently well-educated people still cherish the most banal misconceptions of popular natural history. I found firm believers in the legendary 'elephant graveyard', others who thought that elephants drink directly through their trunks, and still others who lumped elephants, rhino and hippo in a specious little 'family' called pachyderms, regardless of the fact that these thick-skinned animals belong to three entirely unrelated zoological orders.

Almost everyone was curious about *musth*, that strange aberration of elephant physiology which drives most mature bulls twice a year into a state of emotional disturbance. Most of them believed it to be a sort of male menstruation, directly connected with the functioning of the bull's undescended testicles, in spite of the fact that a few females exhibit the same peculiar symptoms. In reality, *musth* appears to be connected with the functioning of two small glands located just beneath slits in the skin of the temples midway between the eye and the ear which periodically swell and become inflamed; they ooze slowly and stain the face with a dark, tarry secretion. The affected animal's behaviour is usually either manic or morose; he may run amok and trample everything in his path, even his own trusted *cornac*, until the madness subsides. Oddly enough, although every elephant on *musth* presents the characteristic physical symptoms, some animals may show active temporal glands and yet remain absolutely normal in their behaviour.

By now both sides of Mambasa's main street were lined with chattering natives, mostly Balese and Babira, wild with impatience to see the two promised *tembo*. Incredibly, although they lived in the heart of the forest elephant's homeland, most of them had never seen an elephant before and knew less about them than white people who all their lives have seen them in circuses, zoos and films. The natives found trampled fields and ravaged groves of coffee trees in the morning and cursed the unseen animals who had done the damage. But the *tembo* generally gave the villages and cultivated fields a wide berth during the day, preferring, like the pygmies, to steal their sweet potatoes and sugar cane under cover of darkness.

When the elephants finally lumbered into Mambasa round the last curve in the road that afternoon, the natives exploded with excitement. '*Tembo!*' shouted the men, jumping up and down like Masai. '*Tembo!*' screamed the women with big, round, astonished, incredulous eyes. '*Tembo!*' squeaked the small children, clinging to their mothers' legs in paroxysms of terrified delight. '*Tembo! Tembo! TEMBO!*' As for the calm, majestic elephants themselves, Bella looked blasé and a trifle condescending, like a stately dowager, but Venus was evidently enjoying the attention and trumpeted softly, which made the natives give a gasp of nervous pleasure. Bokwe grinned from his perch on her back and Bodeko looked a shade jealous.

The crowd gazed up at the *cornacs* with rapt admiration: they must have felt that the two little Balese were real heroes to risk their lives on the elephants' backs, though only the night before Bodeko had confessed that his biggest problem was trying to keep from falling asleep on long rides.

When the *tembo* reached the crossroads, we headed down the road to Beni and camped that night about twelve miles away, near some big cassia trees where Bella and Venus browsed happily and drank from a small stream. Like any other elephants they needed at least a hundred pounds of food every day to maintain their enormous bulk, since their alimentary tracts were able to digest only 44 per cent of their food, compared with 50 to 70 per cent for sheep, cow and horse. Free *tembo* eat even more, up to five hundred pounds a day: vast meals of tender twigs, leaves and bark, fresh green grass and corn, papayas, mangoes and sugar cane, all of which they wash down with thirty to fifty gallons of water. Sometimes they indulge in vast nips of fermented millet or fruit and then get so drunk that they stagger, giggle, squeal, brawl and even play practical jokes.

Fortunately, there were no fermented mangoes on hand, so Bella and Venus preserved their ladylike decorum, until we were all suddenly inundated with a torrential rain. They gave us a little trouble when the *cornacs* chained them to the nearest tree and rushed to take shelter in my tent. Unfortunately, in their haste, Bodeko and Bokwe had underestimated the strength of the elephants: Bella and Venus casually tore the cassia out of the ground and paced off together, dragging the tree between them. I was horrified, less than five minutes later, when I peered out through the tent flap and saw their vast behinds dwindling over the rainy horizon. We rushed after them and caught up very quickly, the dangling tree cut down on their speed, and marched them back to camp, where Bodeko secured their twenty-five-foot chains to a much stouter cassia.

Then the three of us stripped and sat about in blankets while our clothes dried near my little Coleman stove. We dined on bananas, peanuts and cooked corn-on-the-cob, but the elephants seemed to be trying to eat the entire grove. They made an incredible racket as they bulldozed young saplings, tore at the branches of larger trees and rattled their chains like two exuberant ghosts. It went on for most of the night and I couldn't sleep; then the noise subsided and the silence bothered me more.

I left the tent, fearing another escape, but instead, found the two *tembo* lying on their sides fast asleep amid a fantastic débris of broken branches. Bella slept quietly, except for an occasional switch of her tail, but Venus snored loudly from time to time, sounding like a Land Rover in need of a new head-gasket. Less than two hours later both of them were awake again—and eating—but early next morning I saw Venus dozing on her feet for a moment, eyes closed and trunk hanging down with a slightly curled tip.

It was eighty miles to Beni, and by nightfall our slow, steady march brought us within thirty miles of the town. We camped again (without rain) and by the following afternoon were approaching my old enemy's citadel. I could almost see flags of administrative red tape fluttering in the breeze and kept picturing Vermeulen's drab face turning purple when we arrived. I didn't want to spoil the A.T.'s surprise, so I gave no advance notice of our coming even though Beni is much larger and more heavily populated than Mambasa. By now, I had complete faith in *tembo* and *cornacs* alike and expected no real incidents. I toyed with the idea of mounting Bella myself and parading arrogantly round the shaky little territorial building, but decided against it: the big elephant was used to Bodeko, and an unfamiliar *cornac* might have made her nervous in a crowd.

When Vermeulen emerged, like a helmeted mouse scurrying out of the woodwork, he saw the arch-fiend Hallet driving a Chevy truck at the head of a procession consisting of two large female elephants mounted by two cackling *cornacs* and followed by a vast crowd of shrieking, ecstatic Banande. Just as we passed him Venus paused to leave a fifteen-pound pile of steaming brown spheroids in front of his gate (I could have kissed her!). The A.T. glared at the huge heap of elephant *bwa*, while his *Chef de Poste* collapsed against the side of the building in paroxysms of laughter. We camped that night about twenty-five miles south of Beni, and the next day's march gave us our first real difficulties. The road passed over a series of serpentine hills, with constant changes in altitude, and the *tembo* were very tired when we settled down for the cold, almost alpine night in a little Balunda village. For an elephant-parking fee of fifty francs the local *kapita* let me tether Bella and Venus in a big *matete* thicket; for another fifty he let the *cornacs* and me sleep in one of the warm, smoky huts.

Another day's march through intermittent showers brought us to the Hôtel des Trois Canards near Luofu. We were welcome there, since the owner was a fellow animal-man currently harbouring two young gorillas, three chimpanzees, several baboons and a small fleet of antelope. (There were no ducks.) We slept well, and at 6.30 next morning started out on the most critical phase of the journey: traversing the great Kabasha Escarpment and the Ruindi sector of the Albert National Park with its vast herds of free *tembo*.

The elephants laboured over the eleven-mile escarpment road for the next four hours, while I worried about the effects of possible underfeeding, over-exposure to sunlight and rapid changes in altitude. My predecessor, Hannibal, had lost many of his thirty-seven elephants crossing the Alps and most of the rest when he crossed the Apennines; by the time he got to the Arno he had only a single *tembo* left—an important reason for his failure to take Rome.

We had one close call when a big truck nearly clipped us going round a curve, and I felt tremendous relief when we finally left the escarpment. I let Bella and Venus take a long break at the first good-sized stream we came to; they drank endlessly and sprayed each other with water. Then, when they started to eat, they gave an impressive demonstration of elephant co-operation. The trees here were a little too tall for either of them to reach, so Bella tugged at the springy saplings with her trunk, bending them down far enough for Venus to get at the branches; a few minutes later they reversed the procedure so that Bella could eat.

That scene was very touching, but it came as no great surprise. Several years before, at the Queen Elizabeth National Park in western Uganda, I had witnessed a much more striking example of the elephant's ability to co-operate, his intelligence and warmly gregarious nature. I was sitting in my truck, watching a small herd of *tembo* move through heavy bush about a hundred yards away, when suddenly I saw something that brought me bolt upright behind the wheel: a tantalizing glimpse of a strange beast almost hidden in the thickets of false bamboo. It vanished, and I jumped down from the cab to follow the herd on foot. I had just seen an animal which could not logically exist: an elephant without a trunk.

A trunkless *tembo* would have starved to death within a few days. The proboscidean mouth, relatively small, undershot and set back too far behind the tusks, is useless for gathering food. The trunk is the organ of touch and smell, a nose and an upper lip prolonged into a strong, adroit and extremely sensitive hand. As such, it is never used, either by wild or trained *tembo*, for any really heavy or dangerous work; they fight or haul with the tusks, the feet, the back or the head—never with the precious trunk.

After sneaking from bush to bush in pursuit of the slowly travelling herd, I found myself following an elephant whose trunk ended in a huge scar just below tusk-level. He must have been wounded in a fight with a rival bull whose tusk had probably stabbed through the middle of the trunk; and later, following severe infection, the whole lower part had sloughed off. The scar was obviously several years old, but the elephant was healthy and must have been well fed. I trailed the herd for nearly two hours until they finally settled down and I found what I suspected to be true.

The trunkless *tembo* stood by idly while his companions tore into the trees, then he opened his mouth and every member of the herd moved towards him with trunkfuls of twigs and leaves. Two of them jostled each other, anxious to feed him first, but the rest waited their turns patiently. In all, they brought so much food that he hardly had time to chew it; he gulped furiously until, finally, he closed his mouth tight and shook his mutilated head from side to side. Only then did the other *tembo* move away and at last start to feed themselves.

* * *

Our trip through the Albert National Park, which had really worried me, proved to be almost without incident. We passed several groups of elephants quite close to the road, including some really magnificent bulls, but Bella and Venus seemed absolutely indifferent. Even when we bisected a herd of twenty, clustered on either side of the road, my two tame *tembo* scarcely bothered to look. They were far more interested, towards the end of the day, when we encountered a small band of baboons. The monkeys screamed insults, from a safe distance, and Venus looked very angry. She trumpeted, snorted, sneezed and switched her wiry tail until Bokwe pounded lightly on top of her head with the butt end of his *hawkus*. Bella stood by and watched with amused condescension.

As soon as we crossed the southern edge of the Park I left the *tembo* behind me and drove a few miles farther to the large coffee plantation of an old friend, Georges Pierra. 'You wouldn't mind putting me up for the night?' I asked him. 'Of course not, Jean-Pierre,' my poor victim answered, 'it's such a surprise to see you again!' The real surprise came a little after seven o'clock, when Bella and Venus arrived and I added casually, 'By the way, Georges, I've brought two elephants with me. . . .'

The next day's march brought us within a few miles of Rutshuru, the largest town along our route towards Kisenyi. This time, since a population of two or three thousand natives was involved, I made an advance visit to the territorial office. Unlike his colleagues at Mambasa and Beni, the A.T. of Rutshuru was enthusiastic at the prospect of a small-scale elephant invasion, explaining, 'We have so few diversions here. Your animals will give my people something to talk about for the next six months. I want you to march down our main streets, all three of them, and we'll take you past the hospital and the Mission. I'll see that all the children are released from school, so that no one will miss the fun.'

An A.T. like that was almost as rare as a trunkless elephant.

By the time Bella, Venus, Bodeko, Bokwe, the Chevy and I entered the town less than an hour later, the streets of Rutshuru were lined with wildly cheering natives, the lawn of the Hôpital pour Indigènes was solid with stretchers, wheel-chairs and bandaged but happy patients, and the big Catholic Mission school had disgorged three hundred children. '*Tembo!*' they all saluted, '*Tembo! TEMBO!*' Men in litters sat up and those in wheel-chairs almost stood, forgetting their pain. Children laughed and giggled, women trembled with mock or real terror, and men talked and shouted. Then, at the very height of all this frenzy, the sky opened up and down poured a fantastic torrent of rain. Nobody seemed to mind at all.

I gave Bodeko and Bokwe the two sections of the tent to drape over themselves, and as I drove ahead I heard them clapping their hands under the canvas and singing the Hindu elephant songs of *cornacs* who had died or returned to India decades before. The big ovation had been a tremendous thrill for both of the little Balese, and now they were overflowing with praise for their elephants and themselves.

I raced on to Mugwata, a rolling, tree-clad savannah about twenty miles north of Kisenyi. I had to negotiate with the local Bahunde chief for nearly an hour before I got what I wanted: permission to use about sixty acres of land along the Rutshuru road for a gift-rent of 2,500 francs a month. Then, in a fever of action, I hired thirty-five natives at thirty francs each and put them to work felling trees to build a temporary log kraal for the *tembo* and a small hut for the *cornacs*. When there was time I would build a larger establishment for my new gamekeepers, a stable to shelter the elephants from the sun and a much more extensive fence. Then I would stock the park with rhino, buffalo, antelope, zebra and other large savannah-dwellers.

The last big tree trunk was heaved into place about five hours later, and the hut was just getting its thatched roof of elephant grass when the two enormous grey masses loomed up on the northern horizon. I escorted the *tembo* into their new kraal, installed the *cornacs* in their hut and drove off to Kisenyi.

During the next month, while some thirty acres of land were being fenced at Mugwata, I resumed my customary rôle of art collector, businessman and part-time lion-tamer. Gradually I started to stock the new game park and was able to spend more time with Bella and Venus. I made a few little experiments with the two *tembo*, but found them quite unexciting: there is almost no challenge or danger involved in educating tame elephants, only plodding, repetitive work until they learn, very slowly, what is expected of them; once learned, the action is repeated without error even after long lapses of time. Their memory is remarkable and they are extremely gentle with trusted friends; the man who puts his nose under a trained *tembo*'s massive foot runs less danger than one who merely comes too close to the bars of a lion's cage. A billy-goat or even a militant goose is far more likely to attack, except, of course, when the elephant goes on *musth*.

The so-called 'wild' elephants of the forest and savannah lead a life in some respects even more sedate and respectable than that of their tame colleagues. The herd is almost invariably ruled by a bossy old cow. The intelligent males retreat from the main body to form a separate alliance. The cows have their own club and spend virtually all of their time fussing over the baby elephants, petting them, washing them, attempting to educate them, and occasionally spanking them when they run out of patience. The entire herd is reunited at the swimming hole, generally at sunset, where the bulls show off, the cows splash coyly and the calves misbehave.

Serious arguments occasionally develop. The cows never really fight, but they have been known when vexed to pull each other's tails; bulls sometimes engage in real battles, usually for reasons of prestige, and the contest may end in death for the weaker or less experienced male.

The most striking feature of elephant social life, and the proof of their gentle, good-hearted nature, is their penchant for falling in love. Sex is not enough—they insist on romance as well and their love affairs have certain well-marked phases: a period of allegedly platonic friendship, a courting stage enlivened by necking and petting and, when the female comes into season, a grand-scale orgy culminating in the real thing. Gentle head-butting, roguish lip-pinches and amorously entwined trunks are not uncommon, but only once was I fortunate enough to witness the full flowering—or deflowering—of elephant passion.

It happened early in 1957 while I was travelling with Yoma and Ebu along the southern shore of the Ituri River. We were headed for the pygmy camp near Moguda, and it was almost twilight. Just before we reached the camp I went off on a little side-expedition of my own, attracted by an incredible volume of monkey chatter two hundred yards away from the trail. After fighting my way through vicious thorn bush, I stopped dead in my tracks and ducked behind a huge *khaya* tree with Gallic curiosity.

There was a small clearing about twenty yards away, occupied by two amorous *tembo*. The cow was a *svelte* little creature, about three tons with very short tusks, probably only twelve or thirteen years old and just on the threshold of sexual maturity; the bull was enormous, nearly five tons, with heavy, symmetrical tusks. They were engaged in a ludicrous little ballet; she swayed sinuously round the edge of the clearing, waggling her baggy behind, and when he came closer she whisked her tail, turned and rubbed her body along the length of his and fondled him with her trunk, caressing his ears and flanks and lingering over the lower part of his body. He grunted and lunged, whereupon the diabolic female retreated, only to repeat the whole series of erotic manœuvres.

This went on for the next ten minutes, until the bull was obviously more than ready. Still, I found it difficult to imagine how the two animals could culminate their eight-ton affair, since the cow's sexual apparatus is not located at the site traditional in most female mammals, but lies instead considerably forward, almost in the same position as her partner's equipment. It seemed more reasonable, under the circumstances, for the lady *tembo* to face the issue rather than turn her back on it, but that idea proved wrong. The bull approached from behind in the classic style of male quadrupeds, rearing up on his hind legs and extending his front feet towards the little cow's shoulders. She grunted, squealed and widened her stance. He trumpeted nervously for the next five minutes as he tried to squeeze and manœuvre himself towards the difficult goal; then he sank down on his hind legs, almost to a sitting position and succeeded. The two elephants maintained that strange posture in silence for the next few minutes until, gradually, the bull rose again, assuming an almost vertical stance with his front feet resting on his partner's rear. Afterwards, he moved off and tried to look casual about the whole thing, while the cow flapped her ears and trumpeted softly.

Subsequent procedure generally follows a definite pattern: the mated pair continue their dalliance for several months, until the pregnant lady *tembo* loses interest in romance and grows cold to her lover, who accepts the situation with admirable calm and goes off to find another sweetheart. The cow also searches for a female, but for entirely different reasons: her new girl friend keeps her company for the rest of her twenty- to twenty-two-month pregnancy and helps protect her calf when it is finally born.

The blessed event is usually without complications: twins and breech presentations are both rare. After a short labour the new mother finds herself burdened with a hairy, two-hundred-pound infant three feet tall who can walk in less than an hour. The baby suckles with his mouth, not his short trunk, from the two mammary glands located just behind her forelegs. He is weaned by six months, starts to grow tusks at the age of two, and doubles his three-foot height within his first five years. He generally reaches sexual maturity at twelve, comes on *musth* for the first time at fifteen or sixteen, and is full grown at twenty-five. Then the whole bourgeois cycle begins all over again.

My two lady *tembo* seemed quite typical of their species and I found them to be pleasant, reliable but rather stodgy animals, until Venus became involved in the most unlikely affair since the elephant jumped into bed with the elephant-shrew: she fell in love with a stubborn, irascible and thoroughly dim-witted black rhino.

19

A Timid Rhino and a Sleeping Lion

'Nature teaches beasts to know their friends.'

WILLIAM SHAKESPEARE, *Coriolanus*

MY friend Pierrot was five feet tall and nine feet long, he weighed a ton and a half. He had fringed ears, a tufted tail, a prehensile upper lip, a long horn on his nose and a short one in the middle of his forehead. He usually wore a little brown tick bird on his back and a nervous expression on his front. He belonged to that vanishing race of monumental animals which bear the absurd name *Diceros bicornis*, the 'two-horned two-horn'.

I bought this African black rhino from an officer of the Public Works Department in western Uganda for £160, and he arrived at Mugwata two weeks later, riding backwards in a huge crate on a five-ton truck which we drove into his new kraal, a 250 by 200-foot enclosure. At a slight natural dip in the terrain we started digging. Since we had no heavy equipment the huge animal had to leave the truck under his own power; a rhino distrusts any footing except good solid earth and, unlike a horse or an elephant, will not walk on a ramp.

We dug until the truck's carrying surface was level with the ground, lowered the tailgate, backed up and it then took three men standing on top of the crate to raise the massive sliding door. Instead of bolting to freedom the rhino stood there, swaying his head and peering suspiciously through the open end. I felt like prodding him, but there was no way to predict his reaction.

He thought over the situation for nearly five minutes before he sniffed, snorted and lumbered out of the crate. Then, as soon as he had all four feet on the ground, he went galumphing off

A BUSH BABY IN ACTION

The Author with the only animal he took with him when he left
Africa in August 1960.

THE AUTHOR WITH GENERAL EISENHOWER AND DR F. D. MURPHY, THE CHANCELLOR OF THE
UNIVERSITY OF CALIFORNIA AT LOS ANGELES, WHICH HAS ACQUIRED THE AUTHOR'S
COLLECTION OF CONGOLESE WORKS OF ART. APRIL 1963

towards the other end of the kraal. After thirty yards he heard
the two elephants trumpeting in the next enclosure and veered
towards them, turning his charge only when he got within a
few yards of the fence and heading back towards the truck. This
time he veered at about five yards and thundered off to the far
end of the kraal, where he snorted, growled and pawed at the
earth. We made a quick escape with the truck and closed the
gate behind us.

'*Kifaru yote iko pumbavu!*' Bodeko sighed. 'All rhino are
crazy!'

'He's just nervous and frightened,' I told the frowning little
Mulese. 'He may look tough, but underneath I think he's just
as good-natured as Bella and Venus.'

'Could that thing ever work for its living as an elephant does?'
Bodeko cried indignantly. 'Could he haul logs like Bella or
carry a man on his back?'

'*Tembo* are smarter than people,' Bokwe chimed in,
'but *kifaru*? They are monsters! They kill for the pleasure of
killing!'

I glared at the two *cornacs*. It was bad enough that most
Hollywood films portrayed the rhino as a 'vicious monster'
that rammed his horn into every passing Land Rover, but to
hear the same kind of nonsense from natives was even more
trying. 'Bodeko,' I said ominously, 'I'm going to prove something to you, and to everyone else in Kivu. I'm going to show
you that this animal is really a kind, gentle, misunderstood creature—'

'Oh, *Bwana*,' they protested, 'you must be joking!'

'Give me a few weeks,' I insisted, 'and you'll find out just
how serious I am. I'm not only going to make friends with that
rhino—I'm going to be his *cornac*.'

*   *   *

Until now I had often seen the African 'monster' in action:
black rhino in Katanga, Ethiopia, Sudan and East Africa, and
the rare, almost extinct white rhino in the Congo's Garamba
National Park and South Africa's Umfolosi Reserve. There are
many important differences between them, but colour, ironically,
is not one of them: both animals have the same sombre complexion, a dark slaty grey.

The 'white' rhino, *Ceratotherium simum*, may have acquired
his popular name because he spends his spare time rolling in
light-coloured mud; or it may be a corruption of the Boer

word '*weit*'—'wide'—with reference to his broad, square snout. His upper lip is not prehensile, his front horn is somewhat longer (up to five feet) with a squared-off base, and he has a fleshy hump at the nape of the neck. Above all, he is much bigger: up to six and a half feet tall at the shoulder, fourteen feet long and weighing nearly two tons—the world's second largest land mammal. Yet, for all his size and power, his disposition is relatively placid and he lives in small herds that travel across the open savannahs with bowed heads, cropping the grass like cows.

The 'black' rhino is also a confirmed vegetarian, with no real motive for assaulting his neighbours, but he leads a much more active, varied and nervous life, preferably in acacia thickets near a river or a stream. He forms no herds but trots along by himself, head held high as he browses on leaves, twigs and fruit, except when he lowers his horn to grub for roots or to excavate and inspect any souvenirs he may find in his path, especially those left by his own species. He covers his excrement carefully, like an enormous, wary cat, and suspects the motives of anything he may encounter, a bird, a flower or even a distant tree, and usually decides to fight with it.

This seemingly paranoid behaviour results from a conflict of two basic instincts: the animal is extremely timid but insatiably curious, although his mentality is relatively low. This built-in dilemma drives the frightened, worried rhino into trying to bluff his way through a life consisting of one baffling problem after another. To make matters even worse, the animal is constantly goaded on and frustrated by a severe physical handicap: although his hearing and sense of smell are superb he is abysmally myopic. Some naturalists claim that the rhino cannot see objects more than fifty feet away; personally, I think he is unable to distinguish between a man and a tree at thirty feet and cannot see any object distinctly when it is more than twenty or even fifteen feet away. So he hears and smells a whole world of intriguing phenomena, which he can't see. He wants to investigate, but is afraid. He hesitates and finally decides to approach, but he lacks the elephant's self-assurance, intelligence and calm determination and has the skittish temperament of his distant relative, the horse.

The result of these deep-seated emotional and physiological problems is one of the world's most farcical demonstrations of noise, wasted energy and sheer ineptitude: the notorious rhino 'charge', one of the most glaring examples of which was provided by a typically addle-pated rhino I once watched near the Upemba National Park in Katanga. He was quite busy with a big mouthful of twigs when he heard a frog croaking. He stopped chewing, cocked his head and listened, while several leaves fluttered out of his mouth. Then he trotted anxiously in the direction of the sound, but as he approached, the frog emitted a loud croak and sailed towards him with unwitting defiance. The rhino made an abrupt U-turn and retreated to safety. He sulked for a few minutes before he advanced again, and this time the frog jumped in the opposite direction, making the rhino feel more confident; so he lowered his horn and charged, smashing the frog under his hooves without even knowing it. Afterwards he pawed at the little spot of pulp with a puzzled expression.

What the rhino really needs is a good psycho-analyst, but the only human attention he receives usually comes in the form of bullets or poisoned arrows: the native poacher hunts him for his horn, a curious mass of stiff, compacted hairs which the Indian traders buy at up to five times the price of ivory and ship to the Orient as an alleged aphrodisiac; the more civilized white hunter and his wealthy clients from Texas or Beverly Hills go after him with heavy-calibre rifles, bent on converting the monumental animal into a mounted head and a set of matched rhino-foot ashtrays.

The result of those encounters is usually a dead rhino but occasionally a dead or punctured human. An inexperienced hunter, especially a native, may panic at the sight of the huge animal charging towards him in a cloud of dust, and if he misses with his hasty, badly aimed shot, may throw his weapon aside and try to outdistance the galloping rhino. The noise he makes running away merely gives the animal a chance to correct his aim; then, since the rhino can make forty miles an hour over a short distance, versus twenty-five for the fastest man, he catches up and either gores the retreating hunter with his horn or smashes him under foot.

That was the fate everyone predicted for me when word got around that I intended to tame and train a black rhino. Nobody took my theories seriously, especially since I had indulged my sense of humour by giving the grim-looking behemoth the lilting, light-hearted name of Pierrot.

The first time I stepped into his kraal Pierrot heard me and stared nervously in my direction from his position fifty yards away, worrying about the new problem for several minutes before deciding on the traditional answer: charge. He trotted towards me, accelerating, his head held horizontally. In that position, his already defective vision was blocked by his front horn so, as he launched himself into a furious gallop, he cocked it to the side to get an unobstructed view with at least one small, myopic eye. When he reached a point about ten yards away where he could vaguely distinguish my shape, he adjusted his angle of charge, lowered his horn, and then thundered towards me—a blind, determined juggernaut committed to a certain fixed direction.

I had about half a second to make my decision: if the rhino's angle of attack appeared to be dangerously accurate, I could make a quick sideways jump; if the direction of the charge was comfortably wrong, I could stay where I was, like an arrogant matador with an oversized bull.

That idea was attractive, but Pierrot's aim looked rather too good, so I stepped aside in a hurry and he shot past, majestic but futile, his tasselled tail held high in the air. He decelerated to a stop about ten yards beyond me, turned round and peered anxiously in my direction, trotting back and forth while he tried to locate the target. I moved back about twenty feet. He heard me, snorted indignantly, and charged again.

This time I didn't have to move: Pierrot misjudged his angle badly and missed me by a wide margin. His third attempt was even worse, and after five or six failures he stopped charging and instead, frustrated and confused, he began brooding over his troubles, snorting, growling, shaking his head and pawing at the ground. I watched quietly for about ten minutes and then gave him a broad hint by jumping up and down and hooting like a baboon.

Pierrot raised his head, started to trot, spotted a small cassia tree at a 90-degree angle, veered, galloped towards it under full steam, veered again and wound up fifty yards to my left. He spent the next ten minutes trotting back and forth with his head cocked, trying to find me. He was obviously concentrating very hard, but wasted his energy on two more small trees and a big clump of thorn bush; then, when he finally spotted me, he charged, missed, charged again and, of course, missed by an even wider margin.

This last fiasco disgusted him, so he sat down, grunting un-happily. That was the moment I had been waiting for: I charged the rhino, yelling like a Masai. Appalled, Pierrot stared at me until I got to within twenty feet, when he fled in terror to the far end of the kraal. He had been outfaced and outbluffed—and he knew it.

During the next week I drove up from Kisenyi several times and repeated the whole ludicrous game. I wore the same clothing and tried to strike the same pose whenever the rhino came close enough to see me clearly, hoping to make myself familiar to him as a specific, unvarying image. I never charged him again or tried to provoke him after the first day's experiments, for I felt certain that if I could put his fears to rest, he would be eager to satisfy his vast curiosity and abandon his manic, aggressive behaviour.

Pierrot continued to charge—and to miss—and to try again. I dodged or stood my ground for three days, approaching as closely as I dared to let him get a good look at his supposed enemy. Then, towards the end of our fourth session, the first signs of understanding and confidence appeared: I moved to a point within ten feet of his head and he neither charged nor retreated but watched me quietly. After a moment, he started to worry again and backed off in confusion. I tried to reassure him by making a short, noisy retreat; this brought him back, but he didn't charge: I was well within his range of clear vision and was becoming a familiar if somewhat baffling phenomenon.

Encouraged, I took a step towards the rhino, he took a step backwards. So I took a step to the rear, and Pierrot moved forward one step. That peculiar little minuet continued for the rest of the afternoon, and with variants for the next three weeks. We must have looked incredibly foolish, but we were gradually learning to relax and get acquainted with each other while acquiring the necessary feelings of equality and mutual confidence.

During that period rumours of my atrocious death began to circulate throughout Kivu, Rwanda and western Uganda. Ironically, while all the talk had me trampled to a pudding under the rhino's hoofs, my closest call came in the arena at Kisenyi when I slipped on a small piece of meat and skidded past my old friend Simba, who was so startled that he swiped at me and just missed removing half my face.

With Pierrot the big breakthrough came about a month after his taming period had started. I was standing a couple of feet away from his head, when he suddenly turned with his massive front horn towards me. I didn't move an inch, feeling certain that it was psychologically impossible for Pierrot to attack now that he knew me and no longer had any reason to worry.

The great leathery head moved towards me and the rhino rubbed his cheek along my arm like a giant house-cat. I returned his gesture by giving him a few hearty slaps on the neck. I swung my body round to do so and Pierrot nudged me in the ribs with his front horn; I felt a trifle uneasy, but he rubbed it along my body without any menace. After that little exchange, I took a dozen steps away from him, curious to see his reaction. Pierrot didn't move. Then he decided to follow and came towards me with a slow but accelerating trot. I was in the direct line of charge, but I stood my ground as the enormous animal advanced and then ground to a halt, his big horn less than two feet from my chest.

I let out my breath, gave him another friendly slap on the neck and led him on a long walk around the edge of the kraal. I kept a position three-quarters forward so that he could see me without any trouble; he followed obediently, kept step with me, turned whenever I turned and surprised me from time to time with a playful nudge in the back.

Our friendship started that day, but we became real pals about a week later when I taught him how to play ball. The game was extremely simple: we used a three-foot sphere of cattle hide stuffed with straw which I bowled to Pierrot with my hand; he bowled it back with his horn. He thought it was thrilling, but I got more exercise than he did: the rhino had enthusiasm and power but very poor aim.

His other physical handicaps made it difficult to teach him more sophisticated games: he was too near-sighted, unable to jump or even to scramble over any kind of barrier, and he lacked grasping equipment comparable to an elephant's trunk or even a lion's adroit paw. Riding Pierrot was a far more practical project, but it wasn't as easy as I had thought to become a real rhino *cornac*.

The first time I jumped on to his back Pierrot shuddered, heaved and stamped angrily. He was quite unable to buck like a bronco but he could have rolled on the ground had he wanted to hurt me. He relapsed instead into cold, motionless disapproval after the brief storm of protest had failed. I sat on his wide, extremely uncomfortable back for at least five minutes while he waited for me to dismount. Then, experimentally, I kicked him in the ribs, hoping to make him go. He went— like an express train—and I bounced several times before finally coming to rest in the middle of the thorn bush.

The next time, I put a rope halter around his neck and kicked him a little more gently. He broke into a fast trot instead of a gallop and I managed to stay on board by clutching at the rope, but there was absolutely no way to make him turn, speed up, slow down or stop, although I tried every variety of nudge, gesture and verbal command during the next few sessions of rhino *dressage*. Finally, I had to accept the fact that while Pierrot might let me sit on his back, he was simply not intelligent enough to take directions like a horse or an elephant. So, with a joint feeling of relief, we went back to our ball games.

By now there was no trace of fear or anxiety in our friendship. Pierrot was probably the happiest and most relaxed black rhino in Africa, and consequently one of the fattest. Both the great bales of food that the keepers brought him and the relative tranquillity of his captive life were reflected in his physical appearance: the folds of flesh on his sides filled out and disappeared, so that from a distance he looked almost like a white rhino. He was now a kind, sweet, good-natured animal—as predicted—and, of course, he was starting to bore me. Still, I felt guilty about leaving Pierrot alone, now that he had developed a taste for companionship, and worried about him until I had a sudden inspiration—two potential friends named Bella and Venus.

According to popular legend, both rhino and elephant are not only 'pachyderms' but born enemies who attack each other on sight. According to fact, they are two large, totally unrelated animals who generally avoid any real contact. Here at Mugwata they were quartered in adjacent kraals, and Pierrot and Venus sometimes exchanged insults over the back fence. The rhino's antagonism was based, as usual, on bad eyesight, timid curiosity and chronic fear; as for Venus, she was just having fun: no elephant has an inferiority complex, or needs one.

The moment I got the idea I played ball with Pierrot until he was completely relaxed and happy. Then I opened the big double gates between the two kraals and walked towards Bella and Venus. Pierrot trotted after me obediently and the elephants, intrigued, started towards us. As soon as we all were within ten yards of each other and the rhino was able to see them clearly, he stopped dead and snorted anxiously. Bella and Venus stopped also and peered down, much more calmly.

I gave Pierrot a friendly slap on the neck and moved forward, waiting for him to follow. He pawed at the ground and for a moment I thought he was getting ready to attack. If he did, I had a quick answer: I would jump between the charging rhino and the two elephants. I knew that Pierrot would never deliberately hurt me; we were very different animals, perissodactyl and primate—an immense antediluvian horse and a rascally bearded ape—but we were friends and I was ready to trust him with my life.

This time I didn't have to: Pierrot responded to a few more slaps on the neck and a little sweet talk, and calmed down enough to follow me all the way to the waiting elephants. The gap closed, the three enormous animals met: Bella edged forward and shook her great head, unfurling her ears like two wrinkled grey sails; Venus raised her trunk, trumpeting shrilly; Pierrot sniffed, and watched them with a worried expression, but stood his ground without wavering.

For about five minutes they eyed each other nervously until I escorted the rhino back to his kraal. Next day there was another meeting and even less friction. On the third occasion, however, they had some kind of quiet, mysterious disagreement; Pierrot moved off in a huff to brood about it, and I had to play ball with him for half an hour before he finally relaxed. The next two rhino-elephant dates went off without a hitch, and I felt so reassured that I let the animals meet without benefit of chaperon. Nothing changed: they lumbered around the kraal together like a prehistoric gigolo with two elderly dowagers, and when the *cornacs* brought the elephants' bundles of fodder, Pierrot hovered beneath them like an enormous pigeon snatching at crumbs.

From then on, the rhino was never alone. The big double gates remained open between the adjacent kraals and the three animals moved from one to the other according to their whims, their unique community life unflawed by any discordant emotions—until Venus began growing a trifle too fond of Pierrot.

Gradually the smaller, more emotional elephant paired off with the rhino, leaving Bella shocked and extremely unhappy. The big *tembo* watched jealously as Venus and Pierrot strolled around the two kraals; sometimes she shouldered her way between them, but they ignored her and went off together again. Occasionally Venus played with Pierrot's short tail, and he responded by scratching his back on her legs, at which Bella looked as though she had just been stricken with anthrax.

When the rhino accompanied the two *tembo* to the nearby stream for the first time, there was a minor incident. Until now, the *cornacs* had always brought him water, but since the flowering of his elephant love affair, Bodeko and Bokwe found it almost impossible to leave Pierrot behind, so they let him follow. He showed absolutely no interest in bolting for freedom and was extremely polite and well behaved—until Venus playfully gave him an unexpected shower with a trunkful of water. The indignant rhino raced away down the river-bank, but he was back in a few minutes. According to Bodeko the *tembo* never tried it again.

After two or three weeks their romance began to lose the charm of novelty and Venus drifted back to an overjoyed Bella; from that time on, the reconciled elephants shared the henpecked rhino. This sedate, platonic *ménage à trois* astonished all visitors to the Mugwata game park. The other animals were beautiful—my two Grant's zebra, a melancholy-looking gnu, a red forest buffalo and the mixed group of young antelope: four cob and four bushbuck, one pongo, two waterbuck, seven small forest *mboloko*, and an eland from Kenya—but people usually made a quick survey, and then went back to marvel at the elephant-rhino trio.

I found myself spending less and less time at Mugwata. I went up north for a long visit to the pygmies and soon afterwards launched four branches of my business at Goma, Usumbura, Elisabethville and Stanleyville, all relatively respectable establishments—unlike the original Central Africa Curio Shop —which ran like lucrative clockwork.

In Kisenyi, I was having a good deal of trouble with the animals. The run of bad luck began when a prowling dog sneaked into the back yard and dug under the wire into the big aviary, where he killed the twelve hyraxes with casual zest, cracking their necks and tossing the bodies aside without bothering to eat them; I found the corpses and the footprints in the morning. A few days later, for no apparent reason, the big silver monkey attacked Mugerero, the animal keeper, biting a huge chunk out of his calf, so that the man had to spend nearly six weeks in hospital.

A new animal, Queen Sirikit, a beautiful cheetah from Kenya, figured in a distressing episode. I had tied her in the far corner of the back yard on a twelve-foot chain and cautioned all my people not to take any liberties with this rangy, dog-like cat. She was basically docile and good-natured but, like all cheetahs, nervous and very wary with strangers.

The old Muhutu who delivered our vegetables ignored my repeated warnings, and when he tried to play with Sirikit, as I did, she attacked him savagely. The man was bitten in a dozen places and nearly died of his wounds. I paid his hospital bills—and quite a bit extra—but he complained to Kisenyi's Chief of Police. I received a court order to put the cheetah to death.

I killed my elegant Sirikit with a bullet through the temple. Her death was almost as senseless as the medieval trials and executions of suspected animal 'witches' and 'murderers'. Perhaps when men stop killing each other with the latest, most sophisticated scientific discoveries, they may become civilized enough to understand and forgive the instinctive behaviour of an unsophisticated animal.

The day after Mugerero was released from the hospital in Kisenyi, I became a patient at the Mission of Rwanguba near Rutshuru. Animals had nothing to do with it: it was simply the chronic, acute pain in the stump of my right arm which had continued unabated for the past four years.

Dr. Robert B. Salter, a leading orthopaedic surgeon from the University of Toronto, had passed through Kisenyi during a lecture tour for medical missionaries. He examined my arm and recommended another operation. So, early in December 1959, I climbed into my new Chevrolet Impala and drove to the Rwanguba Mission where an American surgeon, Dr. Donald Nelson, reamputated my right wrist; he took another half-inch off the distal end of the ulna, excised several small neuromas and freed the forearm flexor muscles from the scar at the end of the stump.

The post-operative pain was almost as great as I had suffered when I originally lost the hand, but I anticipated a relatively comfortable future. Unfortunately, that proved to be an illusion and the pain continued almost unchanged, apparently the result of a volatile, highly strung nervous system with a permanent short circuit at one end.

I left the Rwanguba Mission after ten days and drove back to Kisenyi with a heavily bandaged forearm. I had to take it easy for a while, so I decided to catch up on office work, reorganize my book-keeping system and take a complete stock inventory. I was shocked to discover a small but appreciable discrepancy between the cash receipts and the amount of merchandise sold. Since the pilfering was of a specialized nature—only leather wallets, coin purses and key cases had been taken—shoplifting seemed unlikely, and I reached the sad conclusion that it must be an inside job.

I suspected the *moke* who did the dusting and asked Kamende, André and Serukenyinkware to keep a sharp eye on him. None of them saw anything out of the way, but the tall Tutsi drummer intelligently volunteered to make inquiries in the *belge*—the native quarter of Kisenyi—to find out if anyone had been selling stolen goods, so I gave him two days off for his detective work. The only result was that he got monumentally drunk in half a dozen native bars.

The mysterious pilfering continued and I grew thoroughly exasperated. Kamende, the 'witch doctor', was wonderfully sympathetic and tried to solve the mystery for me with his *imbehe y'inzuzi*; he threw the black metal triangles, the white bones and the solitary red wooden chip on a long, concave divining board with a look of demonic concentration, and produced an answer which at the time made no sense to me, 'Look under a white cloth to discover the secret.'

The first real clue came when my ivory carver told me excitedly that a friend of his had just met a Batwa-Bahutu half-breed sporting a new, heavily-embossed red-leather wallet, the type I imported from Nigeria. I made a quick trip to the *belge*, accompanied by two *polici*, and located the shack my ivorist had described. When we arrived the indignant man protested that he had bought the stolen item—from a tall, skinny Mututsi who beat the drum in front of a local curio store.

I gaped at him stupidly for a moment and winced as I remembered how my Tutsi Sherlock Holmes had gone off to 'investigate' the crimes. Serukenyinkware had undoubtedly used the opportunity to sell more stolen merchandise and get drunk on the proceeds.

Next day I set a trap for him: as soon as he showed up for work, I suggested an afternoon trip to the *belge* for further research into the mystery. He agreed gravely, and I spent the rest of the morning in the back yard, leaving the shop unattended except when he beat on the big drum. Then, about one o'clock, when I sent him off on his sleuthing mission, Serukenyinkware sailed down the street with his customary majestic arrogance, only to be stopped by the two *polici* I had stationed at the corner.

They asked for his ID book and announced their intention of frisking him for concealed weapons, a frequent and very necessary procedure among the intrigue-ridden natives of Rwanda. The tall Mututsi glared down with scandalized outrage while the stocky blue-clad Bahutu prodded at his toga. In the pockets of the *kapitula* which he wore underneath they found two brand-new wallets—hidden underneath the immaculate white cloth, just as Kamende had prophesied.

When they questioned him, Serukenyinkware had the calm audacity to insist that I had given him the merchandise. In reply the *polici* marched him back to the store where I contradicted this desperate explanation. The tall drummer never said a word to me, but for the first time in our long acquaintance he lowered his eyes in defeat, for he knew that he had lost face among all the Batutsi, not for having stolen but for having been caught. Then he straightened his shoulders and—as arrogant and noble-looking as ever—strode off to prison between the two little *polici* while Kamende watched with a small satisfied smile.

Old Tureko beat the big drum very badly for three or four days until I found a replacement. The new recruit was a far less typical Mututsi, but seemed honest and was much easier to handle. Still, I missed Serukenyinkware.

*   *   *

A few weeks later I was back in the arena again, working with Simba. By now he was not only the best-educated lion in Central Africa but one of the largest, close to 500 pound and much more powerful than his free, savannah-dwelling colleagues (whose weight rarely exceeds 400). He was big, clever and as completely tame as any born predator can ever be, and therein lay my real danger; if I ever let myself forget, even for a moment, the feline instincts, moods and capabilities behind that docile façade, I was headed for real trouble.

After the very sporadic work-outs I'd given the lion during the past few months, he was balky and slow with most of his tricks. Working steadily, I re-educated him patiently, spending nearly two months perfecting his performance. As time passed I made certain psychological experiments which elicited very strange reactions. Certain tactics seemed to make Simba feel uncomfortable, almost embarrassed: any monotonous move-ment, such as swaying my head from side to side very slowly, made him wince, draw back and usually close his eyes; some-times he looked almost dazed and reminded me, irresistibly, of a human being entering the very first stage of hypnosis.

I had never seen, heard or read of anyone having hypnotized a lion, although I have since learned that a Florentine psycholo-gist, Dr. Enrico Ceccarelli, once succeeded in performing this feat in a circus somewhere in the south of France. The process implies far more than keeping the lion at a distance by a fixed, resolute stare: it means leading him into a deep trance during which the unconscious animal is subject to the hypnotist's control.

This would be far more difficult than hypnotizing a man, as I had often done in the past. With a human being, I could use verbal suggestion to subdue the reasoning or critical faculty and approach progressively the subconscious mind of a co-operative subject. With a lion, that method was obviously useless. I could spend days explaining to Simba that his eyelids were getting heavy or his paws were falling asleep, but as far as he was concerned I might just as well have been reading La Fontaine's fables or discussing banana prices.

With an animal, a combined psychological-physiological approach would have to replace suggestion. In other words, I would have to play upon the weaknesses of Simba's nervous and muscular systems to induce a trance, much more complicated than putting a bird or a reptile to sleep. Turning a chicken or a lizard on his back and stroking the underpart of his body produces a superficial locomotor ataxia resulting from the direct tactile stimulation of certain nerves. I had no intention of stretching my lion out on his back with all four feet in the air and massaging him into insensibility—even if he would have permitted it. Instead, I intended to lay siege progressively to all his muscles and nerves with a series of strange sights, sounds and motions.

I made some tentative experiments, trying to determine which were the most effective attitudes and gestures. I succeeded in producing definite indications of fear, malaise and pronounced drowsiness. That encouraged me to continue, and I kept studying different techniques until the beginning of May, when I decided to make the first real test of my theories.

I issued a general invitation and on the afternoon in question I had nearly two hundred people, twenty-five of them sceptical Europeans, waiting to witness my début as the animal world's amateur Rasputin. I began to wish that I had proved my thesis privately before risking a public demonstration.

Everyone gasped when I stepped through the iron gate and Simba rushed up to bite me gently on the knee—his usual way of greeting me, which he followed with a long, luxurious rub against my legs. 'Simba!' I shouted, staring at the big lion coldly to show him that, for once, I didn't want to play games. He sat down and stared back, interested by my unusual attitude.

I gestured and he jumped on to his four-foot pedestal. Then I sent him down again, and up—and down—until, after twenty leaps, he was so disgusted that he sprawled out on his belly. Immediately, I sat down on his back, took a scissors hold on his hind legs with my own, and wrapped my arms around his neck. While the amazed spectators watched we rolled together on the ground just as the leopard and I had in the Watalinga.

Simba outweighed the spotted cat by more than four to one, and, of course, I could never have held him if he wanted to struggle. By now, however, he was so thoroughly convinced of my mastery that he didn't contest it. So, after tiring him out with the hectic jumping routine, I used the close physical contact to reinforce the illusion of my superior strength and authority.

As we finished rolling, I jumped to the side but kept my hold on his neck until I forced him to sit. Then, standing a little to his left, I moved my hand in a circle over his nose. He stared uneasily and rotated his head, trying to catch my hand. I continued, and whenever his interest started to lag, I moved the hand closer and dangled the fingers enticingly. His head turned round and round slowly, a movement entirely new to him and obviously very fatiguing. After ten minutes of it he was dazed and pathetically bewildered.

Now I squatted down about three feet away so that our faces were level. I stared into his eyes while I inched towards him, still squatting, with infinitesimal movements of my feet; at the end of half an hour, my face was about six inches from his and he was blinking every seven or eight seconds. I kept staring at him from that position for another half-hour, moving my head from side to side like a Balinese dancer. He disliked it intensely—who wouldn't?—and several times closed his eyes for four or five seconds. Then he decided that he'd had enough and lay down on his belly, his paws stretched out in front of him.

I lay down facing him, supporting my chin on my fist, and kept gazing at him steadily. 'S-e-e-mba,' I said softly, 'you're a small, tiny, little lion!' He peered at me uncertainly. 'Little Simba!' I repeated. 'Tiny little lion!' He started to growl, annoyed by my sneering tone, and I slapped him gently on the nose—the first time I had ever struck him. He flinched and closed his eyes, obviously afraid. Taking advantage of that temporary fear, I raised my hand again to threaten his nose. He opened his eyes, saw it, and closed them again very quickly lest I give him another little tap. That happened several times, and his eyes remained closed for longer and longer intervals.

I began to feel that he was definitely headed towards a true trance, but I was growing increasingly nervous about all the noise in the background: the native spectators were getting bored with the long-drawn-out procedure and chattering more and more loudly. '*Tulia!*' I yelled at them—an angry Swahili 'Shut up!'

Unfortunately, the word affected the lion more than the natives. He started to pull his front paws back, trying to sit up, and I menaced him with my hand to keep him down on his belly. Then, after experimenting with several different techniques, I returned to my Balinese posturings, moving my head back and forth while reciting some unfamiliar rhythmical words —several hundred resounding alexandrines from Corneille's *Cinna*. Now Simba not only closed his eyes but squeezed them shut so tightly that the surrounding skin was a network of wrinkles.

'Little lion,' I repeated endlessly in varying tones, and his eyes remained shut for more than five minutes. Then, very slowly, they opened. I leaned forward a few inches and touched his nose with my own. It was almost like pressing a switch: immediately, his head drooped and the exhausted animal lay down heavily on his side.

That provoked incredible excitement in the audience and once again I had to ask them to keep quiet. 'The lion isn't really asleep yet,' I tried to explain and Simba, whom the conversation had jarred out of his incipient trance, proceeded to prove it; he staggered to his feet. I was outraged at the prospect of losing more than an hour of hard work, so I grabbed him by the mane and tipped him over sideways. In normal circumstances I couldn't have done that with five hundred pounds of lion, but Simba was still in a daze: I took him off-balance and he fell back without even trying to struggle. I spent another ten minutes trying to re-create the previous atmosphere. Finally, the lion stared at me with a dead, glazed expression until, like a fading light, his eyes closed very slowly and his mouth sagged open. The big tongue lolled out from between his front teeth, he twitched once or twice and he lay there as though he were dead.

I stood up slowly, motioned for silence with a finger held to my lips and then pulled Simba's tail—something which no lion will normally tolerate. There was no reaction. I walked to his head, took off my shoe, and put it into his mouth which was dribbling saliva. Again there was no reaction. I removed the shoe and after making a big gesture to the crowd, put my hand all the way into the lion's mouth. Nothing happened.

For a final test I asked André for a piece of fresh bloody meat

which I held next to the lion's nose and then put into his mouth
with no reaction. I pulled at the meat slowly and removed it,
but the next time I tried it and pushed his lower jaw shut, I felt
a slight tension as I took the meat away. His head lifted a little,
his back legs started to twitch, and I knew that the sleeping lion
was starting to come out of his trance.

'Simba!' I called to him. His eyes opened slowly and he
stared at me with a stupefied expression. 'SIMBA!' I roared.
He jumped to his feet, completely awake. I petted him and gave
him the piece of meat he had ignored a few minutes before. He
took it very carefully from my hand, to avoid hurting me, and
while he was gulping the bloody reward, I stepped out of the
arena.

Naturally, the natives called it *mayele*.

*   *   *

In June 1960 I received the Gold Medal of the Royal Order
of the Lion from King Baudouin of the Belgians, not for lion-
taming but 'as a testimony of gratitude for services rendered to
his country'. A Silver Star of Service accompanied it. The two
decorations were a reward for my ten years as a bush agronomist
and sociologist for the Belgian Colonial Government, during
which I had worked with seventeen different tribes representing
more than 650,000 natives.

In some respects my life in Africa had been most unusual, but
in many others I was typical of thousands of my countrymen:
Belgian doctors, nurses, social workers, missionaries, technicians, administrators. Most of us had come to the Congo very
young and full of altruism. We lost our illusions quickly enough,
yet we had continued to struggle against the indifference,
lethargy, ignorance and superstition of some 13,000,000 Congolese natives. Our goal had been to heal them, feed them, educate them, and somehow to build a self-supporting nation here
where disease, sorcery, inter-tribal warfare, cannibalism, human
sacrifice and the scourge of the Arab slavers had decimated
nearly a million square miles of tropical wilderness.

Now it was June 1960—eighty-four years since Leopold II had
first conceived the vast dream of *l'œuvre civilisatrice* and gone
on to form the old Congo Free State with the aid of Henry
Morton Stanley; sixty-six years since Baron Francis Dhanis had
driven the Arab slavers out of Maniema, and fifty-two years
since the Belgian Congo had officially come into being.

It was June 1960, and within a month the Congo, Belgian no

longer, would slide back a hundred years into the crude, abysmal savagery of Stanley's 'Darkest Africa'. All its people would suffer, but the black man would lose far more than the white. Ironically, paradoxically, tragically, he would lose it in the name of 'freedom'.

20

'Dépendance!'

' "Hallet will be the last to leave", was the general opinion, for he is held in high esteem by all natives who know him.—"and he is widely known. "When he leaves—then we know the Congo is finished", they have been saying. Now Hallet has left.'

African Life, Vol. IV, No. 1 (1960)

'Dépendance!' they shouted at me, a few miles south of Mugwata. *'Dépendance!'* A stone bounced off the rear end of my Chevrolet Impala, and I pulled over to the side of the road to confront the small group of sullen-looking Bahunde, who were still screaming the Congo's version of *uhuru* and, like most of the natives, failing to pronounce the first syllable of the French word *indépendance*. Thus, the people who had been taught by their new leaders to demand freedom were raising a wild outcry for the opposite.

I got out of my car, the four Bahunde retreated and stopped about twenty yards away, staring defiantly at me. 'What do you think you're shouting about?' I called.

'Dépendance!' they echoed, and one man stepped forward to expand on the theme. 'We want our freedom!' he said angrily. 'We're tired of waiting!'

'You've got it. You've been "free" for more than a week—'

'No! When we are really free, things will be different. We'll have big cars and lots of money, we'll live in the white man's houses and we'll all have white wives. They promised us that— and we want our freedom!'

'It's been eight days now,' I said patiently, 'since the Congo received its independence from Belgium. That means you're as "free" as you'll ever be—to build your own country by your own work. Nobody gets cars or big houses without paying for them, whether his skin is black or white. People have to *work* to get what they want, and go on working to keep it. What are your wives and children going to eat while you waste your time on the road, shouting at cars? Go back to your fields and work, so you can feed your families!'

They walked away, smouldering with rage, and I returned to the car. It was only fifteen miles to Kisenyi, but as I drove south I must have heard the shout of '*Dépendance!*' a dozen times.

*   *   *

Although that same slogan was ringing across the entire Congo, most of the natives had no understanding of the new 'nationalism'. Nearly ten million people—75 per cent of the total population—still thought of themselves as Baluba, Balega, Bena Lulua or any one of more than six hundred separate and entirely distinct tribes, and followed their traditional way of life in the bush villages. They didn't even know that a new entity called the Republic of the Congo existed, just as they had never really been aware of the Belgian Congo or the old Congo Free State. They recognized their villages or tribes and distrusted, feared, hated or despised everyone else. 'Nationalism' was about as comprehensible to them as chamber music or nuclear physics.

The real trouble had begun, not so much with these simple people of the bush, as among the Congo's 1,750 *évolués* and 38,500 semi-*évolués*, most of whom lived strictly non-tribal lives in the large towns and cities where 25 per cent of the Congo's black population was concentrated. Their chronic dissatisfaction had been stirred up to a fever pitch by Communist-indoctrinated native politicians, and their troubled mood was communicated to the hordes of unemployed, unskilled people who had left their homes in the bush to come to the big cities.

'Those dirty *wazungu* have sucked our country dry!' the *évolués* theorized. 'If we can get rid of the white men, then *we* can take over the soft jobs, the titles, the prestige and the big money!' That was the constant whispered refrain in government offices, where native typists and clerks dreamed of becoming Provincial Governors; in mines and factories, where semi-skilled technicians decided that they were all frustrated executives; and in the barracks of the Force Publique, where the native soldiers all wanted to become officers. Why not? Their leaders had promised that *everyone* would get what he wanted when the Congo won its freedom.

An army of generals but no privates . . . a nation of white-collar executives but no clerks or technicians . . . a world of wealth, pomp and prestige but not the need for any degrading manual labour. That was the new 'free' Congo the *évolués* pictured: a comic-opera Utopia where they were going to live like Ruritarian kings on the vast natural treasures which the Belgians had allegedly been stealing from them for the past half-century.

It was pure fantasy, but they managed somehow to believe it and to ignore the economic realities by which the Belgians had built their country and maintained it in a state of relative prosperity.

'Without a railway from Matadi to the Pool, the Congo isn't worth a penny!' Stanley had said, concerning the route to Léopoldville. It had taken 132 Belgian lives, 9 years (from 1889 to 1898) and 60,000,000 francs to build that first 260-mile 'Cataracts Railway' round the 32 murderous stretches of white water by which the Congo River descends furiously to the sea. The steep, tortuous route had presented fantastic difficulties: from the Léopold Ravine to the Mpozo bridge, a distance of four miles, the track bed had to be carved through solid rock in terraces, along the side of the cliffs; the notorious ascent of the Pallaballa Mountain, with grades of 150 feet per mile, was so nearly impossible that building the 26-mile stretch actually took four years. Still, the Belgians refused to give up, and pushed on until they completed one of the great engineering feats on the African continent.

Now, half a century later, the Congo had some three thousand miles of railways, ninety thousand miles of highways and roads, twenty thousand miles of inland airways, forty-five thousand business establishments and factories, twenty-seven thousand schools and two full-scale universities, five hundred hospitals and two thousand rural dispensaries. Equally important were ninety thousand resident Belgians, whose technical, administrative and other skills kept the whole complex machine running.

Contrary to popular belief, Belgium's profits from the Congo were relatively small: a complete loss of her Congolese interests would have an impact on Belgium's economy amounting to less than 5 per cent of her gross national product. The Plan Décennal, inaugurated in 1952 for the long-term economic and social development of the Congo, was budgeted at £350 million;

earlier the expense of heavy capital installations and grand-scale social programmes had been almost incalculable.

There were, of course, strong economic ties between the two countries, but Belgium's emotional attachment to the Congo was even stronger. The hard-working people of this small European nation, the most heavily industrialized and overpopulated on the Continent, doted on their vast, sprawling, exotic and wildly beautiful Congo. Ever since the days of Leopold II, Belgium's great dream, challenge, adventure, obsessive hobby and perpetual excitement, main topic of conversation and chief source of controversy had been its 'work of civilization'.

As a result, according to 1958 UNESCO surveys, the thirteen million natives of the Belgian Congo had the highest wage scale, the finest social services and the best standard of living in Central Africa. Half the native babies were born in hospitals, 35 to 40 per cent. of the adults were literate (as compared to about 10 per cent. in neighbouring French and British colonies), and 14 per cent. of the total population—nearly 1,800,000 natives— were enrolled in the schools, a much higher percentage than in Egypt and seven times greater than in Ethiopia and the Sudan.

Those astonishing statistics should silence the repeated charge that Belgium 'hadn't educated the natives'. The figures are even more remarkable considering that the entire life-span of the colony called the Belgian Congo covered only fifty-two years, 1908 to 1960. At least ten of those years were lost because of two World Wars, during which Belgium was occupied and the progress of the Congo greatly impeded. In all, the Belgians had a little more than forty years in which to work, but they had succeeded in creating a vast, constantly broadening educational pyramid with 1,700,000 school children at the base, 60,000 high-school and college-level natives towards the centre and, at the peak, more than 600 working towards university degrees at the Lovanium University of Léopoldville and the State University in Elisabethville.

Yet the Belgians have been criticized because they concentrated on elementary-school education, to keep some kind of reasonable balance within the native population and produced 'only thirty-one Congolese with university diplomas'. What critics fail to realize is the fallacy of attempting to create a large class of intellectuals whose lives will have no relevance to those of their own people and can provide no answer to their country's problems. The Congo, a vast, only partially developed expanse of land in the heart of Black Africa, derived 33 per cent. of its gross national product from agriculture and 25 per cent. from mining; it needed technicians, artisans, farmers—not politicians, philosophers or poets. No country in the world, African or otherwise, can afford to support a heavy intellectual upper crust before it develops a solid technical centre to keep its industry and agriculture going.

From that point of view the Belgians had actually given the natives too much education instead of too little. There had been an unrealistic emphasis on classical learning, due to the influence of the Missions, and insufficient vocational training; thus the *évolués* and the educated population in general had developed an even stronger distaste for any really productive labour. As soon as the average Congolese learned how to read and write, any other tool except the fountain pen became a symbol of primitive servitude and he fled to the big cities, looking for a desk job, and afforded the people of his own village or tribe no benefit from his education.

That was really the Congo's biggest human problem; it was almost impossible to exert any control over the educated natives' arrogant discrimination towards their own people. If they were criticized in that respect, or any other, the unhappy, supersensitive *évolués* complained that they were being persecuted by the white men. Now, as one might have expected, these same *évolués* were leading the cry for freedom, but the freedom they demanded was the right to dominate and exploit their unsophisticated brothers. They had no real desire to alter the established system; instead, they simply wanted to seize control and run it for their own narrow profit, unlike the Belgians who had always tried to aid *all* the Congolese people.

Why hadn't the Belgians prepared the natives for responsible self-government by granting political responsibility and offices to the *évolués*? The answer to that question is terribly simple: there hadn't been enough time.

The Congo has often been compared, unfavourably and most unfairly, with certain former British colonies in which the natives had more political preparation for their new rôles and the transition from colonial status to independence went much more smoothly. Ghana, above all, has been cited as a striking example of enlightened British policy which the Belgians might well have followed. What escapes most is the elementary fact that the Congo was just about the last part of Africa to be discovered, explored, tamed and, to some extent, civilized, while the 'progressive' nations of West Africa had been in contact with European civilization for five hundred years. Ghana, the old Gold Coast, was occupied by the Portuguese in 1481, invaded by the English in 1553, taken over by the Dutch in 1642 and progressively assimilated by the English until the Crown Colony was created in 1874.

With those five centuries of white occupation and influence, the natives of Ghana were culturally and economically more advanced than the Congolese; yet they displayed a tragic innocence when they tried to play politics: in Mr. Nkrumah they have saddled themselves with a self-seeking, pretentious dictator who likes to be called *Osagyefo*—the 'Saviour'—and a government which is, according to young Winston Spencer Churchill, on the 'march towards totalitarian socialism'.

That was the legacy of the political preparation which the British had given to the relatively civilized natives of Ghana. The Belgians had had only a tenth of that five-hundred-year span to work with in a territory ten times larger than Ghana: nearly a million square miles of superstition and disease, inhabited by a profoundly divided population of more than six hundred warring tribes. During the Congo's forty years of effective development as a Belgian colony, medical, social, economic and educational programmes were given priority and political preparation had to wait: you can't teach a man the principles of constitutional government if he is wasting away with malaria, sleeping sickness or yellow fever, starving to death during an unexpected dry season or plotting to murder and eat his enemies in the next village.

As the base of the educational pyramid broadened to include the entire population the two universities at the apex were to produce thousands of mature, educated Congolese to govern a healthy, literate and economically self-sustaining people. In an estimated thirty to fifty years, the Congo would be ready for real independence. But now the wind of 'nationalism' had started to blow a flatulent blast from Ghana and Guinea fanning native unrest in the Congo—and the Belgians began to realize that their vast, long-term programmes would never have time to ripen.

So, in December 1957, the Brussels Government, which formerly had denied suffrage to any resident of the Congo, black or white, ordered local elections at Léopoldville, Elisabethville and Jadotville, and countenanced the formation of political parties. The results of that experiment were what many had predicted and feared: the entire Congo boiled over with agitation, controversy and collective hysteria as *forty-eight* squabbling political parties mushroomed into existence. Virtually all of them were organized along strictly tribal lines, in-including ABAKO, headed by Joseph Kasavubu, formerly a Bakongo ethnic organization, BALUBAKAT, UNIMO (Union Mongo), Lulua Frères, Front Unité Bangala, ABAZI (Alliance Bayanzi) and many, many others. Only a few were in any sense 'nationalist', such as the MNC (Mouvement National Congolais) whose leader was an ex-Batetela tribesman, post-office clerk and convicted embezzler named Patrice Lumumba.

The steady progress of the Congo gradually slowed down to a shuffle as the *évolué* population effervesced into a frenzy of office-seeking, jostling each other for commanding positions in the newly spawned political parties, while the bush natives, stirred up by the growing ferment, started to renew their ancient inter-tribal feuds. It was in that atmosphere, fully aware that the Congo was not ready to strike out on its own, that on 30 June 1960 Belgium granted its seething young colony complete, unconditional independence.

The only alternative would have been another Algeria, a long, futile and blood-drenched colonial war.

Africa was rapidly becoming a Communist sphere of influence, just as the Russian and Chinese leaders had planned at the Bandung Conference in 1956. There were seventeen new 'emergent' African nations by 1960, and for several years Ghana and its Prime Minister, Kwame Nkrumah, had played an increasingly prominent rôle among them. Throughout 1958 Nkrumah organized regular indoctrination courses for the new Congolese leaders: Patrice Lumumba, Antoine Gizenga, Anicet Kashamura, Thomas Kanza, Alphonse Kalonji and Joseph Kasavubu. Thoroughly brainwashed, they returned to their homeland and launched themselves into a mad career of incendiary agitation.

To make matters even worse, President de Gaulle made a thoroughly irresponsible speech at Brazzaville, capital of the French Congo, on 20 August 1958. When the natives of Léopoldville, the Belgian Congo's political hotbed across the border, heard France's Chief of State declare, 'Independence—whoever wants it, can take it on the spot!' they started to smoulder. They belonged to the same tribe, the Bakongo, as the natives of Brazzaville on the other side of the river, and it seemed grossly unfair to them that their fellow tribesmen in the French Congo had more political freedom than themselves, especially since the

Brazzaville Bakongo were, in comparison, poorly educated and economically far less well off.

Then, in January 1959, Lumumba set them on fire with wildly provocative speeches. Riots went on in Léopoldville for two days, followed by similar outbreaks in Matadi, Thysville and Luozi. In October that year Lumumba incited even bloodier insurrections at Stanleyville, his own stronghold of power in the eastern end of the Congo.

'Total independence NOW, NOW, NOW!' shrieked Lumumba to the crowd. '*Pika wazungu!*' they rumbled in return, 'Strike at the whites!', but, ironically, the seventy people killed by the rampaging native mobs were all natives. Hundreds were wounded; the ex-postal clerk Lumumba, who had served a prison sentence for embezzlement, issued a stark, terrible warning: 'Divorce between Belgium and the Congo is complete! 1960 will be a year of war and misery! I launch a vibrant appeal to the oppressed peoples of the Congo to mobilize and put an end to Belgian domination. Better to die than continue under this rule of subjection!'

Once that emotional state had developed and accelerated so rapidly Belgium could have refused to grant independence only by waging that colonial war which the Brussels government refused to consider. The idea of hanging on to the Congo by brute force was abhorrent to a people like the Belgians who had fought for hundreds of years to win their own freedom from the Spaniards, Austrians, French and Dutch, and who had always believed their tenure in Central Africa to have a solid humanitarian basis. Moreover, even if the Belgians decided against their principles to fight that war and succeeded in winning, they would be faced not only with the undying hatred of the Congolese but the odium of the entire world.

The Russians and Chinese had already accused them of 'imperialism' and 'exploitation', simply for administering the most healthy, prosperous and progressive country in Central Africa. The Americans, apparently unaware that they were echoing Moscow's favourite slogans, denounced them as an 'old-fashioned colonial power'. The United Nations expressed a middle-of-the-road opinion by approving a declaration that 'the lack of political, economic, social or educational preparedness should never serve as a pretext for delaying independence'.

In that position, under moral fire from the two coldly warring powers of the East and West, and confronted by the simple-minded opposition of the UN, what else could the Belgians do but grant the Congo a premature, problematic and perilous independence?

On 29 June 1960 the two countries concluded a Treaty of Friendship, Assistance and Co-operation. Belgium literally gave away £30,000,000 in financial assistance and promised to place at the disposal of the new Congolese government ten thousand Belgian civil servants: administrative, judicial, military, cultural, scientific, medical and educational personnel to help the Congo weather the first stages of freedom. The document was signed in Léopoldville by two Prime Ministers, Gaston Eyskens of Belgium and Patrice Lumumba of the Congo.

On 30 June 1960, at the Palace of the Nation in Léopoldville, King Baudouin spoke with gracious generosity as he formally ceded sovereignty. The same Patrice Lumumba, who had written with unfeigned enthusiasm of Belgium's 'very sincere and humanitarian idealism' only two years before and signed the Treaty of Friendship only a day before, answered the youthful monarch with a grotesque tirade: 'We are no longer your monkeys! . . . A humiliating slavery was imposed upon us by force! . . . We have had to submit to mockeries, insults and blows, morning, noon and night, just because we were black!' More than seven hundred assembled dignitaries stared in stupefaction at the posturing Prime Minister of the Congo, and millions of natives listening to the radio broadcast of the ceremonies burned with a new passion.

On 1 July, as the three-day Independence Festival began—sponsored and paid for by the Belgians!—there were incidents in ports, railways and offices where native employees demanded immense raises and threatened to strike if they didn't receive them. On 2 July open war broke out between employers and employees, chiefs and subordinates, in offices and factories throughout the six provinces of the Congo, and bands of sullen strikers began to patrol the streets. On 3 July crowds at Léopoldville went wild when they heard the announcement of the new salaries that Congolese legislators would receive: up to 800,000 francs (more than £5,000) per annum plus 'supplementary allowances'. Most of those politicians had been averaging under £350 a year, just like the men in the crowd, from whom they differed very little in talent or education.

On 4 July there was savage fighting at Coquilhatville, capital of Equator Province, where the Mongo tribesmen demanded their independence four days after they had officially received it, and the forces of the new Congolese government answered them with bullets. Bitter inter-tribal warfare burst out simultaneously in Kasai between the Baluba and Bena Lulua.

On 5 July Lumumba criticized, in the presence of their own troops, the Belgian officers of the Force Publique who had remained at their posts in accordance with the terms of the Treaty of Friendship. Next day the Second Battalion of the Force Publique, stationed at Camp Hardy in Thysville, rose in mutiny, humiliating, beating and torturing their Belgian officers and repeatedly raping the white men's wives.

That fatal sequence of events was only the beginning: other battalions of the Force Publique joined in the mutiny, other tribes took advantage of the anarchy to renew their hereditary feuds and all over the Congo the hated *wazungu*—Belgians, other Europeans and a few Americans—started to flee for their lives as the rampaging Congolese looted, pillaged, raped, tortured and murdered. The entire country was exploding into that savage, uncontrollable chaos which has since come to be known as the Congo Disaster.

Inter-tribal conflicts were, of course, a standard feature of Central African life which the Belgians had managed to keep to a minimum for the past fifty years. The rest of it was, for the most part, the inevitable reaction of people who felt cheated: the great miracle of '*Dépendance!*' had finally come to the Congo, but the promised pie was still firmly fixed in the equatorial sky. The natives still had to work for a living, and since there were no mass distributions of mansions, cars and white women, they decided to take them.

They were goaded on by constant incendiary propaganda from the same source which had originally engineered the disaster in the hope of reducing the peaceful, prosperous Congo into a stricken chaos which could be taken over and incorporated into its own colonial empire of European and Asian satellites and 'emergent' African nations. Radio Moscow flooded the Congolese airwaves with broadcasts in Swahili, Lingala and other leading languages, inflammatory tirades about Belgian 'plots', 'aggressions' and 'massacres'.

The radio barrage was climaxed by an amazing outburst from the Communist-trained Congolese Minister of Information, Anicet Kashamura: 'We were a people numbering twenty-five million! After a century of slavery, our population has been cut in half! It was the Belgians who were the first to rape our women! Their King Leopold II ordered the hands cut off from those men and women who didn't gather enough rubber for him! Everywhere, the Belgians buried our ancestors alive!'

'Our population has been cut in half . . .' Kashamura's statistics were wildly inaccurate. In 1860 there had, of course, been no way to estimate the population of the unexplored wilderness that was eventually to become the Congo. Prospective census-takers would have found themselves impaled on stakes or cut into pieces and eaten. It was only in 1879, when Leopold II became the sovereign of the Congo Free State, that the first geographical surveys were made, and in 1900 the population was estimated at seven million. No complete official census was feasible until 1944, when the native population of the Congo was determined at 10,389,155. By December 1956 the figure had risen to 12,843,574 and in 1960, when 'Independence' came, there were roughly 13,000,000 natives. Thus, the Belgians had apparently succeeded in *doubling* the population of the Congo rather than halving it.

'King Leopold II cut off our hands!' cried the Congolese Minister, repeating a fantastic myth which still survives in some parts of the world, although I have never heard it in Europe. False charges that the Belgians had mutilated natives originated during the late nineteenth-century struggle among the English, French and Germans to snatch African colonies. They had all been envious of Belgium, but the English had been the keenest critics of the flourishing Congo Free State. 'British Africa from the Cape to Cairo!' had been their avowed slogan, but the Belgian territory lay in between.

In launching their defamatory campaign against Leopold II and the men who had freed the Congo from the yoke of Arab slavery, the English used the perjured testimony of merchants, mercenaries, politicians, crackpots, dismissed employees and rival missionary sects. Some typical examples included the claims of Captain Guy Burroughs, who was found guilty by an English court of libelling three Belgian officers, and the notorious report written by the former British Consul at Boma, the Irish rebel Sir Roger Casement, whom the English later hanged for treason.

All the charges were refuted decisively and many prominent authorities stepped forward of their own initiative to dispel the obnoxious lies. Both Lord Curzon and the American Cardinal Gibbons defended the Congo Free State; James G. Whiteley of Baltimore, a member of the Institute of International Law who represented the United States Government at several international congresses, made an important statement of some little-known facts:

> It is unfortunate that so many false impressions about the Congo have been accepted without examination. For example, there is a popular belief that the King runs the Congo 'for revenue only', and that he oppresses the natives in order to extort money from them. The exact opposite is the truth. The King receives no revenue from the Congo Government; on the contrary the State owes its very existence to the generosity of the King, who advanced several million dollars to keep the Government going in its early struggle for existence. It is true that there are in the Congo extensive Crown lands, the revenue from which belongs to the King, but his Majesty refuses to take the receipts from this land and has turned the money into a fund for the erection of schools, the encouragement of science, and similar purposes. He does not even manage the fund himself, but has placed it in the hands of three trustees.

Whiteley concluded, 'A great work has been accomplished in Equatorial Africa, and, as a distinguished missionary said, "Posterity will place the name of Leopold at the head of human benefactors for the princely enterprise, perseverance, and sacrifices contributed by him in such a cause." ' It is one of history's great ironies that posterity should have so tragically misjudged and maligned one of the nineteenth century's most remarkable monarchs.

There were, of course, widespread instances of amputation and other physical mutilations in the Congo, as in most of pre-colonial Africa, since it had been an established practice since time immemorial among the natives and the Arab slavers. It was described vividly by Sir Harry Johnston, the pioneer British administrator of Uganda, who defended the Congo Free State on many occasions:

> In spite of an element of Arab civilization which the slave-trader had certainly implanted in the Congo Forest, he had made himself notorious for his ravages and cruelties. Numbers of natives had been horribly mutilated, hands and feet lopped off, and women's breasts cut away. These people explained to me that the mutilations—which, as only a Negro could, they had survived—had been the work of the Maniema slave-trader and his gang, done sometimes out of wanton cruelty, sometimes as a punishment for thieving or absconding.

J. A. Maloney, another Englishman, recounted how Msiri, the native despot of Katanga, had delighted in 'diabolical refinements of cruelty' and punished even trivial crimes by cutting off a hand or an ear. Commander Verney Lovett Cameron, Dr. William Junker and a host of others described the natives' almost casual attitude towards amputating parts of each other's anatomies, and Cardinal Lavigerie told the horrified world of how 'King Wemba, near Tanganyika, finding the wooden drumsticks too harsh for his ears, cut off the hands of his slaves so that they might beat the drums with their stumps.'

H. M. Stanley summed up the whole ugly libel against Belgium and its King in 1903: 'The sentiment that inspires the charges against the Congo is jealousy. The Congo is succeeding better than any other State of Africa.' But, significantly, he added, 'The white man must remain master of the Congo. Drive him out of it, and you will see war arise between one native village and another, a return to barbarism.'

Fifty-seven years later the people of the new Republic of the Congo proved Stanley was right. They drove out the Belgians and used their 'independence' to revive the worst horrors of their pre-colonial past: inter-tribal warfare, cannibalism, sorcery, ritual murder. That was to be expected, but the real shock came when the natives of the Congo were joined in their wild mêlée by the multi-racial soldiers of the United Nations.

The first UN 'Blue Helmets' arrived on 15 July 1960; in August 1961, after spending a futile, ineffectual year occupying the rest of the Congo, they were sent to Katanga to crush the secessionist movement of Moise Tshombe, the most enlightened of Black Africa's new native leaders and practically the only one who was openly anti-Communist—that same grossly slandered Tshombe who today is the free world's one hope in the tortured Congo.

The incredible violence, rapine and destruction that followed the UN's invasion of Katanga, reaching a climax in December 1961, are described in the vivid text and photographs of a little-known book, *46 Angry Men: The 46 Civilian Doctors of Elisabethville Denounce U.N. Violations in Katanga*, edited by Dr. T. Vleurinck, who has since died at his post in the Congo. The '46 angry men', including Italians, Swiss, Hungarians, Brazilians and Spaniards, as well as the Belgian majority, offer documented proof that the UN forces were guilty of the murder, wounding or rape of unarmed civilians, of arbitrary and often brutal arrests and taking hostages; of multiple thefts and looting; of

bombing the Prince Léopold, Queen Elisabeth, Shinkolobwe
and Lubumbashi hospitals, and other non-military buildings;
of machine-gunning and directing mortar fire on houses, schools,
post offices, churches, missions, factories, fuel tanks, railways,
highways, trucks, cars and Red Cross ambulances; and of
detaining in concentration camps thirty to forty thousand
Baluba under living and hygienic conditions bordering on geno-
cide (an estimated three to five thousand deaths in less than six
months).[1]

The UN's 'peace-keeping' record might have been even more
imposing had Secretary General U Thant succeeded in his
attempt in December 1961 to solicit thousand-pound 'block-
buster' bombs from Great Britain, allegedly for use against
military aircraft and airstrips, although 90 per cent of the
UN's Katangan targets had been strictly civilian.

Dr. Albert Schweitzer, perhaps the man who best knows the
heart and soul of Africa, expressed his feelings on 26 October
1962, when he said, 'The policy of the UN in the former Belgian
Congo causes me great anxiety because it proceeds from total
ignorance of the country's problems. It is a grave error to try
and unite by force people so profoundly divided among themselves. If Katanga is unwilling to be reunited with the Congo,
the UN should respect its wishes and not try to impose its own
will at any cost.' A year later Dr. Schweitzer used far stronger
language. He said of the international peace organization, 'They
are bandits! Assassins!'

On 7 January 1963 the Pulitzer Prize-winning journalist,
William S. White, summed up the course of recent history:
'The ugly truth is that deceit, evasiveness and incredible arrogance have marked the UN's course in the Congo from first to
last.'

Since then, the new state's political and tribal catastrophes
have continued to fill the headlines. In November 1964 they
reached a dramatic peak with the mass slaughter of hostages
halted by a joint U.S.-Belgian rescue operation—but not in
time to save the American medical missionary Dr. Paul Carlson,
and hundreds of other innocent victims, black and white alike,
some of whom were eaten by the *Simba* rebels or fed to the local
crocodiles. The Communist bloc's reaction to those bloody

[1] Copies of *46 Angry Men* can be consulted at any Belgian Embassy or
Consulate, or obtained (in English, French or Spanish) by writing to Dr.
Roger van Grunderbeeck, the Dean of the Elisabethville Medical Corps,
at 65 Avenue de l'Opale, Brussels 4, Belgium.

events resembled their July 1960 outbursts when Belgian para-
troopers landed to rescue trapped civilians and restore order in
Léopoldville, Luluabourg and the other cities of the convulsed
Congo.

There was, however, one significant difference: now the
Americans were sitting in the same uncomfortable boat with the
Belgian paternalists they had criticized so harshly in the past,
branded, as a result of their humanitarian efforts, as 'murderers'
and 'imperialist aggressors'.

The story of the new Republic of the Congo is an immense,
complex panorama of human greed, error and ineptitude, an
epic tragedy far beyond the scope of this brief and incomplete
outline. Perhaps it was best delineated on 1 July 1961, the first
anniversary of the Independence, by *Actualités Africaines*, an
official publication of the new Congolese Republic: 'A year of
misery, 12 months of misfortune, 52 weeks of fratricidal murder,
365 days of anarchy! That is the balance-sheet. This damned
independence, which should have meant joy, good fortune and
prosperity, has been the cause of our sufferings, our misfortunes
and our pains.'

Moise Tshombe summed it up even more strongly on
the same day, at Elisabethville, when he said: 'Who does
not remember having clenched his fists with rage and impotence before the destruction and ruin which—in ten days
of folly!—crushed more than eighty years of labour and
effort?'

*   *   *

In Kisenyi, during those first days of July 1960, tension was
mounting at an alarming rate. Ruanda-Urundi was not scheduled
to receive political independence for another two years, but the
fear, confusion and violence of the turbulent Congo had started
to seep across the border from Goma, less than a mile away. The
situation erupted on 8 July, the day I returned from my trip to
Mugwata, when Goma's detachment of the Force Publique
staged a small-scale insurrection.

When I drove into town that evening, the main street appeared deserted. Just before I reached the big traffic circle, I
saw two jeeps parked near the post office and a swarm of loud,
excited native soldiers armed with machine-guns and rifles. I
put on speed, but as I swung round the central island of trees,
shrubs and green lawns, a car came shooting out of a side street
and we narrowly missed a collision. I had a brief glimpse of the

passengers—a weeping housewife in a blue dressing-gown and
four frightened children—before it rocketed away.

I headed down the Avenue des Volcans, but was soon caught
up with nearly a hundred others in a flood of traffic slowly
boiling towards the border of Rwanda. Rifle bullets and sporadic bursts of machine-gun fire cut through the air as hidden
snipers fired on our trapped, crawling vehicles; some of the cars
were hit but, miraculously, there were no serious human casual-
ties, although more than four hundred people—three-quarters
of the European population—were fleeing to Kisenyi, fearing
that the mutiny would whip seven thousand natives of Goma
into a frenzy of destruction.

When I finally reached the border, after ten agonizing minutes
on that mile-long strip, it was terribly ironic to see Belgian
commando squads rumbling back and forth in their armoured
cars and jeeps, cursing at being forbidden to cross over and help
their beleaguered countrymen a few hundred yards away in the
Congo.

At least 150 of the harried people who fled from Goma took
shelter at the newly established official Refugee Centre: the
Hôtel Beau Séjour, next door to the Central Africa Curio Shop.
Fifty commandos were quartered in the Palm Beach Hotel on
the opposite side. None of us was able to sleep during that long
nervous night: the shooting in Goma lasted until morning and
the mutineers amused themselves from time to time with random
bursts of machine-gun fire into Kisenyi.

During the next few days things calmed down as the Belgian
officers of the Force Publique gradually managed to put down
the mutiny; but the economic situation started to disintegrate.
Postal and bank connections between the Congo and northern
Rwanda were disrupted, and even the elementary supplies of
food were beginning to fail: meat, flour, sugar and salt became
increasingly scarce, and soon the grocers, butchers and bakers
of Kisenyi were forced to go out of business.

To make matters worse, many of our natives, seeing the
violence just across the border, assumed that they had acquired
the same rights as their emancipated brothers in the Congo,
especially the right to highway robbery and looting. The presence of the commandos prevented any outbursts in the town,
but on the highways dozens of native gangs preyed on the white
refugees who had fled from the Congo and headed across
northern Rwanda towards the safety of British East Africa with
the few valuables they were able to carry.

The climax came on 20 July, when a heavily loaded C-119 transport crashed into a volcanic peak near Goma, killing thirty-four Belgian soldiers and badly injuring seven. Crowds of natives rushed to the scene of the accident but not to help. Instead, they carried off a sizeable stock of guns and ammunition, after stripping the victims of their clothing, wallets and watches. The mutilated bodies, living and dead, were covered with bloody red footprints where the Congolese had casually trampled on the naked white flesh. I saw the corpses in Kisenyi, after a band of civilian volunteers crossed the border in cars, station wagons and trucks to bring back the bodies and search for survivors, and descriptions of what happened on the flanks of the dead volcano were almost Dantesque in their horror.

I listened, tortured by the growing conviction that the Congolese might be preying on some other innocent victims: my pigmy friends in North Kivu and my animals at Mugwata. I found no peace, thinking about it, and early next morning set out on the long, dangerous trip into the Congo.

There was no way of telling how bad the situation actually was, but I knew that a battalion of the Force Publique, based at the Rumangabo camp about ten miles north of Mugwata, had joined in the general mutiny. Some of their Belgian officers, badly beaten and half-starved, had made their way to Kisenyi and taken refuge at the Hôtel Beau Séjour, merging with the stream of terrified *colons* who had been driven from their plantations in Goma, Sake, Kirotshe, Masisi, Rumangabo and Rutshuru. As to North Kivu, 250 miles away, the radio reports were incomplete, confused and conflicting. It was simply a mystery, a lethal one, according to most of my friends, who urged me not to attempt the journey.

I had a brief encounter at the border with the Congolese customs inspector, an officious *évolué* seated at a wooden table littered with rubber stamps under an incongruously gay-looking orange-and-white-striped umbrella. He peered suspiciously at the pass which I had obtained from the new native administrator of Goma, checked my car for weapons and waved to a couple of soldiers who raised the wooden barrier arm to an upright position.

Things seemed deceptively normal at first, as I headed north around the huge Virunga volcanoes, but soon I began to encounter gangs of natives along the side of the road, still clamouring for '*Dépendance!*'—three weeks after they had received it. Then, at Mugwata, twenty miles north of Lake Kivu, I was tremendously relieved to find my game park intact, my animals untouched and my two *cornacs* almost cheerful.

'Have you had any trouble?' I asked them.

'Don't worry, *Bwana*!' Bodeko assured me. 'A few drunken soldiers came down from Rumangabo and tried to tease the elephants. Pierrot charged them from the other end of the kraal and they ran like hell! We'll be all right.'

'They'll be back,' I said grimly, 'and with guns. Either that, or the poachers will come to kill the elephants for their tusks and the rhino for his horn. They'll slaughter the others for meat and kill the two of you if you try to stop them. There's only one thing we can do: turn all of the animals loose before they get here.'

'Does that mean we'll lose our jobs?' Bodeko asked me with obvious terror. 'What will we do? Where will we go?'

'Maybe I can smuggle you across the border into Kisenyi.'

'Can you smuggle the elephants too? We don't want the soldiers to kill them. And Pierrot?'

I wondered what the Congolese customs inspector's reaction would be if I brought two refugee elephants and a rhino to the border; he would probably order the soldiers and *polici* to open fire. 'I'm afraid not,' I told them. 'We'll have to let them take their chances.'

'Give the *tembo* to us,' Bodeko pleaded, 'and we'll stay with them. We'll go north and try to take Bella and Venus back to our old home in Epulu. Pierrot can come too—we don't really like him, but the elephants do. Maybe we'll all be safe there.'

'*Iko muzuri!* The two *tembo* are yours!' I said, sealing the gift with a solemn handshake.

The scenes that followed were terribly painful to me. All my beautiful animals wandered about hesitantly, reluctant to leave the familiar kraals where they had been well treated and well fed. The antelope, buffalo and gnu wanted none of their new freedom and—like most of the Congolese natives—had no idea what to do with it. We had to drive them away repeatedly, especially the eland who kept returning with a gentle, baffled look. Finally it was over, and as I started out towards the north, I watched three massive grey forms dwindle away in my rear-view mirror; Bella and Venus were beginning the four-hundred-mile trip back to Epulu in the Grand Forest . . . and Pierrot was walking behind them.

I drove on, preoccupied with my memories of the three

animals, until I got to within a mile of Rumangabo, where a
swarm of khaki uniforms suddenly blocked the road, at least
twenty mutinous soldiers of the Force Publique, armed with
automatic rifles, machine-guns and hand grenades. They waved
me to the side of the road and surrounded the car in a sullen
circle bristling with blued steel barrels. One of them, a tall,
husky sergeant with tattooed cheeks, kept a machine-gun
trained on my chest. '*Toko ya motokaa!*' he growled, 'Get out
of the car!'

I slid out from behind the wheel and stared at the sergeant
with deliberate arrogance. The soldiers gaped at me: they were
obviously accustomed to dealing with panic-stricken *colons*, and
my unfamiliar attitude astonished them. All of them stared
avidly at the exposed stump of my wrist and I heard one of them
mutter, '*Sasa, ye iko napoteza kichwa yake*', 'Now he will lose
his head as well.'

I ignored that ominous remark. Instead, with the haughty,
supercilious air of a superior officer, I strolled round the little
group, almost as though I were passing them in review. I took
a step backwards, staring at them intently, and barked an unexpected order, '*Garde à VOUS!*'

At least ten of them clicked their heels together and lowered
their guns, following the drill command they had been trained
to obey. The others looked at each other in worried confusion
but their weapons continued to point in my direction. I noticed
that one of them, a skinny young private with filed teeth, was
holding a Sten gun without a clip in it. He glared at me and
pulled the bolt back in a gesture that was intended to be
menacing, apparently unaware that it showed his weapon was
empty. I walked towards him, looked him in the eye and said
with studied insolence, 'I am a white man, and a Belgian. Shoot
me!'

The little private was stunned. Then the rest of the mutineers,
seeing his empty gun, started to laugh in derision. 'Give me
your gun,' I ordered, 'and your clip.' Shamefaced, he handed
them over without hesitation. I slipped the clip into position
and tossed the loaded Sten gun back to him with a casual
'Now you'll have better luck.'

Most of the soldiers grinned appreciatively at that swaggering
little stage play, and I felt the atmosphere lighten perceptibly.
'You're pretty sharp,' the husky sergeant remarked, 'for a
muzungu.' Most of them seemed to agree, but a moment later I
heard a short, coal-black private turn to a friend and remark in

Kikongo, 'He may not be so bad, but that car's too good to let go.'

'*Kuteki nkanda mbulu ko go kani kubaka yo ko!*' I called out to him loudly, a Kikongo proverb meaning 'Don't sell the jackal's skin before you have killed him.'

Their reaction resembled a delayed explosion. Three or four of the mutineers understood Kikongo, and they stared at me, open-mouthed, until they burst into gales of loud, overjoyed laughter. Then they translated for the benefit of the others, eager to show them that a white man actually knew and respected the proverbial wisdom of their ancient, powerful tribe, the Bakongo. By the time the excitement had died down, none of them remembered to point their rifles.

'Where are you going, *Bwana*?' the sergeant asked me, in a friendly, easy tone.

'Up north. To see some friends.'

'White men?'

'Pygmies. Near Beni—'

'Bambuti?' cried one of the youngest soldiers. '*Mi bado kuona Bambuti! Mi nataka kwenda na we!*, I've never even seen a pygmy! Let me go with you!'

'*Na mi, Bwana!*' most of them echoed, and the sergeant said gravely, 'It is very dangerous up north. There are lots of *bashenzi* on the road, wild natives who stop cars, rob them and kill the white men. They think that they're tough, but they'll run away from big guns like these! If you take *me* along, I can protect you.'

It would be almost like using lions for protection against leopards—but I decided to take several of them along. I had a four-hundred-mile round trip ahead through a series of unknown dangers, and at the moment the dreaded mutineers of the Force Publique seemed to be the least of them. 'All right,' I said quietly, 'I'll take three men, one in the front seat and two in the back.'

A wild argument about which three would go went on until I stopped it by announcing I would choose the men for myself. The sergeant silenced their protests with a loud, authoritative '*Bwana* will choose and we will be quiet!'

'What happens if I don't choose you?' I asked him.

He grinned, showing his large square white teeth: the three vertical scars on each of his cheeks stood out sharply. 'I will be quiet.'

'Then I'll take you.'

He rushed to my car, anxious to install himself in the front seat. He was obviously one of the most intelligent in the group and, as such, more easily handled than some of the others, who looked brutally stupid. For my second man, I chose the squat little Mukongo whom I had rebuked with one of his own tribal proverbs. From the rapt expression on his face when he looked at me, I felt sure that he would obey my orders without making trouble. For the third and last, I chose the skinny youth whose gun I had loaded. He couldn't have been more than nineteen, and I hoped that he would try to imitate the two older men without getting any dangerous ideas of his own.

Both hurried to take their places in the back seat of my dark-blue Chevrolet Impala, fingering the upholstery with childish delight as they sat down with their gun stocks propped between their legs. The rest of the mutineers stared at them with envy and disappointment, looking like overgrown, petulant brown children equipped with toy weapons. Some started to grumble, but subsided when the sergeant barked a few reprimands in Lingala, the northwest Congo's *lingua franca* and the official language of the Force Publique.

I hadn't gone very far before I became aware of a heavy human miasma. The soldiers' regular army routine had included daily showers, but now, with the coming of independence, it was obvious that none of these three had bothered to wash for days. Even at high speed with the windows open the stench was intolerable. I put up with it for about fifteen miles until we crossed the wooden bridge over the Rutshuru River, and the sight of all that water inspired me. I pulled off the road beyond the bridge and produced a bar of soap and a towel from the glove compartment.

They took my suggestion very nicely and climbed down the small cliff to bathe in the fast-running river. I watched them for a few minutes as they stripped and waded cautiously into the shallows; none of them could swim and they were obviously afraid of the water. Then, after I saw that they were really using the soap, I started to walk back to my car.

Quite a surprise awaited me. Ten Bahunde natives had gathered round it and one was inside, fumbling with the glove compartment as he searched for something to steal. Three large bows armed with hunting arrows turned in my direction as I yelled '*Kuya!*', 'Come here!' to the three mutineers below, hoping to frighten away the gang of raiders. The natives stared at me warily, apparently under the impression that I had asked *them* to come, until the leader, a grizzled, tough-looking old man, decided to waste no more time, whatever I was up to. '*Ua ye!*' he shouted. 'Kill him!'

Just as he bent his bow and I got ready to make a quick sideways leap, a rapid-fire salvo split through the air. I whirled and saw the sergeant, stark naked, poised near the edge of the cliff, brandishing his machine-gun. His two comrades were close behind him, raising their own weapons.

Almost simultaneously I shouted 'Don't fire!', they fired, an arrow whizzed past my left ear, and the old Muhunde screamed once and clutched at his shoulder. I ran towards the mutineers, trying to stop them, but they fired again, narrowly missing me and hitting another native. The band of Bahunde dashed off into the bush, half-dragging the second victim. Just before they disappeared from sight the first—the old man—shrieked curses at me, still holding his wounded shoulder.

I was furious at this unnecessary bloodshed, when a burst of fire near the raiders' feet would have chased them just as effectively. 'We were only trying to help,' the sergeant grumbled, and the youngest man was obviously bewildered. 'Why are you angry?' he asked. 'They were just some stupid natives.' I stared back at him, shocked. 'What if they belonged to your own tribe?' I demanded angrily. 'That would change everything, wouldn't it?' He smiled at me, revealing his filed central incisors. 'I'm a Muhunde, *Bwana*. They *do* belong to my tribe. Why, that old man I just shot reminded me of my father's older brother . . . I never liked my uncle, even when I was little.'

After that appalling incident, I sat down and had a talk with the three of them. The young private, Buega, refused to admit that he had done wrong in shooting a man simply because he resembled a hated relative. The other private, Bamuke, produced a Kikongo proverb about respect for one's elders—to please me—but I could see that he sympathized with the action. The sergeant, Evariste, simply shrugged with a blasé little smile; I got the impression that he wouldn't shoot anyone unless he could make a profit on the deal. None of them showed any enthusiasm when I sent them into the bush to find the wounded men so we could take them to the hospital at Rutshuru. I watched them drag their feet through the motions of a search for ten or fifteen minutes before I finally gave up and decided to drive on. I did succeed, however, in making them promise not to use their weapons unless there was no other way out.

At Rutshuru, which was very quiet, a native poacher tried

to make a deal with me for a huge quantity of ivory. His road-side hut was stacked with it, all fresh tusks from the past three weeks. He had stolen a white man's rifle and found easy targets in the confident elephants of the Albert National Park: after thirty-five years of complete protection, the animals had for-gotten the very meaning of guns. Later, as we drove through the Ruindi sector of the Park, I was appalled by the carnage in this former sanctuary where once even a blade of grass or a pebble had been sacred. The Belgian Congo's oldest and richest national park was a welter of decomposing corpses. The poachers must have killed at least a thousand elephants during the three-week history of the new Republic and other animals, buffalo, antelope and hippo, had been slaughtered in such incredible numbers that the scavenging hyenas and vultures were unable to handle all the corpses.

At one point close to the road there were six bloated elephant cadavers within two hundred yards: their tusks had been chop-ped off with an axe and the ivory stubs jutted bleakly out of their fly-covered jaws. I was sickened by the sight of the murdered animals and flew into a towering rage a few miles farther on when we spotted half a dozen poachers stalking a small herd of elephants. Seeing my anger, the soldiers pleaded for the chance to wipe out the hunters with a spray of bullets. I refused. Instead, I had them place a burst of fire midway between the huge animals and their pursuers. Elephants and poachers shot off, equally terrified, in opposite directions, while the three mutineers went into frenzies of laughter.

The long climb up the Kabasha Escarpment was like an ascent from that inferno of death; the downgrade brought me into a new one, with huge gangs of drunken natives lining both sides of the road, armed with stones, hunting bows, obscene insults and the endless, nauseating cries for '*Dépendance!*' Had I been alone, I doubt that any bravado, proverbs or other psychological manœuvres would have saved me from the hys-terical mobs which advanced on the car . . . and retreated at the sight of armed soldiers.

I drove at top speed through Alimbongo, Lubero, Butembo and Beni. Then, at Mbau, which was relatively quiet, I forced the car down the overgrown trail that led to the *paysannat* at Ebikeba. After the first deserted half-mile, I saw an old pygmy woman and a tiny child, walking along the trail side by side. She gaped at the car, jerked at the child's arm—hoisting it into the air—and ran into the bush. 'Don't be afraid, Grandmother!' I yelled in Kimbuti, as I jumped out of the car and ran after her. 'There's no trouble—it's just me.'

She turned in astonishment at the sound of my words. Then, recognizing me, she ran forward, screaming with joy, '*Bapa! Bapa!* You've come back!' The child, a naked little boy, was still dangling from her right hand. I tried to talk to her, but she gasped and clutched at my shirt when she saw the three soldiers sitting in the car. I ordered them to stay there and started to walk down the trail towards Ebikeba with the old woman and the baby, but I hadn't gone more than a dozen steps before another pygmy suddenly materialized out of the bush and raced towards me. It was Yoma.

He snatched my hand, pressed it between his own, and rested his head on the lower part of my chest while tears welled out of his big, expressive eyes and dripped off the tip of his nose. I stood there for a moment, hugging him, until two more of my old friends burst on to the scene and the three soldiers, growing excited, jumped out of the car. The startled pygmies promptly retreated into the bush, all except Yoma, who was still clutching my hand.

'*Bapa*, why did you bring the soldiers here?' he asked me anxiously.

'They want to meet the Bambuti. They won't hurt you—'

'Soldiers have been here before. From Mbau. They asked us for meat and we said we had none. We told them we'd have to make a hunt, and if we were lucky we might have meat in one or two days. They didn't like that . . . they said that pygmies can always get meat when they want to! So they beat us up and called us little monkeys. One of the old men died the next day. That is why most of the people have run away. Now there are only fourteen of us left at Ebikeba.'

'Yoma, trust me! Call our people back and tell them that *these* soldiers want to make friends with them. If we don't let them have their way, they may decide to become enemies. Then we might have real trouble.'

He left, scratching his neck with a worried expression, but returned very quickly with the two pygmies who had fled from the scene. They stared at the three soldiers with nervous defiance, but the wild mutineers of the Force Publique responded with almost timid curiosity. Finally, Evariste extended his big hand in a gesture of friendship and one of the pygmies shook it warily. Bamuke and Buega imitated their sergeant and I breathed a sigh of relief: I had spotted another pygmy, hiding in the bush, ready to let fly with a hunting arrow.

I left the young private, Buega, to guard the car, while the rest of us walked down the overgrown trail until we reached the *paysannat*. The sight and smell of it were even more of a shock than I had expected. The edge of the clearing was littered with offal, like the Ebikeba of old. Most of the *pisé* huts were deserted, but I found several old people who looked as though they were starving. The fields were a shambles, probably untended for the past month, like those of the Bantu villages I had seen along the way. The old friendly atmosphere and good humour were gone: like everyone else in the Congo, the people of Ebikeba were gripped by obesssive tension and fear.

I stared at the ruins of what I had struggled so hard to build —the pygmies' new world of freedom and dignity!—until I reached a painful but inevitable conclusion. I walked from one end of Ebikeba to the other, gathered my people together and urged them to abandon the *paysannat* and retreat into the deep forest to take up their old nomadic ways. It was their best chance to survive the chaos and destruction that were swallowing up everything else.

They were baffled and terribly confused by advice which they had never expected to hear from me, and debated the question interminably. They were still arguing when I forced myself to leave and sped towards the north with the three soldiers, anxious to see my other *paysannats*.

The four northernmost *paysannats* (Erengeti, Kasana, Lisosisene and Kakola) were all completely deserted, probably because the camps were located closer to the road than Ebikeba and the people had been more exposed to the recent events. It was twilight by the time I left Kakola, and I was unable to visit the rest of the *paysannats*. They, too, had probably been abandoned.

Mile after mile of dark, silent highway flashed past my headlights as I sped through Mbau, Beni and Butembo. The three mutineers talked incessantly in Lingala; then, just as I approached Rutshuru, the big sergeant, Evariste, made an astonishing statement: '*Bwana*, we've seen a lot of things today, and we've been doing some thinking. Now we have a proposition for you: if you will stay with us and be our officer, then we will be your soldiers. We'll get some other men to join us, and soon we'll have an army all our own. Then we can really show those stupid *bashenzi* how to run things around here!'

Evariste slapped the stock of his machine-gun, and the two

younger men grinned eagerly. It was obvious how they would 'run things'.

'You *had* white officers at Rumangabo,' I pointed out to them, 'and you decided you didn't want them. I met some of them in Kisenyi, and they told me how the men at the camp beat them and threw them into jail. They nearly starved before they were finally turned loose.'

'That's true,' Evariste admitted, 'but now we don't know what to do! Please, *Bwana*, won't you be our officer?'

'I don't want anything to do with it. Besides, I'm going back to Kisenyi.'

'Then take us with you!' he implored me. 'We don't want to keep going on our own. We've been having a lot of fun but everything's getting too mixed up now . . .'

'It's getting harder and harder to steal food, and I'm always hungry,' said the young private, Buega, unhappily. 'I'm sick of this wretched *uhuru*!'

'Even if I wanted to,' I explained wearily, 'I couldn't take you to Kisenyi. It's full of refugees—the people you beat up and insulted. Do you think they'd welcome you with open arms?'

'If we had civilian clothes,' Evariste said shrewdly, 'they wouldn't know that we're soldiers . . .'

The three of them talked rapidly in Lingala while I wondered what they were up to. I found out when they asked me to stop at the *magazini* in Rutshuru, where they pounded on the door until they woke up the native shopkeeper. They rushed into the shop, stripped off their khaki tunics, tore at their puttees, and started trying on shirts, brandishing five-hundred-franc notes at the frightened proprietor.

'Look, *Bwana*!' Evariste cried excitedly. 'We don't look like soldiers any more, do we?'

I glared at the mutineers as they paraded before me with plaid cowboy shirts tucked into their khaki *kapitula*. Bamuke had missed a button doing up his shirt and Buega nearly tripped over his trailing puttees. I knew precisely how senseless and brutal their recent actions had been . . . but I knew also that they were victims as well as culprits, swept along by collective hysteria. In a strange way, I couldn't help liking them, especially Evariste, who was a rather colourful scoundrel.

'All right,' I sighed, 'we'll try it. But you'd better stow those uniforms and weapons in the back of the car. You won't make very convincing civilians armed with machine-guns.'

They did as I suggested and sat quietly as we headed south again. As we came back to the Rutshuru bridge, where the skirmish with the band of Bahunde had taken place seventeen hours earlier, a strange vision loomed up in the beam of my headlights and the mutineers cried out in terror at the sight of three enormous spectral grey forms.

Bella, Venus and Pierrot were still together, marching north on their long, uncertain journey towards the Ituri.

I stopped the car, calmed the soldiers down and said a final farewell to my animals and their *cornacs*. Since then I have often wondered how the natives along their route reacted to the unique spectacle of a tame rhino trailing after two mounted elephants, and whether they all reached safety. Pierrot may have run off by himself when they reached the Albert National Park or, as I hope, he may have followed his friends all the way to the Grand Forest. In either case, he would have been the one and only rhino in the area. Then again, the three of them may have been killed somewhere *en route*. I hope I may some day find out.

There were no other real incidents until, at about three o'clock in the morning, we reached Goma, and a yawning Congolese sergeant in charge of the border patrol asked for our passes. I produced my own, but all the mutineers could do was to smile feebly. Fortunately, I was able to save the situation by joking with the sergeant until he passed us through without even bothering to ask for their ID books.

Five minutes later, after a twenty-two-hour round trip of nearly five hundred miles, I was back at the Central Africa Curio Shop, where my animals stirred uneasily as we sneaked into the back yard. Evariste and his companions were startled when the parrots shrieked curses at them and nearly ran when Simba growled. They were still trembling when I bedded them down in the storage shed with a big pile of blankets.

Exhausted as I was, I slept for only a few hours. Then I lay awake until dawn, considering the decision I had been trying to forestall since the first announcement of the Congo's premature independence—the decision to leave Africa.

There was no place left for me or my kind in the new 'emergent' nations. We no longer had the authority to help and protect the people we loved; we could only stand by, sick with pity and frustrated rage, while they tortured, murdered and obliterated each other in the holy name of freedom. I knew that Ruanda-Urundi would follow the Congo on the long backward slide into barbarism and that the rest of Black Africa would trail after them. It was only a question of time—and nobody knew how long.

If I left at once, I would have to put everything behind me: my native friends, my business, my animals, even Simba. Nevertheless, I decided to go. It was my only chance to rescue the most important thing in Kisenyi—the world's largest and finest private collection of Central African arts and crafts. My collection was far more than a pile of beautiful or intriguing inanimate objects: it was the irreplaceable record of traditional cultures which were themselves being destroyed, a living chapter in the long, complex evolution of mankind.

I was determined to save that historic document from the hands of the looters, but I knew that it wouldn't be easy. The gigantic collection comprised more than five thousand individual pieces—some 750 sculptured figures and statues, 225 masks, 100 carved boxes, 100 carved cups, 50 incised horns, 325 drums and tom-toms, 250 other musical instruments, 200 necklaces, 300 bracelets, 100 belts, 100 amulets, 50 anklets, 50 earrings, 50 armlets, 50 jewelled tribal insignia, 75 headdresses, 125 combs, 45 examples of copper, iron, ivory and shell money, 75 shields, 250 spears, 200 knives, 130 axes, 20 hoes, 50 bows, 100 swords, 100 bill-hooks, 500 arrows, 25 adzes, 45 stools, 15 sculptured paddles, 60 baskets and trays, 25 antique native fabrics, 35 potteries and gourds, 125 spoons, 50 wooden pots, 100 pipes, and 150 objects of witchcraft and magic—representing at least thirty-five different traditional cultures.

It weighed more than thirteen tons.

* * *

At eight o'clock that morning I put all my men to work building heavy wooden crates to hold the hundreds of cardboard boxes in which the precious collection was stored. At nine I approached an Italian trucker in Goma and attempted to rent an eight-ton truck with a seven-ton trailer for the 850-mile journey from Kisenyi to Nairobi. He refused, point-blank, to hazard his vehicles on my unpredictable venture.

We argued and haggled for nearly three hours, until he finally accepted an exorbitant rental fee: 100,000 francs in cash (£700) plus £1,400 worth of stock of curios from the shop with office furniture, equipment and refrigerator thrown in. His own driver would accompany me to Nairobi and bring the empty truck back to Rwanda. If it was lost, stolen or destroyed *en route*, I would pay a forfeit of 500,000 francs (£3,500). The terms were outrageous but I signed the agreement: I had no alternative.

It took three days to finish building and packing the big wooden crates, even though I saved some time by making use of an enormous furniture box which my parents had brought from Belgium years before. Fully loaded it weighed more than three tons, occupied the greater part of the trailer, and took the entire nineteen-man staff of the shop as well as my three mutineers and six commandos from the Palm Beach Hotel who volunteered their services, to get it on board. Ironically, the Belgians and former Congolese soldiers worked on this job side by side without any friction while Belgians and Congolese were fighting bloody battles in Katanga.

The car, truck and trailer were loaded by the evening of 25 July and a grand-scale departure for Uganda was scheduled for next morning. André cooked five chickens for a big farewell dinner, and I turned my attention to the animals, dreading the task ahead. I planned to take the baby chimp, Sophie, as well as Kikihibou, the owl-monkey, a handsome crested mangabey I called Spirou, and my two young Siamese cats. The rest would simply have to be turned loose to take their chances with unexpected independence.

I first stepped into the aviary, with its two thousand orioles, weaverbirds, widow birds, mouse birds, budgerigars, lovebirds, serin finches, ring-necked doves and bright red Bengali birds, stood among them for a few minutes and then walked out, simply leaving the door open behind me. I took a few steps and entered the monkeys' noisy domain, where Jeune-Homme, the baboon, rushed up to greet me, along with his best friend, a small silver monkey; Jeune-Homme picked through my hair and beard while the monkey checked my pockets for candy, a little ritual they had performed regularly during the past year. I broke loose with difficulty, stepped out of their cage and, once again, left the door open behind me.

After that, I drove the antelope out of their pens and chased them across the Avenue des Palmiers into the grassy park that ran parallel to the beach, hoping that they would be able to get out of the town before they wound up as the main course of a native barbecue. Next I released the pangolins and pottos, freed the monkeys who were tied out under the trees and tried to drive the strutting crested cranes out of the yard.

The lions and snakes were more of a problem. I planned to release the big cats late at night when they could make a quick escape from the town without any fatal encounters. The two pythons could be turned loose at the same time, but I couldn't free the viper, cobra and mamba: it was too dangerous for the people of Kisenyi and too cruel to the snakes, which would probably starve to death with no one to feed them. I hated to do it, but I picked up a .22 rifle and shot the three poisonous snakes through the head, two bullets in each, to make sure of the ugly job.

That last operation took away most of my appetite, but I forced myself to eat roast chicken with my people, after which I sent them home for the night and had a brief but important conference with the three ex-mutineers. Since I had taken the decision to move the immense collection to safety, I had been growing more and more concerned about the first leg of the journey, those sixty-five perilous miles between Kisenyi and the British Customs Station of Kisoro on the southwestern border of Uganda. Very few cars had passed unscathed through the Ruhengeri territory along the route, and I knew that a heavily loaded car, truck and trailer would be a sitting duck for raiders.

It had taken twelve years of hard work, patience and ingenuity to assemble my historic collection. To lose it now, to see it plundered and dismembered by unknowing hands, would be intolerable.

'We'll go now, *Bwana*,' Evariste said confidently, after the four of us had worked out a plan. 'We'll pick up a khaki-coloured jeep in an abandoned yard or somewhere along the road. Then we'll meet you tomorrow by the place called Nyundo Hill, just as you told us to.'

'Ten miles east of Kisenyi,' I said emphatically, 'at ten o'clock in the morning. It's easy to remember.'

'Don't worry, *Bwana*! We'll be there.'

They packed their guns and uniforms in an old tin trunk I gave them and started to leave. Evariste led and the two others walked behind him carrying the large, heavy trunk. At the last moment, the big ex-sergeant stiffened, presented his hand, and spoke the first and last French words I ever heard him utter: '*A demain, mushew!*' he said melodramatically, with a thick but touching accent. '*A demain, monsieur!*' I echoed gravely.

I waited for almost two hours, until I felt sure that most of Kisenyi was sleeping. Then I opened the gate to the young lions' cage. One of them leaped out and stood uncertainly just

as a *mboloko,* a small antelope, made the fatal mistake of returning to his home, trotting daintily in through the open front gate.
The lion sprang and seized the antelope, cracking his neck, the
second cat joined his brother and the two of them started to
work on the corpse. It wasn't a pleasant sight, but I knew how
the lions felt: they had been watching the antelope for more than
a year without being able to reach them.

By now Simba was in a passion, seeing his two colleagues
with their kill. I opened the iron gate of the arena and he
bounded towards them. They turned defiantly, ready to protect
their prize. The three cats sniffed, grumbled and roared their
challenges. Hearing them, some of the animals who still remained in their open cages cried out in terror: the monkeys
hooted while the parrots shrieked and swore in Swahili. I
broke up the argument by challenging all three lions with
a kitchen chair, and Simba took advantage of the confusion
to snatch up the kill. Flanked by the two young lions, his
head raised defiantly, he ran off with it through the open front
gate.

I stood there, remembering the most vivid incidents in my
long friendship with Simba. Then, growing more and more
furious over the futile loss of such a magnificent creature, I
threw the chair across the yard, smashing it to pieces. The
violent action generated a new cacophony of monkey hoots and
parrot curses. 'What are *you* doing here?' I shouted in Swahili.
'Run away, you're free!'

'*Pumbavu! Pumbavu!*' one of the parrots answered me,
'Imbecile! Imbecile!' '*Kwa heri! Kwa heri! Kwa heri!*' another
one kept repeating, a raucous, ironic 'Good-bye'.

Then I remembered the pythons. I started towards the far
end of the yard but after the first few steps I stopped short:
something was gripping my leg. It was Jeune-Homme. I went
on walking, thinking that the baboon would run off when we
came near the snakes. Unfortunately he had the opposite reaction, and instead of running from the two pythons, scuttled up
my leg and jumped on to my shoulder, clutching my hair with
both of his hands; then he urinated on my neck. I tried to dis-
engage him, but the baboon only tightened his grip on my hair,
determined to stay. I opened the door of the pythons' cage,
hoping that he might panic and take flight, but Jeune-Homme
only shrieked and clutched me even more tightly.

The larger python was asleep, but the smaller snake was
awake and rather nervous with all the noise and confusion. He

poured out of his cage, passing over my feet with his heavy body. Jeune-Homme made guttural noises in his throat, paralysed with fear. I picked up a snake hook and pulled at the big python until he uncoiled and slowly followed his friend. The baboon cachinnated as they wound their way out of sight, nearly unscrewing my right ear in his frenzy. Again I tried to free myself, but once more the stubborn animal clutched on to my hair. Finally, in exasperation, I rushed indoors and jumped under the shower where I pulled at the rope and a flood of cold water descended on to my head. Jeune-Homme screamed and flew through the air; I followed and chased him out of the house. I could hear the wet, unhappy baboon talking to himself for nearly an hour before I eventually fell asleep. He was still angry at seven o'clock next morning when I went into the back yard to check on the liberated animals.

There were three other monkeys left; they peered at me defiantly through the open door of their cage, determined to stay in captivity. The two guib antelope were back home, strolling casually round the yard. Seven of the eight crested cranes had returned, two parrots remained of the original twenty, and at least two hundred birds were still fluttering about in the open aviary, including most of the red Bengali finches. The big iron arena was painfully empty.

I felt a tremendous wave of pity for the uncomprehending animals who had refused to accept their freedom. I wanted to take them all with me but it was impossible, so I compromised and decided to rescue the two parrots. I coaxed them into a small travelling cage and fastened it under the truck bed, next to the cage which held the owl-monkey and the mangabey. Then I imprisoned a wildly protesting Sophie in an old wicker clothes-basket, trapped the two Siamese cats in a second and put both wailing baskets into the back seat of the car.

André, Kamende and my other native friends watched unhappily as I made these final preparations. Their expressions were strained, even when I gave them my parting gifts: 1,000 francs to Kamende, the same amount plus all the kitchen equipment to André, and at least 250 francs to every member of my staff. I would have given them more if I had had it, but hiring the truck had taken most of my cash. By the time I was finished, I hadn't a single Congolese franc to my name, and I was glad of it.

After I gave them the money all my people hurried out of the front door, and I naturally resented such abrupt departures after our long friendship. Then, when I stepped out of the Central Africa Curio Shop for the last time, I discovered that our final moments together would be far from unfeeling.

A crowd of at least fifty natives was forming a long, excited line under Kamende's anxious supervision. My wonderful 'witch doctor' bustled up and down the line in a whirl of bells and dangling civet-tails, putting the finishing touches to a precise hierarchical order: *moke*, 'boys', gardener, carpenter, ebonist, ivorist, *Ntore* dancers and drummers, and a large group of local chiefs and sub-chiefs who had apparently gathered for the occasion. The Belgian commandos at the Palm Beach Hotel stared in amazement, and a large group of refugees looked on with obvious disapproval from the grounds of the Hôtel Beau Séjour.

I shook hands with each one of them as I worked my way down that long, colourful line. At the end, when I had to say good-bye to my two oldest and dearest friends, Kamende and André, I was still unprepared for the force of our mutual emotions. André embraced me, abdomen to abdomen, in the classic style of Rwanda's blood-brothers, and Kamende, whom I had never known to shed a tear, wept unashamedly. I came very close to tears myself.

As I walked to my car, I waved to the white spectators. The commandos waved back and shouted '*Bonne chance!*' but the glum-looking refugees at the Hôtel Beau Séjour glared, apparently resenting the unusual magnitude of my thirteen-ton exodus from Belgian Africa. Many of them had lost everything they possessed and fled from the Congo with little more than a toothbrush before coming to rest, ironically, at their inappropriately named hotel.

I took one last look at the people and the place I loved, and saw Kamende trying to grin with a face still wet with tears. I realized that this was probably the saddest moment of my life and I tried to memorize every detail of it. Then I stepped on the gas.

*   *   *

I left Kisenyi and drove rapidly through the hills towards Nyundo, followed by the huge truck and trailer. At the appointed rendezvous my three armed, uniformed Congolese soldiers awaited me in a battered khaki-coloured jeep. It looked military enough, but carried no identifying insignia. I suspected that it might be an army surplus vehicle belonging to a Belgian contractor in Kisenyi, but I didn't bother to ask.

The Italian truck driver slowed down and started to turn when he saw them. I reassured him and had a small conference with my private army. As we moved off towards Ruhengeri, with Evariste at the wheel and Bamuke and Buega sitting behind him, bolt upright and holding their rifles as though on military parade, our united Belgo-Congolese convoy was a wonderfully impressive spectacle. We passed several big gangs of natives who were obviously looking for trouble, but the sight of our weapons sent them racing into the bush. Then, suddenly, there was a large eucalyptus tree lying across the road with at least two hundred natives standing behind it. Our caravan screeched to a halt; Bamuke and Buega jumped out of the jeep, brandishing their guns, and ordered the natives to remove the road block; I pulled up as close to the jeep as I could, followed by the truck, preparing to make a run for it as soon as the way was clear.

The huge gang of raiders stood their ground. Cursing, Evariste stood up in the jeep and cut loose with a burst of machine-gun fire, shooting into the air to frighten the angry mob. The Siamese cats twanged like banjos when they heard that, and Sophie started to scream in terror. '*Ta gueule!*' I said nervously to the shrieking basket. Then a spear flew by, narrowly missing Buega, and a stone crashed into the windscreen of the jeep. Enraged, but faithful to their orders, the three soldiers sprayed the ground near the raiders' feet with a hail of bullets.

That convinced them: the tree was removed, and jeep, Impala, truck and trailer started to accelerate down the road. Then, as we passed, one of the natives managed to leap on the truck's running-board. Fortunately, the driver had enough presence of mind to open the door abruptly, catapulting him into the road. He scrambled to his feet, dusty but uninjured, shaking his fist with fury.

We passed the post of Ruhengeri at full speed. I suspected that there might be a detachment of Belgian commandos in the area, and had no doubt that even a single one of them could polish off my three-man Congolese army. On the sixteen-mile stretch of road between there and the Belgian customs inspection station at Cyanika, we passed at least five gangs of native highwaymen who took one look at the jeep and wisely decided to refrain.

About half a mile from Cyanika, I signalled the jeep to stop and told my soldiers that our private war was over. I felt in my pockets, anxious to reward them for their rôle in saving the historic collection, but I had given away my last franc in Kisenyi and had to borrow three five-hundred-franc notes from the truck driver. I pressed them into the soldiers' hands and urged them to return the jeep, get rid of their uniforms and weapons, and go back to civilian life. I hope they were lucky. They may have been brutalized by the rough life of the army, but at bottom, they were no worse than any other Congolese and considerably more natural and sincere than many of their better-educated brothers.

The Belgian Customs at Cyanika passed me through with a minimum of formalities. British Customs, twelve miles farther on, was a much more serious problem. I was penniless, and if they insisted on opening, checking and sealing for transport my thirteen tons of assorted crates and cartons and the five thousand ethnological treasures they contained, and if they demanded the usual fees, I could see myself becoming an almost permanent fixture on the Rwanda-Uganda border.

I drove up to the barrier slightly ahead of the long truck-trailer and ignored it completely, as though we were separate parties. I presented my various documents to the Hindu Customs inspector, who scrutinized each of them with slow, maddening attention to the minutest details. He began to look more and more dubious—until he came to the rabies inoculation certificates for the two Siamese cats. He looked at me significantly. 'I always dreamed of having a Siamese cat . . .' he said, in a low, persuasive tone.

I rushed back to the car, picked up the cat basket and hurried with it to the office. 'Which one do you like?' I said winningly.

'This one!' he answered, picking up the male and fondling it.

'You'd better close the doors and windows,' I advised him gravely. 'Cats usually take quite a while to settle down in a new home. You don't want him to escape!'

'Oh, no!' he said anxiously, and bustled about with the cat under his arm, sealing the office with such fervour that he seemed to be shutting down Uganda Customs for good. As I walked back to the car, the native guard at the barrier shot a questioning look towards his chief. Through the closed window, the Hindu made a sweeping gesture indicating 'Let him go through!' as he peered lovingly into the big, light-blue slightly crossed eyes of his new-found treasure.

His tender expression vanished a moment later when he saw the long truck with its huge trailer following in my wake. He ran to the door, started to open it, stopped, clutched at his cat, shook his head—and decided to forget the whole thing.

So, at the cost of a Siamese cat, I passed into the haven of Uganda with thirteen tons of African history intact and untaxed.

21

A Plan to take Africa with Me

Aata 'n-dapan ainei are naarisyo—'I have two skins, one to lie on and the other to cover myself with. What are they?'
En-gop o eng-ai—'The earth and the sky.'

MASAI RIDDLE

UGANDA was only a temporary haven, that was obvious. When I arrived at Kampala, on the northwest shore of Lake Victoria, after a four-hundred-mile journey, my caravan passed right through a demonstration that featured two vitriolic slogans: '*Uhuru!*' and 'Belgians, go home!' I watched as flag-decked cars, bicycles, scooters and crowds of excited natives circled the streets in the wake of a loudspeaker van. I listened with growing disgust as an African politician, microphone in hand, shouted incendiary words, 'The Belgians have no right to take refuge in Uganda! They killed the Congolese in the past, now it's their turn! Send them back to the Congo!'

The speaker was J. W. Kianuka, Chairman of the Uganda National Congress, whose prominently displayed black and red flags showed an unconscious but extremely appropriate symbolism: black for the credulous, easily misled Africans and red for their shrewd Communist backers.

The demonstration was reported in the *Uganda Argus* of 28 July 1960, under the headline '*Anti-refugee Parade*'. Ironically, there was a much longer story directly above it, '*Refugee Took his "Zoo" Along*', which began: 'Two monkeys, a young chimpanzee, two parrots and a cat are among the latest "refugees" to arrive from the Congo. . . .' The Nairobi *East African Standard* echoed that theme on the same day with a startling

396

front-page headline, '*Monkeys Latest Refugees to Leave Congo*' —words which may have given many casual readers the impression that the new republic had even more grotesque political troubles than they suspected.

At the Nakawa Refugee Reception Centre in Kampala nearly a hundred Belgians were awaiting Brussels-bound flights from Entebbe airport a few miles away. My arrival, complete with 'zoo' and thirteen-ton collection, created a fantastic commotion and I had to tell my story several times before everyone was satisfied. I spent the night at the Centre and left next morning for Nairobi, 450 miles away, equipped with tickets for free petrol and food, by courtesy of the Belgian Consulate in Kampala.

All through Uganda and Kenya groups of natives congregated on the highway with frenzied cries of '*Uhuru!*' Some pitched stones at my caravan as we passed. The whole scene was grimly reminiscent of the Congo with one outstanding exception: many of the natives had picked up a smattering of English, just enough to interlard their cries for freedom with casual obscenities. 'Bloody fucking Belgian bastards!' they screamed from the side of the road. '*Uhuru!* Shit! *Uhuru!*' As for that last juxtaposition, I could only agree with them.

In Nairobi that evening I made for the British Red Cross Refugee Centre where my driver and I were cordially received, but Sophie quickly became the real centre of attention. The little chimp peered out of her soiled basket with childlike, imploring eyes which won immediate sympathy from the lady volunteers at the Centre. Two of the gentlemen were considerably more practical: they offered to help me give her a bath.

Sophie snarled, shrieked, struggled, splashed, spat and tried to bite all three of us during the course of that memorable bathroom ballet. Finally, she was radiantly clean while we were not only soaked but spotted with ordure. The chimp stared at us and wrinkled her nose with supercilious disdain until we locked her in a small room and ourselves took baths. Then she screamed without stopping until I brought her some bread and carrots.

I spent that evening in conversation with one of my fellow chimp-washers, a warm and extremely sympathetic man named Robert Ely, an executive of the East Africa Tobacco Company. He invited me to stay at his house, but wisely suggested that we find a separate haven for Sophie: the Nairobi National Park, where he felt sure that his friend the Chief Game Warden,

Mr. S. I. Ellis, would willingly put her up until I found somewhere to settle down.

Bob and I drove to the Park early next day and Mr. and Mrs.
Ellis welcomed the diabolical little chimp into their house.
Sirikit, the remaining Siamese cat, named after my dead cheetah,
went to a lady volunteer at the Refugee Centre for temporary
safekeeping, and I found a willing victim in the person of an old
friend, Dr. I. Mann of the Kenya Department of Veterinary
Services, to board my two monkeys and the brace of parrots.

Finding accommodation for the enormous ethnological collection was more complicated. My driver and I took the truck-
trailer to a modern steel warehouse outside Nairboi, where the
huge power winches and cranes of the Express Transport Company took less than two hours to unload the thirteen tons which
twenty-eight men had struggled for a full day to hoist and shove
into place. Once the truck and trailer were empty, the Italian
driver departed with them for Rwanda.

He left with my fervent good wishes: I had £3,500 gambled on
his safe return to Goma and less than £700 in my account at
Barclays Bank, Nairobi.

Without my animals and my collection, I felt almost disembodied and spent the next few days wandering about Nairobi
from my base at Bob and Shirley Ely's hospitable home. It
didn't help when I learned from Dr. Mann that the two parrots
had died, apparently of penumonia; but things looked brighter
when I received a telegram announcing the truck-trailer's safe
return. I had a few tentative ideas concerning the future, but I
didn't make any real decisions until 1 August, when I accompanied the Chief Game Warden on a private tour of Nairobi's
world-famous National Park. Mr. Ellis and I drove together in
a Land Rover especially adapted for rough terrain and saw a
fine selection of game: lions, zebra, giraffe, gnu, hartebeest,
impala, and baboons. Then, noticing a large snake-track in the
dust of the trail, we followed it into the tall, tussocky grass and
discovered an eight-foot rock python with a shaggy aardwolf in
his coils; he was just about to kill and engorge the victim.

Their meeting, its climax and our presence at the scene constituted a miraculous combination of chances which could happen only once in a lifetime. The rock python (*Python sebae*) is an
enterprising, versatile, daytime hunter who will seize and devour
almost any small mammal or bird that may blunder into his
path; he rarely takes large prey, only once every three or four
months, and prefers to dine in seclusion. The aardwolf (*Proteles*

cristatus) is a rare, burrowing, nocturnal animal resembling a striped hyena reduced to the size of a large fox; almost never seen outside the limits of South Africa or, for that matter, seen at all, the timid, nearly defenceless creature prowls by night, excavating termite hills with his blunt claws and masticating the insects between his weak, degenerate teeth.

According to Mr. Ellis rock pythons were practically never seen in the Nairobi National Park and the presence of aard-wolves had never been officially recorded. It was highly unlikely that the two animals would meet here, and the possibility that anyone would find the scarce diurnal snake in the very act of preying on the rare nocturnal mammal was almost unthinkable. Fortunately, I had brought a loaded 35 mm. Kodak, and so could record the different phases of their strange, fatal encounter.

Apparently the thirty-pound buff-and-black aardwolf had been searching for termite mounds in the grass. As his scrawny appearance indicated, he must have been driven by extreme hunger, otherwise he would never have travelled so far from his burrow in the middle of the day. The eight-foot python, patterned in grey and brown, had seized the unsuspecting animal's left foreleg with his teeth and thrown his coils around the body, but had not killed his prey by constriction. When we arrived on the scene, the aardwolf was very quiet, probably weakened by internal injuries, but still alive.

The python had the slender, almost prehensile end of his tail wrapped around the animal's neck and held its pointed muzzle between his jaws. The aardwolf twitched and kicked feebly for a few minutes while he smothered to death slowly with his nose inside the snake's throat. Once the aardwolf was dead, the python dilated his jaws and took a quarter-turn on the head so that he might swallow the victim with its legs towards his belly rather than his back. It took about two hours before the aardwolf's bushy tail disappeared completely into the snake's gullet. Then the python moved off slowly through the grass, his sinuous beauty marred by a large bulge which had been one of Africa's rarest, most elusive mammals.

My photographic record of this encounter created a sensation in British scientific circles. The pictures were published in the *East African Standard* of 3 August 1960, and I received many requests for prints, including a letter from Colonel Mervyn Cowie, Director of Kenya's Royal National Parks. The three finest photographs were reproduced in the magazine *Wild Life*, official journal of Kenya's Wild Life Society, under the headline

'*Pictures of unparalleled interest to Scientists and Naturalists. Python and Aardwolf: Nature takes its course in the Nairobi National Park.*'

The magazine reproduced in the same issue three other photographs which I had taken the same day, also depicting a strange death, but one in which nature had taken no part. Under the headline '*Poaching again! Tragedy in the Nairobi National Park*', *Wild Life* told the story of a badly wounded zebra which Mr. Ellis and I had seen and chased and, unfortunately, had had to destroy.

This young zebra was found in the Nairobi National Park dragging a 7 ft. 6 in. steel rail behind it. The rail, which weighed 160 lb., was attached to its rear leg by a length of steel cable.

Despite this burden the zebra made every effort to get away and outpaced those who were trying to help it. When it was eventually caught and brought to a halt it was seen that the hoof and fetlock were so badly damaged that they were past healing. The animal was shot to put it out of its misery.

These photographs were taken on a recent routine round of the Park Warden, Mr. S. I. Ellis. They were taken by Jean-Pierre Hallet, famous Belgian naturalist, ethnologist and photographer from the Congo, whose magnificent photographs also make our centre spread on pages 28 and 29.

The poaching campaign seems to be growing in intensity. A few days after these photos were taken, a gang of poachers with their equipment and booty was seen leaving the Nairobi Park via the main Mombasa Road.

The story should have mentioned that the poachers were fleeing from a dark-blue Chevrolet Impala driven by a man who had spent the previous two days pursuing them while seeking out and removing their lethal slip-noose wires. I realized, though, that chasing a dozen poachers out of one National Park was a very minor triumph. All over Africa hordes of poachers and other hunters had already brought death to an incalculable number of animals. The natural habitat of others had been destroyed by the reckless over-extension of unsystematic agriculture and cattle grazing which brought no benefits to the people: the fauna of the savannahs had been decimated to make room for groundnuts and other unsuitable crops which only proved to be a ruinous, soil-eroding failure; and the lean, unproductive native cattle, which government veterinary services struggled so hard to keep alive and increase, were good for status-symbols and little else.

Now, with the advent of the new 'emergent' African nations, the ecological tragedy would accelerate until the people destroyed, without realizing the extent of their loss, the richest, most beautiful and most fascinating animal heritage in the world. I had already seen the carnage in Kivu's Albert National Park, and I knew that similar scenes must have taken place in Orientale's Garamba and Katanga's three-million-acre Upemba National Park, as well as in the Congo's two dozen General Reserves, where all hunting had been prohibited, and in the many partial reserves for the protection of threatened species. According to Park authorities, at least ten thousand elephants were wiped out in the Congo during the first month of 'freedom'. Their ivory was piling up in Mombasa warehouses, where the price had dipped to the lowest on record.

Ruanda-Urundi was scheduled to receive its political independence in July 1962, Uganda in October of the same year, Kenya and Tanganyika in December 1963. It was not difficult to predict the outcome. F. K. Onama, a special elected member of the Uganda Government, had made a speech on 'economic development' in his country's Legislative Council: 'If you are short of money, just shoot all the elephants and sell the tusks.' That brief exposé of scientific economics was grimly prophetic of a future in which the new breed of African politicians would reap quick but short-lived revenues by opening the former sanctuaries and game reserves to hunting safaris, organized and widely publicized by those shrewd businessmen, the 'romantic' white hunters, who apply their expertise with firearms to massacring African fauna and their knowledge of psychology to mulcting a credulous public. Simultaneously, a much larger army of black hunters and poachers would plunder and loot on a still more disastrous scale, killing for tusks, horns, hides, hoofs and tails—to be sold for a few francs or shillings—and only occasionally for meat to fill their bellies. Inevitably, the source of the 'sport', animal trinkets and meat would dwindle away to extinction.

In the whole of Africa (and the world) only seven hundred white rhino remained, including a couple of dozen specimens in zoos; less than 2,500 black rhino were left in Kenya, the species' ancestral stronghold. Mountain zebra, greater kudu, sable and roan antelope were all approaching minimal populations, and cheetah, eland, leopard and gorilla were following them towards the biological point of no return. Even lions were threatened: there were less than two thousand left in Kenya, heart of the classical lion country.

In only thirty years, between 1930 and 1960, fully 90 per cent of African game had been slaughtered. 'Independence' would obliterate the surviving tenth, and some of the most familiar species would disappear completely within fifteen or twenty years. Elephants, lions, rhino and giraffes would become no more than museum specimens or textbook illustrations, like the trilobites and brontosaurs, or the extinct African blue-buck (*c.* 1800), the black-maned Cape lion (1865) and the zebra-like quagga (1878), and—vanished from Morocco alone since this century began—the North African hartebeest, cheetah, mohor gazelle and the glorious Atlas lion.

It was too late to take any practical action on their own continent. The principles of conservation were poorly under-stood in many parts of the world which had been civilized for centuries. By the time the natives of tropical Africa could be taught to respect the meaning and importance of the magnificent living creatures they called *nyama*—meat—most of the threatened species would have passed into oblivion. The only hope lay in re-establishing the animals in similar surroundings on some other continent where the idea of conservation was understood and accepted, where the climate was suitable, where people had vision and where the economy was dynamic enough to support such a gigantic enterprise.

Only one place in the world fitted that description: the United States of America.

I had saved thirteen tons of Africa's past, and now I saw a way to save at least part of its living present. A scaled-down version of the doomed National Parks could be built in Southern California, at least a thousand acres where the animals could roam and breed freely as they had done on their ancestral terrain. There would be no cages, no bars, no kraals. Visitors would explore the grounds in their own cars and *discover* the animals, just as they did in the Albert, Kruger or Nairobi National Parks. Unsurmountable barriers such as cliffs, pits, moats, lakes and other natural fencing would separate the animals into compatible groups and prevent their escape.

A museum of tribal life would be an integral part of the game sanctuary, a place where my ethnological collection could be presented in a series of vivid displays and show all major aspects of Africa's traditional cultures. It would even be feasible to bring the living representatives of those cultures—native dancers, musicians and craftsmen—to the New World. Their six-month visits, carefully and tactfully supervised, would make it possible to create authentic replicas of typical African villages with all their local colour and exotic appeal.

As far as I was concerned, there was only one logical, inevitable name for the entire project: Congoland U.S.A.

To establish and maintain Congoland would require more than knowledge, experience and dedication. It would take money. The initial investment would have to be relatively large —probably a minimum of five million dollars—but the returns could be correspondingly great. Like the African National Parks it was patterned after, Congoland U.S.A. could become one of the world's major tourist attractions.

Nearly everyone dreamed of going 'on safari', but only a wealthy few could afford to spend the thousands of dollars involved. Now, with the recent upheavals on the African continent, safaris were not only expensive but unpredictable. The concept of Congoland offered *everyone* the opportunity to visit the best of Africa for a thousand times less money in perfect safety and comfort. They would find genuine enjoyment, relaxation and increased understanding by spending their precious leisure time in Congoland, rather than searching frantically for 'fun' in the existing highly mechanized amusement parks complete with their 'jungle rides' in wheeled boats along a fake river-bank tenanted by robot cannibals, plastic hippopotami and transistorized elephants, to the tune of tape-recorded lion roars and gorilla howls.

There would, of course, be a tremendous number of problems: obtaining suitable land, securing the various permits and approvals on local, county, state and federal levels, drawing up detailed plans, cost analyses and feasibility studies, getting assured financing, preparing the terrain while the animals were being captured, transported, quarantined and, finally, established in their new home; and completing dams, lakes, irrigation canals, water-purification systems, roads and bridges, as well as the museum and service buildings, motel units, restaurants, shops, parking areas and exotic tropical landscaping. Yet with realistic, logical organization and a highly qualified staff of expert specialists, I felt sure every one of those problems could be solved.

That night, in Nairobi, I drew the first sketches of Congoland U.S.A.; within twenty-four hours one of Kenya's leading architects, Graham McCullough, started work on the general plans; and during the next two weeks I conferred with the most important local authorities.

Derek Fleetwood, Mammalologist of the Coryndon Museum, immediately offered his full co-operation, and Carr Hartley of Rumuruti, East Africa's foremost animal capturer, was eager to help. The Kenya Game Department promised official approval and assistance, and Mr. W. E. Crosskill, Minister for Tourism, Game, Forests and Fisheries, expressed his personal interest and desire to aid. Colonel Mervyn Cowie, Director of the Royal National Parks, wrote to me, 'I am immensely interested in your Congoland project and would be willing to be listed as one of its sponsors', and Dr. L. S. B. Leakey, the world-famed anthropologist who found the fossil man-ape *Zinjanthropus boisei* in the Olduvai Gorge, wrote a splendid letter testifying to the tremendous scientific value of my collection—a letter which secured my admission to the United States.

My next step was to be a visit to Europe, where I intended to confer with leading zoological, anthropological and museum authorities while awaiting an American immigrant visa. There was one complication: Carr Hartley had given me, as a going-away present, a big-eyed, long-tailed 'bush baby'. It weighed less than six ounces and looked like a cross between an owl, a squirrel, a monkey and a shrunken kangaroo. To my considerable surprise I found I had to obtain from the Kenya Veterinary Department a 'Permit to Remove Cattle' before the minuscule lemur and I were allowed to board the plane for Europe.

How I brought the great collection to the United States, where I received—and had to refuse—a million dollars' worth of land in Monterey County, California; how I opened—and had to close—a Congoland Museum in Bakersfield, where I almost succeeded in establishing my project; how my collection was rescued from disaster by Mr. Franklin D. Murphy, Chancellor of the University of California, and acquired by the University; and how I later wandered on a twenty-thousand-mile journey through the troubled Orient, Indonesia and the islands of the South Seas . . . is another, and a very long story.

All of that was in the future; but now, on 22 August 1960, as my Super DC-7 took off from Nairobi, I had only one tiny animal and a vast, exciting dream hanging midway between *en-gop o eng-ai*—what my Masai brothers call the earth and the sky.